Boston's Wayward Children

A Boston "street Arab" before and after the NEHLW saved him, 1880. *(New England Home for Little Wanderers.)*

Boston's Wayward Children

Social Services for Homeless Children
1830–1930

Peter C. Holloran

Rutherford • Madison • Teaneck
Fairleigh Dickinson University Press
London and Toronto: Associated University Presses

Associated University Presses
440 Forsgate Drive
Cranbury, NJ 08512

Associated University Presses
25 Sicilian Avenue
London WC1A 2QH, England

Associated University Presses
P.O. Box 488, Port Credit
Mississauga, Ontario
Canada L5G 4M2

The paper used in this publication meets the requirements of the American National Standard for Permanence of Paper for Printed Library Materials Z39.48-1984.

Library of Congress Cataloging-in-Publication Data

Holloran, Peter C., 1947–
  Boston's wayward children.

  Bibliography: p.
  Includes index.
  1. Children—Institutional care—Massachusetts—
Boston—History. 2. Social work with children—
Massachusetts—Boston—History. 3. Abandoned children—
Services for—Massachusetts—Boston—History. 4. Child
welfare—Massachusetts—Boston—History. I. Title.
HV885.B7H65 1989   362.7'32'0974461   87-46425
ISBN 0-8386-3297-1 (alk. paper)

PRINTED IN THE UNITED STATES OF AMERICA

Contents

Acknowledgments

My interest in the history of social work and child welfare had its beginnings in Robert V. Bruce's graduate course in the organization of modern America at Boston University. He encouraged me to probe deeply in pursuit of working-class history, and the results were refined into a doctoral dissertation under his witty and skillful direction. I am also indebted to many colleagues and teachers who encouraged my research and rewarded my efforts with friendship and advice. Boston University and Pine Manor College provided generous support. Also, I must thank the librarians, archivists, social workers, and court officials who placed facilities and materials at my disposal with good wishes and faith that my research would bear useful results.

The primary sources, in the form of admission ledgers, case records, probation files, manuscript letters, and institutional reports, were drawn from Boston social work and juvenile court agencies, as the notes and bibliography indicate. More than fifty individuals permitted oral history interviews and shared important and often moving recollections with me.

The manuscript benefited from critical advice, comments, and encouragement from many historians and social workers, but none more supportive than Kathryn Ellis Beers, without whom it could not have been completed.

Cambridge
May 1989

Acronyms and Abbreviations

AJC	Associated Jewish Charities of Boston
BAIB	Boston Asylum for Indigent Boys
BCAS	Boston Children's Aid Society
BCFS	Boston Children's Friend Society
BFA	Boston Female Asylum
BJC	Boston Juvenile Court
BPA	Boston Provident Association
BSCG	Boston Society for the Care of Girls
BSPP	Boston Society for the Prevention of Pauperism
CBCC	Children's Bureau Case Committee of the FJC
CM	Children's Mission to the Children of the Destitute
FJC	Federated Jewish Charities
GDSC	General District Service Committee of the FJC
HAG	House of the Angel Guardian
HDCC	Home for Destitute Catholic Children
HGS	House of the Good Shepherd
HIC	Home for Italian Children
HJC	Home for Jewish Children
JBF	Judge Baker Foundation, later Judge Baker Guidance Center
Lancaster	State Industrial School for Girls at Lancaster
Lyman	State Reform School for Boys at Westborough, later Lyman School for Boys
MSPCC	Massachusetts Society for the Prevention of Cruelty to Children
Monson	State Primary School at Monson
NDB	National Desertion Bureau
NEHLW	New England Home for Little Wanderers
Shirley	State Industrial School for Boys at Shirley
NCJW	National Council of Jewish Women
NCCC	National Conference of Charities and Corrections
NCSW	National Conference of Social Work
UHBA	United Hebrew Benevolent Association

Boston's Wayward Children

Introduction

The welfare of children ranks as one of the highest priorities and most pressing social problems facing Americans. Numerous legislative hearings, reports, and statistics in the media and articles in professional journals are striking evidence of the national concern for our children and the fate of the American family. In 1984, more than 3 million children were victims of child abuse and neglect, and 1.5 million children were subjects of juvenile court proceedings. Beyond the human misery involved, the financial burden is staggering. The child welfare and juvenile justice system costs $15 billion annually in direct costs and billions more indirectly. In 1985 taxpayers spent over $1.24 billion to house 49,000 juvenile offenders in 1,000 public institutions and an uncounted sum for 34,000 other juveniles in 2,000 private institutions. Despite our avowed concern for our children, something is wrong, and historians now wonder if it was always so.[1]

The child welfare problem was the subject of White House conferences in 1909, 1919, 1930, 1940, 1950, 1970, and 1980. There will probably be another in the 1990s. At each conference, our national leaders patiently listened to expert opinions by scores of specialists on childhood, adolescence, and the family. They agreed that the largely informal, nongovernmental, localist approach to child welfare should be abandoned, despite Americans' deep-seated fears of government encroachment on the basic values of voluntarism, individualism, localism, and family autonomy.[2]

Child welfare is a complicated subject that includes all the professional activities of individuals, groups, and communities to restore and enhance a minor's capacity for social functioning. The popular and professional literature on child welfare is as ancient as it is voluminous. But it offers agreement on one point, at least; that America fails to provide for the well-being of children and adolescents without adequate parents or guardians. Most experts claim that children have always been at risk of parental neglect, abuse, and exploitation in the family, and any surrogate family provided has been punitive and custodial rather than benign and wholesome. Although the field of social work lacks historical perspective, this is an accurate estimate. Images of harmonious American family life are not borne out by historical evidence, as I will demonstrate. Until recently, however, few historians explored the reasons why local and state governments abnegated (or embraced) their responsibilities toward homeless children or why private individuals undertook this duty.[3]

Early in the nineteenth century, private voluntary associations proliferated in the United States and none more earnestly than those caring for "wayward children." These were youngsters who, for whatever reason, had lost their way, their families, and their homes. Victorians coined many names for them—waifs, little wanderers, guttersnipes, ragamuffins, street arabs and half-orphans—but most were merely poor urban working-class children without intact families. As the Massachusetts urban population rose from 16 percent of Bay Staters in 1800 to 86 percent in 1900, it became easier for middle-class child savers to oversee the growing number of working-class families in cities. The children of families who did not meet middle-class standards were deemed "wayward." They differed from juvenile delinquents (another Victorian term) chiefly because they were accused of no crime. Later these unfortunates were called dependent children, status offenders, or children in need of supervision.

The private charitable organizations for wayward children were called orphanages, asylums, temporary homes, schools, "houses," "homes," child-placing societies, and protectories. Their staffs were called charity workers, matrons, agents, child-savers, and visitors. To be sent to "the home for wayward children" was usually a grim and unwelcome fate, but not always. Despite our Dickensian images, these institutions were far from static or conservative, and antebellum child welfare agencies and asylums were radical and dynamic in origin and design. Striking at the root of traditional child-rearing practices, they removed young children from abusive homes, poor houses, and jails, but like most reform movements the child-saving societies responding to urgent social problems developed in a specific cultural milieu. Once mature, they were slow to alter that character. But the steady and sometimes overwhelming demands of American urban industrial society did change even these pioneer organizations, just as they changed the public welfare system these child-savers had generated.

The choice of Boston, Massachusetts, for this study, dictated by personal and professional considerations, is easy to defend. Boston's history is as ancient and altruistic as any in the United States, and here the prototype of the modern American child welfare system originated as a model for the nation. A pioneer in philanthropy, Boston provides a useful illustration of the complex social, intellectual, political and economic forces that created and shaped social policy and practice for dependent children.

This study examines the development of selected private voluntary charities for children in Boston from 1830 to 1930, as well as the individuals and groups that shaped them. These charities are some of the oldest and most important of their kind in America. Over their long and largely distinguished history, they pioneered new methods to deal with homeless children. This topic has intrinsic interest, not only for the historian or the social worker, because it often reflects the character and tenor of American culture in general. How Americans treated their orphans reveals much about us all.

These small sectarian charities did not function autonomously, and for this reason I refer to the development of public awareness of wayward waifs in the city and the growth of state provisions for the homeless and social deviants. The emergence of an elaborate system of public welfare and carceral institutions in Massachusetts under central regulation and the consequent formation of police, judicial, and administrative policy for children was inspired by men and women experienced in private charities. By understanding the broad social, political, and intellectual framework in which private and public child-savers operated, the particular developments that gave Boston its international reputation for primacy in social welfare become clear. This is more than a study of quaint Victorian charities; it tells of changing social policy and attitudes toward children in America from the age of Jackson to the coming of the New Deal.

Contrary to popular belief and the propaganda of organized social work, child welfare does not have an optimistic record of inevitable progress. In fact, the most innovative and successful period occurred in the mid-nineteenth century. State institutions were probably far more effective in 1850 than they have ever been since. Private agencies enjoyed their greatest confidence and success about that same time, and gradually deteriorated in most respects, though less precipitously than the public institutions for children. Non-professional charity workers—especially the clergy, nuns, and brothers in Catholic orphanages, as well as evangelical child-savers in Protestant asylums and later Jewish social workers—played as important a role in the emergence of social work as a profession as did "scientific" training. Children are not an objective, rational group; they respond to the attitudes and values of the adults supervising them more than to specific techniques used to educate or reform them. Boston child-savers were often child-like in their own subjective response to the wayward child, and analysis of both children and child-savers requires both objective and subjective criteria.

Child-savers accumulated data for their own use—not for twentieth-century historians—and time and neglect deprive us of many of these records. Accurate reconstruction of the daily life in a Victorian Boston orphanage is impossible, although reasonable estimates can be made from some historical evidence. Orphans left few records, but their lives can be traced in the institutional record. Much of this evidence permits us to make justified and accurate inferences. Available statistics are only evidence, not proof, of causal relationships.

Other cautions are necessary. All names of children cited are pseudonymous but preserve gender and ethnicity. The use of the biased terms "immoral" and "intemperate" or "destitute" and "defective" reflect nineteenth century usage and are not intended to offend any readers, although they surely will. These were terms used by Victorians to describe their welfare clients, often not in any derogatory fashion but because of custom, candor, and accuracy. Those were morally intensive religious times in the United States and such emotionally laden descriptions reflect Christian concern that colored American efforts for moral uplift and social control in child welfare.

This study begins in the 1830s when organizations like the House of Reformation, Farm Trade School, and St. Vincent Asylum began earnest child-saving activities. It ends in the 1930s when the Great Depression and Franklin Roosevelt's New Deal overshadowed private efforts to rescue wayward boys and girls from disrupted families. Between 1830 and 1930, Massachusetts and, more slowly, other states developed and maintained a complex and changing system of benevolent agencies and institutions to protect and care for children without homes or guardians. To understand this dramatic process, however, it is essential to recall what preceded antebellum child-saving.

No Americans were greater Anglophiles than Bostonians, who brought the Elizabethan Poor Law of 1601 with them when the city was founded in 1630. This tradition survived the American Revolution, and continuing contacts with Great Britain and the continent greatly affected the American child welfare system. Private and public charity date from more ancient authorities than Elizabeth I. The Code of Hammurabi protected Babylonian orphans two thousand years before Christ, and charity toward the young was preached by the Buddhists, ancient Greeks and the Talmud, which teaches the *duty* of giving and the *right* of the poor to receive alms. But in the minds of the earliest Bostonians, English poor-law practices were accepted as a community obligation. These laws made parents, insofar as they had the means, legally responsible for supporting their children, and grown children liable for the support of their parents and grandparents. Vagrants refusing to work were liable to be whipped, pilloried, branded, imprisoned, or executed. More positive features of the law held the state responsible for supplementing ordinary efforts to relieve suffering or to support the destitute. The helpless and needy child had a legal right to assistance from the state. Such children without homes or suitable parents were to be apprenticed in decent households.

The laws established the principle of local responsibility for the poor and needy, suggested official remedies, and erected a structure at the lowest level of government to implement these remedies. The parish church wardens and a board of respectable householders served as the Overseers of the Poor to collect taxes and spend these funds on the poor. Such laws date in England from 1349 but were codified in the Elizabethan Poor Law in 1601 to secularize poor relief in one coherent statute. The state acted to intervene when poverty and immorality rendered the family impotent and threatened the welfare of the young.[5]

Transplanted to America, the English nuclear family encountered enormous stresses, and despite heroic efforts the seventeenth- and eighteenth-century colonists failed to recreate their traditional society. Although British colonies adopted, sometimes literally, English poor laws from the first; frontier conditions created much family disorder and greater needs for family substitutes. In New England, the smallest unit of government, the town meeting, appointed the selectmen as the Overseers of the Poor in each town. Each colony enacted laws specifying penalties for negligent parents and "stubborn" children. In 1646 Massachusetts authorized the death penalty for extremely disobedient children. Although this draconian penalty was never imposed it indicates that the family was failing as the basis of a well-ordered, hierarchial community. By the middle of the eighteenth century, the isolated conjugal family with a maximum dispersion of the lines of descent, partible inheritance, and multilineal growth was well established. With it came basic changes—blurred social status gradation, achieved rather than ascribed prestige, increased status for women, romantic contractual marriage, and loosened bonds between a child and his community.[6]

Community ties were important, but after the revolution, Massachusetts was a new and unstable society with considerable mobility in which a child had decreasing opportunities to form the elaborate family and community ties that his ancestors took for granted. As a consequence, American children were less deferential and obedient to authority than their grandparents had been. Parents were equally affected by changing social conditions, and new Massachusetts statutes demanded that parents train their children and apprentices in a recognized trade and give them the "ability to read and understand the principles of religion and the capital laws of this country."[7] Passage of such laws suggests that many parents were negligent in raising their children. Fearing that the family was unequal to its traditional roles, Massachusetts had from 1647 passed a succession of laws requiring all town to maintain schools.

This formally transferred the family's educational function to specialized public educational institutions with broad cultural and vocational goals. The little red school house has been enshrined as a cultural beacon in the dim past, but overlooked is the transfer of authority over children from the family to the state. In time other prerogatives of parents would come under increased state scrutiny and control, as children grew restive under the rule of parents less in touch with the requirements for success in an evolving society. Children prompted further variation and innovation in social institutions supplementing the impoverished or unstable family.

Poverty was relieved in early New England by vote of the selectmen or overseers to rebate the taxes of paupers or by sending the pauper and his children to live with other families. Sometimes a pauper child would be auctioned off at the town meeting and sent to live with whomever bid lowest. That child abuse resulted in such a system one can readily imagine. The coldheartedness of this "binding out" or "farming off" system was only the most obvious drawback of the poor laws.[8]

The family performed a wide variety of functions besides child rearing. It was a school for the elementary and vocational education of its own children and of young servants and apprentices who came into the household to work and to learn useful skills from a master craftsman as part of his family. The family was an employment center, with all members working for the household economy. Care of the very young, the very old, and all but the very sick were other family functions. The town fathers assigned the homeless, indigent, disabled, and demented to families for shelter, oversight, and correction. Bastard and orphan children were commonly cared for in this way as servants, apprentices, or merely as adjunct members of a responsible family. Wealthier families often included young unmarried servants, who were regarded as family members despite their servile status. In fact, the early American household was not an isolated, self-centered institution, but rather a semi-public institution with community-ordained and protected roles far beyond modern family functions.

Servants were found in all but the most humble Massachusetts households until the mid-nineteenth century. Domestic service was an honorable though modest calling, and one necessary in the somewhat larger and certainly more labor-intensive households of that period. In this way homeless and wayward children learned correct family discipline and honest work. Their master was officially *in loco parentis,* and his rights and duties over a domestic servant or apprentice included those of a father, as the servant's obligations were, under law and tradition, filial toward the master. This ideal remained common, although slowly declining, until the nineteenth century. In labor-scarce Massachusetts, masters came to regard servants and apprentices more as a badly-needed labor force and less as household or family members. Training in religion and literacy, though contractually guaranteed, was ignored or overlooked in favor of work. Contributing to this breakdown of the master-servant relationship was the fact that by 1800 servants were less likely to be the children of friends or neighbors and more often migrants to Boston from rural New England or Irish, Canadian, or British immigrants. Considered culturally inferior and incompatible by Yankees, they came to be regarded (and to regard themselves) as hired hands or employees rather than as surrogate children. Male apprentices were in service to acquire occupational skills in a trade or craft, and female servants to earn a living before or in lieu of marriage.

One group of masters subject to particular scrutiny were those in charge of public wards, and their performance was often officially deplored. Orphans, bastards, and children of poor or incompetent parents were sent to masters by the overseers of the poor. Respectable householders were asked to rear young paupers under the customary apprentice terms. The indentured servant or apprentice placed by the selectmen or overseers with a family was to receive food; clothing; lodging; training in his master's craft; and instruction in religion, reading, and writing. Sometimes the indenture contract provided for a gift of money, clothing or tools at age twenty-one for a boy and eighteen for a girl.[9]

By 1808, however, problems were so common that law digests published for town officials contained forms for complaints by servants about their masters and for masters about disobedient servants. Boston and Massachusetts legislators passed dozens of laws spelling out the duties of both parties and providing penalties for noncompliance. This too indicates changes in the nature of family government. The personal, nonvocational obligations binding master and servant declined in importance, and the religious, moral, and educational functions gradually shifted from the household to the church, school, and courts for bound-out children as it had for all Boston children. Slowly Bostonians developed and expanded other social welfare institutions to supplement the family in crisis.[10]

Boston built its first almshouse in 1660, and when it burned down in 1682, a larger building near Boston Common replaced it. The pathetic children sheltered there were a notorious feature one Bostonian recalled in 1871:

> At the close of the last century, the Sentry Street of our fathers did not present so inviting an appearance as does the Park Street of our own day. The old dingy buildings and the broken down fences have disappeared, and stately houses have succeeded in their places. No more the staid townsman nor the jocund youth proceeding to the Common in wonted manner on election and independence days, be interrupted by the diminutive hands thrust through the holes in the Almshouse fences, or stretched from beneath the decaying gates, and by the destitute inmates entreating for money; nor will the cries of the wretched poor in those miserable habitations be heard calling for bread. . . .[11]

Mixing children with adults, and especially the assortment of unfortunate and miserable inmates commonly found in the almshouse—the indi-

gent, senile, insane, handicapped, diseased, drunken, and petty criminal—
was early deplored as an unwise practice. Smaller towns quickly placed
homeless children in local families, but often this was not possible in
Boston because wayward children were frequently too many and apprenticeships and indentures not always available. Bostonians suggested the
separation of juvenile from adult paupers by 1700 but this was found too
expensive until 1735 when some separation within the institution was
finally accomplished. One-quarter of the 250 Boston Almshouse inmates
annually admitted in the 1760s were children, and another one thousand
families received outdoor (or home) relief. Poor relief was one of the most
costly items in the town budget before the revolution, and each community
attempted to reduce expenses by "warning out" nonresident paupers,
"idle and vagabond" youths, disowned bastards, and abandoned children.[12]

Physical abuse of children placed out as servants was noted in Massachusetts as early as 1655 and was probably more common than existing
records indicate. A Plymouth jury found Robert Latham guilty of man-
slaughter in the death of his twelve-year-old servant, John Walker. The
boy's body was black and blue, his back marked with stripes of the lash,
and his toes and fingers frozen. He had been forced to carry a log far
beyond his strength. Enuresis added to the boy's troubles, but he was also
deprived of adequate clothing, food, and shelter by his cruel master.
Latham was ordered "burned in the hand" and "all his goods con-
fiscated," but this did little to safeguard thousands of other children bound
out for their minority to whomever wanted their labor. Such neglect and
mistreatment of child servants was probably much more common than
among children at home with their natural parents, but this, like so many
aspects of childhood, is seldom revealed in documents and records available.[3]

Childhood was a vague status in Europe and America until the nineteenth century, and Bostonians gave little attention to the special needs of
the young. The Puritans considered children to be merely undersized
adults of unripe intelligence. Strict discipline by parents was expected to
break innately sinful natures, and this grim attitude prevailed until Horace
Bushnell, a liberal Congregational Boston minister wrote *Christian Nur-
ture* in 1847. This was the single most influential book on children, and it
broke with the Calvinist concept of childhood by stressing the natural
growth of religious belief in the children of pious families. Bushnell
brooded for a decade on the child in Calvinist theology and concluded that
children from pious homes would grow up never having known any status
save that of Christians. This idea became dominant by the Civil War and
prepared Americans for a more humane outlook on children in the Gilded
Age. It also placed great emphasis on family morality, which alarmed

Boston charity workers suspiciously eyeing foreigners flocking to their city.[14]

The first institution to shore up the faltering family was the public school, but New England towns neglected the "common schools" in the 1820s. Horace Mann, Boston's leading educational reformer, found only half of the children in Massachusetts in 1837 had a free public school education. Private schools were more popular with middle-class families and the public common schools had a lower-class or pauper stigma. The Boston Sabbath School movement in the 1820s was an evangelical device to ensnare little souls but became a solution for the educational needs of the town's poor children. Any child aged five to sixteen could attend these free private Sunday Schools to learn to read, write, cipher, and pray. Many pupils were so poor that they had to be provided with shoes and clothes so they could attend without shame. By 1820 the City Missionary Society operated three schools for two thousand children and had an average attendance each Sunday of five hundred pupils.[15]

Boston established free public primary schools in 1818, but excluded illiterate children of over age seven. The City Missionary Society estimated four hundred children roamed the streets daily in search of play, work, or mischief. They were too old, dirty, wild, or illiterate to be admitted to public schools. Congregational charity schools opened to fill this need and prepare all children for the public schools. Despite this, education remained a parental responsibility little interfered with by the state. Massachusetts did not pass a compulsory school attendance law until 1850, and this was unenforced for a decade in most communities. State funds were distributed to local schools in 1834, and the State Board of Education created in 1837. An energetic reformer, Horace Mann, was its secretary, and soon he was a national leader of the public school movement.

By 1851 an influential reform journal, *The Massachusetts Teacher,* worried about the flood of Irish immigrants "pouring like muddy water" into the "pure" Bay State. "With the old not much can be done; but with their children, the great remedy is *education*. The rising generation must be taught as our own children are taught. We say *must be* because in many cases this can only be accomplished by coercion."[16] With the goal of universal education came the erosion of family autonomy and the intrusion of child guardianship by the state.

It is no exaggeration to say that the social and economic organization of antebellum Boston was based on the family. The nonhierarchial church and the distant, ill-equipped government relied on the family as the basis of most social action. Eighteenth-century Boston had no individuals; everyone was required to join a family household and to obey the household head. This would change as the antebellum city expanded, and private charitable associations developed to meet the increasingly complex needs once fulfilled by the family. These charitable endowments attracted bequests and accumulated fortunes in perpetual trusts. Practical trustees invested these funds in far-ranging business activities of capital-craving New England, using the income (but never the principal) to support philanthropic enterprises. In this way Boston merchants assumed governance of Harvard College in 1780, and then created or controlled Harvard Medical School (1782), the Boston Dispensary (1795), Boston Atheneum (1807), Massachusetts General Hospital (1811), McLean Insane Asylum (1816), and many other charitable institutions. Responsibility for the sick and poor shifted from the family to new charitable corporations. Capital was freed for economic expansion and the income controlled by prudent businessmen for the community's benefit.[17]

Some merchant-family sons were encouraged to specialize not in the family commercial or manufacturing firms, where the field would be crowded with competing Bostonians, but rather in newly specialized professions, law, medicine, scholarship and, more significantly, management of social welfare organizations.[18] The famous Boston Brahmin trustee was thus born and a philanthropic legend created:

> This catalogue of names, which fills over one hundred pages . . . shows, like Homer's catalogue of Grecian ships gathered for another warfare, how heartily and readily the men and women of Boston have joined with each other in the great siege, which has been bequeathed from sire to son, of the fortresses of poverty, ignorance, and crime.[19]

Even in this Boston Brahmin war on poverty, ignorance, and crime, it was family that counted and the tradition of patrician philanthropy and noblesse oblige gave a curious continuity to Massachusetts child welfare. The family connection, which failed to protect lower-class children from poverty, assured them that upper-class family charity would offer what their own parents had not or could not provide.

What changes occurred in the New England family to make these new institutions necessary? Americans sentimentalized home and family as the foundation of society and the source of good citizenship in the Age of the Common Man, and declared the home a sacred refuge. But it seemed to be a refuge under siege. Writers made the declining family a new literary convention. Catharine Maria Sedgwick's *Home* was a best-selling story in 1835 of a moral family surviving urban life only by wise parental guidance of their deferential children. Walt Whitman wrote a potboiler novel in 1842, *Franklin Evans,* about the moral danger a farmer's apprentice faced in New York City boarding houses, gin mills, gambling dens, and brothels. Intellectuals voiced dire fears for the future of the Republic as anxious Americans feared the loss of tradition, stability, and piety. Magazines dwelled on moral deterioration, and newspapers regretted the disappearing influence of the family in morals and manners.[20]

The school was seized upon as the best way to shore up the imperiled American family, and Boston led the nation in expanding and improving schools for all children. Antebellum Americans did not distinguish clearly between public and private spheres of social responsibility and seldom even addressed the issue. In education and charity work, this vagueness can be discovered as nowhere else. The two were combined in the shared goals of private and public asylums for Boston wayward and homeless children. Young lawbreakers were a new and growing problem for Bostonians, and characteristically the city's leading ladies and gentlemen responded with prompt, humane, and discreet private action well in advance of public efforts. When noncompulsory schools proved insufficient, Bostonians like Judge William Sawyer blamed poor family discipline and argued in 1846 for reform schools because:

There is seldom a case of a juvenile offender, in which I am not well satisfied that the parents, or persons having the child in charge, is not most blamable—they take no pains to make him attend school—they suffer him to be out nights without knowing or caring where; and, in many instances, they are incapable of taking caring of themselves, much less their children; they have no home fit for as child; their residence is a grog shop; their companions drunkards and gamblers or worse; they bestow no thought upon their child, until he falls into the hands of an officer and is brought before a court.[21]

1
Boston Protestant Charity for Children

I know of no other large city where there is so much mutual
helpfulness, so little neglect and ignorance of the concerns of
other classes.

—Harriet Martineau on Boston, 1836

The unclassified poorhouse was no longer considered suitable for homeless children by 1800, but the traditional alternatives—apprenticeship,
domestic service, and binding out orphans and wayward children to farmers or other respectable householders—were not always convenient or
possible in growing urban centers like Boston, New York, and Philadelphia. America was a more mobile, more populous, and more heterogeneous society in the nineteenth century, and few Overseers of the Poor
or almshouse keepers had the time or interest to find masters for children
in their charge. Reports of neglect and abuse of children in poorhouses or
family placements pointed to the need for new provisions for the homeless
young. To the Federalist and Whig gentlemen of Boston, the well-ordered
asylums established in Europe appeared to be a practical and idealistic
solution.[1]

Like the philanthropic gentlemen who founded penitentiaries and insane asylums, those who advocated the Boston House of Reformation for
Juvenile Offenders in the 1820s were confident that this publicly supported
congregate asylum would benefit the city by ridding the poorhouse and the
streets of destitute and delinquent boys and girls whose parents had
abandoned them or were too poor, immoral, or negligent to provide proper
care. They expected to provide a reform school for the training and
education of wayward children, while at the same time enhancing moral
order in the city.

The Boston House of Reformation for Juvenile Offenders was suggested
first by Judge Josiah Quincy in 1820, and after a study of the problem by
the state legislature and much debate in the newly established (1822) city
government, it opened in South Boston in 1826. It was a congregate
municipal institution like those established in New York (1825) and Philadelphia (1828); part school, part prison, and fully moral in purpose and

24

practice. The inmates were 150 boys, aged seven to seventeen, apprehended by the constable and convicted by the Boston Police or Probate Court of petty crimes, vagrancy, and "waywardness" or those who had been turned over to the police by distraught parents as willfully disobedient and "stubborn." The admission policy was flexible, and school teachers, clergymen, Overseers of the Poor, or other responsible gentlemen who took the trouble to make official complaints about a child could be certain of swift action by the courts.[2]

While the inmates were "guilty" of almost every petty offense or misfortune imaginable, they had poverty and ignorance in common. Few Boston school boys entered the House of Reformation, because regular attendance at antebellum schools indicated a degree of family respectability and stability which usually precluded commitment to this institution. Most of the inmates were not in school due to poverty, parental neglect, and their own preference for street life, nightwalking, cheap theaters, newspaper hawking, and the company of their fellow vagabonds. These were the rowdies and pilfering "street arabs" that shopkeepers and decent citizens found an unseemly nuisance. Proper Bostonians engaged in business and professions began to demand more propriety and decorum of their neighbors in the antebellum era, as the provincial town transformed itself into the commercial capital city, the "Athens of America" and the "Hub of the Solar System." It was a period of increasing social stratification, residential segregation, and rising genteel manners. In this new community roving gangs of unsupervised children were not tolerated by their social betters.[3]

It was also a sentimental age with great emphasis on humanitarianism and evangelical revivals. Ladies and gentlemen formed private voluntary associations to reform the unfortunate and wicked and to uplift the downtrodden. No more pathetic objects could be found than ragged children, and for this reason the House of Reformation suited the changing goals of middle- and upper-class Bostonians. By removing the children of the "unworthy poor" (immoral or intemperate parents) to the House of Reformation on some legal pretext, humanitarians persuaded each other that they did a service to the community and to the child, rescuing him from temptation and moral corruption.[4]

The daily routine of the House of Reformation expressed the core of the child-savers' optimistic belief that the problem lay in a faulty environment and could be cured by the strict regularity of the asylum discipline. To this end, the first superintendent employed was the Reverend Eleazer Mather Porter Wells, a Congregational minister who, like many fashionable Bostonians, had converted to the Episcopal Church. During his tenure from 1827 to 1833, Wells had the full confidence of Boston's leading Federalist and Whig gentlemen and tempered strict discipline with paternal concern for each boy. His personal character and keen judgment of boys promoted self-discipline and voluntary moral reform. Under his human regulations, no corporal punishment was permitted, and the boys governed themselves by daily self-reporting, a merit grading system, and a boys' court which judged violations of the rules. Although the recalcitrant were chained in solitary confinement on a diet of bread and water for serious misconduct, for most boys, the regime was probably superior to the pauper homes they left behind. Each day, the inmates attended school classes four hours, worked in shops for four hours, and had two hours of daily organized recreation in which Wells frequently participated. The extremely high success rate that he claimed—fewer than a dozen of the first three hundred inmates reappeared in court for new offenses—was a fact, at least for the first years of his administration. In 1831 the French penologists Gustave de Beaumont and Alexis de Toqueville judged the Boston House of Reformation the best in the United States, but they attributed its success to the moral atmosphere instilled by Wells rather than to replicable methods.[5]

When Wells resigned in 1833 following a budget dispute with the City Council, the House of Reformation rapidly deteriorated and became a controversial, corrupt, often brutal custodial institution with a reputation as a school for crime from which many boys graduated to the State Prison. It is significant that Wells became superintendent of the Boston Farm School for boys established on Thompson Island in the harbor by a private child welfare agency. This marked the gradual withdrawal of the city's elite philanthropists from the public welfare sector to the smaller, more selective private child welfare system. In doing this, private agency child-savers abandoned delinquent children to congregate public institutions, preferring to rescue the more malleable and less threatening dependent children (i.e., younger, less unruly) with whom they were likely to have less trouble and greater success.[6]

The decline of the House of Reformation after 1834 may be attributed to Wells's resignation or to the tendency of the Boston Brahmins to support their own new private child welfare organizations (rather than the public asylums they originally advocated). Certainly it was also due in part to loss of confidence in large congregate institutions, but these factors do not fully explain the rapid and almost complete deterioration of the South Boston asylum. The initial zeal and pioneering reformist fervor were, of course, impossible to maintain permanently, but the primary cause for the decline of this congregate institution and the public's abdication of responsibility and interest can be discerned in the history of nineteenth-century prisons and asylums of all sorts.

Both prisons and houses of reformation first appeared in the United States in the 1820s, representing the culmination of a long process in which the concept of crime was dissociated from related ideas of pauperism, madness, and sinfulness. Prisons for adult lawbreakers were created with some idea of the inmate's degree of guilt in mind. The House of Industry (opened in 1822) admitted men and women who were not self-supporting, vagrants and drunkards, for the most part; the House of Correction (opened in 1823) admitted adults sentenced to two years or less for criminal offenses; and the State Prison (opened in 1805 as a new penitentiary), admitted recidivists and serious lawbreakers, felons, and those sentenced to long terms. In this hierarchy of crime, the juvenile offender was recognized as a more hopeful subject of the law, and for his moral regeneration the House of Reformation was designed. Sentences from the first were indeterminate (usually to the age of majority or until paroled by the trustees), and the avowed purpose of the institution was to reform and train the children and restore them to decent society educated and with industrious, sober work habits.[7]

These distinctions reflected the belief that the young were more capable of changing habits and behavior than the old, and that the plastic nature of the child made him more amenable to reform efforts. Therefore the therapy that the House of Reformation offered its inmates differed from that in carceral institutions for adults. But as the reformation of delinquents of all ages proved difficult or often impossible, and after the charismatic Wells left (partly because his "lenient" policies disappointed the City Council), the asylum succumbed to bureaucratic pessimism and quickly came to resemble the adult prisons in practice. Although reformation remained the ostensible goal, in daily routine the House of Reformation followed the example of the harsh penal system. In 1831 Toqueville interviewed Elams Lynds, the celebrated warden of New York's Auburn Prison, who expressed the prevailing attitude of the new professional penologists. When asked if inmates could be reformed, Lynds replied:

> I do not believe in complete reform, except with young delinquents. Nothing, in my opinion is rarer than to see a convict of mature age become a religious and virtuous man.

Lynds explained that chaplains had little success with prisoners, but compulsory work in silent gangs and flogging men who violated rules did teach industrious habits. This was the only reform that he expected, "and I believe it is the only one which society has a right to expect."[8] Pessimistic about the moral regeneration of older convicts, Lynds was scarcely more sanguine about wayward children, and it is not surprising that the public lost faith in the ability of the House of Reformation to reclaim youngsters. The Puritan's compulsion to transform the world and the democrat's faith in human progress stumbled on the difficult task of making bent twigs grow straight.

After the departure of Wells to a new private asylum that encouraged leniency and experimentation, the House of Reformation courted failure by adopting the penal methods in which punishment was emphasized. Consequently, an inmate subculture of resistance and sullen hostility developed in competition with the institution's therapeutic program of moral discipline. It became a juvenile prison. When a homeless boy appeared in the Police Court, an almost irreversible process began which ceremonially branded him a social deviant. In the same way that a convict assumed a new identity as a social pariah in the prison; so too, albeit in a less inimical form, did boys entering the House of Reformation (and later the State Reform School in Westborough) undergo rituals of depersonalization. Following arrest and summary trial came mortification: bath, haircut, delousing, physical examination, loss of personal possessions, uniforms, numbering, marching, regimentation, strict military-style discipline, involuntary confinement, asceticism, and enforced celibacy.[9] This penal rule taught the inmate that he was outside decent society with little hope of returning.

The number of escapes (called "eloping") from the House of Reformation attracted the attention of critics as something "which indicated a habit of discontent, and unwilling submission; there was besides but little industry in the shop or schoolroom; few cases of reformation; and generally a state of things affording little satisfaction to the directors or friends of the institution." This unhappy state was compared to the Sing Sing and Auburn prisons in New York. Still, the prescribed remedy was only "unceasing vigilance in government."[10] Wells's success quieted critics for a time, but his less talented successors' difficulty in managing one hundred boys and a small number of girls can be imagined.

All congregate asylums experienced problems with defiant and rebellious inmates, but Victorians had little patience with children who would not learn self-control. It was a central theme of antebellum crusades and reform movements. Restraint and propriety were not simply foisted on the reluctant lower class as part of a hysterical concern for social control, but were generalized goals of mercantile and manufacturing societies in Europe and North America. Specialized asylums for children were especially popular in antebellum America because they were located at a point between evangelical religion and materialism. However, the House of Reformation failed to promote piety and industry in its inmates, and by the 1850s it reflected the impulse (evident in revivals, nativism, asylums, and the urban police forces) to identify and isolate the vicious from the virtuous, the rough from the respectable, and the delinquent from the merely dependent child. The philanthropic gentlemen who founded asylums did so with initial confidence, and as Edward Everett Hale said:

They expected it to succeed. They always had succeeded. Why should they not succeed? If then, they opened a House of Reformation, they really supposed that they should reform the boys and girls who were sent to it.[11]

But disappointment was widespread among the elite supporters of the House of Reformation by the 1840s and the isolation of the socially deviant became as important as their reformation.

Citizens of South Boston complained in 1847 that the institution—together with the neighboring House of Correction, House of Industry, City Lunatic Asylum, School for the Feeble-minded, and Perkins Institute for the Blind—made the area "the Botany Bay of the city," and the House of Reformation was relocated in 1858 five miles away on remote Deer Island, a symbolic transfer out of the sight and mind of respectable Bostonians. It proved that the efficient, economical incarceration, and punishment of inmates, not the moral retraining of children, had become the primary function and bureaucratic goal of the House of Reformation. Its scandalous reputation in the 1840s made judges reluctant to commit minor offenders to this school for crime, but the truancy law in 1850 and the appointment of truant officers in 1852 eventually made it an overcrowded as well as a neglected institution. In 1895 it was moved away from the House of Correction on Deer Island to the even more distant Rainsford Island in an abandoned pesthouse. It was renamed the Suffolk School for Boys in 1901, but this changed little and the boys committed to this training school still did not return to the city educated or prepared for productive working-class occupations. They were stigmatized as social deviants, young rebels who refused to seek respectability by conforming to middle-class values and goals. When Mayor James Michael Curley closed the Suffolk School in 1920, it was a notorious institution in which children were brutally beaten, ill-educated, overworked, abused, and mistreated in a variety of ways by the rigid, inept, corrupt, politically appointed staff at an exorbitant cost to the taxpayers. The respectable community had lost interest in the House of Reformation by the 1850s and those sent to it had long since been labelled by decent working- and middle-class Bostonians as the unworthy poor.[12]

The lesson that the House of Reformation offers is similar to that which historians have seen in Massachusetts state mental asylums in the nineteenth century. Political interference plagued all public institutions, and public indifference or prejudice against "coddling" inmates were common problems in all congregate asylums, but the most important defect of the House of Reformation was its commitment to efficient custodial care above all. This bureaucratic priority precluded its manifest function, namely the reformation of children. Child welfare goals were sacrificed to the requirements of social control in this total institution created in the name of humanitarian liberal reform.[13]

Children were imprisoned for petty lawbreaking or the status offenses or crimes of being poor, stubborn, wayward, orphaned, abused, neglected, truant, or runaway. In the House of Reformation they learned only submission to their keepers, little that would make them self-sufficient, law-abiding citizens upon discharge. Basket-weaving, chaircaning, gardening, and housekeeping were not skills that translated into steady employment in nineteenth century cities. Many boys were paroled as apprentices to craftsmen or farmers in the hope of learning a trade, but they usually worked only as unskilled assistants with little opportunity to learn lucrative trades. Apprenticeship was an obsolete tradition in the new urban industrial economy and more romantic than realistic for the lower-class urban youth.[14]

The regulations of this not-very-well-ordered asylum reflected contemporary opinion on proper child-rearing practices. The prescriptions of Wells's successors followed the advice of the new child-guidance books written in the 1840s by Lydia Child, Jacob Abbott, Catharine Beecher, and other self-proclaimed experts. These were secular works, not the ministers' sermons and tracts of the eighteenth century, and constituted a new and popular genre in American literature. The clergy had diminished status in the Victorian period, and many ministers abandoned obscure rural parsonages for minor positions as chaplains or child-savers in asylums, urban missions, and child-welfare organizations. But the most widely read books on raising children were written by laymen and laywomen who identified with the middle- and upper-class managers of social welfare societies and asylum superintendents. Their domestic advice conveyed a sense of urgency to already anxious parents and guardians while offering calm, practical measures by which erring children could be imbued with the moral character considered necessary for success in the heartless world of Jacksonian America.[15]

They traced the origin of child-rearing problems, problems which they themselves had identified, to the decline of communal life and the consequent deterioration of family government. Worried adults learned standardized parental skills from these books—rather than intergenerationally from distant or deceased grandparents or extended family members—and were encouraged to raise their children by bourgeois Yankee criteria. This *embourgeoisement* of American society can be discerned in many aspects of antebellum life, but in none so palpably as in the institutional discipline of "nobody's child," the inmates of the House of Reformation and other child welfare asylums of Victorian Boston. In the views of the new child-rearing experts, good children were innocent and obedient, and these outcast children formed the juvenile mudsill below which no properly raised child could sink but upon which all genteel society stood. The pariahs of the House of Reformation defined the limits for American children and their anxious parents, a reassuring measure against which naughty middle-class boys and girls could be gauged and a stern caution with which to admonish misbehaving sons and daughters. As Victorian America discovered the importance of careful child-rearing, the deviant child—whether delinquent or merely homeless—received greater attention from the anxious elite.[16]

The traditional placement of socially deviant children in surrogate families was a local, voluntaristic solution for individual children. But superior to this in the eyes of antebellum policy-makers was confinement in a congregate asylum in which large numbers of wayward children could be subject to uniform discipline. This obviated distinctions between native-born and immigrant children and appealed to city and state government as an efficient, uniform, endlessly replicable method without the idiosyncrasies of the almshouse. It is true that the House of Reformation continued to employ apprenticeship for children, as did the State Primary School (for young orphans) established in 1872 in Monson, but only after each child learned asylum discipline prior to placement in a family. The important criteria for social conformity thus became the individual's ability to adhere to a recognized code of morals and manners and his ability to earn a living honestly, not his birthplace or antecedents. Bostonians were repelled by those who were not self-disciplined and self-supporting or, in the case of children, not likely to become so. They scorned those who were satisfied with squalid, clannish slum life and did not make efforts to rise in the world as an individual. To correct these moral deficiencies in lower-class immigrants' children, the character-building program of the Boston House of Reformation was designed. Children who did not learn conformity and control from their parents were removed, as before, but their training took place in a public or private asylum after 1820 because the family no longer offered sufficient oversight for wayward children, and the urban community had fewer substitute parents available. Once a child was trained in the institution, however, he could find a foster home as a domestic servant, apprentice, or "boy of all work" in a shop or farm.

* * *

The sanguine expectations of the 1820s—when Lydia Child advised parents to avoid conflict by anticipating the needs of infants, and Bostonians acted like kindly parents in a plethora of competing charities to elevate the poor—were far from being realized in the result. Under the impetus of liberal Unitarian churches, the community vied to redeem a wide range of social deviants—foundlings, orphans, juvenile delinquents, prostitutes, drunkards, and criminals. But in the haste to help, it was inevitable that mistakes were made. The Reverend Joseph Tuckerman, a retired Congregational minister from Chelsea, established the Boston Society for the Prevention of Pauperism (BSPP) in 1833 to remedy such mistakes by standardizing the city's private almsgiving. Professional beggars and fraudulent widows and orphans were suspected of exploiting scarce funds, and a district committee system to investigate each application for alms was considered necessary. Excessive generosity and duplication of charitable efforts were believed to encourage the unworthy poor to beg rather than to work, and this Tuckerman and his Harvard classmates abhorred.[17]

The BSPP was not successful in imposing order on Boston charity because most private charities were too independent and individualistic to cooperate closely or consistently. They were content to provide clothing, food, fuel, and small sums of money to a few "worthy and respectable poor" applicants, or to refer the able-bodied young to domestic service or farm jobs. Nevertheless, the children of the poor continued to interest the BSPP and many of its sister charities more than adult paupers did. Tuckerman focused on the unemployed children of the lower class who were not in school, seldom in church, and destined to become drunkards, gamblers, and thieves. The depression and the Broad Street Riot in 1837 brought to his attention the large number of illiterate lower-class boys loitering on the streets and wharves and committing petty crimes.[18]

As Irish immigrants multiplied in Boston's North End, Fort Hill, and South Cove slums in the 1840s, the city fathers came under increasing pressure from Tuckerman and his colleagues in the many private charity societies to expand municipal controls and services for wayward children. The image of the city as a center of temptation, vice, crime, disorder, and disease—far different from the idealized farm or small town childhood most moral entrepreneurs like Tuckerman recalled—aroused fear that corrupt individuals would destroy American society. The greatest number of these menaces were found among the urban poor and immigrant Irish. The prisons and poorhouses were crowded with them, and few were considered capable of reform. But their children might be redeemable. To this end, Boston gentlemen sponsored a variety of benevolent enterprises to oversee and control poor children, to rescue them from the dangerous classes by private charity backed by public authority.[19]

The coming of the Irish even before the potato famine led to a heightened sense of ethnicity and class consciousness among Yankees, and along with overt anti-Catholicism—burning the Ursuline convent school, and the Broad Street and Montgomery Guards Riots—came greater municipal surveillance of the children of the Irish poor. As poverty increased in Boston, so did disease, disorder, drunkenness, gambling, prostitution, and squalor, and the City Council reported in 1846 that much of the lawbreaking was due to hundreds of truant and vagrant children on the streets each day. City Marshal Francis Tukey quickly agreed when Mayor Josiah Quincy, Jr., ordered a crack-down in 1849 on vicious boys and idle youth.[20] The arrests of juveniles sharply increased in 1850–65, far beyond the increase in the juvenile population, and the School Committee warned of the menace that truants' posed to public order and safety. Truancy laws passed in 1850 and 1852 and the appointment of three truant officers were official recognition of the gravity of this problem, and municipal responsibilities in meeting it. Still the private charities sought a role in controlling and preventing juvenile delinquency.[21]

Civil leaders who joined private charitable associations like the BSPP and subscribed funds to the Boston Asylum for Indigent Boys or the Boston Farm School considered the public schools one means of disciplining the potentially dangerous children of the lower class. They designed the expanding public school system on the orderly, efficient model "of the cotton-mill and the railroad" and "with the model state's prison" in mind, as Charles Francis Adams recalled.[22] The city's leading gentlemen were thoroughly familiar with voluntary associations created for economic and social purposes and naturally applied methods successful in business to activities in charity, corrections, and education. However, in practice the public school scarcely matched these industrious standards, and antebellum schoolboys led an often riotous classroom existence.[23] Incorrigible pupils and truants were isolated from the docile majority of classmates by sending them to the House of Reformation, especially if they were newcomers to the community from Ireland.

Both the public school and the municipal reform school originated from middle-class determination to impose obedience, order, punctuality, cleanliness, morality, and self-discipline on Boston children, and with the children of immigrants new to Boston ways, the need was even more urgent. Bostonians worried about changes in family government and the disappearance of their small, homogeneous community. Some believed that the disestablishment of the Congregational Church in 1833 symbolized the need for alternative institutions to curb the young.[24] For most boys and girls, parents and public schools sufficed, but an incorrigible minority required compulsory training in the House of Reformation or some other juvenile asylum. Boston followed the examples of New York City and Philadelphia in using these new institutions to teach unteachable children not merely reading, writing, and arithmetic; but, more importantly, appropriate values and behavior.[25]

Thus it was moral training that the founders of the House of Reformation valued, and for which they celebrated Wells's administration. Astute observers like Tuckerman, Louis Dwight, Samuel Gridley Howe, and

Horace Mann, however, were early critics of the House of Reformation once it departed from moralism to mere bureaucratic orderliness. They were committed to science, progress, and republican principles and tended to emphasize the need for practicality and reason in law and government. They believed the new age should not be saddled with the fears and prejudice of the past and should be open-minded toward innovation. Despairing of reforming the reform school amid the chaos of municipal politics, they turned to private charity to find a way to rescue wayward children humanely, efficiently, and economically. Their main objective remained to prevent poor children from falling from the ranks of the respectable and worthy poor into the depths of the dangerous classes. While not willing to disrupt the public schools by admitting incorrigible pupils, who would have a pernicious influence on their classmates, they found the House of Reformation too harsh, inadequate, and inflexible by the 1840s. For their purposes, another means of quarantining morally diseased children from both the terminally delinquent and the morally healthy had to be devised. This "ruling class war on poverty" focused on superior private societies to protect wayward children who seemed still open to salvation.[26]

Romantic reformers—educated men and women imbued with the idealism of the German philosopher Immanuel Kant and Ralph Waldo Emerson, who had celebrated the individual and his perfectibility—likewise found the public congregate institutions unsuitable for antebellum children. Their idealization of preindustrial society and romanticized recollections of happy childhood on New England farms, predisposed them, also, to find fault with the high walls, rigid discipline, and regimentation of the House of Reformation.[27] Such institutions were not suitable for reforming young citizens and were antithetical to life in the new Republic.[28] The antidote they prescribed for the social ills of pauper children was to be found in the same kind of farm family life that had produced (in myth or reality) men and women like themselves.[29] The first private charities for Boston children looked to traditional methods, domestic service, and apprenticeship in rural families. In 1800 Mrs. Hannah Stillman, shocked by the sexual abuse of young orphaned girls in the North End, founded the city's first such private institution, the Boston Female Asylum. This orphanage and child-placing service was joined by the like-minded Boston Asylum for Indigent Boys in 1814, the Boston Farm School in 1832, and the Boston Children's Friend Society in 1833.[30]

Each of these was a small, selective (in membership, staff, and clients), private voluntary association formed to accomplish moral purposes beyond the ken of local government. They all shared the policy of receiving (rather than actively seeking) young, "innocent" (i.e., virginal, noncriminal) boys and girls who were first trained and then apprenticed as domestic servants or farm hands to rural Yankee households, where they would grow up under surrogate parents and learn traditional skills, values, and morals. Rural households and farms needed young hands to replace those who migrated to cities or western states. Concerned with the temptation and turmoil of rapidly expanding Boston, in which the impressionable children of the lower class had diminishing opportunities for traditional family discipline and training, these early child-saving societies volunteered a mixture of religious benevolence and social control. Charity was rooted in their Puritan origins and became possible as merchant princes grew rich. It permitted these bourgeois ladies and gentlemen to fulfill moral obligations, earn social distinction and to display new-found wealth with an aristocratic noblesse oblige.[31]

Hannah Morgan Stillman took the lead in such a society. The daughter of a prominent Philadelphia surgeon and the wife of Boston's leading Baptist minister, she was one of the first Boston ladies to organize women in a charity which extended the "woman's sphere" beyond the home and the church. Maternal concern for the well-being of orphaned girls justified a new form of association for elite women, and the proliferation of such societies in Boston and other cities was prompted as much by the desire to socialize as to uplift. With her husband's consent and the cooperation of a few charitable gentlemen, Mrs. Stillman rallied sixty ladies in 1800 to donate funds to establish the Boston Female Asylum (BFA). Discreet newspaper announcements and private solicitation among friends and acquaintances raised the necessary funds to operate a home on Lincoln Street for a dozen Boston girls aged three to twelve. They were trained in household skills, given a common school education, and then placed out from ages twelve to eighteen as domestic servants in respectable families. Some girls were adopted from the BFA, but most became maids, cooks, or seamstresses. At age eighteen, if not married by then, they were released from BFA supervision, and their employers were required to provide the girl with a fixed sum of money (usually $50 or $100) and some clothing.[32] At the time of admission to the BFA, the following document was signed for each girl:

Form of Obligation to be Signed by a Parent or Guardian on Giving up a Child, or Ward to the Protection of the Boston Female Asylum.
———, I the Subscriber, being solicitous that my child shall receive the benefits and advantages of the Boston Female Asylum, and the Board of Managers of the Institution being willing, provided I relinquish her to them, to receive and provide for her, I do hereby promise and engage, not to interfere in the management of her in any respect, nor visit her without their consent. And in consideration of their thus receiving and providing for her until she shall be of age to leave the Asylum, and then placing her in a suitable home in which to remain during her minority, I

do hereby relinquish all right and claim to her and her services until she shall be eighteen years of age. And I do engage that I will not seek any compensation for the same, nor take her from, or induce her to leave the family, where she shall be placed by the Board of Managers.

About 345 parents signed this form from 1857 to 1887, but 17 percent of them were illiterate and signed with a crossed mark.[33] Their understanding of the legal rights they signed away is reasonably questioned. In its first thirty-three years of operation, the BFA admitted 328 girls, and admissions gradually grew to about forty girls annually by 1860. Thus it was a small institution, housing carefully selected Yankee girls; Catholic, Black, and illegitimate girls were usually refused by the BFA, as were girls with a criminal in the family. Such girls were not considered likely to make suitable maids, cooks, or seamstresses, let alone adopted daughters.

Almost from the first, applicants could not all be accommodated. References were required from applicant families, and BFA members visited a girl when placed, but usually did so only in cases of dissatisfaction on the employer's part. Change of placement was customary if the girl proved unsuitable for any reason.[34] Alone, afraid, ill-informed, and defenseless, these homeless and orphan girls were easy victims of sexual exploitation and mental illness. Husbands, sons, male relatives, tradesmen, and other designing men sought them out, and the BFA records repeatedly list terse, guarded references to girls' sexual misconduct and indiscretion. Despite some efforts to safeguard their young charges, the BFA had chronic problems with "immoral" and "deranged" girls. They were sent away in disgrace to have their bastard babies at the State Infirmary in Tewksbury or committed to the State Lunatic Asylum in Worcester.[35]

The BFA considered its mission to be the training of respectable working-class Protestant Yankee girls to become skillful, trustworthy, honest, and moral domestic servants in the homes of people much like the BFA directors themselves. Their names read like a Harvard College roll call: Adams, Cheever, Hunnewell, Jackson, Lowell, Niles, Paine, and Storrow.[36] Education was deliberately limited to the common school curriculum and housewifery. Several cases mention approval by the managers of employers who refused to enroll girls in local schools.[37] In 1894 one girl was brought back from New Hampshire by the BFA when town selectmen insisted she be sent to the public school. Her employer and the BFA stoutly maintained she was hired to work and not to attend school, and that she was "not bright and would have bad influence on the boys at school."[38] Clearly, the class consciousness of these philanthropic ladies was not in doubt. To keep one of their charges from being "over-educated," they did not hesitate to impeach her intelligence or character or to change her family placement.

In 1844 the directors moved the BFA from its original Lincoln Street house to the fringe of Boston at 1008 Washington Street, where an imposing brick building had been built just east of Dover Street. The BFA remained here until 1896, by which time "it was felt to be a very disadvantageous background for the wholesome, natural out-of-door life which should be led by children." The South End had become a teeming immigrant quarter, so the orphanage was moved to the nine-acre Bartlett estate in Lexington. About twenty orphans attended the local churches but were educated in their own private school, presumably to prevent their "bad influence" on Lexington boys and lest they inadvertently be taught something in school beyond their station in life. By 1906 deinstitutionalization was sweeping charity work and was recognized as more economical, so the BFA (renamed the Boston Society for the Care of Girls in 1909) sold the home, invested the funds in solid State Street securities, and established an office in Boston at 184 Boylston Street. There the BSCG attracted the Back Bay matron who "finds time in her busy life to interest herself in the poor and needy girls who come seeking help," as well as professional social workers who "help any girl in need with no question as to race or creed."[39]

But for more than a century, the BFA persisted in teaching the cult of domesticity by its apprenticeship program. Homeless girls were taken up by this Brahmin ladies' charity and trained to be the faithful servants the upper class found so difficult to keep. The Irish colleens gave the BFA girls some competition after 1840, but what New England family would not prefer a BFA swamp Yankee maid to a priest-ridden Irish biddy? It was not immigration that ended the BFA, but rather the belated realization that apprenticeship was obsolete, a vestige of the eighteenth-century society of status, order, deference, and authority. The nineteenth-century Industrial Age had little place for individuals bound to community, family, and craft.

Before the advent of modern social work in the 1890s, BFA admissions policy was determined by whim and sentiment. Bastard daughters usually were not accepted; but if contrition was manifest, as in an 1890 case in which the mother "had written a very repentant note," an exception could be made. Moral character weighed very heavily with these do-gooders and a latter-day Hester Prynne had to be very convincing to have her "Pearl" accepted by the BFA. Daughters of inter-racial unions were sometimes accepted but most often refused. Vocational training gave a girl a bare literacy but a thorough grounding in housekeeping and sewing to fit her for service or marriage. Typing and music lessons were rejected by the BFA for fear that they would make the girls unsatisfied with domestic service or raise their expectations. Did the BFA have the girls' best interests in mind? Probably, but they were undoubtedly blinded by the class, race, and religious bias of their time and place. Social mobility was proper for an ambitious middle-class individual whose pluck and luck took him up into the upper classes, but it was almost taboo for a lower-class girl to attempt to rise too far in status in the highly stratified Boston of the nineteenth century. It was unwise even to encourage these poor but honest working girls to climb the socio-economic ladder. Rather, they should be made content with their lot in life and grateful for BFA charity in training and placing them with a kind mistress. A girl might hope, perhaps, for a decent husband someday, but this and no more. That was the BFA's prescription for a happy orphan girl's life.[40]

Mrs. Stillman and her elite successors filled leisure hours and widowhood with estimable private charity, using funds raised genteelly by private subscription and bequests from among their own social peers. The BFA was a matronly charity, and most of the officers and managers in the antebellum period were married women (88 percent) from the families Oliver Wendell Holmes dubbed the Boston Brahmins. The act of incorporation in 1803 recognized the legal disabilities of married women (whose husbands legally controlled their wives' property) by providing that the treasurer always be a single woman. This can be interpreted as a common sense precaution or as evidence of protofeminist strategy, but legal changes in the rights of married women to manage property led the founders' granddaughters in 1910 to alter the charter to permit a man to serve as treasurer. Few other changes occurred in the BFA before this, but as twentieth-century professional social workers gradually replaced these philanthropic ladies, the BFA evolved into the Boston Society for the Care of Girls (BSCG). This oldest of the child-saving societies maintained its traditional and conservative goal of helping homeless orphans and other "worthy girls" by affiliating in 1909 (and merging in 1922) with the Boston Children's Aid Society. It relocated to a Beacon Hill office with the BCAS and grafted its Brahmin board of trustees onto the equally genteel BCAS board of State Street bankers and lawyers and clubwomen.[41]

*   *   *

The Boston Female Asylum had a brother institution in the Boston Asylum for Indigent Boys (BAIB), established in 1814 at the corner of Cambridge and Lynde Streets in the West End of the city, and located from 1820 to 1835 in the North End mansion built in the seventeenth century by Governor William Phips at Salem and Charter Streets. Caring largely for poor orphan boys ages seven to fourteen, the Asylum was well fenced to discourage running away or "absconding," but the boys did manage a lively trade in toys and trifles they made and sold to the pupils from a nearby schoolhouse. Although the two groups of boys were forbidden contact, sales were made surreptitiously through the fence in the

1830s. In 1835 the Asylum merged with the Farm School on Thompson Island in Boston harbor and moved to the island under the name Boston Asylum and Farm School for Indigent Boys. This institution was visited by Charles Dickens in 1842, and Nathaniel Hawthorne described the "little tanned agriculturalists" in blue uniforms perched on the fence waving goodbye to him during another visit by Boston literary gentlemen. In 1907 the school became the Farm Trade School and continued to serve the orphan boys of Boston until 1965.[42]

Joseph Tuckerman, George Ticknor, James Bowdoin, Patrick Jackson, Mayor Theodore Lyman, Judge Charles Jackson, Judge William Prescott and other prominent Boston leaders raised $23,000 in 1832 to establish the Farm School for orphans, bastards, and pauper boys too old (over age ten) for admission to the BAIB. These boys were innocent of any crime for which they could be sent to the House of Reformation, but without suitable families. To train poor but honest lads in a practical occupation and Christian morals, the Farm School opened under the supervision of Reverend Eleazer Mather Porter Wells, who had been the superintendent of the House of Reformation and was a close friend of Joseph Tuckerman, the Unitarian minister-at-large to the poor of Boston. Wells bought the 140-acre island from the town of Dorchester in November 1832 for $6,000, and commissioned Charles Bulfinch to design the building. But Wells found island life (and perhaps the boys) too strenuous and resigned his position to Captain Daniel Chandler, a veteran of the War of 1812, in October 1833. The city of Boston acquired title to Thompson Island in 1834, but the school remained and prospered, especially after merging with the well-endowed BAIB in 1835. It sheltered about one hundred boys aged six to eighteen. William Ellery Channing, the city's leading Unitarian, was interested in the school's staff and advised Tuckerman, the most active trustee, "not to be too economical but rather to make changes, till you find a man who can understand the young and reach their spiritual nature."[43]

By 1900 the Farm Trade School was a venerable Boston institution with two thousand worthy graduates who learned printing, woodworking, carpentry, ship-building, painting, and agriculture in the four-year course. Mechanical drawing, music, sports, and the common school subjects rounded out the curriculum, with a major emphasis on practical education suited for a working-class man. The Farm School managed to avoid both pauperization and the reform school stigma. The school prided itself on producing steady, hard-working, sober young men, much as the BFA did for girls. They were both examples of the anti-institutionalism that characterized Boston private charity in the antebellum period and sharply distinguished them from the public welfare system. By carefully admitting only wayward (that is, predelinquent) children to these small, well-man-

Boston Farm School, at Thompson Island, Boston Harbor, 1852. *(Print Departmen* *Boston Public Library.)*

Dr. Samuel Gridley Howe (1801–76). *(Simmons College Archives.)*

Rev. Joseph Tuckerman (1778–184 *(Simmons College Archives.)*

aged asylums they enjoyed a relatively quiet and successful career and a paternalistic, home-like atmosphere in contrast to the more penal county training schools and state reform schools designed for older (or simply less fortunate) youths from the so-called "dangerous classes."

* * *

Both the BFA and the Farm School (as well as its older BAIB component) were private voluntary associations chartered by the state for charitable child welfare work. Elite Bostonians founded, funded, and managed them with the cooperation of the town (and later the city), county, and state governments and the active encouragement of the churches of Boston. It was considered altogether proper for an association of like-minded community leaders to engage in this moral reform charity work, and no one questioned their motives or methods. Even Bishop Jean Cheverus sent children, two Catholic girls, to the BFA; showing his caution only by providing a copy of their parents' marriage certificate to verify the children's legitimate birth. In general, Boston was grateful and supportive of the BFA, the BAIB, the Farm School, and for most of the later private agencies and institutions which emerged. Rivalry was remarkably rare, and although inter-agency cooperation and coordination was to be a twentieth-century phenomenon in Boston social welfare, these early efforts at child-saving prepared the way in the city and state and nation for more expansive kinds of child-saving in the Civil War period, when the large number of wayward waifs and urban urchins demanded new child welfare efforts.[44]

In 1810 the United States had one of the highest fertility rates in the world, and the number of children under the age of five was 1,358 per 1,000 women aged twenty to forty-four. In the 1830s the national birthrate exceeded the average for other Western nations by more than 20 percent. These statistics, however, mask important variations between ethnic groups and social classes. The astonishingly high birthrate for Irish Catholic immigrants and other working-class Bostonians caused great concern to middle- and upper-class Yankees. There were 22,000 children aged five to fifteen in Boston in 1830 and more than 39,000 by 1860. How many of them were wayward waifs is uncertain, but Boston had twenty child welfare organizations by the Civil War as well as fifteen private asylums and three public asylums for orphans, truants, and delinquents. Each religious denomination vied to maintain its own "Home" for dependent children, and it was clear that the philanthropic spirit remained strong in the "Athens of America."[45]

One of these children's aid societies approached the problem of homeless lower-class children in a more aggressive fashion in 1849, and revolutionized the child welfare enterprise and its determination to transmit middle-class culture to the children of the poor. The Children's Mission to the Children of the Destitute was the first major child-saving society in the United States to employ agents to search city streets, wharves, railway stations, theaters, and even jails for children in need of supervision. In 1849 the Reverend George Merrill, a Unitarian Sunday School Superintendent, was inspired by the plea of his twelve-year-old daughter, Fannie: "Can't we do something for these poor little things?" Merrill and Fannie were walking through a South End slum en route to church when they saw ragged children playing in the gutter. Those "poor little things" became the target of the Children's Mission established a few months later. Merrill persuaded his liberal congregation and an association of Unitarian clergymen that Sunday School students would donate enough pennies in mite boxes to support a missionary and a Temporary Home. His goal was to rescue "street arabs" and "guttersnipes" from the dangerous classes, and the perdition they were surely facing.[46]

Although the pennies of middle-class Sunday School children never totally supported the Children's Mission outreach program, the mite boxes were a substantial and steady sources of funds from 1849 to 1950. In cloth bags or paper boxes made by volunteer churchwomen, thousands of dollars annually augmented the Children's Mission budget. When the salary of the first street missionary, Joseph E. Barry, was to be increased in 1850, the directors appealed directly to their young Sunday School patrons:

> By giving up some luxury, or denying themselves a pleasure, they could not only add to their own happiness, but increase Mr. Barry's means of usefulness.[47]

As the Protestant Sunday School movement expanded throughout the nineteenth century, so too did the amount of money raised by the Children's Mission and other church-affiliated charities for homeless children.

This penny ante philanthropy had a dual purpose. It provided charitable resources for the poor and the heathen, in urban slums or in foreign missions; but even more importantly, it taught the children of the affluent the value of religious benevolence. This didactic charity can be seen in another means of fund-raising used by the Children's Mission. Children's fiction published by the Children's Mission especially for Sunday School reading imparted to middle-class readers lessons of moral responsibility. Colorful stories told of starving Irish immigrants in squalid slums who were saved by courageous boys and girls or self-sacrificing Protestant missionaries. These naive stories gave socially insulated children instruction in the need for Christian charity and inspired both funds and empathy for the Children's Mission work with Boston's waifs.

The Reverend Joseph E. Barry was the Children's Mission first "street worker" 1849. *(Parents' and Children's Service Association.)*

William Crosby served as CM treasurer and superintendent from 1858 to 1907. *(Parents' and Children's Service Association.)*

In this Christian propaganda for middle-class children, we discover an early advocate of the Social Gospel. Edward Everett Hale (1822–1909), Boston's well-known Unitarian minister and author, was an active supporter of the Children's Mission and imbued its work with the idea of renovation of society through the influence of a liberal, active Christianity. Hale preached to the young Children's Mission patrons in 1857 on the dangers that well-to-do Christians faced and the benefit that charity provided to the cheerful giver:

> The children of the moderately rich are too apt to envy the splendor and profusion indulged in by the affluent. . . . To counteract this influence, it was a blessed thing for our children to think more of the miseries of the less favored, and to endeavor to relieve them. They should compare their condition, not with those above, but with those below them. Many

a discontented child would become marvelously contented with its own condition, if it could follow Mr. Barry from house to house and see what he sees from day to day.[48]

When Reverend Merrill hired Joseph Barry in 1849 to act as an urban missionary for homeless children, he had few precedents to follow. Joseph Tuckerman had been minister-at-large to the poor of the city, and the Overseers of the Poor sent district representatives to visit paupers at home, but no charity employed an agent to hunt for homeless children in alleys and lock-ups. This kind of outreach program later became common in child welfare, and Charles Loring Brace made his reputation in just this manner in New York City's Five Points slums in the 1850s. However, the Children's Mission deserved credit for inventing this useful policy. It proved to be a widely imitated practice, but one that seemed extraordinary to more conventional charities and the orthodox Protestant churches.

Children's Mission innovation did not stop with mite boxes, children's fiction, and the street worker; in 1850 the first "orphan train" left Boston taking thirty waifs to foster homes in New Hampshire and Vermont. The directors shared the belief of the BFA and Farm School that urban slums were unsuitable homes for children, but placing individual orphans as domestic servants or apprentice boys was too slow and time-consuming. The railroads made it possible to bring large groups of homeless children from the city to rural towns where local clergy and church members would cooperate in placing them out and supervising their care. Although precise details are lacking, by 1850 Children's Mission orphan trains were used to place children on farms throughout New England. Until this practice was interrupted by the Civil War, agents took bands of thirty to fifty children by train to New England and Middle Western communities where local churches made informal indenture, apprenticeship, foster care, or adoption arrangements in respectable families. This practice became so useful that the Children's Mission Temporary Home on Tremont Street organized two or three orphan trains each year. The New York Children's Aid Society (established in 1852 by Charles Loring Brace, a Congregationalist minister and urban missionary) imitated this Boston child-placing method and Horatio Alger, Jr., made the New York CAS practice famous. Brace learned this method from John Earl Williams, the first president of the Children's Mission, who moved to New York City in 1851 to become president of the Metropolitan Bank and a life-long treasurer and trustee of the CAS. The Children's Mission and the CAS saw the orphan train as a modern, economical and efficient way of removing the surplus juvenile population from the overcrowded city. Children living in slums without proper family discipline or moral training were placed in decent rural households in northern New England, upper New York State, and in under-populated Midwestern states.[49]

Exactly why Boston children should be sent to "the West" was never made clear, Horace Greeley's admonition, "Go West, young man," notwithstanding. If the city was so unspeakably foul and dangerous, why did middle- and upper-class philanthropists remain in it with their own children? One Children's Mission sermon in 1859 provided some indication of the child-savers' justification for the orphan train:

> Boston is not large enough. You have not room here to carry out all your plans. It is overloaded already, and, if not relieved, will sink under its own weight. . . . The city is dangerously and alarmingly overcome with a surplus of a mildewing population. We have filled up every place for our criminals. . . . There were a large number of people with nothing to do. Nobody was in fault. Work could not be found for them. But they must be relieved. Their children must be saved; and they cannot save themselves. In this city, you have set a bait for all the country around here by your provisions for the poor. They say, "The Bostonians take good care of everybody who can't take care of themselves; and we will go to Boston."[50]

This clergyman recommended sending more orphan trains to the midwest with larger groups of Boston children under the guidance of one or two agents. By 1859 more than 1,300 children had made the journey under Children's Mission direction. Joseph Barry, who was a Children's Mission agent for fifty years, brought boys and girls to his School Street office, where they were interviewed by the director, William Crosby. If found to be willing and needy, these "orphans" were sheltered in the Temporary Home on Tremont Street until a group of thirty to fifty children were ready to travel. Unitarian and Congregational clergymen in Ohio, Michigan, Illinois, Iowa, and Wisconsin cooperated by screening prospective families who requested a child. In some cases, the children were not actually orphans, but abused, abandoned, neglected, or runaway children; but with limited resources and an overwhelming evangelical zeal, the Children's Mission did not inquire too diligently to locate the relatives of children it found as suitable candidates. In a society familiar with hired hands, apprenticeship, black slavery, and domestic servants, this method of finding homes for poor children did not seem as strange or heartless as it may to modern readers. Because Children's Mission records have not survived, a review of the New York CAS experience may be useful in understanding the Boston orphan train.[51]

About two hundred children were placed annually by the CAS from 1853 to 1876, and this number rose to approximately 3,800 annually from 1876 to 1883. Orphan trains gradually declined in the 1890s and the practice was finally abandoned in 1929. Boys outnumbered girls three to one among those placed by the CAS. The low number of girls placed is probably due to the fact that boys were considered more useful and profitable on Midwestern farms, and also because of the reluctance of many charity workers, including the Children's Mission and the BFA, to become involved with pauper girls. The sexual threat that even mildly wayward girls posed in Victorian American eyes is not to be overlooked. Notoriously fearful of the gentler sex, and misunderstanding lower-class values and behavior as "saucy" or "unfeminine," most charity workers preferred to avoid them. The sexual abuse of servants and foster daughters was known to many charity agencies, and boys were simply a more convenient and safe target for charities. How could one guarantee the virtue and chastity of an orphan girl when even proper middle-class daughters were sexually suspect in Victorian America?[52]

Many of the city children "saved" by the Children's Mission workers were undoubtedly Irish Catholics, although precise data are lacking. It would be remarkable if this were not so, because in 1850, 41 percent of the inmates of the State Reform School for Boys in Westborough were Irish Catholic immigrants or the children of Irish immigrants. This was at a time when the Massachusetts foreign-born population was only 19 percent of the total population, and a year before the first Catholic asylum was opened for Boston boys. The proselytizing reputation of Boston charities—somewhat exaggerated but real enough—prompted a Nova Scotia priest to warn Irish parents emigrating to Massachusetts that Boston had a reputation for making Protestants of Catholics. He urged them to be careful, "especially of the children, or they will get them from you." Although the Children's Mission was an arm of the liberal Unitarian church and more tolerant than the orthodox Congregational and evangelical churches, it shared the common desire to persuade Roman Catholics to assimilate into American society by rejecting the Papacy in favor of patriotic Protestantism. In any case, whether by design or chance, Children's Mission and New York Children' Aid Society orphan trains carried thousands of Catholic children to Yankee families where they generally became Protestant church members, just as the child-savers hoped.[53]

Because the Children's Mission quietly conducted its work with little public notice and in a more tranquil and passive Catholic diocese than the New York CAS did, it avoided the criticism that Brace suffered for the indiscriminate placement of urban (often Catholic) children on unsupervised farms to the west and south. Children's Mission records are mostly silent on this issue, and the elite Boston directors quietly maintained their convictions about the efficacy of the orphan train method, which was imitated by many other organizations. They avoided publicity and controversy and continued this urban missionary work until 1897. Although Unitarian in origin and support, the Children's Mission assumed a nonsectarian posture in the 1860s and cooperated with sister organizations, and by the 1880s this also included Catholic child-savers. Conflict with Catholics was generally avoided in Boston, despite the open hostility Brace faced in New York from the Catholic clergy and press for his "child stealing" methods and for "shipping them by wholesale into the country."[54]

The Children's Mission did have one quarrel with Catholics when Joseph Barry obtained permission in 1849 from city officials to operate a Sunday School for poor children in the District Nine ward room. He prowled the nearby wharves to recruit pupils, and within a few weeks he had about 125 boys and girls attending classes each Sunday. They were attracted by the novelty of attending a free school as well as by gifts of shoes and clothing. One Sunday two Catholic men and two women stood at the door of the school and asked each child entering if he was Catholic. All Catholic children were persuaded to leave and only the non-Catholic minority remained. Attendance fell to fifty-four pupils, and many of the former pupils pelted the door and windows with mud and stones until the police arrived to protect the building. Mr. Barry sorrowfully related the incident in his annual report to the directors in 1850. The Children's Mission reported no further conflict with Boston Catholics after this, perhaps because the following year a Catholic priest, the Reverend George Foxcroft Haskins, opened an asylum for boys, and a network of Catholic Sunday Schools expanded. In any case, the Children's Mission successfully avoided trouble with Boston Catholics after this time.[55]

The permission the Children's Mission received to use a municipal building for sectarian purposes and for its agents to make daily visits to the Boston courts and jails is an indication of the vague lines between private and public authority in the Victorian period and the manifest civic support given moral and spiritual guardians in New England. This is in marked contrast with the denial of permission to Catholic priests to visit jails, prisons, and all public institutions during this time. In a similar vein, the decision to remove orphans by train to new homes to the west shows the interrelated ways of Boston gentlemen. State Street entrepreneurs were overwhelmingly Unitarian and had invested heavily in Midwestern railroads. So the railroad companies, anxious to populate the Midwestern states and accustomed to providing free passes and discounts to clergymen and politicians, were generous to the Children's Mission as well:

> Great facilities were rendered by the various companies on the route, and tickets have been furnished at reduced prices, notwithstanding which it is an expensive method, the distance to transport them being so great; the two companies costing our treasury four hundred and twenty-two dollars.[56]

Thus, with the cooperation of the city government in proselytizing children in Boston and the encouragement of the railroads in taking them

Boston, Mass., May 29th 1890

Dear Mrs Story;—
                I thought I would write
once more before I go West. I am going Friday,
so as I am going West you need not answer
this letter, I hope I will get a good-home Frank
is at the Home, but he will soon go after I
do, My School Teacher wanted me to write
a letter, and I was very glad to write, Mr
cooper thought it not best for Frank to go
West, four children went to homes, Now
I will close my letter,——
                From your friend
                Joseph Wick.

A rare letter by a child going west in 1890 on a NEHLW orphan train. *(New England Home for Little Wanderers.)*

to the underdeveloped Midwest, the orphan train became an accepted method of solving a social problem of growing concern. But it was not accepted by all Bostonians.

No provisions were made for orphan train passengers to contact their families and friends once placed in distant and unknown farms and small towns, and the religious preference of the child was generally ignored. The Reverend George F. Haskins, a convert to Catholicism and former Episcopal chaplain at the House of Reformation and member of the Overseers of the Poor, was very critical of this Children's Mission policy. He was a spokesman for Bishop John B. Fitzpatrick of Boston when he said:

To aid in the work of perversion . . . societies were formed to receive Catholic children and provide for them till a number should be collected sufficient to fill a car, when they should be steamed swiftly off to some western state and there sold, body and soul, to farmers and squatters. Missionaries, both male and female, were hired to prowl about certain quarters of the city, to talk with children in the streets, like the Manicheans of old, and invite and urge them to leave their friends and homes, picturing to them vistas of abundant food, clothes and money. Sunday schools were opened, and teachers employed to waylay children on their path to their own schools and to bribe them into theirs. If pastors and teachers sought their missing lambs in these wolves' dens, they found unfriendly policemen at the doors to prevent them entering.[57]

Father Haskins made this strident complaint about the City Mission, Boston's first Sunday School organization, as well as the Children's Mission. He knew exactly what Protestant child-savers hoped to accomplish. After Haskins became a Catholic priest, he recalled that as the Episcopal pastor of the Grace Church in Boston, he had lured Catholic boys into his church with candy and games on cold winter afternoons. He was unable to win any of their souls, however, and gave up the effort when he overheard one Irish boy tell his playmates he went in just for the candy not the sermon. So Catholics learned to be vigilant, and in 1856 Captain Nathaniel Shurtleff, Haskins's friend and fellow convert and the son of the mayor of Boston, was arrested for disrupting a Protestant Sunday School while searching for his missing Sunday School pupils.[58]

Later critics of the orphan train focused on the sink-or-swim basis of foster home placement in unsuperivsed, poorly investigated families, affording little or no contact with the child by the child-saver or his own relatives. In 1875 the National Conference of Charities and Corrections (NCCC) criticized the New York CAS for these careless practices, but this only resulted in a switch from those states which had complained (New England, New York, New Jersey, Pennsylvania, Ohio, Michigan, Illinois, and Wisconsin) to more amenable states (Virginia, Iowa, Missouri, Kansas, and Nebraska). Despite Brace's rhetoric about sending city orphans west as rugged young individuals seeking their fortune, 42 percent (or 38,719 of the 91,536 children) of the "wayward waifs" placed by the New York agency went to New York foster homes, and nine states received 91 percent of all the children placed from 1853 to 1893. This pattern showed many of the signs of indiscriminate placement where convenience suited the CAS, not the carefully selected individual placement policy Brace claimed.[59]

* * *

The changing concept of children in the view of the new child-rearing experts and professionally ambitious clergymen, and widespread disenchantment with large congregate institutions, had led to child-saving societies like the Boston Female Asylum, Boston Asylum for Indigent Boys, Boston Farm School, and the Children's Mission. In the name of anti-institutionalism and romantic reform, as well as an irresistible conviction that farm or rural life purified children, these Protestant charities sent thousands of urban lower-class youngsters to a wide variety of foster homes in the country.[60] But these Protestants against poverty found the task of ridding Boston of street arabs and guttersnipes an Augean undertaking. The House of Reformation was unequal to the task of reforming its inmates, and the traditional orphan asylums benefited only a small fraction of needy children. The orphan train was one solution, but still the baby boom of the first half of the nineteenth century was coming of age after the Civil War. These were the lower-class children of Irish immigrants and up-country Yankee migrants who persisted in truancy and petty crime and filled the street-hawking trades. They drank, smoked, frequented North End rat pits to gamble and would soon be attracted to grog-shops and brothels. Congregate asylums had done little to reduce their numbers or change their socially dangerous habits. Lack of parental supervision and self-control made them a potentially revolutionary proletariat in the eyes of conservative Republicans. Even the State Reform School for Boys, established by Theodore Lyman's contribution of $85,000 in 1846, proved both controversial and ineffective. The State School Ships in Boston and New Bedford were floating reform schools which trained some boys for the merchant marine and whaling trades, but this was hardly sufficient to clear the streets, courts and jails of juvenile delinquents. In the midst of the Civil War, concerned ladies and gentlemen searched for an answer to the Sisyphean problem of preventing juvenile delinquency.[61]

When a group of prominent ladies visited the Boston jail in 1864 to distribute religious tracts, they were shocked to find dozens of young children behind bars, awaiting trial in clean but grim cells, for want of bail money or because their parents could not be located. These women reacted in customary American fashion. They formed a committee to correct this injustice, from which emerged the Boston Children's Aid Society incorporated in 1864.[62] The BCAS hired the chaplain of the Suffolk County Jail, Rufus R. Cook, as its visiting agent to make daily tours of the jail, courts and truant offices to find homeless children whom he might help. "Uncle" Cook offered advice, bail money and intercession with the court as a voluntary probation officer.[63] He continued the pioneering work of John Augustus (1785–1859), a saintly Boston shoemaker who became the first unofficial probation officer in America at the Boston Police Court in 1841. Cook was even more successful than Augustus, and in 1866 he reported that among the 123 boys on probation to him, only seven were failures. By 1869 Cook had supervised 400 probationers, 320 of whom were without further court appearances. This early success quickly established the efficient reputation of the BCAS.[64]

To shelter homeless boys, the BCAS opened in 1864 a small private reformatory in West Newton called Pine Farm. Thirty boys aged eleven to fourteen were sent there by court or parent's orders. The BCAS usually required legal surrender or court commitment until majority, but most boys stayed at the 27 acre farm for only one year or until they learned farm chores, religious practices, steady work habits, and their common school lessons. The farmer, Wilbur Washburn; his wife; and two young women acted as parents, teachers, and role models for the boys.

When they had adjusted sufficiently to the rural regimen, BCAS agents placed each boy as a foster child on a New England farm.[65] By 1867 BCAS had conceived the idea of paying some families to raise a boy for whom no free foster home could be found. This was a method used in Germany with considerable success and the Boston Brahmin trustees were thoroughly familiar with these European developments from their own visits abroad.[66] Few children were legally adopted from BCAS, despite a Massachusetts law in 1851 permitting legal adoption of children in probate court, and most boys passed through several foster homes before "settling down," but most eventually found a permanent home. They remained in the legal custody of BCAS until age twenty-one, at least in theory.

In 1866 a separate reformatory for girls was established in West Newton, and continued until 1873. Girls were considered much more difficult to reform than boys (as discussed in chapter 3). Both farms held about thirty children each year. In 1868 the legislature granted the BCAS authority to receive children committed by the courts, although the Board of State Charities insisted on its right to inspect and regulate any private reformatory. Sheriff John M. Clark of Suffolk County was very supportive of BCAS goals as were most members of the bench.[67]

The realistic trustees, many of whom acquired administrative experience in Civil War military and civilian roles, acknowledged that some children were incorrigible and even after two years at Pine Farm "a large number will still remain for whom there is most hope in families such as ours, or in the stricter discipline of Public Institutions."[68] Unlike the charismatic Charles Loring Brace, BCAS trustees were not totally opposed to penal institutions for juveniles and never claimed that every child could adjust to family life on a farm. Some "hard cases" pined for the Boston gaslights and street corners.

Nevertheless, by 1896 approximately four hundred boys had passed through the Pine Farm program, and the BCAS trustees were justly proud of their success as child-savers.[69]

The conservative roots of BCAS reform were admittedly located "in the earnest feelings of a few individuals that the large and . . . increasing number of vicious boys is menacing our community."[70] This fear had prompted leading Bostonians, mostly in the Unitarian or Episcopal Church, the wealthy men and women who comprised the so-called Boston Brahmins, to found the BCAS in 1864 with funds raised from their small circle of elite families. They were experienced reformers who joined together for practical, innovative charity with something more in mind than simply another orphanage or placing-out society. They were not pioneers in charity work, but frankly hoped to benefit from the experience of older organizations like the Boston Female Asylum or the Children's Mission. They were neither visionaries nor dependent upon public contributions, state grants, or church affiliation. The BCAS was from the first a well-funded, well-managed, confident, purposeful, secular charity. No scandals, sectarian squabbles, ideological battles or financial crises threatened its work.

Quietly, effectively, privately, BCAS emerged by the 1870s as the state's leading child welfare agency, and by the 1890s it was a national pacesetter.[71] Unlike its sister charities in Boston and throughout New England, BCAS trustees acquired a reputation as broadminded, committed managers who made monthly personal visits to Pine Farm and the Girls' Home in Newton, and later to the Rock Lawn Farm in Foxborough, established in 1885 for younger boys.[72] They amicably referred Catholic children to Father Haskins's House of the Angel Guardian or to the Home for Destitute Catholic Children, and they even admitted Black children at a time when leading reformers were embarrassed to walk in Boston Common with Frederick Douglass.[73]

If the BCAS operated on any fixed philosophy, it was pragmatism with a dose of agrarianism. It epitomized the best of the American private charity spirit and eventually rose above its own elitism to establish Boston child welfare on a more equitable, professional basis. But in Victorian America the managers' faith in the rehabilitative power of the well-regulated asylum, which offered homeless children shelter and training in an ideal rural environment, was an integral part of the national ethos. BCAS policy was supported by a pragmatic, flexible, paternalistic ideology that promised young Yankee and Irish children a place in democratic society, but only if they were willing to conform to middle-class expectations and values.

Children's aid societies like BCAS spread rapidly in the Civil War era. None existed in the eighteenth century, but there were more than fifty by 1867. Small communities continued to rely on the poorhouse, apprenticeship, and "binding out" to care for homeless children, but large cities like Boston, New York, Philadelphia, Baltimore, and Chicago created private asylums for dependent or wayward children. The BCAS is probably typical of children's aid societies in urban centers in the 1870s, but perhaps more elite in its membership and more innovative and progressive in its policies than many. It was a prime example of patrician paternalism mobilized to eradicate public squalor by high-minded, pragmatic benevolence.[74]

The boys Cook removed from jail or court were sent to Pine Farm immediately. Lack of discipline was their most common problem, something the BCAS considered a great fault in the American family, which resulted in children who lacked the self-control to avoid and withstand the temptations of the new urban environment—truancy, gambling, drinking, stealing, and even brothels. BCAS intervened benevolently to remove endangered needy children from the baleful influence of their own families and neighborhoods. A short period of training in the healthy, orderly, natural, and disciplined life at Pine Farm was the remedy prescribed. They hoped that this moral and physical regimen would save children from sin, disease, crime, prison, and the gallows. Rescue fantasies or not, BCAS created a model family farm designed to test new ideas and child-rearing principles by the successful treatment of thirty children. These child-savers expected nothing less than the salvation of American society by reforming individual juvenile delinquents. Pine Farm was a nursery for young children intercepted on the road to ruin, an experiment to train youngsters to avoid or overcome the moral dangers of the modern city. The plastic nature of the child offered realistic hope that these goals could be accomplished without pauperization or incarceration of the child.[75]

Pine Farm was not a reform school (although BCAS called it a reformatory) like the House of Reformation or the Westborough and Lancaster state schools. Nor was it merely another orphanage. It was a working New England farm whose paternal managers were role models of the idealized parents every country boy should have had. As father, farmer, and master craftsman, Washburn governed the thirty boys firmly but kindly. The first priority was obedience, and this was obtained in the majority of cases without corporal punishment, physical restraint, or any discipline not

BCAS operated Pine Farm in Newton from 1864 to 1896. *(Boston Children's Service Association.)*

BCAS sent younger boys to Rock Lawn Farm in Foxboro from 1885 to 1899. *(Boston Children's Services Association.)*

common in a typical family (although the absence of corporal punishment made this an atypical family). The second priority was regularity in work habits as the boys learned the farm and housekeeping chores. BCAS assumed that steadiness in obedience and work inevitably led to reformation of character. Conformity, self-control, and moral regeneration were expected to follow.[76]

The greatest dangers to a boy's success at Pine Farm were parental interference and the lure of the boy's old haunts in the city. To avoid this, parents were forbidden to visit their children without permission and signed a legal document surrendering all rights to the child until age twenty-one. In other cases, the court was asked to commit the child to BCAS custody until his or her majority. This was necessary to remove a still salvageable child from his weak, careless, ignorant, or depraved parents and family.[77]

Acting *in loco parentis,* the BCAS conformed to the child-rearing advice of American experts like Lydia Child, Catharine Beecher, and Jacob Abbott and the example of French, German, and British reformatories. Poverty, immigration, geographic mobility, family deaths, and the heterogeneity of urban industrial life made intergenerational parenting infeasible or impossible, so the authors of child-rearing books became authoritative sources for parents and caretaking institutions after the Civil War. These experts pronounced grave warnings of moral degeneration and social disaster if children were neglected, overindulged, or improperly raised. This note of urgency and panic was characteristic of many reformers who warned of imminent social decay and disorder unless Americans redeemed themselves by one reform or another. In fact, many child welfare advocates had been active participants in evangelical, temperance, health, abolitionist, and other antebellum crusades. In a sense, the BCAS reflected the distillation of the ferment of American reformism.[78] However, earlier uncompromising, fanatical, dogmatic social criticism disappeared as fastidious Mugwumps, like BCAS trustee Robert Treat Paine, succeeded the antebellum reformers.

BCAS offered a private solution for a peculiar public crisis. Americans now feared for their own children. This was because middle-class Americans did not recognize the North End street urchins as *their* children. These uprooted immigrants' children were considered too foreign and unassimilated to be accepted calmly and traditionally as "our children." In reaction to new fears of urban children by Boston's best men, BCAS hoped that social stability would follow its individualized rehabilitation of wayward boys and girls. In their view, the decline of community life as Boston expanded and changed had weakened family government to the extent that wayward city children required specialized training in well-ordered (but not congregate or penal) asylums like Pine Farm. By removal from the slum and isolation from the "disordered" family life that degraded them, children would be restored in most cases to natural morality. The careful admission policy, substitution of BCAS guardianship, Pine Farm environment, and the expert knowledge of the managers were planned to reclaim each child's innate innocence.[79]

The social upheavals on the Civil War homefront, which removed the restraining hands of thousands of lower-class Massachusetts fathers from their families, was blamed for the overflow of soldiers' dependents in city and state charitable institutions. BCAS responded, like the Home for Destitute Catholic Children (opened in 1864) and the New England Home for Little Wanderers (1865), to Lincoln's promise "to care for him who shall have borne the battle, and for his widow, and his orphan."[80]

The nation answered this call from the sacred lips of the fallen president by establishing more than 100 asylums for Civil War orphans and widows. In the Gilded Age, the care of homeless children expanded into a national mania, the most sentimental charity in an age which revelled in sentiment and pathos. By the 1870s, child welfare became an unregulated boom business and a form of private enterprise admittedly in need of leadership and professional administration. It was at this time that BCAS asserted its own principles on the national stage under the direction of an ambitious new child-saver.[81]

When Rufus Cook's health failed in 1885, Robert Treat Paine (1835–1910), president of the Associated Charities and the leading member of the BCAS board of trustees, hired a young Harvard College man who had just graduated *summa cum laude*. Like many others of his generation, Charles Wesley Birtwell (1860–1932) entered social work in an offhand fashion. He was born in Lawrence, Massachusetts, of "sturdy Methodist stock" and considered medicine and law while working his way through Harvard. Professor Francis Greenwood Peabody's course in social ethics, and Birtwell's natural inclination toward experimentation, led to his first position as Cook's assistant visiting agent in 1885. Influenced by the settlement house movement, the National Conference of Charities and Corrections (formed in 1874), and the growing interest of middle-class reformers in social work as a profession, Birtwell made it his life's career.[82]

Since 1880 BCAS had been moving toward the position that its role was to investigate and "adjust" any needy child in Metropolitan Boston and to refer children it could not help to other child welfare agencies. This broad basis of social work gave BCAS a freedom of action and a constituency greater than that of any other private charity in New England. With a substantial endowment and a broad-minded board of trustees, Birtwell, who became the general secretary (or chief executive officer) in 1887, had an opportunity to exercise his vigorous talents. He quickly won the support and admiration of the board and gradually overcame the con-

Charles W. Birtwell (1860–1932) managed BCAS from 1885 to 1911. *(Boston Children's Services Association.)*

Robert Treat Paine (1835–1910) epitomized the Boston Brahmin philanthropist as a BCAS director and president of the Associated Charities, 1879–1907. *(Simmons College Archives.)*

servative suspicion of the older child-saving organizations as he made BCAS a national leader in child welfare.[83]

Birtwell closed the Pine Farm and Rock Lawn Farm homes in 1896 and 1899, preferring to concentrate on foster homes. Other societies continued to care for narrow categories of children—Catholics, Lutherans, Jews, "Americans," orphans, infants, the blind, unwed mothers, the children of seamen or clergymen, Boston residents, and so forth—but BCAS assisted all those who fell "into the gaps that exist between the various agencies." Consequently, its caseload increased, and a better-educated, professionally trained staff was employed. Birtwell built a modern, innovative, expanding child welfare agency while Boston showered him with praise and support. He realized that the day of parochialism and partisanship had passed, and that to survive, private charities must accept the new scientism and changes in religion, ethics, medicine, law, and urban life. Under his guidance, BCAS became the cutting edge of social work for children and families.[84]

Home libraries were a new method Birtwell developed to identify, supervise, and uplift lower-class children in 1887. A small bookcase containing carefully selected children's books and magazines was placed in the home of a lower-class boy or girl, and ten of his or her friends met there once a week for story-reading by a BCAS volunteer. The children exchanged and discussed the books and formed a peer group under the watchful supervision of the "friendly visitor." The visitors were middle-class women trained by Birtwell to discourage street corner loafing, bad manners, rowdyism, and truancy and to teach conformity, politeness, patriotic values, and a love of "good literature." They also kept a record of each family and reported neighborhood crime, housing violations, and sanitation hazards to the police, Board of Health, or Watch and Ward Society. This primitive form of group work may seem trivial, but public libraries were forbidding institutions to poor children in 1887, and reading was an inexpensive middle-class habit which Birtwell recognized as a preventive measure for potential juvenile delinquents. This anticipatory socialization was a fruitful method used by BCAS for more than thirty years to penetrate lower-class neighborhoods without the onus of charity or legal auspices. Like Birtwell's children's savings banks and gardening programs, the home library was an ingenious, economical and effective way to bring bourgeois values to unwitting "clients."[85]

Birtwell avoided the child labor controversy, but lent his support to the industrial trade school movement sweeping urban public schools in the 1880s. He championed a pragmatic, realistic approach to adolescents and challenged the Horatio Alger myth that the messenger boy could become president of the corporation. He knew that many children in the street trades—bootblacks, newsboys, candy butchers, and flower girls—were truants who added to the ranks of juvenile delinquents, criminals, and prostitutes. American society matured quickly in the Gilded Age, and the route to success for the poor child was in education, conformity, and middle-class socialization, not in penny-ante entrepreneurship. Earnestly Birtwell preached this message to the BCAS and its clients. He opened this new mode of social mobility to working-class Boston by carefully planned campaigns for children's savings banks and gardens, vocational schools, kindergartens, cooking classes, gymnastics, playgrounds, supervised foster homes, child guidance clinics, casework methods, and the juvenile court.[86]

BCAS links to the moral supervision of evangelical crusades could be discerned in the 1890s. Birtwell was inducted into the Boston Watch and Ward Society, established in 1873 by Godfrey Lowell Cabot to suppress vice in cooperation with Anthony Comstock. He was one of Professor

A BCAS Home Library group in the North End, June 1889. *(Boston Children's Service Association.)*

Francis G. Peabody's proteges in social ethics and an ally of Phillips Brooks and Bishop William Lawrence. Birtwell, like these Episcopalian leaders, rejected the austerity of the Puritan heritage which was still strong in Massachusetts, and he agreed that the focus of divine attention was on man, not on the churches, which existed only that men might lead better lives. In this new moral tradition, Birtwell became the general secretary of the American Federation for Sex Hygiene and a strong proponent of sex education for school children.[87]

Robert Treat Paine, who founded the Associated Charities in 1879 to introduce scientific philanthropy and business-like methods to social welfare in Boston, urged data collection and accurate statistics as the basis for BCAS programs. Birtwell accepted these changes, and reported in 1890 that "a body of information is thus being created from which may come the enrichment of the whole programme of preventive effort."[88] These new data showed the passing of the apprenticeship system, which was regretted by BCAS managers chiefly because it was not replaced by another method of training boys as skilled craftsmen. BCAS trustees studied the Massachusetts Bureau of Labor Statistics reports which demonstrated that the factory system provided adolescents with only dead-end unskilled jobs at low pay.

Despite this progressivism and statistical gathering, country life continued to hold attractions for BCAS trustees if not for city boys. In 1890 Paine argued that the country should be expected to help BCAS to reform problem children from the city. When the electric streetcars almost reached the doorstep of Pine Farm, BCAS reluctantly accepted the inevitable and closed the home in 1896. Their idealized and obsolete view of rural life reappeared in BCAS support of outdoor recreation, the Boy Scouts, Campfire Girls, summer camps, and placement of Boston boys at New Hampshire summer resorts as gold caddies, waiters and lifeguards. This vision of a purer, cleaner, morally invigorating countryside was a romantic reform concept difficult for the elite BCAS to abandon. It had been their traditional alternative to the well-ordered asylum in which other Boston child-savers continued to treat lower-class social deviants.[89]

As Birtwell became recognized as a national spokesman for the professional altruists in social work, he was invited to advise other Boston private charities on placing-out methods, selection of staff, and even amalgamation with BCAS. As a result of his successful management of the evolving BCAS, mergers and reorganizations with five other societies by 1920 had formed the Boston Children's Aid Association, a parent organization of the BCAS. This became in 1956 the present Boston Children's Service Association, and was the culmination of the new culture of professionalism Charles W. Birtwell brought to BCAS in 1885. The secular, scientific social work methods he introduced led inevitably to the transformation of the entire child welfare network in Boston and indirectly in every American city. The individual child in need was adjusted to society by careful, humane, professional social workers in collaboration with the whole range of services available in the community. The focus was on the positive "personality development" of each child, not on restraining young sinners.[90]

Birtwell's chief contribution, however, was his advocacy of differential casework. The transition from charity work to social work was essentially the shedding of the moralism from which children's aid societies like BCAS had originated. Even the Charity Organization Society and the Associated Charities of the 1880s had clung stubbornly to a notion that irresponsibility and self-indulgence underlay most cases of poverty. Charity workers were quick to punish the "unworthy poor" by denying them assistance and resorting to the police and the courts, when careful investigation of individual family problems could have revealed a non-coercive solution to problems. Birtwell was responsible for shifting BCAS emphasis from moral supervision to the accumulation of comprehensive social data upon which objective casework decisions could be founded. Largely to Birtwell's credit, one recent historian of social work contends that "the Boston Children's Aid Society personified progressive casework ideas and practice in the early twentieth century."[91] Birtwell's high regard for casework, the availability of enthusiastic well-trained staff members, and the rich charitable resources in Boston combined to enable him to transform a good child-saving society into a great child welfare agency. This he did by returning to the eighteenth-century concept of the sanctity of the family. No longer the inviolable domain of the patriarch, the family was to be supported by society when temporarily weakened by poverty, disease, death, or other tragedies.[92] BCAS existed, Birtwell insisted, to support, not to supplant, the family. Pine Farm, foster homes, and institutional placements were only temporary means to help the family regain self-sufficiency, not long-term solutions for children. The use and development of the assets in the child's own family became the BCAS policy as social workers recognized that children could not be divorced from natural family relations without irreparable loss. To help poor children intelligently, these new social workers scientifically investigated the individual child's life and surroundings. Decisions for each child were based on as much accurate, objective data as could be gathered. This was the modern profession of social work Charles W. Birtwell created in Boston from 1885 to 1932, and from the BCAS the new profession spread to child welfare organizations across the nation.[93]

Boston Children's Aid Society had come a long way from Joseph Tuckerman's Society for the Prevention of Pauperism, but both organizations brought to philanthropy the special interest of an elite reeling before the assaults on traditional social order. Coming from the city and state that had long since assumed the role of America's conscience, but well aware of their diminishing authority, Boston Brahmins felt "we are vanishing into provincial obscurity; America has swept from our grasp; the future is beyond us."[94] In the wake of the Civil War, the dark Reconstruction years and the dismal Gilded Age, Bostonians were determined to regain their prestige and power in some sector of the new national life. The sons and daughters of the robust, stiff-necked race of seventeenth- and eighteenth-century dissenters, whose plain living, high thinking, and tenacious, stern beliefs had made Boston the "Hub of the Solar System" and the "Athens of America," turned to the control of society in the nineteenth century by new non-profit enterprises. Colleges, universities, hospitals, museums, and even savings banks were among the prominent eleemosynary institutions used to control and to benefit local and national constituencies.[95] Less obvious, but nevertheless important, were the social welfare agencies, institutions, policies and methods Bostonians devised to regulate the poor. Boston knew that it was superior and that it was right, and no amount of persuasion or philosophy could erase from its collective identity this sense of righteousness and moral superiority. Social welfare became a new weapon by the 1830's with which to isolate, pacify, control, and ultimately to reform threatening members of the native and immigrant poor. When the massive asylums of the Jacksonian period proved incompatible with elite control and ideals, the Boston elite created their own social welfare system for the most plastic and vulnerable of the poor, wayward children. But they faced an implacable adversary in this struggle, the Boston Irish.

2
Boston Catholic Charity for Children

Boston is a dreadful place for making Protestants of people, and you must be careful, especially of the children, or they will get them from you.

—Irish priest's warning to an immigrant, 1854

In contrast to the Protestant child-saving societies in nineteenth-century Boston, which attempted to rescue children from the dangerous classes by teaching them middle-class values, Roman Catholic charities for children reflected a vital and distinctive working-class subculture which had a powerful impact on the community. The aspirations and activities of these Catholic child-savers differed fundamentally from those of Protestant and secular charities.[1]

The greater attention historians give to elite reformers subverts the fact that American working-class immigrants had a robust and expanding culture of their own. With deep roots in ethnic, class, and Catholic tradition; the Boston Irish, for example, resisted (often successfully) the values and controls of middle- and upper-class Yankees. The rise of the American Catholic child welfare system—precipitated by European traditions and proselytizing evangelical child-savers like Charles Loring Brace in New York and the Children's Mission and the New England Home for Little Wanderers in Boston—demonstrates the power and creativity of Irish Catholic immigrants. They refused to be manipulated by patronizing or prejudiced Yankee Protestants. From this child welfare conflict emerged a broad and permanent Catholic system of institutions and agencies in Boston, as in most other large cities, which made unique contributions to American child welfare services.[2]

Yankee-Irish conflict in charities was part of a wider conflict, rooted in recent Irish history. When the potato blight caused devastating famine in Ireland from 1845 to 1849, the British government took full responsibility for dealing with the disaster. The humane and wise men in Whitehall then failed totally to deal with the problems. Seized by that "most horrible, and perhaps the most universal, of human maladies: the belief that principles and doctrines are more important than lives," the British imagined that rules invented by economists were as natural as the potato blight itself. England's statesmen left the Irish to the workings of "natural causes" while millions starved, died, and emigrated.[3] Nearly all Englishmen and their Anglophile Boston cousins regarded Ireland as an inferior version of England inhabited by a lazy, inefficient, backward people. Misadministration and ignorant prejudice by the English resulted in the economic stagnation, heavy taxes, low wages, backward agricultural methods, absentee landlordism, and genocidal policy during the famine which drove 4.5 million Irish to the United States from 1820 to 1870.[4] They arrived on overcrowded, disease-ridden vessels, the "Irish coffin ships" Herman Melville described in *Redburn*. Finding themselves stranded in the most Anglophile city in the United States; too poor, weak, and demoralized to migrate inland; and fearful of returning to the agrarian life they had fled, most of the Famine Irish crowded into North End slums in the 1840s. Close to laborers' jobs, churches, and fellow countrymen, the Irish peasants settled into the inner city and the urban poverty they would not escape for two generations or more.[5]

Largely as a result of this influx, Boston's population climbed from 61,000 in 1830 to 85,000 in 1840 and 137,000 in 1850. The foreign-born population in Boston rose from 10 to 53 percent during this period. More than 72,000 of the city's residents in 1860 were Irish immigrants, and over half of these were manual laborers occupying the lowest place in society, save for the city's small Black population. In response to the immigrants' destitution, expenditures for poor relief rose dramatically in the 1850s and Irish paupers and criminals crowded city, county, and state institutions. By 1870, 82 percent of the manual laborers and 72 percent of the domestic servants in Boston were Irish, and the death rate in Irish districts was triple that of the native-born districts. The Puritan city staggered under the impact of these refugee problems and struggled to cope with them.[6]

Massachusetts had slowly conceded rights to Catholics, freedom of worship in 1780, the right to hold public office in 1820, and freedom from taxation for the Congregational Church in 1833, but the coming of the Famine Irish in the 1840s endangered the gains Catholics had won. Mediating the conflict between Protestant and Irish Catholic Bostonians were the native Catholic clergy who preached assimilation and humility to the working-class immigrants. These Yankee Catholics transmitted New England values to their Irish parishioners by advice on how to succeed in American society. Success, like salvation, was available to all by hard work and faith. American Catholicism embraced the gospel of success designed to shape self-reliant, moral individuals who internalized middle-class American values. As Boston Catholics grew from 26 to 40 percent of the city's population from 1845 to 1850, the Brahmin elite allied with native-born Catholic priests to control the immigrants and to assimilate their second-generation children.[7] Once aroused by antebellum nativists and evangelical preachers, however, anti-Catholicism was slow to subside in New England. It reflected American Protestant fears for democratic institutions as well as the ancient Anglo-Celtic conflict.

In the wake of rapid industrialization, urbanization, and immigration in antebellum Boston, the increasingly Irish Catholic lower-class labor force required new and additional social services. Among Protestants, a variety of such services had appeared, especially for children. Boston Brahmin leaders despaired of reforming adult social deviants, but had hope for their offspring. Hereditarianism had not yet supplanted environmentalism as the rationale for most American reformers and social critics. Children were considered malleable, and optimistic child-savers hoped to restore pauper and wayward children by educational innovation and reforms. Schools of all kinds—Sunday, evening, charity, public, truant, trade, and reform schools—were weapons employed in the war on poverty, as well as the traditional methods of apprenticeship, domestic service and indentured service. Urban missions, temperance, and female moral reform were related national movements common in antebellum New England.[8]

The long tradition of European public and papal charity was well known to nineteenth-century Protestant Americans, but rejected by them. Charles Loring Brace began *The Dangerous Classes in New York* in 1872 with an account of needy children in the Old World mistreated by an indifferent society.[9] Brace, a conservative New England Congregationalist, condemned traditional Roman Catholic practices as invidious pauperization by an inefficient, out-moded system. Brace wrote in the wake of the Civil War draft riots and the Paris Commune with vivid recollections of urban violence by mobs largely composed of young lower-class Catholics. He saw street arabs as potential revolutionaries and criminals who needed better control than was achieved by Catholic charity practices.[10] Catholics, however, regarded the family as sacred and inviolate, to be restored not superseded, and the congregate asylum as a holy refuge, not a temporary receptacle. But Brace and other Yankee child-savers doubted the value of shoring up a pauper family by almsgiving and preferred rural foster family placement to longterm institutionalization. He resented opposition of priests to his orphan trains, and he condemned Catholic orphanages as useless vestiges of medieval monasticism more akin to the *Canterbury Tales* and Maria Monk's *Awful Disclosures* than to modern American philanthropy.[11]

But Yankee remedies were largely irrelevant to the Irish Catholic immigrants and their children. Existing public and private social services were Protestant in all but name, and thus unattractive or unavailable to Catholics. Although not as pious as later generations proved to be, the so-called Famine Irish clung to their ancestral church as a cultural refuge in a hostile community. The Boston Catholic Church became an immigrant church whose largely non-Irish leaders—Cheverus, Fenwick, Bodfish, Tucker, Metcalf, Brownson, Haskins, Healy, and Williams—had to learn to deal with the Celtic Catholics much as other Americans did.[12] The Church's first temporal priority was, therefore, to create social welfare institutions for the dependent and distressed. Monumental church edifices and massive asylums appeared in Boston long before the parochial schools so common in other cities.[13] Schools were considered less important in the Archdiocese of Boston than charitable institutions because timid Catholic leaders were reluctant to challenge the public school system so esteemed by Bostonians and because Protestant child-saving efforts threatened to win large numbers of Catholic children away from the church. The Catholic clergy established their own asylums for children made homeless by the high mortality lower-class immigrants suffered.[14]

Boston Catholics and Protestants shared a Christian concern for the poor, but different attitudes toward poverty prevented cooperation or understanding. Poverty in Calvinist Yankee eyes was public manifestation of moral defects, inner weakness, and sin. Prosperity was a divine reward for virtue and hard work. But Catholics remembered that Jesus said it was easier for a camel to go through the eye of a needle than for a rich man to enter heaven. The road to salvation, while not closed to the wealthy, was encumbered by material prosperity. On this ideological difference alone Catholic-Protestant understanding foundered even without cultural and economic tensions. Thus the Catholic child welfare network was not merely sectarianism or defense against anti-Catholicism, but was the result of different philosophical values, expressed in the concrete form of asylum-building. Boston Catholic asylums for children were a conservative, traditional reaction to urban poverty that only slowly resembled native American child welfare programs.[15]

Catholic charities were intended to mitigate misery, not to eradicate poverty or to reform the poor.[16] These charities constitute unmistakable evidence of the development of group consciousness among the Boston Irish who established an independent institutional life. Even among their fellow Catholic immigrants—German, French-Canadian, Italian, Polish, and Lithuanian—the Irish were unique in their support for independent charities conducted according to Catholic principles and ethnic values. They lagged behind antebellum Protestant and public methods, and not until the end of the Civil War did they experiment with innovation and change, but support was always widespread.[17]

* * *

One Protestant philanthropist had an idea about what changes were needed. In 1830, the Reverend Joseph Tuckerman (1778–1840), a pioneer in what was to become social work, invited Bishop Benedict Fenwick (1825–46) to assign a priest to visit destitute Catholic families as he himself had done as minister-at-large of the American Unitarian Association.[18] Fenwick rejected this suggestion because of a chronic shortage of priests in his expanding diocese, and he refrained from reminding Tuckerman that Boston's first bishop, Jean Cheverus (1810–1823), had impressed Yankees by his regular visits to the poor in 1799. But Fenwick did act when the resources of his diocese permitted. In May 1832, he brought to Boston three Daughters of Charity from the convent founded by Elizabeth Seton (1774–1821) in Emitsburg, Maryland. These sisters established the St. Vincent Female Orphan Asylum on Purchase Street, although their initial duties were only to operate a free day-school for girls and to teach Sunday School for poor children. Almost immediately Fenwick sent the sisters a young girl whose father had deserted their demented mother. The bishop took her brother into his own home and asked Sister Ann Alexis Shrob, the superior, to raise the girl, who later became a Sister of Charity. She was the first of ten thousand orphan or half-orphan (one parent deceased) girls sheltered and educated by the sisters.[19] This was the first important Catholic response to the plight of the poor in Boston following the cholera epidemic of 1832. The legislature incorporated the St. Vincent Female Orphan Asylum in 1843 and by 1850 it sheltered one hundred girls annually. They were trained by six Sisters of Charity in sewing; housekeeping; the common school subjects; and, of course, the Catholic faith. Some girls were sent by parents or relatives to be educated by the nuns, but most came for want of better places to live and were actually orphans. When possible their families paid a modest fee, but about one-third of the girls were totally supported by the diocese. Fund-raising by fairs, public subscription and bequests provided money for operating expenses, and gradually a modest endowment accumulated.[20]

St. Vincent's admitted only pure, virginal, innocent girls aged four to sixteen from poor but respectable Catholic families of the diocese, not the petty criminals, "fallen women," or well-bred young ladies other Catholic institutions attracted. From the first, it was a lower-class asylum offering homeless girls food, clothing, shelter, elementary education, "industrial training," and a safe refuge. It never assumed the character of a reformatory for wayward girls (like the House of the Good Shepherd) and admitted no infants or toddlers (like the St. Mary Infant Asylum and the Home for Destitute Catholic Children), and it attracted no well-bred young ladies (like the Ursuline Convent School), nor did it employ a child-saver to seek out girls in the poorhouse, jails, and streets. The girls came from priests, parents, and relatives and remained until they were old enough to leave (usually at age fourteen or later) for positions as domestic servants, seamstresses, or factory workers. Few girls were adopted, and as late as

Sister Anne Alexis Shrob (1805–75) founded St. Vincent's Asylum in 1832 and managed it until her death. (*Archdiocese of Boston Archives.*)

Charity-minded Brahmins called St. Vincent's Asylum the "Camden Street Home" in 1929. (*Boston Pilot.*)

1930, most girls still took jobs in factories or as servants upon discharge.[21] The changes resulting from the industrialization of the Greater Boston economy were advantageous for lower-class women because they offered income and job opportunities—however limited—beyond domestic service, especially for the respectable, well-discipline graduates of St. Vincent's Asylum. Although exposed to the cult of true womanhood values of the Daughters of Charity, they were clearly destined to be the mill girls rather than the ladies of Victorian Boston.[22]

Surviving records for the St. Vincent Asylum are scanty but interviews with Sisters of Charity who served the institution in the 1920s shed light on earlier practices, which changed slowly in traditional Catholic asylums. All sisters interviewed emphasized that tuberculosis or the death of a girl's parents were the most common reasons for admission. A common case involved the death of a mother and placement of a young daughter in St. Vincent's by her hard-working Irish father who struggled to pay the one dollar weekly boarding fee. The daily schedule was both crowded and strict. The sisters rose at four in the morning to wash, dress, pray, and prepare for the day. At seven o'clock the girls rose, attended Mass with the sisters and ate breakfast. School classes began at half past eight and lasted until noon. The girls marched to school to the accompaniment of a piano when classes resumed at one o'clock and stayed in session until three. Sewing classes, music lessons, house-keeping chores and recreation occupied the girls after school until dinner at half past four. This was followed by a recreation period and bedtime at eight o'clock.[23]

By the age of eight, each girl had specific house-keeping duties and cooking or cleaning assignments. She also assisted in the care of the younger girls. Cleanliness was extremely important, and discipline was strict, although corporal punishment was rare. By 1890 school uniforms were worn, and poor girls received other clothing donated by Catholic women or shops. A pauper atmosphere was avoided when possible, but the St. Vincent Asylum was a classic example of a carefully organized congregate institution. The emphasis on cleanliness, prayer, orderliness, discipline, conformity, and obedience made it a somewhat grim and repressive but kindly shelter for homeless Boston Catholic girls for more than a century.[24]

By 1900 St. Vincent's trained some girls in business subjects—typing, filing, bookkeeping, and so forth—and assisted them in locating office jobs upon graduation from the eighth grade or high-school course. In addition, sewing and cooking classes (as well as daily cleaning and washing chores) trained them to become domestic servants or housewives. A few girls entered convents after growing up in St. Vincent's, but Catholic orphanages seldom produced religious vocations. Domestic service and jobs as seamstresses were the goals of most working-class girls in nineteenth-

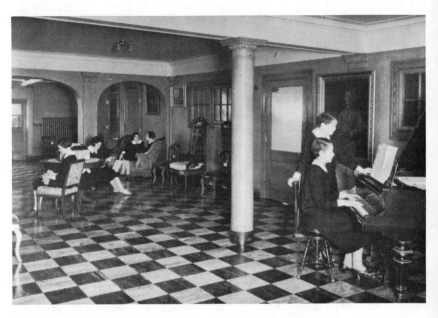

St. Vincent's Asylum girls at recreation in 1930. *(Archdiocese of Boston Archives.)*

Industrial training was provided in the St. Vincent's Asylum kitchen in 1930 also
(Archdiocese of Boston Archives.)

century Boston after discharge. Occasionally feeble-minded girls were retained voluntarily at St. Vincent's and employed as lay workers in the laundry, kitchen, or sewing rooms, assisting the sisters in heavy work. Many girls left at age fourteen for domestic service or to return home to their families, sometimes keeping house for their fathers, brothers, or uncles, or as companions to elderly women. The typical girl worked as a maid or cook from the age of fourteen to her mid-twenties and then married.[25]

Because the annual reports of St. Vincent's Asylum are missing or not consistent, it is not possible to determine exactly how many girls were adopted or placed out at service. Available figures indicate that from 1843 to 1863, approximately 137 girls were admitted each year and about 30 percent were adopted or placed in families as foster children. It is unclear how the terms "adopted" and "placed out" differed, but internal evidence suggested that few girls were formally adopted in probate court and most entered families as domestic servants or (after 1880) as foster children.[26]

From 1873 to 1893 the number of annual admissions rose to an average of 158 and the annual placing out rate increased to 52 percent (adopted, placed out or sent into domestic service). From 1893 to 1913, St. Vincent's admitted an average of 174 girls annually, of whom 42 were placed out. Thus we have a portrait of a large, stable, slowly expanding orphan asylum for Boston Catholic girls, training servants for the middle- and upper-class families in metropolitan Boston.

Personal data on the inmates are unavailable except for the period 1902 to 1909, in which birth places were recorded. Table 2.1 shows that the majority of the girls were native Catholics from the Boston area. Foreign-born inmates numbered only 91 girls or 11 percent in this period.[27]

The steady growth and reputation of the St. Vincent Asylum was due to its foundress, Sister Ann Alexis Shrob (1805–75), who was its superior from 1832 to her death. The official historian of the Archdiocese of Boston credits her administrative and executive ability as well as her gracious personality for making this institution thrive. In forty years, this remarkable women shepherded five thousand girls to maturity. Her grand-nephew, Dr. N. D. Drummey, was the staff physician for many years, and his son, William Drummey, was its architect. Sister Ann Alexis benevolently ruled the home with little interference and much help from the community. She became a symbol of the major role Catholic nuns played in New England child welfare and was regarded as a saintly woman by Boston Brahmin and Irish alike.[28]

St. Vincent's required each parent or guardian placing a girl to sign a form (witnessed and notarized) which said:

For and in consideration of the expenses already incurred, or to be incurred by the Directors . . . in the case of the child, named, _____

Table 2.1

St. Vincent Asylum, Nativity, 1902–1909

Birthplace:	N = 870
Boston	56%
Massachusetts	20
New England	4
United States	4
Canada	4
Ireland	2.5
Italy	2.2
Germany	0.3
France	0.1
British West Indies	0.5
Portugal	0.4
Romania	0.1
England	0.1
Syria	0.1
Native-born	83
Foreign-born	11
Unknown birthplace	6

SOURCE: St. Vincent Home, Register, 1902–1909, Archdiocese of Boston Archives.)

born in _____ and in consideration of a place being found for her in a good family into which she may be adopted and suitably provided for and educated, I hereby engage of my own free will, to give her up to the Directors of the Asylum . . . I will not seek to discover, to molest or to deprive them of the child, but that I will rely upon the Sisters and Directors of the Asylum to dispose of her as they may judge best for the good of the child.[29]

This document is like that used by the Boston Female Asylum and other children's institutions in Massachusetts. A formality required but not used in every case, it gave legal status to the institution as permanent guardian of each child and was meant to avoid legal disputes between parents, relatives, and the directors over child custody.[30] Several such disputes had caused long court battles, and the St. Vincent directors devised this form as a precaution.

Located in the South End, not far from the Boston Female Asylum, St. Vincent's was a physically impressive institution. It occupied one acre of land at the corner of Camden Street and Shawmut Avenue, slightly outside of the downtown Boston business district in 1858 that became a heterogeneous working-class neighborhood after the Civil War. The four story building of red brick was built with a $12,000 donation from Andrew Carney, the city's leading Catholic philanthropist. The total value of the land and building amounted to $120,000, and expenses were $10,000 in 1870 for twenty sisters and four hundred girls.[31]

Andrew Carney (1794–1864) was an important figure in this and other Catholic charities in Boston. Born in County Cavan in Northern Ireland, Carney emigrated to Boston in 1816 and accumulated a large fortune as a tailor and clothing manufacturer. In 1835 he negotiated a contract to supply the United States Navy with uniforms, which resulted in enormous profits for him and his partner, Jacob Sleeper, a Downeast Yankee Methodist who founded the New England Home for Little Wanderers. The panic of 1837 and declining prices for material and labor made both men wealthy. Sleeper withdrew from this partnership in 1850 with profits of more than $250,000, and Carney was even richer. Carney increased his fortune by wise investments in Boston real estate and devoted much of his time and money to Catholic charities. He was a major supporter of Father Theobold Mathew's temperance movement, served as a trustee of St. Vincent's Asylum, and helped found Boston College, Carney Hospital, and the Immaculate Conception Church in the South End. Carney also bequeathed a large sum to the House of the Angel Guardian, an asylum for Catholic boys.[32]

Important Protestant supporters of the St. Vincent Asylum were the Boston Brahmin merchant, John Ellerton Lodge, and his wife, Anna Cabot Lodge. He was a wealthy China clipper merchant who married the granddaughter of the Federalist sage, George Cabot. Both Lodge and his wife were active supporters of the "Camden Street Home" and generous contributors at a time when anti-Catholicism was rampant in the city. After his sudden death in 1862, Lodge's portrait hung in the lobby of St. Vincent's in honor of his generous support.[33] Bishop John B. Fitzpatrick, an intimate friend of many Boston leaders since his Latin School days, introduced Sister Ann Alexis to the Lodge family and to other liberal-minded philanthropists. She won their support and donations as well as much goodwill for the Camden Street Home, as non-Catholics preferred to call St. Vincent's Asylum. Dr. Henry Ingersoll Bowditch, a Harvard Medical School professor and prominent reformer, was a devoted friend to Sister Ann Alexis despite his misgivings about the Irish and their Church.[34]

Despite the overt anti-Catholicism in Victorian Boston, Brahmin cooperation with Catholic charities in the mid-nineteenth century was not unusual. The city's elite leadership, especially liberal Unitarians and Episcopalians, was inextricably involved in all public events, and even Roman Catholic charities were important community enterprises in that period. Joseph Tuckerman, for instance, did not hesitate to advise Bishop Fenwick; Samuel Eliot, another Brahmin reformer, willingly donated his charity school to Bishop Fitzpatrick; and May Collins Warren Dwight, a prominent convert, founded the House of the Good Shepherd reformatory for wayward girls. Later friction between the Irish and the Yankees created the impression that Boston was first besieged by Irish Catholics in the

1840s, but that is only a city of phantoms not of facts.[35] Many Irish immigrants settled in Massachusetts prior to the potato famine of 1845 to 1849 and not all who arrived were penniless paupers. The leading members of the Boston priesthood until the 1880s were neither immigrants nor the sons of immigrants. On the contrary, they were native-born Americans and descendants of pre-famine settlers or Yankee converts, a rather ethnically mixed group. Though the future belonged to the Celts, the leadership of the diocese from 1790 to 1890 was safely in the hands of non-Irish clergymen.[36]

The most vicious anti-Catholicism came from the lower-class Yankee mobs who burned the Ursuline convent school in 1834 and attacked the Irish in the Broad Street Riot and the Montgomery Guards Riot. Like the fanatics who inflamed the school Bible issue and burned Irish shanties in 1859, they were not led by gentlemen of property and standing. On the contrary, upper-class leaders like Horace Mann observed these tumults with dismay, and Boston legislators repeatedly supported bills to compensate the bishop for the destruction of the Ursuline school. While evangelists of the Second Great Awakening intermittently launched "No Popery crusades" between 1820 and 1860, Bishop Fitzpatrick was always welcomed in the Cabot and Lodge family drawingrooms as "Bishop John." Bishop John J. Williams continued this assimilationist tradition as did many priests of the antebellum generations.[37]

Thus the diocese accommodated itself to its immigrant flock by building an asylum for its homeless daughters, the most vulnerable and pathetic of the poor. This was a worthy project in the eyes of the Boston elite as evidenced by their goodwill and support. The St. Vincent Asylum grew from 1832 to 1932 into a major congregate institution protecting innocent girls from poverty and vice. It imitated but did not duplicate the work of the Boston Female Asylum or the Lancaster State Reform School for Girls because St. Vincent's purpose was not to reform the poor or the depraved but rather to thwart evangelical child-savers' designs on the unprotected daughters of the Irish. The city's elite cooperated in this not for love of Roman Catholicism or because of their rivalry with the evangelical Protestants, but to preserve harmony and hegemony in Boston. The Brahmins saw the Catholic hierarchy as useful allies in their struggle to maintain social control and to prevent violence, radicalism, and social disorder. These liberal Unitarian and Episcopal humanitarians—although initially as unsympathetic to "undemocratic foreign Papism" as their Congregational, Methodist, and Baptist fellow Yankees—came by 1830 to forge discreet alliances with the Catholic bishops to cultivate assimilationist conservative tendencies and to prevent violent confrontation between the city's Protestants and Catholics. Evangelicalist attacks on "the corpse-cold Unitarians of Brattle Street" also served to promote Unitarian tolerance and support of elite Catholics, and to divide Protestant critics of Catholicism.[38]

As Irish-Americans won political power in the cities, anti-Catholic tensions waned, despite outbursts in the Know Nothing Party, the American Protective Association, the Ku Klux Klan, and the immigration restriction movements.[39] But social justice and liberal reforms characteristic of some dioceses were noticeably absent in the Archdiocese of Boston, which had become the second most important see in the United States. To the innate conservatism of the Irish immigrant was added more than a little New England Puritanism, and the Boston bishops subtly promoted peaceful assimilationism as part of their bargain with the Brahmins for religious toleration and support. The Boston church was in the control of bishops and priests of native, non-Irish, or pre-famine Irish origins until 1905 when the Vatican installed the imperious William Henry O'Connell as Archbishop over the objections of the local clergy, bishops, and most American prelates. But initially the "Papal Bull," as Archbishop (later Cardinal) O'Connell was dubbed for his beefy appearance as much as for his ultramontanist views, was an ally of the Boston Brahmins.[40] Born in Lowell, the one-time mill boy was fond of high society and more at home in Beacon Hill and North Shore circles than in Hibernian clubs.[41]

Because of the hierarchy's comfortable relations with the Boston elite, the St. Vincent Asylum enjoyed a noncontroversial role in Boston charity. The trustees of the Boylston Fund, a prestigious endowment for children, paid boarding fees for Kate Curran in St. Vincent's, while the New England Home for Little Wanderers plotted to release Alice Crawford from the "Roman Catholic Home on Camden Street."[42] The NEHLW feared "she will certainly be brought up a Catholic if she remains there." Alice's mother, a Protestant nurse at the State School for the Feeble-minded, permitted the NEHLW to place her daughter with the Shakers in Canterbury, New Hampshire, in 1886 rather than allow Alice to remain with the nuns. The difference between the two cases illustrates the continuing antipathy between Yankee Methodists and Irish Catholics in contrast to the paternalism of the Unitarian and Episcopalian child-savers.[43]

St. Vincent Asylum (renamed St. Vincent's Home in 1928) held 218 girls in 1921, admitted forty-six and placed out twenty-seven in what was an average year for that decade. The *Boston Pilot,* O'Connell's newspaper, praised the oldest charity in the archdiocese for its accomplishments and predicted future success:

> As the problems of society increase with its growth, so do the equipments of the Church in her spiritual armor keep pace. Looking back on the splendid record of St. Vincent's Asylum, there is every reason to believe that the future years will unfold even greater triumphs of spiritual achievement than the past, giving the Church an increasing number

of noble-hearted children and to the Archdiocese worthy representatives of their great common Mother.[44]

The *Pilot*'s analysis, however, never mentions the individual needs or backgrounds of these deserving girls. Within St. Vincent's high walls, the girls spent their childhoods in the care of pious nuns. What was this life like for these inmates? How did St. Vincent's Home differ from the Boston Female Asylum? There is no data from which to answer such questions.[45]

Inmate accounts for nineteenth-century institutions of all sorts are very rare. Few prisoners or orphans wrote personal accounts or correspondence describing daily life in congregate institutions. Surviving administrative records are terse and uninformative about the institutional life. Even the most diligent research is unable to recreate the silent annals of the institutional poor. Newspaper accounts of St. Vincent's Home depict a happy, efficient "model" institution presided over by pious and kindly Daughters of Charity with only love and good intentions for the waifs in their care. Members of the Board of Directors are similarly portrayed as high-minded Catholic businessmen and saintly priests quietly devoted to overseeing this home for orphaned girls.[46]

Perhaps so, but some skepticism is warranted. Interviews with priests and Daughters of Charity who lived there in the 1920s and 1930s revealed problems in this "model" institution. Newspaper accounts uncritically celebrating anniversaries of the home or its founders also mentioned that the well-regulated life included numbering clothing, sinks, beds, and other furnishings and items. Although uniforms were not always worn, the girls did have a uniformity of dress that was official policy. They were a quiet, well-behaved group of girls as a matter of course and as a matter of rigid policy. They lived an authoritarian, institutional life modeled after the strict convent training their guardians reproduced according to Canon Law. That the inmates shared some of the restrictions of convent life was unavoidable. As one Catholic orphan remarked, "After years of that life, none of us was ready for a religious vocation." Social workers have long been critical of the repressive nature of Catholic institutions for children, which stifled individuality and self-expression. It is clear that life in the St. Vincent Asylum included this monastic atmosphere and its psychological impact on the children was totally ignored.[47]

Records from the St. Vincent Asylum of the 1920s and 1930s can provide the outlines of its earlier history. Individuals with personal knowledge of this Home emphasized the slow and cautious changes effected in its operation. For example, Sister Rose Quinlivan, who entered the Daughters of Charity in 1919 and worked at the St. Vincent Home from 1924 to 1935, recalled that teaching third and fourth grade girls and supervising the sewing room was a mammoth job. She reported that "great and edifying practice of poverty" was done there.

> Good use was made of donated clothing and hand-me-downs! The laundry was done under the supervision of a Sister with the help of a few older girls. The 8th graders worked in the laundry all day Monday! I also supervised a large dormitory of young girls, and the place was in perfect order before the girls went to school, and before I left for college courses.[48]

Repairing old clothes and making hand-me-downs and donated clothing suitable for poor girls was given as much priority as the new idea of providing higher education for the sisters. This was not only a function of the Home's meager budget, but also a manifestation of the convent virtues of frugality, economy, and humility; and these values were consciously imparted to the orphans as part of their moral training. They were poor children of the lower class and were taught to cope and make do in preparation for life as wives and mothers in working-class families. Spiritual not social mobility was the approved goal for St. Vincent's girls.[49]

Sister Rose remembered: "The children of St. Vincent's in my day were of Irish extraction, by and large. Tuberculosis was rampant at the time and Irish workers were employed at the bottom of the salary ladder!" The sisters did not operate a finishing school and did not urge upward mobility or higher education for the children. Simple and stable habits were the goals of the home. Modern social work methods were considered irrelevant or were unknown in such Catholic orphanages until the 1950s and the Rule of St. Vincent de Paul, by which this community of religious women lived, emphasized the virtues of poverty, obedience, and order. In the absence of effective medical cures for tuberculosis and other diseases, cleanliness was not only next to godliness, but also preventive medicine. It coincided with the most progressive hospital methods employed by the Boston medical community of the late-nineteenth century, but first in the minds of the sisters was their rule and their religion.[50]

The tuberculosis mortality rate in Massachusetts fell from 368 deaths per 100,000 in 1865 to 190 per 100,000 in 1900, but it remained a major public health problem until the 1930s and far exceeded the death rate for smallpox, typhoid, diphtheria, and scarlet fever. Sanitation and cleanliness were considered the most effective preventive measures, especially in congregate institutions, so the sisters' insistence on spotless housekeeping was medically and morally sound practice as well as busy work for restless girls. Massachusetts children's institutions of all types were well scrubbed and highly polished in this period, as were the best managed carceral institutions of the day, as much for appearance and health reasons as for reasons of discipline and domestic training.[51]

Sister Rose's recollections of the role played by the five gentlemen on the board of directors ("laymen appointed by the Diocese . . . it was the custom of the day") is a frank admission of the power and influence customarily wielded by the professional women in Catholic congregations like the Daughters of Charity:

> The Sisters of St. Vincent's had a free hand in conducting the institution, and all food bills were paid by the Board. I attended several of those Board meetings and it was quite obvious that those professional men did not have a glimmer of knowledge of the many needs of children.[52]

She was a professional woman in the tradition of Sister Ann Alexis, a highly competent, diplomatic executive whose skillful management of the Board, the clergy, and the institution's public relations guaranteed maximum autonomy and success. There were many such women in charity work, but the peculiar anonymity of convent life concealed individual accomplishments because of the self-effacing humility expected of Catholic sisters and nuns. Yet the sister superior at St. Vincent's Home—like her counterparts at the Home for Destitute Catholic Children, the Daly Industrial School for Girls and the expanding parochial schools—enjoyed much prestige, power, and influence within her institutional walls. On a daily basis, considerable autonomy and discretion was held by the sisters who commanded those badly needed labor forces staffing orphanages, asylums, hospitals, and schools. Bishops, priests, and the laity were reluctant to offend or interfere with the sister superior's decisions concerning children in her custody.[53]

The lower-class origins and poverty of most St. Vincent's girls continued through Sister Rose's tenure. She recalled in 1979 the modest payments made on visiting day at the Camden Street asylum in the 1920s:

> some poor parents tried to give a little when they had it, but I can say from my experience on Sundays when the visitors came, that the pittance I received for the children were a "widow's mite" compared to the upkeep of over a hundred children in 1924.

The lack of an endowment and the chronic shortage of funds at Catholic institutions created a rather cheerless atmosphere for the children and the staff. A Boston philanthropist provided an excursion boat for the girls one day each summer, and the Knights of Columbus arranged a lakeside outing once a year, but in general life for the girls and the sisters was confined to the daily routine behind the high asylum fence. By 1920, a few girls attended a Catholic high school, and a Jesuit priest from a nearby parish served as chaplain, but contact with the "outside world" was minimal. Most girls still left at the age of fourteen or fifteen to work as domestic servants; factory workers; seamstresses; candy makers; and, occasionally, office workers. Sister Rose recalled, "Many girls, after leaving St. Vincent's, came back to visit and to be counselled, but I do not know if a close connection was ever established as a record." The distance between Catholic charities like this one and modern social workers was widening. According to Sister Rose, "Comprehensive personal records were not then used in that day. A bare outline of each girl's history was kept in a card file in the office." Advances in psychology and social work were slow to become accepted or even known at Catholic institutions, and the case histories were too terse to be useful. Those at St. Vincent's sounded a repetitious refrain: born in Boston, mother deceased, placed by father, unable to pay, paying reduced fees, girl homesick, girl doing better, sometimes saucy, First Communion, Confirmation, girl placed in job.[54] The sisters saw thousands of such stories in an endless parade of tragedy. They performed an essential service in providing refuge for the homeless daughters of working-class Boston Catholics, but it was not social work. Yet if these child-care services were deficient by some later standard, these women nevertheless earned the community's respect for their honest efforts. As Sister Rose argued:

> These few human-interest details should be of some value in a study of old institutions. It all happened before State and Federal aid was available, so honor is due to any effort such as the work of our Community, the members of which did their best, *under the circumstances!*[55]

How do we assess St. Vincent's Asylum? Because this institution, like the American Catholic Church itself, was confronted by the pervasive anti-Catholic prejudice implanted by the original English colonists in the seventeenth century, and was overshadowed by entrenched Protestant charities, it succumbed to a ghetto mentality, separatism, timidity, a sense of inferiority, and an overly pragmatic outlook. The staggering task of absorbing waves of nearly 10 million Catholic immigrants to the United States from 1820 to 1920 left the clergy and religious community leaders little time, energy, or resources with which to develop intellectually or to participate in the professionalization of charity work. But in assimilating the dominant culture, Catholics imbibed too deeply, absorbed the worst features of American charity, and institutions like the St. Vincent Asylum overlooked its own strengths. Moral virtue is the *raison d'etre* for any ecclesiastical institution, yet St. Vincent's concentrated on fitting girls for working-class jobs in a puritanized urban society. Piety was a means of self-discipline and social control, as much as it was spiritual or intellectual elevation. Apologists argued that they did their best in the face of poverty, prejudice, and powerlessness to shelter one hundred girls annually. Certainly, St. Vincent Asylum cannot be compared fairly to secular child-saving societies nor faulted for not embracing social work and psychology, because that was not its mission. It was a Roman Catholic orphanage for immigrants' daughters.

Yet the goals to which the daughters of immigrants were urged best reveal the nature of this asylum, the church, and the city. Without power or prestige, the daughters of the lower class were channeled into those economic roles which the middle class avoided but required someone to fill. Economic and social mobility was discouraged by St. Vincent's Asylum so that most inmates took socially acceptable routes to working-class conformity. This was the bargain the Boston bishops made with the city: docile domestics and skillful seamstresses in exchange for religious toleration and social acceptance. It was a high price to pay, but one common to the American Catholic child welfare system.[56]

Having provided for the more vulnerable girls, Boston Catholics turned to the homeless or wayward boy. Elizabeth Oakes Smith, in her 1854 potboiler, *The Newsboy,* depicted Sam, an Irish "newsie" overfond of cheap theaters and pitching pennies, who took his orphaned friend Mary to the Sisters of Charity. Eventually, the two were married by a Catholic priest and died after a melodramatic accident attended by the tearful nuns. Fiction, in this case, had verisimilitude not only in portraying Irish-American slum life but also in the double standard which compelled Mary to enter the sisters' asylum while Sam earned a precarious livelihood hawking newspapers in the streets.[57]

The search for adventure and advancement in the Victorian city was a male prerogative, and Irish immigrant boys were allowed much more freedom to wander the streets in search of play and profit than their sisters. Action-seeking adolescents found peculiarly suitable the episodic life of a newsboy, bootblack, or street peddler. The routine patterns of home, school, and workplace were based on adult rules against which red-blooded boys were permitted to rebel. Boston parents of all classes accepted that their sons could only become manly by being independent. Boys sought adventurous episodes interspersing mundane school, play, and home life. Adults expected that "boys will be boys" before graduating to routine adult lives when they found jobs, married, and established families. Most boys outgrew life "on the street corner" unscathed and adjusted uneventfully to middle-class values, but some did not. Juvenile delinquency was a term coined in the 1840s to describe adolescent boys whose rebelliousness exceeded increasingly strict bourgeois standards, and, not surprisingly, many of these wayward boys were the sons of Irish immigrants.[58]

Irish Catholic boys whose street-corner life was unrestrained by parental discipline filled the House of Reformation and the State Reform School by the 1850s. They clogged the Boston Police Court each morning for a variety of misdemeanors and violations of city ordinances. Protestant child-savers from the City Missionary Society, Children's Mission and the Children's Friend Society were eager to rescue them, too eager to suit the Catholic clergy worried about soul snatching evangelists.[59] The St. Vincent Asylum was adequate for homeless girls, but no refuge for Catholic boys existed in Boston until Father George Foxcroft Haskins (1806–72) founded the House of the Angel Guardian.

Haskins is an overlooked Boston Brahmin child-saver in many respects. Born to a prominent Boston family and educated at the Latin School and Harvard, he was ordained an Episcopal priest in Boston in 1830. He became chaplain of the House of Industry, superintendent of the House of Reformation and an Overseer of the Poor from 1829 to 1840. His public service was interrupted in 1840 when he converted to Catholicism, and he was ordained a Catholic priest in Paris in 1844. He had shown an alarming toleration for Catholicism in 1830 when he summoned a priest to the deathbed of an Irish woman in the House of Industry. This was contrary to Massachusetts practice, which excluded all Catholic clergymen from public institutions until 1879.[60]

In Father Haskins, the Protestant charities encountered a formidable opponent to proselytizing in the guise of charity as well as an influential proponent of the assimilationist tradition of the Boston Brahmins and their Catholic allies. Haskins was one of only thirty priests in the archdiocese of Boston when he returned from France, and he was immediately appointed pastor of St. John's Church on Moon Street in the Irish North End slums. Later he transferred to St. Stephen's Church on nearby Hanover Street, where he remained as pastor from 1862 until his death. Well-acquainted with charity work and institutions for the poor in his earlier career, Haskins quickly diagnosed the problems of the Irish children in his parish. In 1851 he received permission from Bishop John Fitzpatrick to establish an orphanage for boys in a rented house on Moon Street.[61] Haskins believed the antagonism between Protestants and Catholics would diminish if a Catholic asylum diverted homeless and wayward boys from the Protestant-controlled private and public institutions. Because Catholic religious practices were not permitted in those institutions, Haskins would safeguard the boys' faith as well as silence nativist critics. Bishop Fitzpatrick agreed, having the example of St. Vincent's Asylum in mind, but had no funds to offer. With only his own financial resources, Haskins opened the House of the Angel Guardian in 1851 and installed Mr. and Mrs. Cornelius Murphy as houseparents.[62]

To its inmates, the House of the Angel Guardian was known as "the Hag," and Father Haskins supported the institution by his private income,

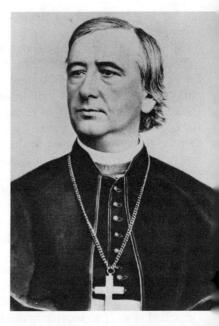

Bishop John B. Fitzpatrick (1812–66). *(Archdiocese of Boston Archives.)*

Archbishop John J. Williams (1822–1907) succeeded Fitzpatrick in 1866 *(Archdiocese of Boston Archives.)*

The Reverend George F. Haskins (1806–72) founded the HAG in 1851. *(Archdiocese of Boston Archives.)*

Bishop James A. Healy of Portland, supervised Boston charities from 1854 1900. *(Archdiocese of Boston Archives*

contributions from wealthy Protestants, some funds from the struggling diocese, and fees from the parents or guardians of one-third of the boys. It was a boarding school for boys aged nine to sixteen who were orphans, half-orphans, or simply too poor to attend academies but eager for a good Catholic education with which to rise in the world. As a member of the Boston School Committee and a former teacher at the Boylston Asylum for Boys, Haskins was familiar with the goals and methods of private and public education. He agreed with many of these goals; nevertheless, he established the House of the Angel Guardian to counter child-saving and school policies contrary to Catholic principles.[63]

Haskins was sharply critical of the orphan trains sent west by the Children's Mission, but even more threatening in his view were the self-righteous policemen and overzealous judges in Boston who arrested young Irish boys for pitching pennies on Sunday or playing truant from school and sentenced them to reform school for their minority.[64] He recalled an instance in his own parish in which an off-duty Yankee policeman did precisely this:

> Now I am far from approving of boys' pitching coppers on Sunday, or playing truant from school. But what I do think is, that the punishment is barbarous and cruel. . . . When they do wrong and violate the law it is seldom with malice or thought on the subject. What does punishment concern them? What dread have they of REFORM SCHOOLS UNLESS THEY MAY HAVE BEEN IN ONE?[65]

These harsh words did not, however, characterize Father Haskins' relations with Protestants. The overwhelming task of caring for the spiritual and temporal needs of the laity in nineteenth-century Boston, as well as the nonmilitant, conciliatory stance of Bishop John B. Fitzpatrick (1846–66) and his timid and aloof successor, Archbishop John J. Williams (1866–1907), prompted Haskins to exploit his friendships with Harvard classmates and former co-religionists.[66] Haskins became a spokesman and liaison between the Catholic Church and secular leaders. As a result of his diplomacy, state funds were appropriated for the House of the Angel Guardian because it was less expensive and more humane to aid this sectarian asylum than to allow Irish boys to wander the streets as beggars and thieves. Haskins served the diocese well and, with the patient strategy of Bishop Fitzpatrick, gradually Catholic priests could visit the Houses of Industry, Correction, and Reformation; the Suffolk County Jail; and the City Lunatic Asylum. State institutions, however, barred priests until 1879, and not until 1905 did the legislature safeguard the religious freedom of Catholic children in public institutions and foster homes. Irish political influence won religious toleration first in Boston and more slowly in the hinterland, but the career of Father Haskins and Bishop Fitzpatrick demonstrate the key role Boston Brahmins played in assimilating the Irish and deflecting the bigotry of the Yankees.[67]

Father Haskins maintained friendly relations with his Protestant colleagues and with the police and judges of the Boston courts. Frequently, he interceded in the courts to save boys from commitment to the House of Reformation or the State Reform School.[68] Gradually his boarding school for poor boys became a reformatory for wayward or predelinquent adolescents. Father Haskins admitted no "confirmed thieves" but many "street arabs" and homeless or unsupervised bootblacks and newsboys, whom he was careful not to pauperize or institutionalize. Their stay was limited to about two years, after which they went home to relatives or to an apprenticeship in which they lived with a family while learning a trade or skill or business.[69] Haskins retained the Protestant dread of pauperization, but not their predilection for farm family placement for "bad boys." He was a native Bostonian and tried to adjust these Boston Irish boys to urban society (see Table 2.2).[70]

On a daily basis, Mr. and Mrs. Murphy managed the House of the Angel Guardian, but Haskins played a major role in its operation from 1851 until his death in 1872. When the growing number of inmates over-crowded the Moon Street house, he purchased an abandoned foundry on Vernon Street in Roxbury. He converted the large brick building in 1860 to a congregate asylum housing as many as five hundred boys. They received a common school education and moral training similar to that Wells introduced to the House of Reformation earlier. Haskins had been denied permission by his former colleagues on the Overseers of the Poor to take Catholic orphans from the almshouse—his desertion to Rome being too serious to overlook—but he found an ample supply of boys without their cooperation.[71]

Haskins discouraged lasting relationships among the boys by substituting numbers for their names whenever possible and by stressing military-style drill, monastic silence, and self-discipline.[72] A former inmate, James Judge, acted as First Prefect overseeing meals, marching, recreation, deportment, and dress. Haskins had definite ideas about the discipline and education of wayward boys based on his broad experience and close study of European asylums, and he did not hesitate to offer them to the public. He incorporated some concepts from the monastery and the seminary and some from European penal institutions—group prayer, public confession of misconduct, a choral group, and marching bands—and rejected others from Massachusetts reform schools—manual training, flogging, and the idea of a self-supporting institution—as he saw fit.

He considered the care of boys younger than nine years of age to be the natural responsibility of women or the Daughters of Charity, as well as "the infirmary, washing, and scrubbing." Unlike the Sisters at St. Vincent's Asylum, he expressed high hopes for his students, claiming in 1864

Table 2.2

House of the Angel Guardian, Nativity, 1877–1927

Birthplace:	1877 N = 113	1887 N = 258	1897 N = 224	1907 N = 456	1917 N = 368	1927 N = 246	Total N = 1165
Boston	41%	20%	31%	26%	30%	30%	28%
New England	40	43	37	42	56	54	47
United States	4	4	4	3	3	4	3
Native-born	84	67	71	71	89	88	78
Foreign-born	16	12	15	7	7	10	10
Unknown birthplace	0	21	14	22	4	2	12

SOURCE: House of the Angel Guardian, Registers and Ledgers, 1877–1927 Archdiocese of Boston Archives.

that "hardly a years passes that we do not hear of some of our boys being students in some provincial college, or in the College of the Holy Cross, or in the St. Charles seminary."[73] Besides Protestant rivals, indulgent parents were the "most terrible enemy to encounter" because they generally blamed Haskins when their sons did not reform. He conceded, "the institution must suffer and be silent." Still, he was proud of the boarding school/orphanage/reform school he founded singlehandedly. He was prouder still of the unusual grants he obtained from the state legislature. Although refused access to the boys in public institutions, Haskins did obtain state funds: $2000 in 1868 and $3500 in 1870.[74]

Father Haskins appealed successfully to the non-Catholic community because the House of the Angel Guardian cared for hundreds of homeless boys more effectively and economically than the public sector could hope to do. Elite agencies like the BCAS referred Catholic cases to him; and, in general, Boston was openly supportive of the House of the Angel Guardian by 1860.[75]

But strident criticism by the evangelicals and the press in 1871 and 1872, which condemned the use of public funds for sectarian purposes, ended this support. The Board of State Charities objected to this financial aid as a violation of separation of church and state, and the legislature's Committee on Public Charitable Institutions in 1872 reported unfavorably on all petitions for such grants. The House of the Angel Guardian, the Home for Destitute Catholic Children, and eleven Protestant charities were denied grants because "it could be construed as aiding any one religious faith more than another." After heated debate, the legislature accepted this view, cutting off charity's nose to spite Catholicism's face. Although the House of the Good Shepherd did receive a state grant of $10,000 in 1870 "for once only" because of its special mission to protect wayward girls and to reform fallen women, the less threatening boys in the House of the Angel Guardian did not require such precautions. The trend in Boston charity in the 1870s was clearly toward secularism, sometimes masking anti-Catholicism, but in any case preferring scientific philanthropy over private charity, which was largely denominational.[76]

Like other Boston child-savers and reformers, Haskins visited Europe to investigate charitable methods, and he toured French, Irish, English, Belgian, and Italian reform schools in 1843, 1851, and 1870. He applauded the Irish and English support of Catholic (or sectarian) asylums for homeless and wayward boys but admitted ruefully that no American politician would dare suggest such a policy. He also advocated educational rather than vocational training in the American juvenile asylums and remarked that as superintendent of the House of Reformation," I must have known at least two thousand boys; I have met many of them since, but I never knew or heard of *one* that followed, or ever tried to follow, the trade or occupation that he was taught in the institution."[77] Caning chairs, making nails, or other manual labor in institutions he dismissed as useless busy work by the "insatiable vortex of misguided philanthropy" which drew boys into the reform school or prison and discharged them as ignorant and unrehabilitated as they had entered.[78] Haskins's preference for academic and moral training was confirmed by field trips to reform schools abroad where he was "informed that not one in thirty ever follow the trade he learned at the school."[79]

Haskins also disdained reform by rustication for his largely Boston-bred boys (60 percent in 1867), perhaps recalling the folly of punishing suspended Harvard students by "sending them to Coventry" for a term. His English informants said, "When boys are discharged, it is seldom that they leave London; they seek employment in the city, scarcely ever in the country."[80] As a result, House of Angel Guardian policy was to find jobs in Boston for graduates or apprenticeships with carefully selected craftsmen or businessmen rather than to use the orphan train to place city boys on farms or to send them to the western frontier.[81]

He also avoided corporal punishment, claiming: "Our system of government is simply that of a well-ordered family. Beating, pinching, kicking, and flogging are expressly forbidden, and if an officer is known to have recourse to any of these modes of discipline, he is promptly rebuked, and if he cannot govern otherwise, he is considered unfit to govern at all." Flogging was rarely used, perhaps once or twice a year, and then only for hardened offenders, "crusty" boys who were unresponsive to all other discipline.[82] As rector, Father Haskins administered the flogging himself in a calm manner after a fair hearing. In the classroom, the rattan, common in Boston public schools until 1960, was rarely seen, a stern reprimand by the teacher or rector usually sufficing. Minor infractions of the rules were punished by loss of privileges or recreation or by demerits. The merit system invented by Wells at the House of Reformation was adapted for the House of the Angel Guardian. Rewards for good behavior were stamped cards redeemable for pennies or small items in the boys' store, and bad conduct cost a boy some credits. At night each boy reported his own daily conduct to the prefect on an honor system. The best behaved boys formed a Class of Honor with special status and privileges, and the least disciplined formed a Class of Penance, but most boys fell into the middling group. All inmates, however, prepared for life in the capitalist marketplace by speculating in buying and selling merits to one another. In Father Haskins' moral economy, there was room for Yankee trading.[83]

Despite high hopes for his boys, Haskins realized that most did not graduate to college or the seminary, but entered urban working-class occupations. Inevitably, this asylum assumed a working-class ambience similar to the St. Vincent Asylum or the House of the Good Shepherd.

Some boys never escaped the poverty that brought them to the institution, like Steven Whelan, who was born in Boston in 1852. His widowed mother placed him in the House of the Angel Guardian in 1860 at the suggestion of Father James A. Healy. Steven spent a year and a half there and next contacted the House in 1929 when he wrote from the San Francisco Almshouse requesting proof of his birthdate to qualify for old age assistance in California. He apologized for not enclosing a fee for the documents, admitting he was destitute. This case of chronic poverty from cradle to grave was not typical of the graduates and the inmates, and staff took great pride in the low incidence of crime, poverty, and social deviance among the alumni. Haskins and his successors created a reputable Catholic institution which, if it produced no great men, produced no notorious men either.[84]

House of the Angel Guardian supporters organized in 1855 as the Society of the Angel Guardian to find jobs for boys, to raise funds, and to marshal community support for the asylum. By 1885 this society included successful alumni who regarded it as their home. They assisted the staff and each other and befriended recent graduates. It became an extended family for many young men without families or relatives who were alone and friendless in the city. The group identity and peer support it offered was much like the Young Men's Christian Association, established in Boston in 1851, or the Sons of New Hampshire Society for rural migrants to Boston. Because of Father Haskins's careful admission policies and strict disciplinary practices, as well as the support of the Society of The Angel Guardian, the boys did not see themselves as juvenile delinquents. Like most single-sex institutions, the "Hag boys" developed their own inmate subculture with strong loyalties to their home and to one another.[85]

One alumnus observed that "many boys found the routine and regimented life comforting" after the poverty and disorganized family life they had known as children and "this is probably why so many of them liked military service in World War I and II." The House of the Angel Guardian was "certainly no bed of roses under the strict rules," but it inculcated manly virtues, self-discipline, independence, and respect for authority in its graduates, qualities useful in the military and industry.[86]

This successful asylum became an even more strict institution after Haskins was succeeded by the Belgian Brothers of Charity, whom Bishop Williams persuaded to operate the asylum as they did reform schools in Montreal and Detroit. In January 1874, Brother Justinian, the new Superintendent, arrived with Brothers Michael, Edward, Thomas, Theodore, and Linus. These Belgian and French-Canadian religious men efficiently transformed Father Haskins's idiosyncratic asylum into a large, congregate, industrial reform school. The debt was expunged in 1884, new buildings erected in 1887, and a trade school opened in 1892. Baking, shoemaking, tailoring, bookbinding, and printing classes trained three hundred boys for remunerative jobs. Income from a weekly newspaper, *The Orphan's Friend,* and a quarterly magazine, *The Orphan's Bouquet,* paid a substantial portion of the expenses as did the printing shop. By 1917, the House of the Angel Guardian trained 450 boys yearly and had 15,000 graduates. Brother Jude, the next superior (1889–1920), who had managed the Montreal reform school, expanded his staff to 25 brothers and 10 laymen to better manage the increasing number of boys.[87]

The brothers, most of whom were working-class French Canadian or Irish, changed Haskins' policy of admitting "any worthy boy of good character" even if his parents or guardians could pay nothing for his care. No truly needy boys were denied admission, but the brothers insisted that someone be responsible for each boy, whether parents, guardians, relatives, friends, the boy's parish, the St. Vincent de Paul Society, or the local Overseers of the Poor.[88] They engaged a collection agency to dun delinquent accounts and managed to support four hundred boys in 1915 on a modest budget of $14,981. The boys lived an extremely frugal, almost monastic, life; rising for prayers at six o'clock, followed by a simple breakfast of oatmeal, bread, and milk; four hours of classes; lunch; three hours of shop classes; and two hours of sports. The monotonous diet of oatmeal, bread, milk, stew, potatoes, and peanut butter was "nourishing but plain and unappetizing in the extreme."[89]

More important than food, however, is affection in the emotional well-being of children. On this score, the House of the Angel Guardian performed poorly. It was a difficult task for thirty brothers to manage five hundred young boys confined behind high walls, and there was little incentive to provide individual attention or counseling. Discipline was harsh, corporal punishment was introduced, and at least some boys matured as "emotionally stunted men," unable to express love and affection as freely as men "raised in their own families." Escapees were punished by having their heads shaved and were dubbed "baldies" by the brothers. Homosexuality was seen as a serious threat which inhibited the staff and prevented the boys expressing affection or emotion. The picture that appears from interviews with the alumni and staff is one of a cold, distant, harsh "total institution" more like a military post than a children's home. Fiercely competitive sports and a boys marching band, both of which attracted financial contributions and favorable publicity, were the major emotional outlets for most boys.[90]

Cardinal O'Connell, always critical of his subalterns, surveyed the House of the Angel Guardian in 1910 and decided to institute "strict economy and the practice of businesslike methods." This was hardly what the overburdened school needed. O'Connell's chancellor, Monsignor Richard J. Haberlin, tightened admission and payment policies and purchased the former Perkins Institution for the Blind in Jamaica Plain for the school. Installed in larger quarters in 1915 under the close review of the chancery, "practically a new institution came into existence" and the "ramshackle, tumble-down makeshift of a house on Vernon Street was sold to advantage." At the same time, the cardinal discharged a layman in charge of the printing department for secretly printing risque books and pamphlets, "the reading of which would be to any Catholic conscience a matter of grave offense."[91]

Despite these changes, however, the inmates themselves changed little. The average age was eleven for the period 1877 to 1927, just as it had been in 1868. Few immigrants (10 percent) entered this largely Irish-American (40 percent) asylum. Almost half of the boys were discharged (40 percent) or escaped (3 percent) within three months of admission, and by the end of six months, another 15 percent left. Relatively few boys remained for one (10 percent) or two (16 percent) years. Foster home or adoption placement was seldom done by the House of the Angel Guardian (10 percent) and the recidivism rate (14 percent) was high.[92] This reflects Father Haskins's complaint that many exasperated parents brought their wayward sons to the home, perhaps a few steps ahead of the truant officer of policeman, but "on the first visiting day after his admission, those same indulgent parents will declare to me their satisfaction and delight at the improvement in their boy, and their determination to take him home and give him another trial."[93]

About half of the boys admitted were orphans or half-orphans without "indulgent parents" to remove them, and 4 percent of these homeless and wayward boys were taken directly from the courts. Both the Boston Children's Aid Society and the courts cooperated with the House of the Angel Guardian from the first, a tribute to Haskins's reputation as a child-saver and to his Brahmin connections. He claimed, "I have never yet had to contend with any religious prejudice or scruple in my application for boys. On the contrary, the Judges and prosecuting officers have frequently expressed their satisfaction that guilty boys of good character would be spared the shame of incarceration."[94] After his death in 1872, however, his role as a volunteer probation officer went unfilled until the Boston Juvenile Court's St. Vincent de Paul agents referred some boys to the House of the Angel Guardian. From 1906 to 1911, for example, this court sent 128 boys there instead of to a foster home or public institution "because it was less agreeable to them and therefore constituted a sort of punishment." Judge Harvey H. Baker admitted this was unfair to the other boys in the House of the Angel Guardian, but he considered this compromise between probation and reform school preferable to foster care for many wayward youngsters. This expanded Catholic asylum also served as a temporary detention home for boys from the juvenile court, and the brothers cooperated willingly with the court probation officers.[95] In general, however, the

House of the Angel Guardian did not depend upon courts for referrals. Very few boys were admitted officially from Massachusetts courts from 1877 to 1927 (0.4 percent) and few were transferred from it to public reform schools (0.6 percent) once the Brothers of Charity succeeded Father Haskins.[96]

The majority of House of the Angel Guardian boys (88 percent) "went on their own" after discharge, and only 11 percent returned to parents. This reflects the facts that 49 percent were orphans and that the average stay in the House increased after 1877. Under the brothers' aegis, it became a permanent home for some boys (16 percent) by 1890, an orphanage as well as a reformatory for homeless, wayward boys. They entered at age ten or eleven and remained until graduation from high school at seventeen or eighteen, with an average stay of 18 months, comparable to that of the State Reform School (19 months) in 1913.[97]

Often House of the Angel Guardian graduates lived near the institution in boarding houses and tenements in working-class Irish-American Jamaica Plain and Roxbury neighborhoods until jobs, marriage, or military service drew them away from their only real homes. Few boys attended college, and as late as 1955, most found working-class jobs in Metropolitan Boston, often using their training and contacts from the house to become printers. By 1900 this asylum was a large congregate industrial school for homeless or mildly delinquent Catholic boys. It evolved into a massive asylum with five buildings on seven secluded acres, training wayward boys to be the willing workers Boston's varied economy demanded. The House of the Angel Guardian had changed from the boarding school Father Haskins opened in 1851.[98]

More importantly, the House of the Angel Guardian had discarded the last vestiges of Father Haskins's boarding school notions and hopes for social mobility by higher education. The Brothers of Charity did not encourage boys to attend college and no scholarships or resources were available to the graduates. Like the St. Vincent Asylum and the House of the Good Shepherd, the "Hag" rescued the homeless and wayward from the dangerous classes by training them for respectable working-class occupations. This does not demean this valuable work, but it does indicate the low aspirations Boston Catholics had for their dependent children after the 1870s. Security, piety, and respectability were more important than mobility, and thousands of Angel Guardian boys filled jobs as printers, bakers, bookbinders, and factory operatives and rarely entered the "provincial colleges" or seminaries Father Haskins had envisioned.[99]

*   *   *

The same conservative and cautious approach to child welfare was not found, however, in the third Catholic asylum for children established in Boston, at least not for its first generation. The Home for Destitute

Catholic Children was a temporary home and child-placing agency founded in 1864 by Bishop Fitzpatrick. Like the St. Vincent Asylum, the House of the Angel Guardian and the House of the Good Shepherd, the HDCC also had Brahmin origins. It began as a charity school opened in 1850 by Samuel Eliot, the president of Trinity College and superintendent of the Boston Schools. He donated the Eliot Charity School on High Street to his friend Bishop Fitzpatrick in 1856, and by 1864 it was incorporated as the HDCC by the Association for the Protection of Destitute Catholic Children in Boston. This association was composed of Bishop Fitzpatrick; his chancellor, Father James A. Healy; and six prominent laymen and Sunday School superintendents. It created a child-saving, child-placing organization rather than duplicating the work of congregate asylums like the St. Vincent Asylum or the HAG.[100]

Most prominent among these "foundling fathers" were Patrick Donahoe and Charles F. Donnelly. Donahoe (1811–1901) emigrated from Ireland in 1821, attended Boston public schools, and became a printer's devil at the age of fourteen. By 1836 he owned the Boston *Pilot* and was the city's first Irish publisher, bookseller, banker, and travel agent. The Boston Fire of 1872 and two subsequent smaller fires bankrupted him, but he recovered sufficiently by 1890 to repurchase his newspaper, which he had made an influential national weekly with a circulation of 100,000 by 1870. Irish eager to hear news of home or to contact relatives and friends in America read the *Pilot* avidly, which gave Donahoe and the archdiocese of Boston (often using the paper as its organ) enormous influence. Donahoe applied his talents to many business enterprises, but he gave his heart to charity and church work.[101]

His friend and fellow immigrant, Charles Francis Donnelly, was the city's leading Irish lawyer and chairman of the Board of State Charities from 1875 to 1907. Donnelly served as legal adviser and lobbyist for the archdiocese and as the HDCC lawyer, and he was equally committed to Catholic charities. Together they—and the other men whom Bishop Fitzpatrick and Father Healy summoned to the basement of the Cathedral of the Holy Cross in May 1864—represented the most experienced and accomplished Catholics in Massachusetts. They swiftly transformed the Eliot Charity School into a temporary asylum for Catholic children, obtained a corporate charter in 1864, and larger quarters on Common Street in 1865. By 1866 the Daughters of Charity came from Emitsburg, Maryland, to conduct the HDCC as they did orphanages in a dozen other cities. In 1869 construction of a large building on Harrison Avenue in the South End began, and in 1871 the new Home for Destitute Catholic Children opened with elaborate ceremony. The building cost over $100,000, proof of Bishop John J. Williams's words, "Next to the Church, the most important subject for Catholics is the care of destitute children."[102]

By the end of the Civil War, in which American Catholics proved their loyalty, Boston was recovering from a series of incidents which convinced Catholic leaders that their children would never be safe from Protestant proselytizing until a separate Catholic charity system was available. The issue erupted in 1859 when a teacher at the Eliot Public School in the North End, McLaurin Cook, brutally punished a young Irish pupil, Thomas Wall, for refusing to read the Protestant Bible in class. His parish pastor, Father John Wiget, had instructed the pupils not to recite any Protestant prayers in daily classroom opening exercises, and Wall was identified as a ringleader of the Catholic rebels. He relented after half an hour of rattaning on his hand, but the next day three hundred Irish boys boycotted school.[103] The incident was explosive until Father Haskins and Bishop Fitzpatrick persuaded the school committee to require only the teacher, not the pupils, to read the daily prayer. Later that year Haskins was elected the first Catholic member of the school committee and city officials forced stiff-necked school masters to keep the peace by evading this divisive issue.[104]

Despite this highly-publicized incident, Boston Catholics remained hostile to parochial schools and instead invested their ecclesiasticism in monumental churches and massive asylums. As late as 1880, only ten of the twenty-seven parishes operated schools. Unlike New York, Chicago, and most Catholic centers, Boston Catholics relied on the public schools (at the insistence of Bishop Fitzpatrick) supplemented by a vigorous Sunday School system.[105]

The HDCC benefited from this because talented laymen like Donahoe, Donnelly, and William Pelletier, a wealthy merchant and banker, devoted their efforts to Sunday Schools and charities rather than to parochial schools. It was a resourceful and well-assimilated group that established the HDCC. Moreover, in Father Healy they found an experienced charity worker and administrator who worked with Haskins at the House of the Angel Guardian and was known for his ability "to tame hostile Irish Catholics" offended by his mulatto origins. His role as overseer of all diocesan charities was a strong foundation upon which to build this new asylum. The construction of such an impressive building to house the HDCC was evidence of the ability of the directors as well as a concrete symbol of Catholic determination to rescue their own homeless and wayward children.[106]

The need for a Catholic asylum for children too young or too innocent for the St. Vincent Asylum or the House of the Angel Guardian was growing. The Famine Irish produced thousands of children by the 1860s who were driven by poverty and family crisis into Protestant public and private institutions in which they lost the faith or disappeared on orphan trains to the Midwest. Already the Eliot Charity School had sheltered four hundred children by 1856 and two hundred more by 1864, partly as a result of the Civil War's impact on the homefront. The HDCC cooperated with existing Catholic charities, but it was a very different institution. Unlike the House of the Angel Guardian, which aped the Boston Farm School, or the St. Vincent Asylum, which imitated the Boston Female Asylum, from the first, the HDCC was a temporary home and child-placing agency more like the Boston Children's Aid Society or the Children's Mission than any existing Catholic asylum. The founders frankly admitted to imitating "Protestant Associations" in Boston and New York whose "principal subjects are the destitute children of Catholic parentage." Children stayed for only a few months and were either returned to parents and relatives, if they proved fit, or placed out as foster children in Catholic families under the oversight of the local pastor. Pauperization or institutionalization was less feared than the cost of supporting young children in an orphanage.[107]

The diocese had too many healthy but homeless children to shelter them all in orphan asylums, and in response to advertisements in Donahoe's *Pilot,* thousands of Irish farmers in the Midwest and in Northern New England applied for foster children. Applications usually outpaced available children, and by 1865, inquiries came from as far away as Indiana, Illinois, Iowa, and Missouri. Most children, however, found homes in Massachusetts, and as early as 1865, the question of permanent adoption and parents' rights arose.[108] A foster mother in Sharon, Massachusetts, had one boy from the HDCC in 1864 and a few months later also took his brother. "She is anxious to have papers signed, so that she can keep them. They have no relatives that I know of, except a Grandmother & a Sister 15 yrs old. I do not know where to find them. Has the Association the power to give papers, & if so what is the form?" Superintendent George W. Adams wondered.[109] The HDCC was sensitive to the charge of child-stealing, and Adams defensively noted his self-restraint:

> In the Police Court, a little boy was up for stealing. Judge Maine asked me if I could take him, found he had a Father & Mother who were in Court, and were able to provide for him; declined to take him.[110]

Neither was HDCC willing to take "confirmed thieves," no matter how young. As Adams reported in his daily journal," To the Police Court, 2 small boys sentenced for larceny, no use to take them as they had been up before, these were all the cases in Court of interest to me."[111] The unwed mother was a favorite target of child-savers eager to save a baby from an obviously immoral mother and aware that good mothers were easily found for a healthy, white infant; but, again, Adams was patient and discreet:

> Received information of a young woman at the Charles St. Home having a child 4 months old, she is anxious to give it to a Catholic family,

several Protestant ladies are willing to take it and provide for her if she will give up all claim to the child, but she will not consent to it at present.[112]

Irish Catholics were not as docile or desperate as they had been in the antebellum era when Protestant child-savers preyed more easily on their "homeless" children. The Children's Mission agents complained to their directors:

It is within the experience of your missionaries, that parents who have been sentenced to Deer Island for drunkenness, and whose children are left unprotected, prefer to have them sent to the almshouse, rather than to accept the offer of your missionaries to place them in good families in the country.[113]

Adams persistently applied to the Boston Directors of Public Institutions for a "general permit to allow me to visit the Island at any time," which was a privilege enjoyed by his Methodist rival, the Reverend R. G. Toles of the New England Home for Little Wanderers, and many other Protestant child-savers. When the permit was finally granted in 1865, Adams made full use of it to visit Catholic prisoners in the House of Correction and Industry. He inquired about inmates' children left at home or in the streets or sent to the Almshouse while their parents were serving sentences for misdemeanors and petty crimes.[114] Visitors were permitted at the Deer Island institutions only on the first Wednesday in January, April, July, and October. This made it difficult for inmates to maintain contact with relatives and neighbors who might care for their children; and without an official permit, Adams's work was hopelessly delayed. He made regular trips to Deer Island with an aptly-named truant officer, Mr. Fetch, often in the company of his dreaded adversary, Toles. Adams talked with the Irish inmates convicted of drunkenness, larceny, or prostitution whose children were in the HDCC awaiting their parents' release or to be placed out.[115] One distraught mother told him that "she has suffered more from the thoughts of her children than from her own imprisonment." Most promised to reform when released and to provide better homes for their children, but some were "miserable creatures," who refused his help. Molly Geary, for instance, paid board for her two sons in the HDCC while serving sixty days in the House of Correction. She told Adams not to place them out or she would have them sent to the Almshouse "so she can get them as she wants to."[116]

Judge Sebeus C. Maine, the Boston Police Court justice who befriended Adams, often suggested placement in the HDCC to mothers he sentenced to jail:

> To the Police Court, Ellen Sullivan sentenced to 6 months in House of Reformation had 2 children, the Judge requested me to take them or he should be obliged to send them to Bridgewater [State Almshouse]. Took them & brought them to the Home.[117]

If he did not find any children in the courtrooms, Adams visited the "Tombs" beneath the courthouse, and there he encountered the most pathetic sights. Mothers were permitted to take nursing infants or even toddlers to jail with them, although the courts discouraged this practice:

> Went to City Prison, found there a woman just going to the Island for six months, having a little boy who was to be sent to the Almshouse. This little fellow was nearly naked, brought him to the Home. Mr. Nagle and Ring [directors] saw this boy & kindly furnished him with shoes and clothes.[118]

While these intemperate, larcenous, or immoral parents were in jail, the HDCC placed their children in foster homes, usually in suburban Boston, but this led to problems, as in the case of Robert Maloney:

> Mr. Daley of Neponset called, he took a boy named Robert Maloney from here June 25, says the boy was doing well. Yesterday the boy's Mother went there, saw him in the street and took him away. Mr. Daley wants to see if he can make arrangements for the boy to go back with him, says he will do well by him. I will see her about it.[119]

Because of such problems and the difficulty of finding Catholic foster families near Boston, the HDCC adopted the orphan train method used by the Children's Mission and the New England Home for Little Wanderers to bring Boston waifs to rural families. Notices placed in *The Pilot* were an effective means of locating foster and adoptive families, especially good Irish Catholic farmers:

> Received a letter from Patrick Walsh of Edgeworth, Illinois enclosing $40.00 to pay expenses for 4 boys of from 10 to 14 yrs. of age to Chicago, Ill. We are now incapable of furnishing them, they not being here. We have now applications for 8 boys & 2 girls to go West.[120]

Less than one month later, however, Adams had forty-eight children available for the first HDCC orphan train, and he made preparations to take a company of children to Illinois farmers:

> Went to the office of the New England & Western Transportation Co. to see about the fare for children to the West. The regular half fare is $13.87 but if a number should go at one time, it would be much less.[121]

HDCC children were not the only Catholic children on his mind, however, and Adams asked the City of Boston and the Board of State Charities "about taking some children from the State Institutions to send West." In this he was frustrated by delays in the state's new welfare bureaucracy: "To the Directors of Public Institutions about getting the children [released], after spending the greater part of the afternoon there, was told I must come again Friday next."[122]

HDCC records, unfortunately, do not reveal what happened to these orphan train passengers, but the tracks ran both east and west, and a child could be retrieved from the foster family to which he or she had been sent:

> Received a letter from James McDonough of Cambridge, he wants to have his children sent for & returned to him, he says he will pay their expenses when they arrive in Boston; one of them is in Vermont & one in Illinois. I will send for them when I receive the money to pay their expenses.[123]

Frequently, a child proved to be unsuitable or unwanted, and in such cases the foster parents simply sent him back to the HDCC with a note of explanation:

> Mr. Thomas Allen of Marblehead sent by Express the boy James Donlon who was sent to him 2 years ago; he says the boy is constantly running away and can do nothing with him. It took him a long time to find it out.[124]

This attitude toward foster children was not uncommon in a society accustomed to slaves, servants, and hired hands. In 1867 Wisconsin and Iowa farmers wrote to the HDCC to obtain boys "physically and mentally sound" with as little sentiment as they might buy a horse.[125] The HDCC considered these requests carefully, requiring letters of reference from local pastors or physicians, but the most important criterion was religion. An Irish name almost deceived Adams in an 1866 adoption application:

> Mr. & Mrs. Patrick J. Kelly of Randolph came, they want to adopt the baby. I found out they were not Catholics, declined to give the child.[126]

Another important criterion was the foster family's willingness to pay expenses for clothing and railroad fares. The HDCC budget was meager and contributions or "subscriptions" were constant themes in the superintendent's journal:

> Mrs. Margaret M. Lally of Trenton, N.Y. wrote asking for a boy, she keeps a Dairy and 40 cows. I answered and stated I would send them

one by sending a reference from her Pastor, the boy's fare and a little to clothe him. I prepared a list of names of those who subscribed and Christmas gifts and left it in the *Pilot* office.[127]

Five weeks later the Lally family had a strong and healthy Boston Irish boy, who was familiar with farm life. Bernard Cullen, who succeeded Adams as superintendent (1866–1878), found most of the Catholic inmates he counseled at the House of Correction were recent immigrants to Boston from rural Irish villages and towns:

I have conversed with 90 Prisoners this morning, about 12 of those were Females. I think ⅔ of the entire number were from the Country.[128]

Cullen continued the practice of placing children on farms and he had wide acquaintance with Catholic clergy throughout New England to whom he sent boys for placement at the pastor's discretion. If the child "did not suit" the farmer, he was returned to Boston, but mistakes occurred that proved embarrassing to the HDCC:

Michael Lydon of Claremont, N.H. sent a boy named Michael Curran back in conductor's custody. Boy sent to "the Wanderers' Home." I called there and took him to the Home.[129]

Cullen, like Adams, was suspicious of the New England Home for Little Wanderers agents he encountered as he toured the courts and jails on the watch for Catholic children. Parents sentenced to the Deer Island prison were the most likely sources of children and many different charity workers approached them, but Cullen, the new visiting agent, observed:

It is really touching to see with what tenacity these people in the midst of all their misery cling to their children. They are perfectly willing that the Home may have them, but the bare idea of some other woman taking them sets them wild. Yet, in the end they prefer this to the thought that their children might lose their faith. After a hard fight I got the releases. . . . Several took the papers home to have their husbands sign them, whilst several refused outright to sign any paper.[130]

John A. Duggan, who served as superintendent (1883–1900) after a long career in Boston politics, also kept an active schedule which won the admiration of the first historian of the HDCC.[131] "The special work of the superintendent is to scour the courts, newspapers, and other sources of information for deserving cases" and to use judges, truant officers, the St. Vincent de Paul Society members and the Massachusetts Society for the Prevention of Cruelty to Children (MSPCC) agents to relieve "a large proportion of the misery which exists among the offspring of unfortunate parents in our midst." Placing children "in good homes, vouched for by the local pastor, constitutes another important department of the superintendent's duties. In many cases the children are restored after a time to their parents—the hope of recovering their custody forming a powerful motive for reform, especially with mothers."[132]

Duggan, however, found a large number had to be separated from their natural guardians and distributed throughout the country where they would be useful. He crossed the Mississippi River several times, traveling as far as the Dakota Territory to inspect personally the surroundings amid which his wards were to spend their lives.[133] In 1877 the HDCC took eleven orphans to Baltimore and placed them in rural Catholic families using St. Mary's Female Orphan Asylum, a sister institution to the HDCC, as a base. The congregation in one church where the children attended Mass (after which they were frankly inspected by potential foster parents) was mostly "coloured" but apparently pious because the superintendent noted one half of them took Holy Communion. He thought the Maryland countryside a "poor place to live" because "there is no grazing land to speak of," nevertheless he placed all the children in good families. The cost of this orphan train was only $121.50, and each of the applicants paid $13.50 for his foster child, so the HDCC was encouraged to compose similar companies later.[134]

Duggan brought twelve boys and eleven girls to St. Louis in May 1887, stopping en route at Syracuse, Rochester, Buffalo, Chicago, and St. Paul to deliver children or to visit those previously placed. He noted with satisfaction that "all are doing well with one or two exceptions" and found that four boys placed in Chicago were well and two of them were studying for the priesthood. The entire trip was completed in three days, so successfully that Duggan returned to St. Louis three months later with twelve girls (from seven to thirteen years of age) whom he left at St. Philomena's Industrial School for foster placement by the sisters. Two months later he was again in Buffalo, Chicago, and St. Louis with twenty-two children, and despite two railroad washouts he was home in ten days.[135]

By 1896 the HDCC had admitted 12,825 children aged from three to fourteen, usually with "conditional surrender papers" signed by parents or legal guardians. The HDCC sheltered three hundred children at a time, and the average length of stay was about four months. One-quarter of these waifs were received from the Boston courts as abused or neglected children, and all but a few were eventually placed in foster families. Although the HDCC claimed to select carefully and supervise every foster home, in practice this amounted to a semi-annual form letter inquiring about the child. The HDCC actually depended on the interest and ability of the parish priests to protect the children's interests. Thomas Ring, the president of the Boston Society of St. Vincent de Paul, told the National

Conference of Charities and Corrections in 1896 that families seeking
"free maids" are forced to pay wages to the girls, but this was a hollow
promise considering the scarce resources of the HDCC, which relied on
the superintendent and one visiting agent to oversee thousands of children
in placements.[136] About one-quarter of the foster children were returned
to the HDCC by foster parents or local priests for unexplained (or unre-
corded) reasons. For example, six boys and four girls were placed in
Brandon, Vermont, in 1901 by Robert A. Lynch, the visiting agent, with
the help of Father Daniel E. Coffey but five were returned.[137]

In 1891, Duggan described with uncharacteristic wit his method of
dealing with two difficult cases:

> Having received a letter from Mrs. Collins of Swampscott asking me to
> remove Maggie Gavin, whom I had left with her the week before, I came
> to the Home and took Mary E. Palmer to her. It is true that Mary
> Palmer has acquired quite a reputation, but I thought I would give her
> one more chance, this being the fourth. As Mrs. Collins lives in the
> country I am in hopes that Mary will do well. The next question was
> what to do with Maggie Gavin, as she appeared fit for nothing. Re-
> collecting that Mrs. Kelly in Lynn had no children and wanted a girl for
> a companion I carried Maggie to her. As her only occupation there will
> be to talk, she probably will succeed.[138]

The child welfare business, as Duggan demonstrates, had its light mo-
ments, and his instincts were apparently correct because there was no
further mention of Mary or Maggie. Most cases, however, were more
tragic than comic. James Brady, a sixteen-year old "half-orphan" (his
mother died and his father was in prison) returned from a foster home in
Tolland, Connecticut, in 1887 at the request of Father Lee because the boy
was being "ill treated." Previously he had been rejected by his cousin in
South Boston because he was "uncontrollable." One reason James was
"difficult" was that his younger brother, John, was placed in another
Connecticut family, and the boys had no opportunity to visit or write to
each other. Child abuse was a chronic problem only tacitly acknowledged
in the HDCC records. Duggan had "several applications on file from Lynn
which cannot be filled as they wish girls at least ten years old," which
suggests another form of child abuse and exploitation.[139]

Many foster families wanted cheap labor, girls to be domestic servants
or boys for farm work.[140] The children were reluctant to complain about
being overworked or abused. Furthermore, to whom could they complain?
Their foster parents (or employers) had the confidence of parish priests
who wrote letters of recommendation to the HDCC. The visiting agent
communicated only with the parents or priests by mail and seldom returned to visit the child unless the foster parents complained.[141] It was

very difficult for a mistreated child to complain except by running away (called absconding or eloping in the HDCC records). One HDCC half-orphan bitterly recalled: "I had no idea where my mother and father and sisters were and no way to contact them. Those people (in the foster home) worked me to death and the nuns and social workers didn't believe anything I said."[142] Another neglected child placed by the House of the Good Shepherd also recalled "terrible beatings" and "working on the farm from dawn to dusk" and always "being uncertain about where my relatives were and who was responsible for me." Foster homes were "so bad that I was glad to be sent back to the HGS."[143]

As more children, "failed in placement" (in the twentieth-century social workers' phrase), the HDCC gradually sheltered more children for longer periods, slowly evolving into the congregate asylum and orphanage its founders deplored. One reason for this development concerned the role of the American Catholic nun, particularly the Daughters of Charity under Cardinal O'Connell. By 1917, Canon Law, under which all religious orders functioned, expressed a new wave of papal conservatism. This Great Repression tightened the regulations under which religious women lived, and was quickly reflected in the policies of the ultramontanist archbishop of Boston, Cardinal William Henry O'Connell. He ranks high as an administrator who centralized Catholic charity and social welfare programs.[144] But O'Connell was very critical of the sisters and brothers operating children's institutions and suspicious of upper-class liberal philanthropists, whom he denigrated as "this cod-fish aristocracy, this Jamaican rum nobility" who flirted with reform and charity as a hobby.[145] Settlement houses and social workers were often anti-Catholic secularists in his view, and child-placing smacked of Protestantism.[146]

By 1900 O'Connell broke with the Boston Brahmins he once cultivated and despaired of obtaining state funds for Catholic charities. He ordered his chancellor, Monsignor Richard J. Haberlin, to revamp the existing institutions and to monitor them closely. Amid this reorganization, the HDCC escaped with little criticism and even modest praise. The self-effacing sisters were an example of the church as a mother who "reminds him that the world is not a little red schoolhouse and that humanity is a family, not a formula." O'Connell regretted the trend "to turn over its problems to the professional social worker trained along purely mathematical lines," and charged these "paid people produce reports but they don't solve social problems." He warned Irish Catholics not to foolishly imitate Yankee Protestants but to have confidence in themselves; what the Catholic charity system needed was "a good strong dose of vigorous, genuine, fervid and thorough medievalism."[147]

The HDCC responded to Cardinal O'Connell's centralization of power and to his conservative view of social work. By 1907, the agents relied

Cardinal William Henry O'Connell
(1859–1944) reorganized Catholic
charities on an efficient basis by 1907.
(Archdiocese of Boston Archives.)

Thomas F. Ring (1841–98) founded the
Vincentians in 1888. *(Boston College Archives.)*

increasingly on the Boston Juvenile Court for admissions, and most of the
neglected child cases in that court were referred to the HDCC: 62 percent
in 1907, 57 percent in 1917, and 52 percent in 1927.[148] From 1906 to 1917,
the presiding justice, Harvey H. Baker, committed 638 children to the
HDCC and Superintendent Daniel J. Pyne was a daily visitor to his court.
In Pyne's absence, the Vincentians or the Irish Catholic probation officers
working in the court were sure to refer neglected or abused boys and girls
to the "Harrison Avenue Home."[149]

At the same time, the total number of children admitted to the HDCC
rose from 229 in 1867 to 1,512 in 1917, while the daily inmate population
rose from 48 to 248.[150] The HDCC became a traditional orphanage, the
overcrowded congregate asylum its founders rejected. Moreover, as non-
Catholic agencies professionalized by adopting new casework, psychological and psychiatric techniques, the HDCC continued to ask subjective
questions on admission forms (immoral? intemperate? insane? shiftless?

criminal record?). The switch from moral to medical questions (diph-theria? chicken pox? shick test? scarlet fever? vaccination?) came only in 1928, and psychologists were not employed until 1952.[151]

One reason for this "retrograde attitude," as one HDCC chaplain termed it, was the greater authority the Sisters of Charity wielded. The sister superior became the chief executive after Daniel Pyne died in 1917, and as she and her nuns retreated from things secular, they disparaged foster care and "were completely innocent of social work and psychol-ogy." Boston Catholics were more respectful and trusting of nuns than they originally had been, and the Sisters of Charity won greater influence in proportion to the distance they placed between themselves and the Jazz Age. Otherworldliness was a feature of twentieth-century American Ca-tholicism akin to the "medievalism" Cardinal O'Connell favored.[152] Sister Aloysia devoted fifteen years to the HDCC (1783–88) and Sister Dolores twenty-three (1900–1923), and such long tenure gave the sisters consider-able influence in Catholic welfare despite the misogyny of the Church.[153]

With a diminished role for the male child-savers who had been managing the HDCC, and less emphasis on foster placement, new methods were created to support HDCC children. The orphan trains discontinued by 1900, but were succeeded by the "streetcar orphan train" and the "parish slave auction."[154] On Sunday mornings each Spring, the visiting agents took groups of twenty children by public transportation from the HDCC to parish churches throughout metropolitan Boston.[155] They attended Mass in local churches at the end of which the priest invited parishioners to examine the children at the altar rail and, perhaps, take a child home for a few weeks "vacation."[156] This often became an indefinite foster family placement or an adoption. The HDCC agents wrote or called (and occa-sionally visited) the foster family and the pastor was asked to "check up on the child from time to time, but often he didn't have the time to do so."[157] It was that simple and callous. This slave auction was an annual feature of parish life in Boston from 1890 to 1940 when Bishop (later Cardinal) Richard J. Cushing ended this "hit or miss, barbaric but well-intentioned practice."[158] One HDCC agent remembered being embar-rassed at delivering "slave auction kids in an old pick up truck," but the "kids never complained, they had lived through much worse than that and sometimes even looked forward to trying out a new foster family."[159] Many Boston Catholics recall these parish slave auctions and seeing groups of "orphans riding on the streetcars with one man herding them along" in the 1920s. One priest who witnessed this annual rite "now shudders at the brutality and insensitivity of it" and he went home "grate-ful for my own family."[160] Another priest, who later became director of the Catholic Charitable Bureau in Boston, recalled this phenomenon in 1925 and saw the last remaining child dolefully standing at the altar waiting to be selected, and "your heart went out to him." His own middle-class family took an HDCC foster child twice, as did many well-meaning Catholic families.[161]

The HDCC Ladies Aid Society, organized in 1887 to "aid the Sisters in carrying on their good work" by fund-raising, sewing bees and charity balls provided clothing for the children to be placed in this way. It was a small, elite organization for Catholic matrons that met one Sunday afternoon each month at the HDCC "for a pleasant hour of social, business and inspirational get-together." It too attempted to recruit foster homes for HDCC girls, but the homeless girl was a much more "hard to place" child than her homeless or wayward brother. Most of the children on the streetcar orphan train were boys, and for Boston Catholics and Protestants, the wayward girl continued to provoke great anxiety in child-saving efforts.[162]

3

Wayward Girls in Boston

The homeless or unsupervised girl posed a special problem to nineteenth-century Bostonians, one very different and more perplexing than that of the wayward or delinquent boy. Charity workers took a generally pessimistic view of their work with homeless girls and women, one reflecting the double standard imposed on the "weaker sex" and supported by a variety of moral and medical opinions that the female invariably had a weaker mind to match her more delicate body. If women were still spiritually superior to men, their moral lapse was all the more awful. Even sympathetic women engaged in child-saving expressed doubts about the reformation of homeless girls who had known the seamy side of slum life:

> The homeless boy is a sufficiently pitiful object, but the girl child fares even worse. The boy is often less perverted than he seems. His sins belong to his ignorance and his condition, and drop away under an entire change of environment. . . . For the girl there is less chance in every way.[1]

Why should girls be less susceptible to social and moral reform in the eyes of Victorian child-savers? Aside from male supremacist notions, tradition saddled the homeless and wayward girl (the two being considered inevitably linked) with a much heavier penalty for her sins than boys had to bear. The girl who lived in urban slums without proper guardians was believed vulnerable to moral temptations almost impossible to resist. Her past was held against her as his seldom was, and she felt herself handicapped socially by poverty and the lack of respectability. Child-savers expressed hope for virtuous poor girls, but for those who sacrificed virginity for pleasure or profit, the "angel corrupted became a devil, and a woman abandoned to treachery and lust became a mournful wreck" in Victorian America. Boys were considered more redeemable than girls because a vagabond boy might, in the popular imagination, be strengthened by the school of hard knocks and mature into a successful man like the impoverished bootblack, Ragged Dick, in Horatio Alger's novels.[2] The loss of sexual innocence was irreversible for the female, and her sin was believed to doom her to a life of total corruption or at least to place her

St. Mary's Infant Asylum displays the foundlings on the lawn, 1855. *(St. Margaret's Hospital.)*

outside the bounds of normal society, like Hawthorne's Hester Prynne. She was a fallen angel tempting weak-willed men to sin. The leading expert of the period on child-saving, Charles Loring Brace, said that street life destroyed girls' souls beyond all possible cleansing, and the Boston child-saver Rufus R. Cook agreed.[3] But this disdain for and despair about rescuing girls who fornicated tells more about the reformers than about reforming. In the female, the loss of virginity can (sometimes) be determined by the rupture of the hymen; in the male no equivalent physical evidence exists. It was thus earlier to focus on the verifiable and concrete female stigmata than to speculate on the male's sexual misconduct. As late as 1915, the Boston Juvenile Court routinely used gynecological examination of female defendants to determine virginity and relied upon the opinion of the Massachusetts Society for the Prevention of Cruelty to Children (MSPCC) physicians concerning the moral character and sexual experience of girls.[4]

Most "bad girls" caught in the child welfare nets were generally guilty of no specific crime, but were considered to be in moral jeopardy. They were often charged with vague status offenses as "stubborn" or "wayward" children under Massachusetts law due to assumed or anticipated sexual activity. Today sexual acting out by adolescents is considered symptomatic of peer pressure, or family and personal psychopathology, but in the simpler, pre-Freudian Victorian era it was a sinful tragedy. The fact that poverty made prostitution an economic strategy for poor women was beyond the comprehension of middle-class child-savers.

Urban boys constituted a real threat to people and property, a social menace that middle-class Boston had no reluctance to curb by court sentence to institutions like the State Reform School for Boys in Westborough. This institution, like the House of Reformation or the Parental School in Boston, was created as an instrument of social control. Bourgeois reformers treated wayward boys strictly and directly to curtail their criminal behavior and to train them to become productive, orderly working-class men. But girls were a very different problem because their illicit and shameful sexual activity (or even the suspicion of sexual activity) threatened the moral order without which nineteenth-century Boston could not function. This was a more serious, sinister threat than the rowdiness of boys, so the responses to it were much more complex, reflecting the Victorians' view of woman as the spiritual superior and moral guardian of man.[5]

The attributes which antebellum Americans associated with the ideal woman, the "cult of true womanhood," consisted of four cardinal virtues—piety, purity, submissiveness, and domesticity. These were the standards by which every woman was judged and by which she judged herself. Middle-class women were expected to represent, conserve, and transmit moral and cultural values, while their men were expected to fall prey to lust and moral lapse in the tumult of the marketplace. Sexuality was denied decent women, and in the absence of effective birth control methods, men who could not restrain their lust were permitted to visit secretly Boston's brothels and professional prostitutes. These fallen women were tolerated tacitly to preserve the American family and the purity and sexlessness of good women.[6] The morally inferior lower-class women who lost their virtue provided recruits for prostitution—often the unsupervised daughters of the poor who sold candy, fruit, matches, or flowers on city streets.[7] Many of these girls became prostitutes in a desperate search for economic security and material comforts after casual encounters with men cost them their virginity and reputation and their parents had expelled them from the home. Others were the orphaned, abandoned, abused or runaway girls George Templeton Strong saw roaming the streets in 1851 "with thief written in their cunning eyes and whore on their depraved faces . . . a gang of blackguard boys is lovely by the side of it."[8]

As nineteenth-century ladies expanded their moral guardianship from the family and the church to new reform movements, they encountered the problem of prostitution and poor girls in the city. The Boston Female Asylum arose from one such incident, but it early decided to accept only young virginal girls. On the other hand, the Boston Penitent Female Refuge Society reformed prostitutes, especially rural New England girls entering Boston's growing ranks of fallen women. The elite reformers found this sexual license shocking because it violated the rigid standards of chastity expected of all women, because it increased the number of illegitimate children, and because it denied lower-class children proper moral guardians as mothers. These children, they feared, would swell the ranks of juvenile delinquents and fill the asylums for homeless and wayward children.[9]

Boston had a dozen child-saving societies and institutions by the Civil War. The treatment was more or less similar: girls found in moral peril were taken up by an agent; investigated; sent to a temporary home; trained in religion, manners, housekeeping, and the common school subjects; and then placed in middle-class suburban or rural Yankee families as servants. There they were expected to work diligently and learn to be the moral, obedient young women respectable men of their class would want to marry. Their employers were surrogate mothers who prepared the girls for marriage and motherhood in exchange for faithful service.

Yet as a sort of indentured servant, these lower-class Boston girls had to overcome the stigma of poverty and the suspicion of immorality shared by the child-savers and the employers, both of whom watched carefully for any signs that the girls were about to lapse into sin, mischief, or immorality.[10]

Since the reforms of Horace Mann, the public school was expected to enculturate lower-class children, particularly the children of the 35,000 Irish immigrants who crowded into Boston by 1845. But American school books were written to appeal to the middle-class native-born teachers and school committee members.[11] The values, attitudes and mores in these textbooks were alien and even absurd in the eyes of poor urban immigrant pupils, and the high truancy rates in nineteenth-century schools can be attributed partly to the alienation, apathy, and frustration the curriculum created in many pupils.[12] By 1860 Boston teachers were predominantly (77 percent) Yankee "spinsters" who found the conservative, traditional tenor of the texts and curricula more compatible with their own backgrounds than those of the Irish "Paddy" children in their classrooms. The public school Americanization process convinced many lower-class girls that they were different and inferior and their family customs worthless. Their accents, language, religion, and traditions were badges of inferiority, and the slow progress the immigrants made contrasted with the egalitarian values and social mobility the school books promised in America.[13]

Consequently, Boston truancy rates in 1838 were 33 to 40 percent overall and higher among Irish and black families (34 and 42 percent respectively) than among native-born white families (24 percent). Girls attended school less often than boys, even after Boston opened its public schools on an equal basis in 1828. It was clear by the 1840s that the public school was not a solution for the restraint of all girls. One judge remarked on the number of truants filling street corners each day who

> present the miserable spectacle of idle, untaught children, male and female—a crop too rapidly ripening for the dram-shop, the brothel, and the prison—and that too under the shadow of spacious and admirably kept schoolhouses, into which all may enter free of cost.[14]

* * *

To supplement the failing family and school antebellum reformers turned to the new public asylums. When Boston opened the House of Reformation for Juvenile Offenders in 1826, girls were among its first inmates, and by 1830 even a few young prostitutes were admitted. They were segregated from the boys and the small number of young girls lest they corrupt them. But the difficulty of distinguishing between the sexually depraved and the merely sexually curious girls, as well as a general distaste by the staff and directors for contact with wayward girls, was obvious from the first. The Boston Police Court repeatedly committed girls who were turned away for one reason or another by the unwilling directors. They persistently avoided the more volatile and embarrassing female delinquents. Few girls were admitted thereafter, and by 1834 the

House of Reformation was a reform school for boys and a few prepubescent girls. In 1840—when the directors had been convinced that the presence of "immoral girls" led to the moral contagion of the boys despite high walls and strict separation of the sexes in every activity—the superintendent released every girl and started over with a new group of females under age twelve and limited to twenty-five at any time.[15] After the institution relocated on Deer Island with the other county asylums, a new building was opened exclusively for girls. Still they continued to trouble the city government with fears of moral contagion and rumors of sexual misconduct between the inmates or between girls and male staff or visitors. The establishment of a state reform school for girls in 1856 permitted the House of Reformation to reduce the number of girls to a handful (usually less than twenty-five). With an official sigh of relief, Boston finally closed the Girls' Department in 1890, although boys were committed to city care until 1920.[16] The opening of the Marcella Street Girls' Orphanage by the city government in 1878 also relieved the House of Reformation of many females it would have admitted.[17]

The House of Reformation was clearly never comfortable in treating delinquent girls, especially those whose "sexual powers" had been unleashed. Boys, of course, were another matter; the male directors could punish and reform them without embarrassment or moral danger, and sexual misbehavior was seldom a problem. It remained for the state and a few bold private asylums to cope with the perplexing problems of wayward girls in Boston.

Encouraged by the initial success of the State Reform School for Boys established in Westborough in 1847, the Massachusetts legislature in 1849 considered opening a similar institution for girls, and asked for the advice of Samuel Gridley Howe (1801–76), a well-known physician, prison reformer, Boston School Committeeman, House of Reformation director, and superintendent of the Perkins School for Blind Children. Howe quickly disparaged the project because he preferred a placing-out system for girls, who he believed would benefit even less than boys from a congregate asylum. The legislature studied this proposal for four years and in 1854 authorized the State Industrial School for Girls in Lancaster, a small farming community thirty miles west of Boston. The state appropriation of $20,000 was matched by an equal amount in private funds, and in 1856 the first girls were admitted from the Boston courts.[18]

Howe's advice had not been totally ignored, however, because the Lancaster School (as it was known) was the first American reform school to use the family cottage plan of the French Mettray and German Rauhe Haus schools for delinquents. Howe, Horace Mann, Theodore Parker, Father Haskins and other Boston reformers had studied European asylums carefully and advised key legislators, state Senators Bradford

Kinney Peirce and Frank B. Fay, who sponsored the Lancaster School legislation. Peirce, a Methodist Sunday school organizer and editor, became the first superintendent and chaplain at Lancaster (1856–62), and Fay was a trustee and neighbor of the institution.

Instead of cells or dormitories, like most nineteenth-century asylums, Lancaster housed the girls in four small cottages. Each was a self-contained family unit, sheltering thirty girls ages seven to fourteen and two matrons, with its own bedrooms, kitchen, parlor, classroom, and sewing room. Girls were assigned to a cottage according to their individual background and needs. Cottage inmates mingled with the other girls only at chapel services, and were otherwise prevented from indiscriminate mixing in this decentralized, home-like environment. This cottage method became highly regarded in penology and was still in use at most institutions for juveniles when Lancaster School was closed in 1976.[19]

From the first, Lancaster was "designed for those who are wayward, obstinate, or who from the poverty, ignorance, neglect or abuse of parents, are exposed to, or have become, vagrants." The sexually depraved were not admitted, although girls who "have taken the initiatory steps in crime"—usually truancy or petty theft—were admitted "to save them from inevitable ruin, and from becoming a nuisance to society." The institution was to be a home, and "each house is to be a family under the sole direction and control of the matron, who is the mother of the family." Mixing younger girls (ages seven to twelve) with older girls (ages twelve to fifteen) served to create a family atmosphere with a tattle-tale pattern in which the young impressionable girls policed their older "sisters" by snitching to the matron about minor infractions. This infantilization of the inmates created tranquility and consequently there were few escapes under Superintendent Peirce, despite unlocked doors and the absence of restraining fences or walls. This pleasant state continued from 1856 to 1870.[20]

Lancaster succeeded most often with young girls who had come to court through no fault of their own, but due to the poverty, neglect, intemperance, or desertion of their parents. Most were orphans (52 percent in 1860) and came into state custody for truancy, shoplifting, or gross destitution. Prior to 1870, Lancaster admitted few young prostitutes, partly because the steady stream of wayward virgins or relatively inexperienced girls excluded the fallen women, and partly because the directors refused to accept hardened offenders. But in 1870 the Board of State Charities authorized its visiting agents to attend all court trials of minors from which boys and girls could be taken for foster family placement without any period of institutionalization. This was a major victory for Dr. Howe's supporters because these children avoided even brief confinement in a jail or asylum and went directly from court to a farmer's household. A

Table 3.1

Lancaster School Admissions, 1857–1937

Year	No. of girls admitted	Average age	Average stay (months)
1857	92	13	9
1867	141	14	—
1877	110	16	—
1887	67	15	12
1897	167	16	18
1907	250	16	15–36
1917	340	16	24
1927	297	15.5	19
1937	251	16	—

SOURCES: Lancaster, *Annual Reports*, 1857–1937, and the State Board of Education, *Annual Reports*, 1857–1937.

committee of "lady volunteers" or the state visiting agents made quarterly home visits to oversee the "indentured" wards of the state, much as public welfare social workers do today.[21]

The impact of this change in state law was immediately apparent at the Lancaster School. Gardiner Tufts, the chief state visiting agent, drew off the younger, more innocent girls for foster care or sent them to the new State Primary School, a public orphanage opened in Monson in 1872. This left only the older, chronically delinquent girls for Lancaster; naturally the directors protested against this new policy and defended their large institution (with over one hundred inmates) as a necessary and effective child-saving asylum. These dedicated gentlemen resisted any Massachusetts policy or practice which changed the character and number of inmates from the merely destitute wayward child to the seriously delinquent adolescent. Nonetheless, after 1870 the age and length of stay of the inmates rose while the number declined (see Table 3.1). Lancaster became a juvenile jail, a junior league prison, and in response to the increasing outbreaks of violence, arson, disorder, and escapes, recalcitrant inmates were transferred to any other state institution that would admit them—the Sherborn Reformatory for Women, the Tewksbury State Infirmary, the State School for the Feeble-minded, and the Bridgewater State Farm. Superintendent Peirce complained about the admission of older, "immoral" girls, whose presence justified lowered expectations:

It was intended in the commencement, that the school should be particularly one of prevention; but the necessities of the case, and the success of the experiment, have made it a home and a refuge for "brands plucked from the burning." Most of its inmates would have been subjects of criminal law; so whatever we accomplish is almost an absolute salvation.[22]

Many of these brands plucked from the burning were sexually active lower-class Boston Irish girls charged as stubborn children by parents or police for vague moral offenses such as nightwalking, being idle and disorderly, lewd and lascivious carriage, or fornication. This was just the kind of criminal conduct Dr. Howe hoped to prevent by scattering pre-delinquent, homeless girls in rural families. Lancaster was created in the idea that "it is hard work to make straight a single crooked stick—harder yet a bundle of them taken together." The girls admitted originally were only slightly "crooked" and housed in small bundles that could be individually straightened by family cottage treatment. Dr. Howe was convinced that "viciously depraved youth should not be brought together but put far asunder," and the inmates in the first era (1856–72) tended to be young, innocent, and carefully selected and sorted girls. They were easily trained in a year and placed out in the foster homes as Howe and his allies planned. This was in accord with the House of Reformation experience "that some of the most satisfactory cases of reformation . . . were those effected out of the House, and in families, after the Institution had failed to do them any good."[23] Howe and his friends Horace Mann and Franklin B. Sanborn hoped that the "first business of the Superintendent would be to procure places in suitable homes for the girls" because "families were the natural reform schools," and few girls were as bad as they were said to be. This optimistic, anti-institutional view suited the seven men who composed the first Board of State Charities created by Governor John A. Andrew in 1863, especially when Howe joined the Board (1865–1874) and Sanborn became its Secretary (1863–69).[24]

Lancaster was a compromise between the foster family program advocated by romantic Pestolozzian reformers like Howe and the Benthamite school advocates who preferred to punish social deviants as they were reforming them. It never succeeded despite its innovative family cottage system and dedicated staff. Superintendent Marcus Ames resigned in protest in 1875 when the new directors installed workshops and insisted on economical, even profitable, management, much as Wells had resigned from the House of Reformation earlier for similar reasons. When the legislature and Board of State Charities authorized the commitment of older girls and drew off most young girls to Monson, foster homes, or private asylums, Lancaster was destined to become a school for crime, a last resort for female delinquents too besmirched for family reform and too young for prison. As incarceration levels rose and social surveillance heightened during the Civil War, and as the new private asylums found crimes against chastity too shocking to treat, Lancaster increasingly sheltered chronic juveniles delinquents, the incorrigible, the feeble-minded, and girls with an unusual sexual history—rape, incest, group sex, interracial sex—and those tough cases expelled from private asylums. By 1880 Lancaster had admitted 1,062 girls, but they were no longer the morally endangered waifs of the antebellum era; they were now morally dangerous girls in need of isolation and restraint to protect the community.

The girl who was committed by the court to Lancaster after 1875 was most likely to be charged with a moral offense or a crime against chastity, a separate category of victimless crime almost exclusively applied to females. The average age of inmates in 1877 was sixteen, and the indeterminate sentences usually amounted to a term longer than that served by boys at the Westborough Reform School. This was explained as necessary because girls required more careful oversight, a longer period of training, and a more intimate relationship with the staff. The chastity offenders included adolescents charged as stubborn children for running away from home, truancy, or refusing to work or obey their parents or guardians. Oftentimes they were sentenced at the request of parents, and the length of their sentence was determined by their submissiveness to Lancaster staff. The longer sentences reflected the directors' belief that young, promising girls deserved fuller treatment. The courts sometimes said that the sentence was imposed not as a punishment, but to see what change the reformatory may accomplish in a girl.[25]

The Victorian preoccupation with sex meant that chastity offenders included prostitutes, as well as girls who had engaged in premarital intercourse, chronic masturbators, and girls whose "lewd and lascivious carriage" and "wantonness" foretold immoral conduct even if they were still technically chaste. The other inmates were guilty of various minor crimes against person and property—assault, arson, breaking and entering, and larceny. But all had strayed too far from the cult of true womanhood to merit the attention of selective private asylums, and their only resort was the industrial discipline of the Lancaster School.[26]

Exactly how did a girl become an inmate in the Lancaster School or one of the Boston asylums for homeless and wayward females? Surviving records were not compiled with the historian in mind, but it seemed unmistakable that many girls were the subjects of official complaints by their parents or relatives. This does not mean, however, that every frustrated father or tearful mother dragged his or her promiscuous daughter into the police station. The girls who populated children's institutions in nineteenth-century Massachusetts were usually taken into custody by a Boston policeman for a minor offense. Their parents were summoned to the police station within a few hours for questioning. Facilities for detaining young girls were limited, and Boston Police Department practice dictated that only children charged with serious offenses or those children of unknown origin be detained overnight in the Tombs beneath the Suffolk County Courthouse or at the Suffolk County Jail in the West End.[27] Most girls and boys were released to their parents, once the child's identity and residence was established.[28] The child went home with her parents, probably to a sound beating. Minor offenses by local neighborhood girls did not usually result in a court hearing, but were petty matters settled arbitrarily in the police station and the woodshed at home.[29]

But chronic or serious offenders, or girls obviously neglected, abused, or in grave moral danger were subjects of formal complaints. Many immigrant parents, anxious to pacify the policeman and to avoid blame for their daughter's misbehavior, were easily persuaded to sign an official complaint against them as stubborn or wayward or a school offender.[30] Girls in Boston, under state law amended for Suffolk County only, appeared at a separate court session for juveniles under age seventeen. These hearings were not open to public spectators and a separate court docket was kept. The probate or district court judge sat as a juvenile court justice, usually on one morning each week in the district courthouse, and heard the accumulated juvenile cases. No district attorney acted as prosecutor, but the policeman or truant officer assumed this role. It was to these special court sessions that the Board of State Charities visiting agent came (having been notified by the clerk of court) to act as a sort of defense attorney or friend of the court *(amicus curiae)*. He claimed any homeless or unsupervised girl he found suitable, or one of the private asylum visiting agents was permitted to take a girl he found appropriate.[31]

These judges attempted to treat young girls compassionately, and often this was reflected in long postponements of cases, dismissal of minor charges, small fines, probation, and lenient sentences or paternal lectures. The judges had no special training in dealing with juveniles, and the appearance of a young girl in Boston courts was particularly embarrassing or appalling to many judges. But in some cases of female delinquence the courts relied on new community resources. Child-savers from private asylums frequented the police, probate and municipal courts by the 1850s looking for children to rescue, but these proper Bostonians were reluctant to become involved with sexual offenders. They worked closely with the courts in rescuing homeless orphans, but girls appearing in court for crimes against chastity were unsuitable for genteel asylums like the Home for Destitute Catholic Children (HDCC) or the New England Home for Little Wanderers (NEHLW).[32]

Superintendent George Adams of the HDCC reported in 1865 that he "received a note from Truant Officer Cole that tomorrow he should bring a girl named Kelly for sentence. . . . Her Mother is a miserable creature."

When he was sure that the girl was chaste, although her mother was immoral, Adams decided, "I shall see what can be done for the child."[33] He usually avoided the daughters of unwed mothers, and when Bridget Ryan applied for his assistance "until the Mother comes from Prison," his assistant, Mrs. Ann Leake, "took charge of it" because "I refused to have anything to do with it."[34] The HDCC did admit morally tainted girls, as in 1877 when a ten-year-old Irish girl and her five-year-old sister were taken while their "very intemperate" and immoral mother was in the Boston City Hospital, but only because "the case is urgent as Protestant uncle would have seen them to."[35]

The key role the judge played in mitigating the severity of the law for girls is seen in the case of young Mary O'Neil in 1865. Judge Sebeus C. Maine, who presided over the Boston Police Court from 1858 to 1866, was grateful for the assistance of Adams (HDCC), Cook (BCAS), Toles (NEHLW), Haskins (HAG), and Barry (CM) in dealing with girls, but he was seldom able to persuade them to accept an immoral girl who was bound for the Lancaster School, and often parents were unwilling to consent to a private asylum placement. Mary O'Neil's mother strenuously objected when her daughter was found guilty of truancy, but when Judge Maine "gave the Mother the preference, whether she should be sentenced to the Island [House of Reformation] for 2 years, or to let [the HDCC] take her," she also objected to that disposition. The judge told Mr. Adams privately that he could take the girl in a few days if he wanted to, but Adams, although pleased with his access to the bench, declined. Mary was too wild and her mother likely to disrupt the HDCC or a foster home looking for her daughter.[36]

Sometimes the HDCC assisted girls of questionable character while not admitting them to the asylum. In 1866 Adams "furnished with places 12 girls . . . whose names do not appear on the books," primarily because they were "stubborn, disobedient, violent in temper, and idle" and had lived the street arab's life too long. Their chastity could not be verified and they might spread moral contagion among the younger, more innocent girls in the HDCC.[37] Occasionally girls were admitted who later proved to be "stubborn," which was a reference to the state law making stubbornness a status offense punishable by commitment to reform school. Stubborn girls were usually immoral girls sent to the Lancaster School. The HDCC transferred Catherine Sullivan to the House of the Good Shepherd in 1877 as a "stubborn girl" because the HGS specialized in reforming prostitutes. Such girls were too threatening and too much trouble for an orphanage or child-placing agency like the HDCC or the NEHLW, and this was reflected in both institutions' preference for boys. By 1917 the HDCC admitted 1,512 children, of whom 56 percent were boys; and a majority of the 1,300 children taken "from the streets" of Boston by the Methodist NEHLW from 1865 to 1892 were male.[38]

Even a girl whose sister was immoral was considered unsuitable for the gentle HDCC, as in a case in which the Boston truant officer, Mr. Cole, asked Adams "to investigate an orphan Irish girl in East Boston" in 1867. When Adams discovered she had "2 sisters, young girls whose reputation is not good," he refused to help her. Street life did not necessarily make a girl ineligible for private asylums, but sexual transgression did. When Ellen Ryan, aged ten, and her sister, Anne, aged eight, were sent to the HDCC "in custody of 2 Sunday School Lady Teachers from St. James Parish," they were accepted although they were "regular St. Arabs and tried very hard to get away."[39] Chronic theft, like precocious sexuality, also disqualified girls in the HDCC view. Adams saw "4 little girls arraigned for shoplifting. Judge Maine asked me if I wished to take one or more of them. . . . Informed him we had no place for them. . . . They are confirmed thieves."[40]

If a girl was without family or friends, and her offense was not sufficiently mild (that is, not sexual, violent, or chronic) to interest the private asylum child-savers who happened to be in the courtroom, the judge had no alternative but to commit her to the Board of State Charities, the Lancaster School, or the House of Reformation. After 1870 the Board's visiting agents attempted to place out the homeless girls or first offenders, but this was not always possible and, of course, serious offenders were ineligible for foster homes without a period of institutional training. So the girl whose misfortune or misconduct placed her outside the purview of private charities was soon on a train to the State Primary School in Monson (if she was under age twelve) or to the State Industrial School in Lancaster (if she was over twelve or seemed "too saucy" or "too immoral.").[41] After 1880 Massachusetts child-savers redefined waywardness to include sexually active girls who engaged in immoral behavior with boys or men but had not yet fallen into the ranks of streetwalkers and the chronically promiscuous. Previously, even a single incident of sexual experimentation was sufficient to condemn a teenage girl as immoral. But this view gradually moderated from 1880 to 1910, as American sexual standards altered in the maturing urban industrial economy. Middle-class women learned to value virginity less and to risk premarital sex more, and this phenomenon altered child-savers' perception of lower-class girls as well.[42]

Although Lancaster was originally intended for girls in moral danger, not for young prostitutes, most female delinquents from 1875 to 1915, whatever the exact offense listed in court records, were usually accused of sexual misconduct. Most private child welfare agencies preferred to deal with non-sexual cases, leaving the "immoral, wanton girls" to the public institutions. As a result of the fastidiousness and prudery of the private social welfare sector, Lancaster School, like its older brother, the Lyman School in Westborough, was filled by the mid-1870s with older, more hardened offenders—criminals and prostitutes—than was intended or desired by the directors. During the Civil War, charitable and carceral institutions in New England and New York had an influx of dependents of men under arms. Mothers, wives, sisters, and children of soldiers and sailors were said to be corrupted by bonus money and the new financial aid for military dependents. This wartime demoralization on the home front led to increased vigilance by charity workers to safeguard the poor from their own vice and hedonism.[43] The reformers and child-savers were still reluctant to dirty their hands by contact with young prostitutes or "soiled doves," but in the predelinquent girl they found ideal targets for their moral marksmanship. The traditional poor-law distinction between the worthy and unworthy poor expressed itself in the futile attempt to distinguish the dependent girl from the delinquent girl. Wayward girls were especially sought by child-savers because to save one girl was believed to save ten boys from her sexual licentiousness. The already fallen girl was a candidate for some asylums, but the not-yet corrupted, still-virgin girl excited the ambitions of many more philanthropists. Not until the 1880s would sexually experienced girls (although few girls were as "experienced" as reformers imagined) be admitted to most Boston child welfare agencies.[44]

After the Civil War, new private asylums in Boston expanded moral training and placing-out services. Girls who were not seriously delinquent found temporary shelter in private institutions superior in reputation to Lancaster, from which they were adopted, placed as foster children, boarded out, or sent to work as maids, mother's helpers, or old ladies' companions. Child-savers continued to see the New England family farm as the ideal home for these children, but they found in the middle-class suburban family an acceptable substitute. But in creating these child welfare services, little thought was given to the needs of lower-class families. The private agencies were disenchanted with the congregate asylum and with the inflexible public sector as remedies for socially deviant children, but they formed their own alternative system without reference to the needs or desires of their clients. When parents attempted to use child welfare services or adapt them for their own ends—perhaps to place a child temporarily during a parent's illness, child-bearing, unemployment, or widowhood—they were often refused cooperation by the agents. Sometimes a child placed by a parent would not be returned by the institution because the girl was adapting to a foster family which the child-saver regarded as morally superior to her parents' household. Few parents had the wherewithal to wage a custody battle with a respectable charity, and courts were unsympathetic to impoverished parents who signed legal documents surrendering their rights and later reneged on this contract.[45]

The public welfare system for dependent and delinquent children as it stood in Massachusetts by 1870 was widely recognized by charity experts as inadequate, inflexible, and uncontrollable (from the emerging professional altruist's viewpoint). Consequently, new private organizations entered the child welfare field and quickly dominated it, using Lancaster and Lyman (as the Westborough State Reform School was renamed) Schools a negative reference. This elite, private child welfare system itself deserves attention.[46]

* * *

When a group of philanthropic Beacon Hill ladies distributed religious tracts to the inmates of the Suffolk County Jail in 1864, they were astonished to discover many young boys and girls in the cells. If the Good Samaritan had been a Bostonian, he would not have stopped on the road to aid the robber's victim, but instead hurried to town and organized a Travelers' Aid Society. The moral indignation of these good ladies had a similar effect when the Boston Children's Aid Society was incorporated in 1864 to rescue delinquent children awaiting trial in jail.

As we have seen, the BCAS operated a family farm for wayward boys in Newton and Foxborough from 1864 to 1896, but new ground was broken in 1866 when a similar home for wayward girls aged five to sixteen opened in West Newton, about fifteen miles from Boston. These were wayward but virgin lower-class Boston girls numbering from ten to twenty-five in an old school and small farm on Church Street. Newton was not yet the prosperous suburban city it later became and still had an agrarian character although it was conveniently reached by train from Boston, Brookline, and Cambridge where most of the BCAS members lived. This was important because the visitors' committee conscientiously inspected both Pine Farm and the Girls' Home each month.[47]

The inmates were not merely orphans but wayward girls who needed reformation and moral rehabilitation beyond mere custodial care and protection. This asylum was an experiment that the BCAS attempted as a result of its satisfaction with the nearby Pine Farm mini-reform school. The Girls' Home, however, burned down in 1868, due to incendiarism by one unhappy inmate, and the entire project was abandoned in 1872. The reasons for ending this experiment disclose much about the role of private asylums in preventing female juvenile delinquence.[48]

Although the BCAS directors emphasized that this was not to be another orphan asylum for homeless girls like several others in metropolitan Boston, they excluded girls who were "confirmed" criminals or prostitutes, or who were even suspected of sexual immorality. As a result, few "appropriate" girls were available, and most inmates were orphan or half-orphans charged with truancy, shoplifting, or property damage. But even these offenses sometimes masked sexual transgression as did the more frequent charges of being a "stubborn" or "wayward" child. How then did the BCAS screen applicants for admission to insure that they were girls who needed reformation but were not too unmanageable to be safely committed to the small, community-based, family-style asylum? Obviously, there was no sure way to cull the incorrigibly depraved from the less hardened sinners the BCAS imagined would benefit from a year in the country under paternal discipline. The impossibility of separating the wayward from the wicked—even with careful investigation of applicants and with an experienced staff headed by Mrs. Rebecca R. Pomeroy (1817–84), a Civil War nurse familiar with charity work for thirty years—doomed the Girls' Home from the first.[49]

Within three months of its opening, the directors were asked to remove a girl because of her immoral influence on younger inmates.[50] Rebelliousness was a constant refrain in the BCAS records, and the arson in 1868 exasperated the directors. A new building was opened but the BCAS lost its enthusiasm for the project and acceptable girls were difficult to find, even with Rufus Cook's thorough scrutiny of the courts and police lock-ups. In 1872 the BCAS reiterated that the Girls' Home was not simply for orphans; but the "sauciness" and "eloping" and "corruption" of younger girls by more brazen inmates confounded Mrs. Pomeroy and the visiting committee. With the example of the deteriorating Lancaster School in mind and unwilling to duplicate the more traditional work of the Boston Female Asylum and other orphanages, the BCAS decided to close this home and to focus on the more successful and less morally worrisome work with wayward boys.[51] This decision was not unanimous; Mrs. Pomeroy continued to operate the Home with private contributions as an orphanage for destitute girls; and a few BCAS ladies continued to advocate some other kind of work with girls.[52]

The decision to close the Girls' Home had more to do with the prevailing Victorian ideology than it did with the ability of the directors and staff of the incorrigibility of the inmates. It demonstrated the pervasive double standard which condemned the girl more quickly and certainly than the boy. Assumptions of male supremacy and the corresponding idea that girls who were aggressive, independent, self-assertive, or sexually curious were unfeminine and immoral underlay the discomfort of the BCAS directors with their new Girls' Home. Boys were encouraged to develope the skills and strengths of adult autonomy, but girls were confined to the stereotyped traits of the middle-class woman as an emotional, passive, pious, affectionate dependent of her father or husband.

Despite the profound implications of social, economic, and demographic changes in the 1870s, however, gender-role socialization of females by the family remained fundamentally unchanged. Normative prescriptions of proper feminine behavior were taught by the BCAS to lower-class girls plucked from family and friends, and when they reacted by misbehavior to this class and ethical conflict and inevitable emotional trauma, they were labeled "wicked" and "corrupt," while the same misconduct in Pine Farm boys only incurred a paternal lecture and a trip to bed without supper.[53]

For some girls, the traditional female role was functional and appealing, but for those who questioned or resisted or, in relatively few cases, rejected it and reacted to the discontinuities between lower-class urban origins and middle-class pastoral aspirations, there was only moral condemnation. At a time when American society embraced egalitarian democracy and free will as transcendant social values for their brothers, girls were routinely socialized to assume a dependent, domestic, social role and forbidden to express anger, violence, strength, courage, or other masculine traits. Is it any wonder that the BCAS was unable to find "appropriate" girls for this family farm reformatory? Girls who filled the prescribed role were at home or in a genteel asylum like the BFA or St. Vincent's Home, and those who did not learn or accept this role were sent to the Lancaster School. The BCAS sought the middle ground but quickly abandoned its cautious effort to question the double standard because of the conflict between philanthropic intentions and the conservative roots of reform, entangled in sexism. Limited by the ideology which defined a woman as madonna or whore, angel or temptress, the BCAS closed its Girls' Home in frustration and dismay and in doing so consigned wayward girls to the inferior Lancaster School.[54]

Still some BCAS members agitated for a program to rescue mildly wayward girls, so in 1879 the BCAS began placing girls referred to their agents directly into rural New England families as domestic servants and foster children, depending upon the character and age of the child and the needs of the family. These girls were aged ten to sixteen, and one motive for placement was to avoid commitment to the Lancaster School, with its stigma of institutionalism. The label "state girl" implied by this time a strong suspicion of gross immorality, and some BCAS members doubted the efficacy of congregate asylums, despite Lancaster's innovative family cottages. Rural family placement was idealized by many Bostonians, including the BCAS members and patrons, as the best remedy for most dependent or delinquent girls. Poor parental supervision and "bad home life" was seen as the chief cause of juvenile delinquency, and good foster parents were considered the best solution. The cult of domesticity was invoked to save lower-class girls once again. The middle-class Yankee housewives who took these poor girls into their own homes to train them as apprentice housewives were said to be motivated by Christian charity; but they also expected much help in housework and submissive gratitude in exchange. In this they were often disappointed. Many girls were placed and replaced in foster homes and domestic service positions, the frequent turnover and terse accounts in record books indicating that most girls were discontented with their foster mother/employer and that much conflict occurred. The mistresses were offended to find that the BCAS girls were not the submissive waifs they expected, but oftentimes troublesome and troubled lower-class urbanites; lonely, immature, unruly, or mentally ill.[55]

*   *   *

The difficulties the BCAS agents encountered in placing out adolescent girls were shared by the New England Home for Little Wanderers, an orphanage and child-placing society established by Boston Methodists in 1865 to care for the children of Civil War veterans. Parents, policemen, and charity workers brought homeless boys and girls to the asylum on Baldwin Place in the North End, and after a few months of training and education, the children were placed in private families throughout New England. By 1867 nine oprhan trains took Boston children to the Midwest as well. The daily problems faced by the agents left woeful accounts in NEHLW records, indicating that many girls were unhappy with their foster mother/employer and insisted on returning to the city to find their relatives or to remain in the asylum.[56] The Reverend R. G. Toles, the NEHLW visiting agent, reported that Mary, a fifteen-year-old orphan, was placed in a Jamaica Plain family in 1881, but that two years later her mistress complained that Mary was no longer a dutiful child despite all efforts to make her happy:

> This lady however cannot keep her longer and thinks she greatly needs training and a period of some discipline. She has a very high, ungovernable temper, likes the company of boys, and is untruthful.[57]

Mary was born in Portsmouth, New Hampshire, to an Irish mother and a Yankee father who "altho a drinking man, is a skilled workman." She was readmitted to the NEHLW "in the belief that few mistresses of good households could have time or patience to correct and control Mary's serious faults, while in a school, under discipline, they might be overcome." In less than nine months she was sufficiently trained to be placed out in domestic service. This time she had no further trouble.

Was Mary as "ungovernable" as reported, or was she reacting to being uprooted from her family and friends, sent to an asylum and then placed

The Reverend S. S. Cummings, NEHLW Superintendent, and some "little wanderers," September 1879. *(New England Home for Little Wanderers.)*

out as a foster child? Or was her misbehavior in the foster home only a case of normal adolescent acting out? Her mistress, like many others in the NEHLW records, was chagrined to find the girl she kindly took into her household was not the submissive, grateful daughter she had expected. These girls were often the emotionally needy daughters of poor, unhappy lower-class broken families, and frequently defiant, flirtatious, unruly, or hysterical teenagers. Some were destined for the brothel and some for the insane asylum, but most settled into the housemaid's life after two or three "unsuccessful placements," content for a while to earn a meager living in domestic service until old enough for marriage or until other more appealing work appeared.[58]

Much like the BCAS in method, if less prestigious in membership, the NEHLW combined benevolence with social control in a humane but elitist desire to impose restraint and respectability on the unsupervised children of the lower class. The aim was to remove pauper offspring of unassimilable immigrants from the morally threatening slums and place them in middle-class Yankee homes in the countryside for enculturation and assimilation. Each case was scrutinized, and those unlikely to benefit from training were rejected. One Sunday school teacher referred such a girl to the NEHLW in 1899:

> Mabel is in her Sunday School class. [Lives with] Mother and Step-father. Mabel will not go to school, goes away for two or three days & sleeps on steps, has been found by police. The truant officer said he should send her to Lancaster if we did not take her. Mother very weak woman. Child would not speak before her Mother, decided to take her if passed by Dr. Bond. Dr. Bond said she was not at all suitable for our School, having *very* bad habits (self-abuse) and bad in every way. *Refused.*[59]

A similar care was Alice, an orphan thirteen years old, who had been a maid in a suburban family in Milton since the age of nine. She was referred to the NEHLW by her employers because "she has taken money and cannot manage her—needs a reformatory." This girl was a thief from a destitute family and Mabel was sexually active.[60] Both Mabel and Alice were unsuitable for the NEHLW program chiefly because of their moral defects; while Mary, despite her Irish temper, could conform to pious Methodist standards and work as a dutiful maid. How did these altruistic child-savers judge the girls they investigated?

The case of Agnes in 1889 is instructive on this point. When her Canadian mother died in 1882, her Belgian father remarried. The NEHLW visiting agent reported that:

> Agnes has a step-mother who is leading a very bad life, and her father has no steady employment, as he speaks but little English. Her own

mother was well-born and educated, and her father's second marriage has brought her under evil influences and subjected her to cruel treatment, therefore it is most important that she should be cared for and protected . . . a girl of sweet disposition but no great strength of character. Pretty and in good health.[61]

Agnes was admitted immediately to the NEHLW and after nine months of training in the asylum, she was placed in a foster family in New Hampshire in 1890. She was placed again in 1891 and 1892. Each time she was transferred from one family to another by the solicitous visiting agent when she was unhappy. Fortune smiled, however, when a lady "interested in charity work" sent Agnes to an Episcopal boarding school in Wisconsin. When last heard from, Agnes was a dressmaker and a mother contentedly married to a respected newspaper reporter. She was one of the "poor girls who have become fair ladies, and are now honorable wives and happy mothers" in the Midwest, where "they shook off the slothfulness of city habits, and put into practice the fatherly counsel given them by their rescuers."[62]

This theme is found repeatedly in NEHLW records, a lovely child with a wicked step-mother, and this became a characteristic rescue fantasy of the Victorian child-savers. The daughters of "well-born and educated" mothers are worthy and suitable objects of sentimental Protestant charity workers who impart a fairy-tale spirit to the shabby and mundane business of sheltering "street arabs and guttersnipes." More importantly, the story of little Agnes, which is representative of both the BCAS and NEHLW most successful cases in the 1880s, reveals the class bias and hereditarian or environmentalist assumptions under which Boston child-savers operated. Some girls received the benefit of private charity and the advantages of foster family care and boarding school educations, and the agency proudly followed their subsequent (and very satisfying) success in marriage, motherhood, and homemaking. But other less suitable girls, of lower origin and refinement, were accused of precocious sexuality, dishonesty, and theft. They were consigned to poorly paid domestic service or sent to the Lancaster School, and agency records blush to mention their sordid stories. It demonstrated that "blood will tell" and that the daughters of superior breeding and grace somehow deserved charity while base-born girls usually failed to benefit from opportunities offered to them.[63]

The New England Home for Little Wanderers did not enjoy the elite support of Boston Brahmins as did the BFA and the BCAS, but its *nouveau riche* Methodist patrons compensated with enthusiasm for what they lacked in social cachet. A $500,000 endowment was quickly accumulated from pious businessmen like Governor William Claflin (bootmaking), Jacob Sleeper (clothing), and Isaac Rich (fish-dealing). The NEHLW moved from the Irish North End to the more respectable South End and

The NEHLW *Advocate* raised funds and public support for its child saving and orphan trains to the Midwest. *(New England Home for Little Wanderers.)*

later to a suburban Jamaica Plain neighborhood where a large asylum housing one hundred children was built. Orphan trains were dispatched throughout the 1870s to Iowa, Minnesota, and Wisconsin, much as the Children's Mission had done in the 1850s. Still the problem of wayward girls remained unresolved by the placing-out system and child savers were increasingly aware of the abuse and sexual exploitation foster girls and domestic servants encountered. These problems were under-reported, but the fact that some cases were mentioned in NEHLW, BCAS, Children's Mission, and the Board of State Charities reports indicates that it was a continuing issue in child welfare. Even the assurances in these official reports that girls were not abused by foster parents or employers were couched in defensive terms. Consequently, the new private children's agencies, which appeared after the Civil War intent upon expanding the number and scope of child welfare services, quickly avoided the wayward girl and concentrated their limited resources on the dependent children or mildly wayward boys much as earlier charities had done.[64]

* * *

A new solution to the problem of the wayward girl appeared in Boston in 1867 when the Sisters of the Good Shepherd arrived from their asylum in New York City to found the House of the Good Shepherd. Bishop John Fitzpatrick had been persuaded by a group of prominent Catholic ladies to invite these French nuns to establish the House of the Good Shepherd (HGS) in 1859, but a lack of funds and the coming of the Civil War delayed the project. However, the success of the HGS in Philadelphia (1856), New York City (1857), and Chicago (1858), encouraged Fitzpatrick's successor, Bishop John J. Williams to undertake this new charity in 1867.[65]

French convents were established as early as the fifteenth century to reform prostitutes and even to transform some of them into cloistered nuns devoting their lives to prayer and penance. The Religious of the Good Shepherd (RGS), or, as they were popularly called, the Sisters of the Good Shepherd, began in France in 1641, and by 1835 the congregation spread across Europe. Widespread prostitution was a distinctive feature of urban culture, a consequence of industrialization and capitalism, and it constituted a persistent social problem, but one with which few private charities were willing to grapple and one for which public asylums were notoriously unsuccessful. Consequently, the specialized treatment offered to inmates of the HGS found public approbation even in non-Catholic communities. The reputation of the Sisters of the Good Shepherd won them public funds and popular support even during the nativist campaigns in the United States.[66]

The first American HGS opened in Louisville in 1842, and by 1867 convent-reformatories were established in eleven major American cities.

The nuns specialized in being "true mothers" to girls and women of the "most depraved" sort, and their skill in dealing with the emotional needs of wayward girls and prostitutes anticipated in some respects modern behavioral-psychology techniques. In each HGS, the sisters lived a semi-cloistered life under the strict Rule of St. Vincent de Paul and carefully adhered to the organizational plan of HGS foundress, Rose Virginnie Pelletier (called Mother Euphrasia), which was described in the *Practical Rules for the Use of the Religious of the Good Shepherd for the Direction of the Classes.*[67]

This wise and pithy book taught each sister how to cope with the daily problems of managing large groups of delinquent girls in a congregate asylum. It instructed the novice sister or "Mistress" of the "children" (as all inmates were called regardless of their age or marital status) to use outward calm and authority to impose order and obedience on even the most recalcitrant girls. For example, the *Practical Rules* advised, "It is not by speaking that a Mistress imposes silence; an authoritative look, a dignified manner, a calm countenance, and a self-possession, have more effect than the noisy movements and loud voice of a Mistress." This was useful advice because only thirty sisters managed as many as three hundred inmates in the HGS and a young, inexperienced sister often taught a class of thirty teenage girls.[68]

The *Practical Rules* distilled the accumulated wisdom of two centuries of experience with delinquent lower-class girls, and it reflected the sisters' familiarity with working-class social problems. Oftentimes widowers sent their wayward daughters to the HGS as affluent parents sent their children to boarding schools, and the HGS handbook advised compassion for them:

> Go promptly to the parlor when you are summoned, that you may not excite the impatience of visitors, or prejudice them against us. Sometimes a poor workman deprives himself of his dinner to come to see his daughter, if you keep him waiting, he may lose the forty cents he has gained, and then who will give supper to his little ones in the evening? We must be kind, extremely kind to working men.[69]

Such compassion won the HGS warm support from the Boston Irish at a time when immigrant Catholics were cool to parochial schools and not as pious as later generations of Irish became.[70] A majority of the girls in the first St. Joseph Class in the HGS were the daughters of Irishmen (see Table 3.2) but had been born in Boston or elsewhere in Massachusetts (see Table 3.3). As might be expected, most of them were orphans or half-orphans (see Table 3.4) who were destined for the Lancaster School until "voluntarily placed" in the HGS by parents and courts. This was often an informal court disposition or crude form or alternative sentencing in which

Table 3.2

House of the Good Shepherd, St. Joseph Class, Ethnicity, 1887–1917

	1887 N = 47	1897 N = 46	1907 N = 104
American	4%	19%	2%
English	4	3	6
French Canadian	6	3	18
German	4	0	2
Irish	71	44	61
Italian	0	3	4
Black	2	0	3
Scottish	4	0	1
Other	2	28	3
Unknown	4	22	4

SOURCE: HGS, *St. Mary and St. Joseph Registers, 1867–1927.*

the girl and/or her parents agreed to a term in the HGS instead of a term at Lancaster.[71] The court had no authority to commit a juvenile to a private institution, but the lines between public power and private influence were sufficiently vague in the nineteenth century to permit arrangements between the courts and the HGS comparable to those made with other private asylums.[72] In fact, some of the first HGS inmates in 1867 were "sent" by the Boston Municipal Court in lieu of commitment to the House of Reformation. Of course, these "wild" girls were hardly desirable candidates in the eyes of most asylums, and the HGS did not have to compete for them. But most inmates, whatever their legal status, were placed by parents, relatives, priests or child welfare organizations rather than the courts (see Table 3.5) to save young girls from the shame of Lancaster incarceration.[73]

The scarlet reputation of some inmates and the semi-cloistered nature of the HGS made it a fascinating and even titillating institution to Protestant child-savers. In 1871 one critic noted that:

Being an enclosed order, a veil of secrecy is thrown over most of their doings. The Lady Superior converses with the outside world through an iron-gated ceiling, inside of which the curious are seldom permitted to step, and the order, except for a few outside Sisters, are forever concealed in the shadows of the cloister.[74]

Among these doleful stories were the public lectures given by Margaret L. Shepherd, an English prostitute who spent two years in the HGS at Bristol, England.[75] In 1890 she began a profitable career lecturing on the alleged abuse and cruel punishment she suffered in the HGS. Mrs. Shepherd published her recollections enlivened with tales of gross immorality

Table 3.3

House of the Good Shepherd, St. Joseph Class, Nativity, 1887–1907

	1887 N = 47	1897 N = 46	1907 N = 104
Inmates born in Boston	31%	30%	47%
Inmates born elsewhere in Massachusetts	49	24	29
Inmates born elsewhere in New England	5	13	9
Native born	92	78	88
Foreign born	8	22	12
Unknown	17	20	3
Foreign born parents	72	63	91
Native born parents	28	37	9
Unknown	0	0	0

SOURCE: HGS, *St. Mary and St. Joseph Registers, 1867–1927.*

much like the earlier claims of Maria Monk about a Montreal convent. *My Life in a Convent* was not as popular as Maria Monk's *Awful Disclosures,* but Mrs. Shepherd was baptized at the Trinity Baptist Church in East Boston in 1891, to the outrage of Boston Catholics and the embarrassment of non-evangelical Protestants in the Unitarian and Episcopalian churches. The American Protective Association, aided by easily aroused British, Scottish, and Maritime Province immigrants in Massachusetts, sponsored Mrs. Shepherd's appearances in New England. In other cases, "escaped nuns" sued the HGS for false imprisonment and unpaid wages.[76]

Despite some doubts about this unusual Roman Catholic asylum and the ravings of a few religious bigots, the HGS was well-supported in Boston from the first. Among its first inmates was a young girl transferred by the HDCC agent, Bernard Cullen in 1867, and St. Vincent's Asylum housed the Sisters of the Good Shepherd until they rented a house on Allen Street in the once-fashionable West End.[77] Bishop John Williams paid all of the HGS bills for one year and encouraged the work in every way. Father James A. Healy, the brilliant young chancellor inherited from Bishop Fitzpatrick, served on the HGS board of directors as a financial adviser as he had done for the HDCC. Later Healy became the Bishop of Portland, Maine, and his sister, a mulatto like himself, entered the HGS convent in Boston as a novice Sister of the Good Shepherd.[78] The ties between the archdiocese and the HGS were cordial and close, but Boston Brahmins were also early supporters. The major force behind the decision to open the HGS was May Collins Warren Dwight, a scion of Boston's most famous medical family. Mrs. Dwight and her son, Dr. Thomas Dwight, the Parkman Professor of Anatomy at Harvard Medical School, were converts to Catholicism and generous supporters of the HGS.[79] Another Brahmin convert was Florence Lyman, the granddaughter of Boston Mayor Theodore Lyman, who founded the State Reform School at Westborough that bears his name. Miss Lyman introduced the HGS superior, Sister Mary Aloysius Charlton (1867–93), to Beacon Hill friends and benefactors and she bequeathed $50,000 to the HGS when she died in 1906. Other benefactors from elite circles included members of the Appleton, Derby, Gardner, Green, Lodge, and Wigglesworth families. In addition, the state legislature granted $10,000 to the HGS in 1870 in recognition of the unique public service the institution performed on a non-sectarian basis.[80]

Sister Mary Aloysius was highly regarded as the foundress of the HGS in Boston, and was "a Southern gentlewoman of strong personality, magnetic, accomplished, endowed with the gift of drawing out the best in her religious and in the girls and women under her charge."[81] Her staff expanded from four sisters in 1867 to twelve by 1871 as the physical expansion and relocation of the HGS permitted a larger number of inmates. The sisters were largely Irish or Irish-American working-class women with a modest education who usually entered the convent in their early twenties. They were capable of controlling and reforming groups of fifty prostitutes and delinquents despite limited education, training, and resources because their pious commitment to this charity was usually a lifetime vocation.[82] Even more important than the religious enthusiasm and dedication of the sisters, was their highly structured organization. Every detail of the daily activities was planned in advance. This gave a steady rhythm and comforting pace to the HGS inmates whose lives had been characterized by poverty, disorder, and depravity. A few inmates preferred the asylum life and became permanent members of the HGS as

Table 3.4

House of the Good Shepherd, St. Joseph Class, Family Status, 1887–1917

	1887 N = 47	1897 N = 46	1907 N = 104	1917 N = 161
Orphan	30%	26%	1%	8%
Half-orphan	65	36	32	38
Parents living	5	37	57	54
Unknown	21	17	4	18

SOURCE: HGS, *St. Mary and St. Joseph Registers, 1867–1927.*

Table 3.5

House of the Good Shepherd, St. Joseph Class, Source of Placement, 1897–1907

	1887 N = 46	1897 N = 104	1907 N = 161
Placed by court	—	52%	28%
Placed parents or relatives	—	41	36
Placed by clergy	—	1	14
Placed by herself	—	3	5
Placed by welfare agency	4%	3	17
Unknown	96	0	7

SOURCE: HGS, *St. Mary and St. Joseph Registers, 1867–1927.*

Penitents (or a trusty) in the industrial laundry or commercial sewing room. Penitents assisted the sisters in supervising the work of the other inmates.[83]

The organizational plan of the HGS differed only in details from one city to another and it reflected a working-class version of the cult of domesticity as well as traditional Catholic convent values. The first department was the St. Mary Class organized in 1867. It was composed of sexually-experienced girls and women—prostitutes, drunkards, thieves, and petty criminals—referred by courts, police, parents, and priests. Each inmate received a "house name" upon admission to protect her family identity from shame. Only the admissions sister and the sister superior knew the identity and the exact nature of the inmate's offenses. She was taught to sew and embroider in order to earn a living upon discharge, as well as the inevitable washing, cleaning, and cooking duties expected of all female asylum inmates.[84]

The second department was the St. Joseph Class, created when space permitted in 1885 at the new HGS (built on Huntington Avenue in Roxbury in 1871). The "Josies" were virgins aged six to seventeen who attended school classes for five hours each day and received music, sewing, and religious instruction after school hours. These girls were sometimes called "Children of Preservation" because the HGS preserved their innocent state until ready to return home or to be placed out as a foster child or domestic servant at age sixteen.[85] They were kept entirely apart from the St. Mary inmates, who were required to avert their eyes and pass silently on the rare occasions when the members of the two classes met in hallways or on the landscaped grounds. Even in the chapel, high partitions between the pews prevented communication between the two groups. Most St. Mary inmates cooperated willingly in avoiding contact with the "Josies," convinced that moral contagion might ruin an innocent girl's life as they themselves had been ruined.[86]

House of the Good Shepherd, Huntington Avenue, Roxbury sheltered 10,000 wayward girls by 1960. *(Madonna Hall Center.)*

House of the Good Shepherd classrooms were very crowded in 1920 but strict discipline maintained order. *(Madonna Hall Center.)*

The third group created in the HGS in 1888 was the Magdalen Sisters, who were members of the St. Mary Class who had become Penitents and later asked to remain in the HGS permanently. As Magdalens, they took the veil of a cloistered nun and lived a life of prayer, penance, and silent work apart from all but fellow Magdalens and the Sisters of the Good Shepherd who supervised them. Because some Magdalens were reformed prostitutes and criminals, they comprised a colorful and exotic addition to the HGS, and lent a mysterious air to the already controversial institution.[87]

The Magdalens were cloistered nuns in the Third Order of St. Teresa following the strict Carmelite Rule. Their besmirched past made them ineligible to become Sisters of the Good Shepherd, "however holy, however gifted and accomplished." To permit them to join the Good Shepherd convent would have placed the reputation of all the sisters in jeopardy. But by 1900 few Magdalens were former prostitutes or criminals, on the contrary most were pious, shy, young women who entered this rigid order to expiate the sins of others. Visitors to the HGS were very curious about the Magdalens, who were never seen by anyone but the sisters and their special chaplain.

These three groups of socially deviant females constituted more than nine thousand inmates of the HGS from 1867 to 1917. By 1917 there were 300 St. Mary inmates, 150 St. Joseph girls and forty Magdalen Sisters in the HGS each year. They were not the sort of females admitted to any other child welfare institution in Boston and even the Lancaster staff might have found them challenging. The St. Joseph girls were "mildly delinquent" only in comparison to the fallen women and vagrants in the St. Mary Class, and few of the Josies would have been suitable for more genteel asylums like the HDCC, St. Vincent Asylum, or the BFA. They were institutionalized because they had no home and were unable or unwilling to live as a foster child or servant. The value of the HGS was chiefly in its realistic appraisal of wayward females and its recognition of gradations of deviance. Inmates in both classes were carefully assigned to dormitories, classrooms, and work by their mistress, who learned the character and habits of each of her "children" over the customary two-year term in the HGS.[88]

How effective was the HGS in reforming wayward girls? The cryptic records surviving and the subjective evaluations and claims of contemporary sources do not permit quantification of this charity. One study of the HGS in another city found that the HGS had at least a benign influence on most girls and tended to improve self-esteem and made other positive changes. This was due chiefly to the girl's identification with institutional goals transmitted by the individual care and attention of the girl's mistress whom she was required to call "Mother." The authoritarian benevolence of the HGS worked well with emotionally deprived, homeless female delinquents in a treatment-oriented, closed institution because young girls are believed to be more impressionable and readier to conform than delinquent boys. The sisters fostered identification with Catholicism, the convent values (which differed only in degree from the cult of true woman-hood and idealized domesticity), and HGS education and training because experience proved this was the most effective way to change deviant behavior.[89]

Conformity to the strict rule of silence for most of the day, for instance, created a predictable, tranquil, and rewarding atmosphere, but nonconfor-mity led to swift, sure penalties. The chief punishment was not corporal but psychological, the withdrawal of approval and affection by the sisters. Most girls found this intolerable because many of them came from cold, abusive, unloving families. They found in the HGS, often for the first time in their lives, the security, love, and approval every child requires for emotional maturation. Few inmates remained in the HGS without identify-ing with the asylum's values. Like all congregate institutions, the HGS was not a substitute for a family, but it did serve a useful and benevolent purpose at a time when sexually-active girls had few alternatives in a generally prim and proper child welfare system.[90]

One Sister of the Good Shepherd, who is today a professional social worker in a Catholic girl's treatment center, noted that most girls in the HGS St. Joseph Class from 1900 to 1950 were "juvenile delinquents who might have been committed by the Boston courts to the Lancaster School." Those who failed to adjust or ran away from the HGS, or relapsed into delinquency after discharge often were sent to Lancaster where they formed a clique of "HGS girls." The Josies were "rebellious and stubborn rather than wayward girls," in another sister's recollection, and remained for about two years to allow the sisters time to teach new values and habits to these "unstable, erratic girls." But all sisters inter-viewed about their work with HGS inmates agreed:

> It is a mistake to impose a social work model on the House of the Good Shepherd and other Catholic institutions prior to 1950 because they performed charity work not modern social work or casework or clinical treatment. The Sisters never claimed to be philanthropists or social workers, but only did God's work and it is unfair to measure them by modern standards.[89]

The HGS existed for females who would have been abandoned by all but the most evangelical charity workers in proper Boston. It amounted to recognition that American attitudes toward sexual deviance had changed and that disobedient girls were no longer tarred with the same brush as streetwalkers. Victorian Boston condemned but did not control commercial sex, and by barring immoral girls from the House of Reformation, the Lancaster School, and a host of child-saving societies, the reformers had consigned girls to the brothels. In the HGS, socially deviant, "immoral" females found understanding and forgiveness, as well as a well-worn path back to respectability. As an example of how girls could be salvaged, the HGS led the way for child welfare agencies in the twentieth century, while at the same time the HGS demonstrated in its recidivist St. Mary Class the perils of moral bankruptcy. The success of the St. Joseph girls and the failure of the St. Mary women taught by example the lessons of moral order, and were both a justification for the expanding network of child welfare organizations.[91]

4

Separate but Unequal:
Black, Jewish, and Italian Child-saving

> For the love of God . . . if ever again you meet me, even though
> they are hacking me to bits, do not aid or succor me but let me
> bear it, for no misfortune could be so great as that which comes
> of being helped by you.
>
> —Don Quixote

By the end of the Civil War, Boston Protestants and Catholics, the
Yankees and the Irish, had established an efficient and humane network of
public and private institutions and agencies for dependent and delinquent
children. These asylums, orphanages, reformatories, and child-placing
agencies flourished in the sentimental Gilded Age (1865–90) and demonstrated the American idealization of childhood. But some children were
less equal than others in this carefully arranged system of philanthropy.
Excluded from the elite private sector and disproportionately served by
the inferior public sector were the sons and daughters of Blacks and the
offspring of the largest groups of New Immigrants in Massachusetts,
Jews, and Italians. These children faced racial and ethnic prejudice in
child welfare services. Ultimately, each of these minority groups devised
its own alternatives to the racist public sector, the discriminatory private
sector, and the Irish-dominated Catholic sector.

Boston Blacks, Jews, and Italians created their own child welfare services as a reaction to discrimination as well as a positive response to their
own needs. Each of these separate child-saving systems demonstrated the
vitality and self-confidence of these largely poor working-class "newer
races," as the Yankees and Irish dubbed them.

Blacks constituted a permanent population in New England throughout
the nineteenth century, but one too small and impoverished to support its
own Colored Orphan Asylum like those established in Philadelphia (1822),
New York (1836), Providence (1838), and Cincinnati (1846).[1] In 1820
Boston had only 1,700 of the 6,700 Blacks in Massachusetts, and the city
included only one-quarter of the state's slowly expanding Black popula-

tion throughout the century. There were only limited economic opportunities for Blacks in Boston, although a small, well-established cadre of
antebellum families occupied a modest position in the crafts and service
industries. Some of these middle-class Black families were descendants of
pre-Revolutionary slaves, and many were mulattoes with Indian, French,
and Anglo-American ancestors.[2]

Residential segregation was the most obvious obstacle Boston Blacks
faced. The modestly affluent South Boston suburb was considered blessed
because it had no Black residents in 1847, leading one Black leader to
comment that "it is five times as hard to get a house in good location in
Boston as in Philadelphia, and it is ten times as difficult for a colored
mechanic to get work here as in Charleston." Despite social and economic
exclusion, however, Blacks had some rights. They could vote in all of the
New England states by 1850 and serve on Massachusetts juries by 1860.
The abolitionist crusade promoted the cause of all Afro-Americans, slave
or free, in the South and in the North, but with uneven results in the
abolitionist center of Boston.[3]

Racial prejudice was an unmistakable problem for Black children in
antebellum Boston schools. When Bronson Alcott, the Transcendentalist
philosopher, admitted a Black girl to his Temple School in 1839, all of the
white pupils were withdrawn by their parents, including the son of Chief
Justice Lemuel Shaw of the State Supreme Judicial Court. New Haven
parents had reacted even more sharply in 1831 when a Quaker admitted
Black girls to her small private school. Clearly New Englanders, no matter
how much they opposed slavery, were not willing to concede social equal-
ity to their Black neighbors.[4] As Black Bostonians struggled for respectability and justice, school desegregation was an early battleground. When
the town refused Black citizens' request for a "colored school" in 1798,
the parents hired a Harvard graduate to conduct their own school. The
legacy of a philanthropic merchant, Abiel Smith, provided funds for a
colored school in 1806 until the school committee assumed responsibility
for the Smith School in 1812 and opened a Black primary school in 1820.
When the state repealed the law against miscegenation in 1843 and deseg-
regated the railways, Black leaders were emboldened to ask the city to
integrate the public school. When they were refused, Benjamin Roberts
retained Black attorney Robert E. Davis and Charles Sumner to sue for
the right to enroll his daughter in a school close to her home. Sumner, an
abolitionist lawyer who was beginning his political career, lost the suit
when Chief Justice Shaw announced the unanimous decision of the Supreme Judicial Court that the city had plenary power to classify and
segregate schools. *Roberts v. Boston* (1849) was a stunning defeat for the
Black community, but it prompted the legislature to amend the law in 185[5]
to forbid segregation in Massachusetts schools. Still, Shaw's separate bu-

equal doctrine, which reflected the prevailing attitude of most white Americans, would continue to deny Blacks equal rights.[5]

Black school children numbered 352 in 1850, and most continued to attend the Smith School because a majority of Black residents lived near it in the West End or on the north slope of Beacon Hill. Although only a few blocks below the city's most fashionable district, the Smith School stood on "Nigger Hill," an unsavory and disreputable area in which brothels, bar-rooms, gambling dens, and cheap boardinghouses stood alongside the homes of respectable Black church members. The city's Blacks comprised about 2 percent of the population from 1830 to 1860 (see Table 4.1); although their birthrate was one of the highest in Boston, their infant mortality rate was even higher.[6]

Most of the Black population was aged fifteen to thirty-five, and these adolescents and young adults contributed most to the incidence of crime and delinquency among Black Bostonians. Frustrated in educational and vocational opportunities, and beset by poverty and squalid housing, some Blacks were attracted to gambling, crime, and prostitution as routes to economic success. These anti-social tendencies were barriers to acceptance of Black migrants in Massachusetts, a state that had easily abolished slavery in 1794 by judicial decree. The Puritans-turned-Yankees feared innate depravity and "criminalism" among Blacks. In 1800 the Boston selectmen "warned out" 239 Black nonresidents, and in 1821 the legislature appointed Theodore Lyman chairman of a committee to study the feasibility of restricting Black migration on the grounds that Blacks constituted "a species of population" that might "become both injurious and burdensome" to the community.[7] Although no legislation resulted from this study, the Boston Prison Discipline Society investigated Black criminality in 1826 and found that Blacks formed a disproportionate number of prison and reformatory inmates in northern states. The directors of this elite reform organization concluded that "the first cause existing in society of the frequency and increase of crime is the degraded character of the colored population." They recommended that funds appropriated for "colored schools" equal those spent on Black prisoners, and were confident this "would very soon raise their character to a level of whites, and diminish the number of convicts from among them about tenfold."[8]

Although sin and criminalism proved not to be inherent in Black Bostonians, their moral elevation by education remained controversial. Racial prejudice persisted in antebellum New England, and the Prison Discipline Society suggestions were ignored. Segregated schools became the common (if not the legal) practice, and Boston's most ambitious Black leaders were frustrated by this policy. By 1820, Prince Saunders, a Connecticut-born Dartmouth graduate who taught at the Smith School and founded the Masonic Society, allied with Thomas Paul, the founder and pastor of the

Table 4.1

Boston Black Population, 1830–1930

	Boston Population	Black Population	Percent of Population
1830	61,393	1,875	3.1%
1840	84,400	1,988	2.4
1850	136,900	1,999	1.5
1860	177,840	2,261	1.3
1870	250,526	3,496	1.4
1880	362,839	5,873	1.6
1890	448,477	8,125	1.8
1900	560,892	11,591	2.1
1910	670,585	13,564	2.0
1920	748,060	16,350	2.2
1930	781,188	20,574	2.6

SOURCE: United States Census, 1830–1930.

African Meetinghouse on Beacon Hill, to advocate colonization in Haiti and Africa. They both despaired of finding equal opportunity for themselves or their children in Boston or in any other part of the United States.[9] Although colonization was not popular among the professionals, artisans, and skilled craftsmen who formed an indigenous Black bourgeoise in Boston, they felt keenly the absence of an open occupational hierarchy in which their children could advance as white children did.[10]

Most Black Bostonians were confined to lower-class occupations, whatever talents they might possess. Among 384 Black household heads in 1837 were: 171 mariners, 112 laborers, 32 barbers, 25 waiters, 23 used clothing dealers, 8 carters, 6 tailors, 4 bootblacks and 3 blacksmiths.[11] A laborer in 1830 was fortunate to earn $200.00 per year while working 260 days, but annual expenses for a family of four were about $450.00. By 1840 the average Black workingman earned one dollar per day for 260 working days. The State Bureau of the Statistics of Labor estimated that frequent periods of unemployment and low wages made most fathers unable to support their families without withdrawing their children from school to contribute to the family income.[12] Black parents were in a precarious economic position in antebellum Boston and racial prejudice hampered their best efforts to support their families. Consequently, we would expect to find the city's Black children (of unemployed or underemployed working-class parents) well represented in charitable asylums and on the Boston charity rolls.

On the contrary, however, few Blacks entered the Boston Almshouse or received outdoor relief. Black children rarely entered the private child welfare asylums, and those few who received the dubious benefits of the House of Reformation were subject to the grossest racial discrimination.

They were only the incidental, unwelcomed recipients of child welfare services designed and operated by child-savers more concerned about the white "dangerous classes" than free Black children.[13] When Charles Dickens visited the South Boston institutions in 1842, he noticed "there were many boys of colour" making palm-leaf hats in the House of Reformation but none at all in the adjacent (non-penal) Boylston School, a jointly managed private and municipal refuge for "worthy" homeless boys. Boston's treatment of Black orphans and delinquents reflected that of the New York House of Reformation, where Blacks committed from 1830 to 1850 were outnumbered ten-to-one by Yankee, Irish, and German children. This ratio increased to twenty-to-one by 1855 although New York City's Black population had continued to expand in proportion to whites.[14]

The few Black children who entered the juvenile asylums in Massachusetts were treated as inferior to white children. They were segregated and assigned to the most menial tasks in conformity with racial prejudice and in order to save white inmates from loss of status. Similarly, the Philadelphia House of Refuge superintendent admitted practicing this type of racial discrimination in 1831 because "it would be degrading to the white children to associate with beings given up to public scorn." In 1849 Philadelphia solved the problem of Black juvenile delinquents and wayward orphans by opening a separate House of Refuge for Colored Juvenile Delinquents, leading the British reformer Edward Abdy to remark:

> It was painful to observe the studied manner in which the white and colored children were separated and distinguished from each other, as if moral improvement could be promoted in either by encouraging pride and inflicting humiliation.[15]

The private sector was no less racist, and William Lloyd Garrison embarrassed anti-slavery leaders Samuel Gridley Howe and Horace Mann in 1831 by criticizing their Perkins Institution for the Blind because Black children were excluded, and Theodore Lyman was abashed when the *Liberator* revealed that the Boston Asylum for Indigent Boys was for whites only. The Perkins Institution did admit a Black boy in 1837, but few thereafter, and this became a typical pattern for most Massachusetts asylums for children—a token Black child was admitted, but only on a carefully selected and racially discriminatory basis. This prompted Frederick Douglass to urge Blacks to establish their own (segregated) schools and institutions, but William Copper Nell, a prominent Boston Black leader and ally of Garrison, insisted that public and private institutions should be integrated. Both men were frustrated by the racism which forced the Black community to rely upon informal child care methods of their own creation and denied Black children equal access to child welfare services and asylums.[16]

Racial discrimination was a serious problem for all nineteenth-century Black Bostonians, but it was especially unjust to homeless Black children excluded from the emerging child welfare system. American social welfare as a whole operated on the principle that all but a few households were self-supporting nuclear families able to care for their own children. Only minimal social services were considered necessary to care for a minority of dependent or delinquent children from broken or inadequate families. This view constrained all ethnic and racial minorities by ignoring social stresses on impoverished families outside mainstream American culture because of their race, class, religion, ethnicity, or recent arrival in the industrial city. The underlying philosophy of the Victorian American social welfare system, which assumed that all families would be in social and economic harmony with the community, overlooked actual urban industrial conditions. These conditions were formidable obstacles for all poor households, but when combined with racial prejudice they often proved overwhelming to Blacks. Together poverty and racism produced stresses on Black parents qualitatively and quantitatively different from those white parents faced. The child welfare system served all children badly, but this problem was exacerbated in the case of Black children in Boston where the Black community was not sufficiently affluent (like the Yankees) or large (like the Irish) to create their own child welfare organizations (see Table 4.2).[17]

Racism not only excluded Blacks from admission to private asylums, but it gradually forced a disproportionate number of Black children into public institutions. Blacks were over-represented in the Monson, Lancaster, and Westborough Schools by 1876 and under-represented in the Board of State Charities' and private agencies' foster homes.[18] Racism also limited the number of Black children occasionally admitted to the BCAS asylums in Newton and Foxborough as well as the number admitted to the NEHLW and Catholic asylums, the HAG, HDCC, and HGS. In addition, racism (and slavery, which was the major child welfare institution for Black children until 1865) denied Blacks a role in managing or influencing child welfare organizations. Exclusive white control was justified by the circuitous reasoning that few Blacks were served by these organizations or contributed to their support.[19] This influenced Massachusetts child welfare indirectly because racism and slavery retarded every type of social welfare reform for American children of all races. It created inordinately low moral standards by which the care of all poor children was measured. As Grace Abbott explained the callous and cruel treatment of pauper children in the antebellum era:

> In a society in which slaves and indentured servants were used and the supply of free workers was inadequate, the employment of children was not challenged.[20]

Table 4.2

Largest Northern Urban Black Populations, 1860

	Black Population	Percent of Total Population
Philadelphia	22,185	3.9%
New York City	12,472	1.5
Brooklyn, N.Y.	4,313	1.6
Cincinnati	3,737	2.3
Boston	2,261	1.3

SOURCE: Hollis R. Lynch, *The Black Urban Condition: A Documentary History, 1866–1971* (New York, 1973), 421.

As the slave system and universal racial prejudice discouraged social reform, it also excused the abuse of apprenticeship, orphan trains, child labor, and reform schools throughout the United States.[21]

Although some Black children were found in American almshouses, the orphanages and the new reform schools were rigidly segregated in the nineteenth century.[22] Most American private orphanages admitted only white children and all homeless Black children were sent to the almshouse. Separate "colored orphanages" were established in some cities, but even this was not a popular solution; in 1838 a Philadelphia mob burned the colored orphanage, and in 1863 a New York mob destroyed the New York Colored Orphan Asylum. Anti-Black attitudes persisted and even deepened when immigrants competed for menial jobs with free Blacks.[23]

Because segregated orphanages were a universal practice in antebellum America, racial bias in charities was not considered remarkable. Child-savers seldom questioned segregation in private asylums, and when poorhouse care was supplanted by the orphan asylum and reform school, Black children were not immediate beneficiaries of the new methods. When orphan trains and foster homes became popular in the 1850s, few Black children were among these rescued children. They could still be found in poorhouses and only rarely appeared among orphanage inmates in the 1870s.[24]

The Children's Mission, like the New York Children's Aid Society, did not place Black children in free foster homes in the countryside or in Midwest farm families because community opinion would not permit such a radical practice. By 1880 a few Blacks were placed out by these child-savers, but only occasionally, because charity workers complained Black children "were difficult to place." This was not only due to the preference of foster families for white children but also because child-savers had little incentive to find Black foster parents for the small number of Black waifs in their charge.[25]

Adoption began in Massachusetts in 1851 as a probate court procedure, but as this new method of child care slowly became general in the United States in the nineteenth century, few Black adoptions occurred. In place of this cumbersome and uncommon practice, Blacks used an informal adoption method developed from African and slave experiences. Because slave parents and children were often separated by the slave trade or work assignments, relatives or friends became accustomed to "adopting" the motherless children. This was similar to the plantation practice of assigning a superannuated slave woman to care for young children while their parents worked in the fields. Surrogate parents became a common phenomenon in the slave society, and after emancipation, this kinship fostering system of child-rearing continued. Until the twentieth century, the vast majority of Blacks lived in the rural South where few orphanages existed and most of those were for whites alone. Informal adoption was approved by Southern courts and custom and Northern segregation made it a convenient and uncontested import from the South as Blacks migrated north after the Civil War.[26]

Even in Boston, Black child welfare, however, did not consist primarily of white philanthropy or enlightened social work. In slavery and in freedom, the American Black family maintained itself largely without white domination. Slavery, poverty, and prejudice had a devastating impact on Black families, but only a minority of Black children in the nineteenth century did not grow up in a two-parent nuclear family. For these homeless Black children, the traditional extended family continued to suffice as a major child-rearing institution. The informal adoption of Black children, a necessity during slavery, remained the most widely-practiced alternative in freedom to white society's child welfare methods. This community-ordained foster care was organized privately within the extended family of kin as the chief strategy of survival for Black children.[27] Apologists for slavery—like Nehemiah Adams (1808–78), a New England Congregationalist minister who toured the South in the 1850s—attempted to show that abolitionists exaggerated the evils of slavery. Adams claimed that Black parents had weak bonds to their children, and that slave families felt little grief or anguish when separated by the slave trade. This belief was based on the pseudo-scientific observations of southern physicians defending their "peculiar institution."[28] It was a convenient racist myth which proved extremely long-lived in America. Of course, Black family members were emotionally tortured by the threat or fact of separation from their loved ones, and accounts of slaves' suicide or pining away for grief constitute substantial evidence. But most Blacks, especially those in freedom, lived in a two-parent nuclear conjugal household just as white Americans did. The nineteenth-century American family was once believed to be typically an extended family, yet 75 percent of the Philadelphia

Blacks in one study lived in two-parent nuclear families from 1850 to 1880. Blacks did have a slightly higher incidence of female-headed households than Irish, German, or native Philadelphians, but this was due to the high mortality rates, poverty, and unemployment of Black males rather than to the cultural heritage of slavery, African-American values or Black matriarchy.[39]

Despite low occupational status, high mobility, morbidity and mortality rates, and generally poor living conditions, the Boston Black family structure did not differ significantly in 1870 from that of white neighbors. Approximately 18 percent of the migrant Black families and 22 percent of the immigrant Irish families in Boston in 1870 were female-headed because of the death or desertion of a spouse. One difference which did stand out was that 12 percent of the Black children in Boston in 1850 lived with a household head other than their natural parents, and 50 percent of these foster parents had children of their own in the household. In 1860 one-third of these foster children lived with a household head of the same surname, and 42 percent lived with one of a different surname.[30]

This demonstrates that Black Boston children were frequently raised in the informal adoption or kinship fostering system created by and for Black families with little or no interference by the white society. These children grew up calling their foster parents Uncle, Aunt, or Cousin; and they maintained a more fluid, extensive, and supportive family network than has been realized until recently.[31] Boston's four largest orphanages sheltered 326 children in 1860, none of whom were Black, but hundreds of Black orphans, half-orphans, and waifs of all sorts were reared in stable, secure Black families of kin. The higher rate of illegitimacy among the urban poor meant that many of these children were born out of wedlock. The rigid moral code of upper- and middle-class Victorians sharply contrasted with the freer expression of sexual mores by rural Blacks. Sexual behavior, like child-rearing practices, reflects class-oriented moral values, and the rural poor tolerated bastardy because they saw children as an economic asset. In the rural Black family, children were indulged while young but expected to contribute to the family income before adolescence.[32] Unwed motherhood was an unfortunate but not disastrous or uncommon feature of rural southern society, and many of these Black children found their way to Boston to live with relatives or friends.[33]

Bastards were usually unwelcome at Boston orphanages, but this does not explain the low rate of institutional care for Black children in Massachusetts. The small size of the Black population, the barriers created by racial discrimination, and the over-representation (by twice the proportion of Blacks in the state's population) in penal institutions also fail to explain fully this anomaly. In times of crisis, the Black community in Boston, as in other cities and in rural communities, possessed a strong sense of solidarity and self-support. Thwarted economically, educationally, and in almost every other respect, Boston Blacks created their own child welfare system by relying on the kinship foster care their ancestors had known in Africa, had used in slavery, and adapted to urban industrial life. Black parents unable to support their families in Boston were supplemented by relatives, friends, and neighbors who, to a remarkable and little appreciated degree, were willing to raise homeless children in their own families.[34]

In addition to the large number of wayward, homeless Black children raised in this "informal" kinship foster family system, small numbers of Black waifs entered Boston asylums for dependent children. Although Jim Crow prevailed in Boston institutions for children, the record of racial discrimination or segregation is an uneven one. Boston Catholics had relatively few Black co-religionists in the nineteenth-century, were known to be antagonistic toward Black workers, and were slow to join the antislavery crusade. Yet Boston Catholics admitted Black children into their charitable institutions in small but symbolically important numbers. The Catholic Church claimed its asylums were doing God's work and were open to all God's children, regardless of race or creed, and to a remarkable extent these words were confirmed by deed.[35] The House of the Good Shepherd admitted its first Black inmate in 1871, only four years after the HGS opened, and the House of the Angel Guardian had two mulatto priests as assistant superintendents, Father James A. Healy (1854–56) and his brother, Father Sherwood Healy (1860–62).[36] Although the records do not identify boys by race, it is likely that the HAG admitted some Black boys from the first, particularly when Father James Healy became Bishop Fitzpatrick's chancellor with responsibility for all diocesan charities for twenty years. His brother was also an influential member of the bishop's staff by 1860. Both men, the sons of an Irish immigrant planter in Georgia and his slave wife, were proud of their Black heritage and not at all cowed by racial bias.[37]

The Home for Destitute Catholic Children also admitted Black children from time to time, not only because Father James Healy was a founder and vice-president of the HDCC, but also because the Daughters of Charity, who staffed the institution, belonged to an order founded by Elizabeth Seton, who was from a New York abolitionist family devoted to the moral uplift of the city's Blacks in integrated schools. Black children were routinely admitted to the HDCC in the 1890s and probably much earlier as well.[38] The Working Boys' Home, an institution established in Boston in 1883 for work similar to that of the HAG, also admitted Black boys from the first.[39]

The Boston Catholic record on the race question was not always liberal, however, and the Daly Industrial School in Dorchester was one of only four of Boston's seventeen institutions for children in 1910 to bar Black children.[40] Also, the HGS record was marred by racial prejudice in 1874 when Amanda Josephine Healy, the younger sister of Father Healy, applied for admission to the Sisters of the Good Shepherd order. The sister superior, Mother Mary St. Aloysius Charleton, an aristocratic woman from Charleston, South Carolina, reluctantly accepted the young mulatto woman as a novice, but Josephine withdrew from the convent after a year because of racial prejudice among the sisters. She entered a more hospitable Montreal convent, but when she died in 1879, Josephine bequeathed her patrimony to the HGS, perhaps hoping to win by charity what she herself had been denied by the sisters.[41]

The first layman to serve as a Boston Sunday school superintendent was "Mr. Heaney, an Irishman who was also a colored person," a well-educated gentleman who successfully managed the Cathedral of the Holy Cross Sunday School in 1813. He was the leader of Boston's small Negro Catholic community which numbered four hundred by 1860 and more than one thousand by 1927. By 1889 there was a sufficient number of Black Catholic men to establish a Society of St. Vincent de Paul chapter for charity and missionary work among poor Blacks. The St. Peter Claver Conference of Colored Men was the most active among the 350 Blacks who attended St. Phillip's Church in Roxbury and the forty children in its Sunday School.[42]

Bishop Fitzpatrick and his successor, Bishop John Williams, were sympathetic to Black Catholics; and John Boyle O'Reilly (1844–90), the Irish rebel, poet, and editor of *The Pilot*, the most influential Catholic newspaper in America, was a vocal champion of Blacks' rights.[43] Most Irish Catholics, however, shared American racial prejudice. They sought some respectability by anti-Negro and anti-abolitionist views and ignored the cooperation and working-class solidarity that leaders like O'Reilly advocated.[44] In fact, Boston Blacks in 1850 were in a better position as compared with the Irish than one might imagine, and a Boston "Negro was as reluctant to have an Irishman move into his street as any Yankee."[45] Only on the lowest levels of Black and white society did one find racial intermingling. Boston Blacks intermarried with whites in 1865 at a rate (12 percent) higher than Irish Catholics married Yankee Protestants. Most interracial marriages and social contacts in New England involved free Black men and white women "of the meaner sort."[46] Boston's "Nigger Hill" and the "Black Sea" waterfront were "vile districts" where underworld desperadoes consorted with degraded women of both races and policemen dared walk only in pairs.[47] The racial toleration Boston leaders advocated was generally absent among the middle class and the respectable working class, but in the red-light and slum areas of the city, inhabited by Irish immigrants fallen into the "dangerous classes," the color line blurred.[48]

Most sectarian reformers were repelled by this unnatural fraternization between lower-class whites and free Blacks in these slums, but racial prejudice compelled them to rescue only impoverished whites rather than to uplift both groups. Aside from Quakers' traditional concern for Black welfare, and the limited interest of Catholics, the Episcopal Church was the only major denomination to devote substantial resources to Northern Black children after the Civil War. Philadelphia Episcopalians established the House of St. Michael and All Angels for Colored Children in 1887 and another asylum in 1889, the House of the Holy Child. Boston Episcopalians, while not aroused to the same extent, did admit Black children to the Church Home for Destitute Children by 1870.[49] The Church Home Society opened this small orphanage on Charles Street at the foot of Beacon Hill in 1855, and after it relocated to larger quarters at the corner of East Fourth and N Streets in South Boston in 1868, a few Black orphans were admitted quietly. No Boston asylum was willing to risk censure as a "nigger charity" in the racially sensitive Gilded Age, but the Church Home Society transcended tokenism and deserved credit as a pathfinder in integrating its orphanage.[50]

*   *   *

When the Reverend Charles Neale Field (1849–1929), an Anglican priest active in the Oxford Movement and a member of the Society of St. John the Evangelist (called the Cowley Fathers), transferred from Philadelphia to Boston in 1891, he brought with him a tradition of active missionary work with urban Blacks. Assigned to the Church of St. John the Evangelist on Bowdoin Street in the racially mixed West End, Father Field quickly established close contact with the Black community. He operated two mission churches in Roxbury for Black Episcopalians and became vice president of the John Howard Industrial Home for Discharged Prisoners. This work made him aware of the problems of dependent and delinquent Black children, so in 1891 he established St. Augustine's Farm in Foxborough, as a summer camp and asylum for Black juveniles. The farm was donated by a wealthy admirer of the Cowley Fathers on Father Field's birthday with the hope that he would build a Black orphanage. Although it did not develop into a permanent asylum, Father Field took children on probation from the Boston courts and those referred by clergymen and social workers for "summer vacations" that could last six months. Thus, St. Augustine's Farm was the first child welfare institution designed exclusively for Boston Black children and was highly regarded by the Black community. Father Field's memory is still cherished by the Blacks he befriended as children at this rustic asylum.[51]

Father Field had sufficient resources for fifty boys and girls at a time, and parishioners at the Roxbury mission churches, St. Mark's, and St.

Episcopalian child-saving focused on the Church Home Society orphanage in South Boston. *(Episcopal Diocese of Massachusetts.)*

Father Charles Neale Field (1849–1929) opened St. Augustine Farm in Foxboro for Boston black children in 1891. *(Episcopal Diocese of Massachusetts.)*

Augustine's, as well as affluent supporters throughout the diocese, contributed food, clothing, funds, and services to make St. Augustine's Farm successful. Field was a frequent visitor to the Boston Juvenile Court interceding for Black children, many of whom Judge Baker and Judge Cabot placed on probation in his custody. In his first court case in 1907, a stubborn Black girl from the West End was "voluntarily committed" to St. Augustine's Farm because Father Field appeared on her behalf. In such cases, the BCAS or the Massachusetts Society for the Prevention of Cruelty to Children (MSPCC) provided casework services while the child was placed in Foxborough. When, however, the girl proved "too stubborn," both Father Field and her BCAS social worker recommended that the court commit her to the Lancaster Industrial School.[52]

A disproportionately high number of Black girls were committed to Lancaster by the 1890s, many of whom had "failed to adjust" to less coercive child welfare services, like St. Augustine's Farm or a foster home. The Church Home Society often cooperated with Father Field in "troublesome" cases but placement services were wholly inadequate. By one estimate 10 percent of the inmates at Lancaster were Black girls between 1895 and 1905.[53] Lacking private institutions of their own, dependent Black children were over-represented in public institutions for delinquents. This resulted in a perplexing problem for child-savers and the Lancaster staff. Institutionalized Black girls frequently became involved in homosexual relationships with white inmates and these "special friendships were shocking and almost impossible to avoid." After Father Field's death in 1929, St. Augustine's Farm was closed as a Black children's asylum because of homosexual incidents and because the opening of a nearby Civilian Conservation Corps camp posed an even greater sexual danger for the girls, if only in the minds of anxious white social workers.[54] This overreaction to what was probably only normal adolescent or situational sexual experimentation was consistent with the racist view of Blacks as more sexually volatile than whites and less capable of moral restraint.[55]

Both the Church Home Society and St. Augustine's Farm were staffed by the Sisters of St. Margaret, a small congregation of Episcopal nuns located in a convent in fashionable Louisburg Square on Beacon Hill. The sisters staffed Boston Children's Hospital from 1871 to 1917, as well as St. Monica's Home for Sick Colored Women and Children, established in 1862 in Roxbury. The sisters also supervised the Girls' Friendly Society, clubs for working-class girls in Episcopal parishes. But the major work the sisters performed for Black children was in operating summer camps in South Duxbury and Rockport from 1870 to 1955. All of these child welfare services offered by Boston Episcopalians, of course, had as their primary purpose Christian charity for poor Black children, but were used by many

Black families to care for wayward or homeless children until other solutions appeared.[56]

Not to be outdone by their sectarian sister charities, after the Civil War non-sectarian private charities also became aware of the needs of homeless Black children, and like Catholic and Episcopalian charities, the child savers responded with a mixture of Christian concern and racial prejudice. The New England Home for Little Wanderers, which began as a Methodist orphanage in 1865, was the first private charity to admit Black children on a more or less equal basis with whites.[57] The NEHLW was one of the first child-saving societies established for Civil War orphans and half-orphans, but "little contrabands" from the South were also welcomed. The term contraband originated in 1861 when General Benjamin F. Butler of Massachusetts used it as a device to free Virginia slaves who fled to Union Army protection. It first applied to Black men used as Army laborers but became a popular term for freed Blacks. Although it suggested that Blacks were property, at least it did indicate that the NEHLW crossed the color line in the name of charity at a time when most American orphanages were rigidly segregated.[58] The Methodist Church was an early champion of Blacks and founded many schools, missions, and colleges in the South and the North for Black children. No precise account was made of the Black children admitted to the NEHLW, but a small percentage of the 3,651 little wanderers admitted from 1865 to 1874 were Blacks. The NEHLW *Advocate* declared in 1865, "The work of the Home is not sectarian, six different denominations being now represented on the Board of Managers; nor are its labors and benefits limited to children of any denomination, sect, locality, or color."[59]

The NEHLW recorded in February 1884 that a "colored girl of 13, her mother in service in Uxbridge, Massachusetts, applied." She was described as a "bright girl" and the admissions committee routinely recommended that she be admitted.[60] Another Black girl, Cassie Hunt, had entered the previous month, and she "belongs to a colored family from Georgia, the father is dead, and the mother is dying of consumption." She too was admitted on the recommendation of one of the 3,500 Yankees sent to the South during Reconstruction as Freedmen's Bureau agents, teachers, missionaries, and charity workers.[61] Among this group of philanthropic carpetbaggers was a later superintendent of the NEHLW, Frederic Harrison Knight (1859–1922), a Vermont Methodist minister who was president of New Orleans University, a small Black college. Reverend Knight, like many of the NEHLW managers, had a deep interest in the moral uplift of the "colored brethren in Dixie."[62]

Boston Children's Aid Society lacked this evangelical impetus and wider geographical ambition, but it too admitted Black children. In 1869 the Pine Farm asylum rescued two Black boys from moral danger in the

West End, and in 1872 the Newton Home for Girls also experimented by admitting two Black girls.[63] Always more cautious than Pine Farm, the lady mangers found it difficult to select "appropriate" Black girls, and the BCAS abandoned the effort by 1879 after the Newton Home closed and foster family placement replaced this mini-reform school.[64] Rock Lawn Farm in Foxborough also admitted young Black boys from time to time. When Charles W. Birtwell became general secretary in 1886, greater efforts were made to offer child welfare services to Black families in what rapidly became the region's most innovative social work agency. Birtwell's Methodist roots and the liberal Unitarian origins of the BCAS predisposed the agency to adopt a sympathetic policy toward Black clients by the 1890s.[65]

The Massachusetts Infant Asylum, another private, non-sectarian charity for Boston children, was founded in 1867 as a foundling home and developed into a small pediatric hospital. Black infants were admitted from the first, but in 1872 the white wet nurses suddenly refused to suckle "colored babies." The Brahmin managers, surprised by this racially prejudiced labor strike, were dependent upon the lower-class white mothers who were paid (slightly more than domestic servants) to nurse sick or motherless infants in the asylum or in private boarding homes. The managers were forced to hire a few Black wet nurses, but this severely limited the number of Black children who could be admitted thereafter, contributing, no doubt, to the already high infant mortality rate in Boston.[66] The rate for Black infants in 1880 was 392 deaths per 1,000 live births compared to 274 per 1,000 for white infants. This was an extraordinary instance in which racial toleration in a children's institution decreased at the very time when most Boston child welfare services were slowly opening their door to Black children. When the Massachusetts Infant Asylum merged with the BCAS in 1914—as the color line was growing sharper—this segregation was still in effect.[67]

The Boston Female Asylum, which was also absorbed by the BCAS, did not admit Black girls from 1800 to 1880, and even after 1880 the number was carefully limited to one or two Blacks at a time. Gradually, however, Birtwell's influence and the spread of modern social work ethics pervaded even this traditional Brahmin asylum. In 1907, three of the forty-seven girls admitted (6 percent) were described as "colored." This sometimes meant, however, only that a girl "had some Negro blood." Lighter-skinned Blacks were preferred to "jet black" girls.[68] But when the Boston Children's Aid Association (the umbrella organization which coordinated BCAS mergers with several senescent charities) formed in 1922, it eliminated much of this racial prejudice.[69] The BCAA of the 1920s "accepted colored cases on an equal basis and tended to stick with them no matter how difficult they might become," as one social worker recalled.[70]

When Birtwell addressed the National Conference of Charities and Corrections in Detroit in 1902, he presented the case of Florence, a fifteen-year-old Black girl. This was an unusual and subtle attempt to demonstrate to a national audience of colleagues and admirers that the new BCAS/BCAA policy of crossing the color line had sound professional results. According to his outline, Florence had been placed by the agency as a domestic servant in Boston, but due to some "indiscreet colored friends," she became dissatisfied with her wages and ran away. After wandering the streets with some wayward boys and girls for a few days, Florence was lured by an old colored woman into "a life of shame." The procuress beat and abused the girl so badly that she escaped and attempted suicide by jumping into the Charles River. Saved by a policeman, she was returned to Birtwell's own home where he and a female social worker nursed her back to health. In most cases, a young Black prostitute like Florence would have been committed by the court to Lancaster, but Birtwell interceded, and she was able to return to her employer. Happily, she adjusted quickly to the workday life of a maid. This was a bold device by Birtwell to challenge racism obliquely, but he was enough of a Victorian to add a pathetic epilogue. Florence was restored to moral industry after her ill-fated stint in the bordello, but she died of tuberculosis six months later. With this dose of Progressive racial tolerance, his NCCC audience received a familiar pinch of moralism.[71]

The case of Roberta Richards illustrates a more common child welfare problem in the BCAS files. She was a Black girl born out of wedlock in North Carolina and raised by her maternal grandmother. At fourteen Roberta joined her estranged mother in Boston and worked in a South End factory. Her employer referred the case to the BCAS because her mother "took all of the girl's earnings, allowed no spending money and did not clothe her properly." It described her as "a good worker and reliable." A female social worker investigated the family and discovered that Roberta's mother had a long court record, had never married, and "lived in sin with a married black man." This was a very difficult case for a white middle-class social worker to "adjust," because the naive girl from the rural South had no relatives in Boston except for her cruel and immoral mother. The BCAS could have easily declined the case, or referred it to the court, and many such cases were "refused for cause" by Boston charities. Surprisingly, the BCAS social worker maintained contact with Roberta for six years, advising her, interceding with her mother, and generally helping her to adjust to life in the city. Only when Roberta was safely married to a respectable man in 1925 did the BCAS close this case.[72] Although this may have been an unusual case or the work of an extraordinary social worker, a review of the cases in the BCAS files from 1880 to 1937 indicates that it was representative of a new trend in Boston social work. Individu-

Table 4.3

Boston Juvenile Court Black Defendants, 1907–1927, Family Status

	N = 19
Both parents in home	26%
Mother only in home	31
Father only in home	10
Parent and Step-parent in home	10
Grandparent or sibling as guardian	15
Both parents deceased	15
Child in a foster family	37

Only 19 of the 514 dependent children in my sample of Boston Juvenile Court cases in 1907, 1917, and 1927 (as stubborn, wayward or neglected children) were black. I estimate that a correspondingly small percentage (about 4 percent) of the delinquent children in this court were also black in these years.

alized casework free of subjectivity with long-term follow-up became the standard by which all child welfare services were measured. Although this professional service was not available to all Black children in need, it gradually became common in "progressive" agencies like the BCAS in the 1920s.[73]

The Blacks who appeared in the Boston Juvenile Court from 1907 to 1927 as dependent children were often living in two-parent households (37 percent) with both of their own parents (26 percent) despite the high degree of family breakdown customarily found in such a population. As Table 4.3 shows, the small number of Black children who came to the juvenile court as dependent children (i.e., status offenders charged as stubborn, wayward or neglected children) rather than as delinquent children (i.e., lawbreakers charged with larceny, assault, etc.) were generally the victims of broken homes but did have stable households in which to live. In fact the status offense for which these Black children were summoned to court often had little to do with home conditions, but rather was a convenient charge masking sexual misconduct (42 percent) by the child or his or her parents.[74] The juvenile court took its moral policing duties very seriously in the days before the Great Depression transformed social welfare, but this analysis of Black child welfare cases tends to support the view that the Black population was composed of stable nuclear families striving for respectability much like their white neighbors.[75]

Many of these Black children were in court because of racial prejudice on the part of the authorities in Boston. Although most of them were born in Boston (43 percent) or elsewhere in Massachusetts (12 percent), their families were regarded as aliens and newcomers, "a youthful, untried race" still unsettled in the city.[76] Racist policemen were extremely suspicious of Black boys known to "hang around the street corners" and "who were lazy and would not work."[77] Black pupils sometimes encountered a teacher "who was down on colored boys and made slurring remarks," which led them to "hook" school and resulted in a court appearance as a truant. One such boy explained that after truanting just once "he was afraid to go home so he bunked out," for which the court placed him on probation.[78] One Black girl with ambitions to become a nurse was told candidly by her BCAS social worker "that the New England Hospital Training School for Nurses admits one colored woman to each training class" and that she had little chance of being selected.[79]

The court could also be quite unsympathetic to Black families in crisis, as in the case of Alfred Norris, a truant whose mother was committed to a mental hospital when his father's express business went bankrupt. His probation officer was suspicious because the family lived in a "racially mixed" boardinghouse in the South End, and Judge Cabot complained that the father was rather "touchy," which "is likely to be greatly to his son's disadvantage." Alfred was "very bold and forward" in court, and, not surprisingly, he was committed to the Parental [truant] School for one year.[80]

Dr. William Healy, the nationally acclaimed director of the new court clinic, the Judge Baker Foundation, also revealed this same insensitivity to Black children. In 1917, Charles Paris, a thirteen-year old "colored boy" abandoned by his parents, was referred to the clinic when he "failed to adjust" to his eighth foster home in five years. Dr. Healy pronounced the boy healthy and fit but reported to the court:

> After observing this boy's attitude and learning his history and knowing the difficulty of getting a colored boy well taken care of in a stable family and knowing that there is no help to be received from his parents, we should feel that this boy probably needs a prolonged training in an institution . . . he needs a consistent, prolonged educational and moral training.[81]

Healy admitted that institutionalization was recommended primarily because white social work agencies did not locate appropriate foster homes for Black children. He justified institutionalization on the grounds that Charles's father was a "genius" but a "destitute lawyer" and his mother was an "immoral woman" last seen in New York or Philadelphia. Yet even this alternative plan provided Charles Paris with little help. Judge Cabot committed him to the Suffolk School for Boys and one year later he was bound out to a farmer. This was scarcely the "consistent, prolonged educational, and moral training" Dr. Healy prescribed, and the rigidly segregated county reform school on Rainsford Island provided neither white nor Black inmates with useful skills or training. It was "commonly regarded as a recruiting post for the State Prison."[82]

A private reformatory like the House of the Angel Guardian in Roxbury was what Dr. Healy had in mind, but even in this Catholic industrial school for wayward and homeless boys, a Black inmate faced overwhelming racism. One Black inmate in the 1930s, Wallace Hicks, was called "Nigger" by the students and staff until a young chaplain insisted that he be called Wallace. This mild reform was not entirely successful, but forty years later the priest insisted that the name, "Nigger," was not intended as an insulting or derogatory term, that it was more unseemly than vicious.[83] There were five other Black inmates in the HAG from 1930 to 1945, but never more than two at a time. Two Black faces were lost in the sea of six hundred white boys; perhaps they felt as Booker T. Washington did at an all-white Harvard University dinner, "like a huckleberry in a bowl of milk." It was not an enviable position for a Black child to gain admission to white-dominated institutions for children, and in Catholic asylums, whether he was Protestant or Catholic, the Black child never truly belonged to the group.[84]

It is clear that the establishment of the Boston Juvenile Court in 1906, and its trend-setting psychiatric clinic, the Judge Baker Foundation in 1917, did little to improve child welfare services or juvenile justice for Black children. Racial prejudice did not abate in the first decades of the century, and the application of psychological and psychiatric techniques only provided new methods by which the inferiority of Blacks could be "proven scientifically." As one critic said of the new laboratory experiments in eugenics and psychology, "even the rat was white."[85]

Most reformers were frustrated by the difficulty of helping poor Blacks in slums, but racial prejudice compelled them to rescue poor whites rather than uplift both groups. Racism was one reason for segregation in child welfare, but a more compelling reason was that the children of European immigrants constituted a large and growing threat to social order. The numerically greater and more urgent problems of the Irish (and after 1880, the Jewish and Italian) lower class, not these of the small Black community, received greater attention to the detriment of Black welfare needs. The major child welfare services in Massachusetts developed at a time when the Black population decreased or was overwhelmed by the post–Civil War immigration. The 1800 census found that Blacks represented 19 percent of the United States population, but this fell to 14 percent in 1860 and 10 percent by 1920. Not until Blacks migrated to northern cities after World War I did urban Black children become a visible and compelling social problem for sectarian child-savers.[86]

* * *

Jews were another ethnic minority present in colonial Massachusetts, although not permanent settlers until the mid-eighteenth century. Newport, New York, Philadelphia, Baltimore, Richmond, Charleston, Savannah, and New Orleans all had earlier and larger Jewish communities than eighteenth-century Boston. Although the Puritans considered themselves God's Chosen People building a new Zion in the wilderness, they refused to admit Hebrews into their colony.[87]

In the turmoil of the Revolution, Boston attracted some Jews from Newport, the most prominent of whom was Moses Michael Hays (1738–1805), a wealthy merchant who settled in a fashionable mansion on Hanover Street in 1782. His sister, the widow of Rabbi Isaac Touro of Newport, and her sons Abraham and Judah joined Hays. Both boys were apprenticed to their uncle and adapted easily to Boston. Abraham Touro (1774–1822) became the city's first Jewish philanthropist when he bequeathed $10,000 to the Massachusetts General Hospital and $5,000 each to the Boston Female Asylum and the Boston Asylum for Indigent Boys.[88]

Later his brother Judah (1775–1854), who became a prosperous merchant in New Orleans, also contributed large sums to these three charities, as well as to five orphanages in New Orleans.[89] Their uncle was an intimate friend of Boston's most prominent gentlemen, grandmaster of the Masonic Lodge, an ally of Paul Revere, and frequent host to reformers and abolitionists like the Reverend Samuel J. May. In fact, May spent weeks at a time in the Hays household and as a result it was natural that the Touro brothers imbibed the ways of Boston philanthropy. Moses Michael Hays made his house "the abode of hospitality," his "family moved in what were then the first circles of society," and he was well known for his liberal charity to the poor of the North End.[90]

This tolerant atmosphere, however, was not characteristic of antebellum Boston, and the small Jewish population (see Table 4.4) suggests anti-Semitic prejudice. The first synagogue, established in 1816, did not survive the decline of the city's small Portuguese Jewish population. Most Jews avoided the socially and economically inhospitable New England states in preference for New York and the South. Not until 1842 was the first permanent synagogue opened in Boston, and Temple Ohabei Shalom consisted of rented rooms until 1851 when a small wooden building seating five hundred worshippers was constructed on Warren (now Warrenton) Street. Still, the school in the rear of the synagogue with scholarships for poor students was evidence of the changing character of the Boston Jewish community. This school had thirty pupils in 1852 from the congregation's 120 families. The director of the Farm Trade School, the Reverend E. M. P. Wells, was an early ally of Temple Ohabei Shalom ("Lover of

Table 4.4

Boston Jewish Population, 1830–1930

	Boston Population	Jewish Population	Percent of Population
1830	61,393	50	.08%
1840	84,400	100	.1
1850	136,900	400	.3
1860	177,840	600	.3
1870	250,526	2,500	.9
1880	362,839	5,000	1.4
1890	448,477	20,000	4.5
1900	560,892	40,000	7.1
1910	670,585	57,000	8.5
1920	748,060	85,000	11.3
1930	781,188	90,000	11.5

SOURCE: *The American Jewish Yearbook* (Philadelphia, 1899–1930); the U.S. Census did not enumerate the population by religion.

Peace"); he attended services in 1844 and wrote to a Boston newspaper urging philanthropic Christians to contribute to its support. Although this benevolent attitude was not widely shared in Boston, when the temple was dedicated Mayor Benjamin Seaver, the city councillors, the Reverend Theordore Parker and other leading clergymen attended the ceremonies.[91]

The Jews, however, assumed a very low profile in Boston. Judah Touro's contributions were made anonymously, and as a result, the British consul, Thomas Gratton, mistakenly wrote in 1859, "Boston does not, I believe, contain one individual Israelite."[92] The failure of the liberal revolutions of 1848 in Germany led 15,000 Bavarian Jews to emigrate to America, but few came to Massachusetts and those who did intermingled with Catholic and Protestant Germans in Boston, making the consul's error understandable. Although the American Jewish population reached 50,000 by 1850 and 160,000 by 1865, Massachusetts had fewer than one thousand Jews in 1860. The reason for this had as much to do with the economic stagnation and well-entrenched Yankee family business class of New England as with anti-Semitism. New York, Philadelphia, Baltimore and expanding western cities simply proved more attractive to Jews than Boston.[93] Because Boston was the last of the largest northeastern cities to become a major Jewish center, its sectarian charity system cannot be considered typical of American Jewry. The Jewish charities in Massachusetts matured only after 1880 (with considerable influence from New York) when large numbers of pious Eastern European Jews settled in New England.[94]

Jewish charity was a more religious impulse than a humanitarian one, because the Jewish concept of charity was an ancient injunction dating from Biblical times when taxes were levied to aid the poor and the homeless. Tithes are an example of traditional Jewish charity for the unfortunate poor, and all pious Jews understood that the needy had a right to receive aid which the almsgiver was obliged to contribute. All wealth emanated from God and the almsgiver honored God and himself by acts of charity (called *mitzvah*). These included, besides almsgiving, visiting the sick, burial of the dead, free loans, free schools, and voluntary associations to provide dowries, clothing, food, shelter, and advice to poor Jews, travelers, or newcomers to the community. Widows and orphans were a basic concern of every congregation, and so fundamental was this form of charity that many Jews neglected to record it as noteworthy.[95]

Charity of all types played a major role in every Jewish community, but Charleston, South Carolina, established the first Jewish orphan asylum in America in 1801, an example followed by Philadelphia (1819), New York City (1827), San Francisco (1870), and Baltimore (1872). Every synagogue formed charitable societies (called *chevra*) and Boston's congregation followed this custom in 1850. This was direct almsgiving on an informal basis. Members of the *chevra* had first call on its resources, but any poor Jew could ask for assistance. This charity operated much like those in Protestant or Catholic churches, but with a different spirit. Protestant charity emphasized the dangers of indolence and wastefulness, and Catholic charity focused on "good works" that earned a specific amount of "grace" for the charitable soul. But Jewish charity valued the cheerful, discreet donor who respected the dignity of the poor. Honor, prestige, and other intangible benefits rewarded the charitable Jew, whose prosperity found social and religious justification in acts of charity. Jewish charity was based on the demonstration of piety, tact, generosity, humane feelings, social conscience, and moral responsibility. This was the ideal to which all good Jews aspired, because it protected the historically embattled minority and embodied the Talmudic injunctions of brotherhood and love. In this respect, Calvinism was the antithesis of Judaism, and Catholicism was a half-way convenant. Only in Judaism did one discover the idea of charity as a communal well from which all could drink freely.[96]

Tzedakah is the Hebrew word for charity or acts of righteousness, especially giving alms or assistance to the poor. Closely related to this is the phrase *gemilut hesed,* which refers to all other acts of charity of a non-material kind. The very word *tzedakah,* however, shows that the relief of poverty is a matter of sacred duty and not voluntary philanthropy.[97] It is an unceasing obligation, and Judaism lays great stress on the spirit in which this charity is given, and the consideration of the feelings of the recipient, rather than on the act of giving or the amount given. Tithes of 10 to 20 percent were recommended for prosperous Jews and the highest form of charity was the anonymous donation for care of homeless children.[98]

Orphans were among the most deserving objects of charity in Judaism,

counted among the most helpless members of society and special objects
of solicitude in Biblical legislation which emphasized the orphan's claim to
justice. The Talmud and the Old Testament repeatedly mention orphans as
deserving objects of charity, and the prophets frequently condemned the
wickedness of exploiting or mistreating them. Orphans were to be treated
with dignity and gentleness, to be addressed kindly and to have their rights
and property guarded. It was particularly meritorious to provide a home
for a poor orphan and Talmudic law encouraged adoption. Moses himself
was a precedent for foster family placement when the pharoah's sister
found him in the bullrushes.[99]

This outlook influenced the American Jewish view of charity and explains why few Jews sought public charity or the aid of Christian welfare
organizations. American Jewish population growth from 2,700 in 1820 to
160,000 in 1860—primarily due to emigration from Bavaria, Bohemia, and
Hungary in the economic depression and repressive aftermath of the
continental revolutions of 1848—resulted in the rapid expansion of Jewish
philanthropy and its separation from the synagogue.[100] The scope of
Jewish charity necessarily grew with the size of the Jewish population.
Each community had a Hebrew Benevolent Society and an equivalent
charitable association of Jewish women. These organizations were autonomous with only loose ties to the rabbinate. Unlike their Christian counterparts, they were fraternal organizations dominated by businessmen rather
than clergymen or charity workers.[101] They seldom reached above the
municipal level due to the difficulties of communication and transportation in the antebellum era and the apprehensiveness of many American
Jews over an anti-Semitic reaction by the nativists.[102]

German Jews, the largest and dominant group by 1850, formed many
mutual-aid societies or *Landsmannschaften* to assist fellow countrymen
in adjusting to American life. The most important of these was the Independent Order of B'nai B'rith, founded in 1843 for self-help and fraternal
charity among American Jews. The rapid growth and permanence of this
organization outside the orbit of the synagogue provided a prestigious
alternative form of Jewish identity and cohesion. This was important as
American Jews divided into Sephardic, Ashkenzai, German, Dutch, Polish, and Hungarian congregations as soon as their numbers permitted, and
especially when new waves of Eastern European Jews arrived after the
Civil War.[103]

With this proliferation of Jewish charitable organizations separate from
the houses of worship came increased variety and independence, which
influenced Boston Jewry. When Yankee merchants turned from commerce
to manufacturing in the 1840s, Boston offered new economic opportunities for Jews in the New England peddling and retail trades. By the end
of the Civil War, the city had a permanent population of two thousand

German, Dutch, and Polish Jews, with each group establishing its own congregation and charities to aid countrymen *(landsleit)*. Temple Ohabei Shalom spawned Temple Adath Israel in 1854 and Temple Mishkan Israel in 1856. All were separate Orthodox congregations which rarely mixed or coordinated social welfare services.[104]

As a center of social reform, Boston transformed its own philanthropy, as we have seen, and this strongly influenced Jewish practices. In this milieu of social welfare reform, Boston Jews took a bold step in 1864 by creating the United Hebrew Benevolent Association (UHBA), which frankly drew inspiration from the Brahmin's Boston Provident Association founded in 1851. The UHBA incorporated the Provident's idea of secular organized philanthropy as well as the practical standards of coordination, cooperation and community responsibility among like-minded charities.[105]

The members of Boston's three synagogues who formed the UHBA were chiefly businessmen made prosperous by Civil War wool, leather, shoe, textile, and drygoods business. They were independent of the rabbinate and motivated more by the example of the Yankee and Irish charities than by any crisis within the Jewish community. Soon, however, the immigration of destitute Jews from Eastern Europe in the 1880s—from Russia, Lithuania, Latvia, Galicia, Poland and Hungary—provided ample scope for UHBA largess. These refugees from pogroms and persecution were economically, religiously, and ethnically distinct from Boston's assimilated bourgeois Jews led by elite Bavarian and Westphalian Germans.[106]

Fearful of anti-Semitic reaction to these poor, backward Jews, whom they derisively labeled "Russian Jews," the UHBA aroused itself to meet this challenge. They recognized that Christians considered all Jews a single group, and partly for self-protection, Boston Jews assumed responsibility for their co-religionists who arrived in the city after the Russian pogroms of 1881 and 1882. Imbued with traditional notions of Judaic charity and the example of Boston philanthropy, the UHBA applied scientific charity to help the immigrants efficiently and humanely.[107]

Community-wide secular philanthropy, however, was still a concept unappealing to most Boston Jews, who clung to national origin ("Hollanders" or "Polanders") and the local neighborhood (the Ladies North End Benevolent Association) as natural limits to Jewish charity. While the progressive UHBA accepted the goal of unifying and coordinating all Jewish philanthropy, most Jews resisted it. The members of Temple Adath Israel, who were more affluent and assimilated than others, assumed leadership of the UHBA, and it was they who perceived the need to organize on a wider scale as needs changed. Members paid three dollars as annual dues and referred the needy Jews they encountered to the directors' homes or offices. Direct almsgiving was common, and record-keeping was still lax.

The most frequent aid was in the form of interest-free loans to Jewish peddlers. Boston drygoods firms specialized in outfitting peddlers who traveled through New England selling household goods, novelties, and mail order clothing to farmers and rural villagers. The North End in the 1870s had dozens of poor peddlers who came home only for Friday Sabbath and departed on Sunday morning with packs and wagons replenished for another week on the road. In distress or crisis, their wives and children were given alms by small charities or the UHBA, but usually only on a short-term basis.[108]

During the long depression of 1873 to 1878 in Massachusetts, members of Temple Ohabei Shalom organized a new charity which for a time rivaled the UHBA. The Young Men's Hebrew Association began in 1875 "for the moral and intellectual advancement of the Jewish population and for the relief of the deserving poor." It was quite unlike the later YMHA, which was modeled on the Young Men's Christian Association, and this earlier YMHA was almost wholly charitable in purpose. Mayor Samuel C. Cobb invited the YMHA in 1875 to use a room at City Hall as an employment bureau, and each afternoon advice and relief were provided poor Jewish boys. Information about peddling, licenses, medical care, and legal problems also occupied the YMHA agents, but this promising charity was overshadowed by the expanding and well-funded UHBA under its new leadership.[109]

Jacob H. Hecht (1834–1902), a Bavarian immigrant wealthy from his family's shoe business, invigorated the UHBA after he and his talented wife, Lina Frank Hecht, settled in Boston in 1868. Jacob and Lina Hecht devoted themselves to scientific philanthropy in a manner worthy of the most philanthropic Boston Brahmins.[110] In this they were ably assisted by Boston's leading Reform rabbi, Solomon Schindler (1842–1915), who was called to Temple Adath Israel from New Jersey in 1874. Schindler mingled with radical reformers and the progressive Protestant clergy and introduced the most advanced child welfare methods to Jewish organizations.[111]

When Hecht became president of the UHBA in 1876, he implemented Schindler's recommendations—regular office hours for relief applications, accurate records, careful investigation by paid agents (Schindler or Rabbi Raphael Lasker of Ohabei Sahlom) and friendly visiting by district. These systematic techniques, borrowed from the Associated Charities, the BCAS and the NEHLW, transformed the UHBA from a traditional *chevra* into an effective and economical family agency for the entire Jewish community.[112]

More importantly, these changes occurred just before the waves of Jewish immigrants swept over Massachusetts in the 1880s, severely taxing existing Jewish charity resources. Although New York City continued to receive the majority of Jewish immigrants, Boston had a significant influx. The Hebrew Emigrant Aid Society, founded in New York in 1882, opened a Boston branch under the leadership of Israel Cohen, the president of Temple Ohabei Shalom. Cohen raised four thousand dollars to meet the needs of Russian refugeees, but due to a misunderstanding, the first group in 1882 was directed to the Provident Society.[113] The Yankee charity workers, unable to speak Russian or Yiddish, and always on the alert for fraud, suspected the worst and dispatched sixty of these immigrant Jews to the State Almshouse at Tewksbury as paupers to be deported. When Almshouse officials discovered that most of these immigrants had sufficient funds to enter the country legally, they returned them to Boston. Still, this incident embarrassed Cohen, Schindler, and other Jewish leaders, who quickly improved methods of receiving immigrants at the East Boston piers.[114]

Jacob Hecht informed the public and private welfare representatives that the UHBA assumed responsibility for all Jewish immigrants and insisted that any doubtful cases be referred to his office. Quickly, the city's charities recognized the UHBA as the only agency competent to deal with Eastern European Jews and invited Hecht to open an office in the municipal Charity Building at 43 Hawkins Street. Soon a Jew became a Overseer of the Poor, which hired a Yiddish-speaking visiting agent. The first refugee crisis ended happily with new respect for the UHBA and new understanding of the unique problems the "Russian Jews" presented to Bostonians.[115]

Rabbi Schindler, greatly influenced by the Associated Charities, persuaded Hecht to reorganize the UHBA in 1883 as an association of all of the Jewish charities in Boston for economy, efficiency, and uniformity. This step was a drastic departure from traditional customs, and national or regional origin still divided the Jews. Cooperation, however, was customary in Boston child welfare, and the traditional Judaic concern for homeless and wayward children was a compelling reason to overcome intra-ethnic conflict. Both the UHBA and Lina Hect's Ladies' Sewing Society, which made clothing for poor children by 1876, hired Schindler as a visiting agent and listened sympathetically to his argument for a Jewish orphan asylum. Still the cost and the difficulty of overcoming the mutual mistrust of the Russian and the German-American Jews deterred them.[116]

Less discouraged, however, were City Councillor Isaac Rosnosky and Congressman Leopold Morse, who purchased a large house in the Mattapan section of Boston in 1887 as an orphanage. The Montefiore Home Society, which had planned to establish an orphanage, contributed its funds for this purpose; and other donations accumulated from wealthy Jews, the UHBA, and the Ladies' Sewing Society. On 3 April 1889 the Leopold Morse Home for Aged and Infirm Hebrews and Orphans opened on the principle that elderly and convalescent Jews could care for orphaned children more effectively than a paid professional staff. Actually, more adults than children were admitted, and this principle was quickly abandoned. The home's president, Godfrey Morse, reported only twenty-three children in the home in 1892. Even the arrival of Schindler as superintendent in 1899 did not increase the number significantly. The Morse Home was embarrassingly underpopulated throughout its existence.[117]

It had other problems as well: it was too remote, ill-adapted for its purpose, and inflexible. The managers accepted only orphans who had been Boston residents for at least three years prior to admission, which eliminated many immigrant children who were the most needy candidates for admission. Although the neighboring town of Milton permitted the children to attend its public schools free of charge, and Rabbi Schindler supervised religious and music lessons, few children were referred. The Home's location on the southern fringe of the city and its German Reform management made it inaccessible and repugnant to the poor Orthodox Russian Jews who lived in the North End and West End tenement districts.[118] With these problems in mind, Samuel H. Borofsky, a Russian immigrant lawyer and politician, founded a Jewish orphanage more suitable to the needs of his countrymen. The Russian Jews still distrusted the Germans, who dispensed charity with a haughtiness they found impious and whose scientific philanthropy the immigrants found even more insulting than that of the Yankees. They feared the Reform Jews' orphanage almost as much as they feared Protestant, Catholic, and public institutions for children.[119]

With the colorful and sympathetic Borofsky as president, the Ladies' Helping Hand Society Temporary Home for Destitute Jewish Children opened in 1897. Located in the former St. Elizabeth's Hospital on Fort Hill Avenue in Roxbury, the Home quickly filled under its beloved superintendent, Louis "Papa" Cohen. It sheltered sixty-five boys and girls, most of whom were half-orphans whose parents paid low weekly fees and brought the children home when they remarried or resolved the economic or family crises which had made the placements necessary. The Helping Hand Home, as admiring immigrant Jews dubbed it, was little concerned with "fancy schmancy social work" and emphasized a "warm and loving atmosphere and Orthodox religion with kosher meals" and a liberal admission and visiting policy.[120]

Before Boston Jews were able to address the problem of child welfare and to provide modern social casework services to Jewish families, they had to overcome the financial devastation following the extraordinarily harsh winter of 1892 which was followed by an economic depression from 1893 to 1895. These tragedies bankrupted most private charities and convinced Schindler and Hecht that fund-raising efforts must be coordinated. Brahmin critics of private philanthropy, like Harvard Professor Francis Greenwood Peabody, had long advocated the same goal, but the UHBA acted first. Schindler and his dynamic lieutenant Max Mitchell (1871–1929), a young Hungarian journalist, united the UHBA, the Hebrew Ladies' Sewing Society, and the Morse Home fund-raising efforts under one appeal. This new organization, the Federation of Jewish Charities, formed in 1895 and gradually attracted other charities. One novel feature of the FJC was the addition of three women to the board of directors. But only dire necessity drove the independent-minded into the FJC fold. Children suffered most from the economic depression, and Boston's 30,000 Jews taxed the meager resources of the city's twenty *Landsmannschaften* and the ladies' *chevrot* for sustaining destitute families.[121]

Schindler was dismissed from his pulpit at Temple Adath Israel in 1895, ironically because his accent and Teutonic socialist manner offended the younger, assimilated members of the congregation, so he was free to devote all of his energy to social work. Increasingly, the children in the Morse Home intrigued him, and in 1899 he resigned as director of the UHBA and FJC to become superintendent of the Morse Home, where he served until his retirement in 1905. Max Mitchell succeeded him at the UHBA and FJC (1899–1914), and he too was immersed in child welfare problems, spending many afternoons in Mattapan or taking children on hikes and drives in the Blue Hills. Other members of the FJC board accompanied Schindler and Mitchell on these visits, and as a result the Jewish waifs occupied a more central position on the FJC agenda than ever before.

Even these two Jewish institutions for homeless children, however, were not adequate for Boston's increasing Jewish population, which reached 40,000 by 1900. Jewish children continued to enter Catholic asylums, particularly the HDCC, HAG, and HGS, and Protestant agencies like the BCAS, CM, and NEHLW. Moreover, the Lancaster and Lyman reform schools had substantial Jewish populations by 1900.[122] The UHBA deplored the need to place Jewish children in Christian or public institutions or in gentile foster homes, but it lacked an alternative. Few immigrant families could afford to take a foster child into their own crowded and (in social workers' view) "unsuitable" homes, and even if assimilated Jews were willing to take a child, his Orthodox relatives were outraged by the idea of "irreligious" Reform Jews taking their son or daughter. They often preferred institutionalization to such foster homes.[123]

By 1908 the Helping Hand Home outgrew its quarters and faced an increasing demand for admissions, so the managers bought vacant land on Canterbury Street in Dorchester and began construction of a large modern institution. When the cornerstone was laid with elaborate ceremony in

1910, the only representative of the German Jewish establishment who bothered to attend was Lehman Pickert, the diplomatic president (1904–08) of the FJC. This insult caused considerable scandal among Boston Jews, and the Ladies' Helping Hand Society redoubled efforts (by holding dances, concerts and fairs) to raise $100,000 for the new building. By November 1911 they were only $30,000 short of their goal when the new Home for Destitute Jewish Children opened.[124]

Meanwhile, Lehman Pickert had persuaded the still underpopulated Morse Home to amalgamate with the new orphanage. By 1912 the two rival institutions merged as the Home for Jewish Children, and the assets which the Morse Home trustees contributed made the HJC solvent and gave it a claim to FJC funds and ties to the affluent Jewish community. The new asylum sheltered two hundred boys and girls annually. They were aged six to eighteen and attended school on the grounds until old enough for local public schools. Daily activities included religious training, music lessons, participation in a marching band, publication of a monthly magazine (in the children's own print shop), woodworking and sewing clases, Boy Scout membership, gymnastics, and other sports. Few children were adopted. Some were placed out as foster children, but for most, the HJC was home until old enough to work.[125] It was a medium-sized congregate institution, a three-story brick building on spacious grounds, and generously supported by the Jewish community from 1911 to 1934. As immigrant Jews adjusted to Boston, many of them moved by 1910 from the North End and West End to middle-class neighborhoods in Roxbury, Dorchester, and Mattapan, street-car suburbs bordering the JHC grounds. This created a supportive Jewish suburban community into which the HJC children easily blended. The inmates had many opportunities to mingle with classmates and friends who lived nearby, and this prevented the institutionalization of the children that was so characteristic of Boston Catholic asylums.[126]

The most common reason for placing a child in the HJC differed from the reasons listed in the HDCC, HAG, and HGS records, or for those in CM and NEHLW files. Although some were children born out of wedlock or were orphans, many were children whose parents had deserted, divorced, or separated. When the parents or relatives could no longer maintain the family, often a child would enter the HJC until a permanent solution was found.[127] This corresponds with the observation of one Boston critic who noted that "the family life of the Jews is, on the whole very wholesome," but "strangely enough, however, desertion by the men is noticeably frequent" and the "desertion of women with helpless infants is one of the causes of extreme want among the Jews."[128]

This problem concerned the National Conference of Jewish Charities from its beginning in Chicago in 1900, and led to the creation of the

Home for Jewish Children on Canterbury Street in Dorchester (1912–34) coordi-nated Boston Jewish charities for "wayward children" and orphans until modern casework methods emerged. *(American Jewish Historical Society.)*

National Desertion Bureau in New York in 1911. This national register of deserting husbands (and a few wives) canvassed labor, religious, welfare, and social organizations to trace missing parents. Abraham Cahan published inquiries and photographs in his newspaper, *The Jewish Daily Forward,* by 1908 to assist the effort. The National Conference of Jewish Charities heard discouraging reports on the high desertion rates as social workers and rabbis debated the causes and solutions. The New York legislature eventually responded to Jewish lobbyists by making child abandonment by parents an extraditable offense, but this had only a limited impact on the problem.[129]

More than one hundred and fifty organizations cooperated with the National Desertion Bureau, which gradually decreased the number of Jewish families receiving welfare.[130] Rabbis who granted divorces by rabbinical decree *(ghets)* to Jews not legally divorced curtailed this prac-tice in an effort to uphold family life among immigrants.[131] By 1915 the NDB had greater influence when Professor Felix Frankfurter of Harvard Law School and leading Jewish social workers and businessmen became trustees. The National Probation Association also cooperated with the NDB by lobbying for new family and juvenile courts as another solution to this perplexing Jewish child welfare problem.[132]

In Boston the FJC cooperated with the NDB to trace irresponsible (or simply desperate) parents who abandoned their children and spouses, and demanded child support payments if they refused to return home. One such case involved a girl placed in the HJC after her mother died and her father suddenly moved to New York. When located, he agreed to pay her boarding fees if the FJC dropped legal proceedings against him. The anguish and grief in such pathetic cases is concealed by the terse style of social workers in the 1920s:

> Report from district worker that National Desertion Bureau had traced man in New York, and he is willing to pay $6.00 per week for girl's care in Home for Jewish Children.[133]

Although the desertion problem faded, it never completely disappeared and the FJC cooperated with the Massachusetts Society for the Prevention of Cruelty to Children (MSPCC) to compel parents to support their children under the neglected child law. When a Jewish girl was ostracized by her grandparents because she contracted venereal disease, the FJC placed her in a foster home with minimal payments from her impoverished family. The directors attempted to find a Jewish foster family, "but no Jewish home will take her if told of her present condition, it was moved that an attempt be made to place her with a Gentile family who would accept the fact of venereal disease."[134]

When a Jewish drycleaner "ran off with his housekeeper leaving the children homeless," the MSPCC investigated the case for the FJC. The five youngsters appeared in the Boston Juvenile Court as neglected children, but could not be placed in the Helping Hand Home or the Morse Home because "one is a temporary home and is overcrowded and the other is for orphans only." The NEHLW refused the case because a social worker suspected the family "had $500.00 in assets," but BCAS accepted four of the children for foster family placement. The BJC committed the eldest sibling to Lancaster "though the poor child is not so much feeble-minded as she is untrained and ignorant." Whatever the merits of this social service plan, Jewish and Yankee child-savers cooperated to care for these abandoned children with the authority of the juvenile court supporting the best available casework.[135]

Despite increased cooperation between the city's Protestant, Catholic Jewish, and public agencies, however, the FJC directors did not share a common tradition with these other charities. Most Jews still looked upon their colleagues as *goyim* (non-Jews) who could never provide satisfactory care to homeless and wayward Jewish children. As soon as their numbers and resources permitted, Boston Jewish leaders created their own sectarian charity and social welfare system for Jews. Unlike the small and impoverished black community, Boston Jews were able to form a child welfare system which rivaled, and in some respects surpassed, other child welfare services.[136]

One result of this attention to child welfare was the Country Week Committee which sent three hundred poor Jewish children to the seashore or mountains each summer. Lina Hecht began these vacations in 1891 for her Hebrew Industrial School girls. When Max Mitchell became superintendent of the FJC, he continued Mrs. Hecht's program as part of his work with the Baron de Hirsch Fund. Mitchell's Industrial Removal Office resettled forty West End families on dairy and poultry farms in Millis and Medway, Massachusetts. These Jewish farmers were eager to supplement their income by boarding city children in the summer. Unlike the still-functioning orphan trains of the CM, NEHLW, and HDCC, these waifs were temporary visitors not expected to work for their keep.[137] It was an inexpensive and healthy opportunity for Boston children to enjoy rural life and country kosher cooking. Hopes that the children would later abandon tenements for the countryside were largely unrealized, but it was a step in the direction of foster care and adoption. Social workers were satisfied that the children at least returned suntanned, invigorated, and aware that America was wider than the West End.[138]

Schindler and Mitchell carefully studied the Massachusetts record of foster family care, as well as the experiences of the CM and BCAS, before they organized Jewish child-placing services. Despite exhortations in the Bible and Talmud to provide homes for orphans, few Jewish families had taken homeless children into their homes.[139] Consequently, the FJC was compelled to refer children to the CM, BAS, and NEHLW for placement. This dilemma prompted Mitchell in 1902 to devise another strategy. He announced in the Jewish press that FJC children were available as "boarding children." He paid suitable families $2.50 per week to care for a child and provided the clothing and medical care. Mitchell personally investigated these rural or suburban foster homes and required letters of reference from rabbis or physicians before placing children. The first year he placed thirty-two of the fifty-four available children at the modest cost of $940.00. He found that most children had a parent or relative willing to pay part of the cost. Families were permitted to visit their children at the foster home, but in "troublesome" cases, the child was brought to the FJC office by a volunteer who supervised visits with the family. To comply with new State Board of Charity regulations, state visitors inspected the foster family quarterly, but the FJC had primary casework responsibility.[140]

Mitchell aroused considerable interest in this program when he described it to the National Conference of Jewish Charities in 1902. He cautioned the delegates that several years of ground work were required to establish a corps of "proper homes for children of different temperaments." The FJC endorsed this "new method" as preferable to congregate asylums for most children, although the difficulty of finding and supervising satisfactory foster homes for wayward (and often emotionally disturbed) children assured that the HJC would continue to fill a need in child welfare for a generation longer.[141]

Many Jewish families were troubled by the placement of their children in public and Christian institutions and foster families. They feared their children would lose their faith and ethnic identity in Christian surroundings. The FJC created a Children's Bureau to respond to these objections and to coerce some parents who were able but unwilling to pay for the child welfare services their children received. Some Jewish parents concealed their assets and denied their ability to pay the modest, flexible fees for a child in the HJC, and this "free-loading" drained scarce financial resources. The Children's Bureau adopted a forceful posture to prevent this abuse:

> Case discussed, and it was voted that Mr. Kessler pay $6.00 per week to the Home for Jewish Children for the care of his children, and until he agrees to do this, no action is to taken for the transfer of girl from the [City of Boston] Trustees for Children.[142]

When Governor Curtis Guild appointed a Jewish attorney, Philip Rubenstein, to the new Boston Juvenile Court in 1906, the FJC acquired stronger influence in the juvenile justice system they had lobbied to create. Judge Rubenstein was a strong ally of the FJC and met monthly with the Children's Bureau staff to discuss problems and methods of resolving them.[143] Another FJC ally in dealing with wayward children was the Boston chapter of the National Council of Jewish Women, which provided voluntary probation officers to the Boston courts by 1895. NCJW agents attended the BJC from the first and enjoyed full cooperation from the court. Many Jewish children committed to reform schools or to the custody of the State Division of Minor Wards (an agency of the Board of Charity) were diverted to the HJC or to a FJC foster home through the efforts of Judge Rubenstein and the NCJW agents in court.[144]

In some cases, knowing that immigrant parents preferred a Jewish asylum to a public institution, the FJC used admission to the HJC, and the unwelcomed alternative of Lancaster or Lyman reform school, to compel uncooperative parents to pay for boarding their children. When Simon Dubinsky, a fourteen-year-old son of well-to-do but miserly immigrant parents, was placed in a foster home by the court, he repeatedly ran away

His foster parents and FJC social worker complained he "does not obey, stays out nights, parents run a lunch counter and can't control Simon." Judge Rubenstein committed him to Lyman School, but suspended the sentence when the boy and his parents agreed to a "voluntary commitment" to the HJC. Having had difficulty with the parents before, however, the Children's Bureau, which controlled admissions, "voted to place him in the HJC if father pays in advance 2 weeks and thereafter in full."[145]

This coercion was not as hardhearted as it might seem, because many immigrant parents misconstrued private and public institutions like the HJC or Lyman School as a kind of free boarding school. Their troublesome "American" sons and daughters were sent "away to school" at no cost to the families during periods of adolescent turmoil or family crisis, and they returned home subdued, educated, and trained in useful skills.[146] In some cases, at least, this period of incarceration proved beneficial. No doubt some parents abused their children by manipulating the police and the court to commit an unwanted or burdensome child, and Yankee child-savers had long suspected this was so. Few Jewish immigrants from the Eastern European village *(shtetl)* were familiar with orphanages or reform schools, and to many hard-pressed parents these asylums merely seemed another of the wonders of America, a generous invention of the *goyim*. If rich German Jews or the Yankee do-gooders wanted to take one good-for-nothing son or a wild daughter for a year or two, perhaps it was best to cooperate, if only to appease the officials and to protect the family from further scrutiny.[147]

For every distraught mother, prostrate with grief as her son or daughter was led away by a probation officer to reform school, probably there was a relieved parent who hoped his wayward child would learn a useful trade. Was Lyman, Lancaster, or the HJC so different from the Country Week vacation the neighbors' children enjoyed? With this attitude in the minds of at least some impoverished working-class Jewish parents, it is understandable why the Children's Bureau was adamant in cases like Simon Dubinsky's. If his parents could afford to pay the low weekly fees, but refused to do so, let them prove their good faith by advance payments to the HJC. Actually, the directors appeared to be harsher than they were. Simon was admitted to the HJC and his father made the weekly payments, but no cases were discovered in FJC records in which a child was denied admission or discharged for lack of funds. By all accounts it was a warm-hearted charity generously supported by the Jews of New England. If there were some cases in which avaricious, miserly, or uncomprehending parents were cajoled or coerced into meeting their financial obligations to the Jewish charities caring for their children, this does not obscure the high-minded social service the FJC constituent agencies performed as they both aided and policed the children of the poor. It does highlight the difficulty Jewish social workers faced with immigrants accustomed to only brutality and injustice from the rapacious government of the Czar. Jewish charities Americanized the immigrant poor in many ways, borrowing from the Brahmins in some instances and from their own rich religious and cultural traditions in others.[148]

An important difference existed, and may still exist, between Jewish child welfare concepts and Yankee ideas about vulnerable children and their families. Jewish culture condoned need as a socially acceptable condition, unlike Yankee culture which deplored dependency. When Jews expressed emotions freely and voiced the need for assistance, they offended Yankee values and provoked an anti-Semitic reaction. Jewish immigrants, faced by a family or financial crises, were "likely to demand relief with the stance of a social debt collector."[149] In the *shtetl*, the impecunious rabbincial scholar held higher status than the prosperous merchant, and this equation of piety with poverty was jarringly upset in the United States. The aggressive custom of demanding community help without shame or guilt made even the most tragic Jewish pauper a repulsive *Schnorrer* (beggar) to his German-American cousins and appalled the Yankee charity workers.

This explains why the existing Jewish and Christian charities were antagonistic to the Russian immigrants in the 1880s and 1890s, but it also reveals why a fifteen-year-old South End boy was unembarrassed to beg the Boston Juvenile Court to send his two younger sisters to Lancaster "because if you don't, you will be getting them into the Court for bad girls." As adolescent head of his fatherless immigrant family, he preferred reform school for his sisters to prostitution or pregnancy.[150] It was to meet these compelling needs in the immigrant community that the Children's Bureau created alternatives to incarceration and crime for the Jews without money who adjusted too slowly, or not at all, to urban industrial Boston. This was the reason the Helping Hand Home and the Morse Home appeared in Boston, but even the consolidated, modern HJC was not sufficient. Having imbibed deeply at the well of Brahmin philanthropy, Boston Jews thirsted for something better than almsgiving and the congregate institution.[151]

Jewish agencies learned from their Yankee colleagues to scrutinize each applicant carefully, perhaps more so than in Jewish charities in other cities. Not only was the FJC extremely wary of imposters and malingerers, but FJC caseloads were heavier than those of Jewish agencies in cities with larger Jewish populations. Also the backlog of pending cases, those applicants awaiting investigation and social services, exceeded those in all other cities reviewed by the Russell Sage Foundation in 1926 (see Tables 4.5 and 4.6).[152]

Table 4.5

Selected Federated Jewish Charities Cases, Pending, December 1926

	Total # Pending Child Welfare Cases	Average # Cases Per Worker
Boston	347	13.3
New York	210	2.8
Chicago	177	4.0
Cleveland	79	3.6
Baltimore	74	3.5

SOURCE: Jewish Family and Children's Service, Archives, General District Service Committee, Minutes, 17 March 1927.

The number of cases treated each month by the Boston FJC staff was very high, exceeding even New York City, which in 1927 had 1.6 million Jews compared to 90,000 in Boston. Moreover, the total number of active child welfare cases was much higher in Boston than in five other cities.[153]

The 1,185 cases the Boston FJC investigated in December 1926 were pending applications for child placement, financial aid, medical care, or counseling by working-class Jewish families in Boston, Chelsea, Revere, and Winthrop (or Suffolk County). All applicants were interviewed at one of the five Jewish Welfare Community Centers established in 1917 in the West End, South End, East Boston, Roxbury, and Dorchester. Unsatisfied with the existing methods of the UHBA, which the FJC believed smacked of almsgiving and old-fashioned charity, the entire child and family welfare system was revamped in 1917. The directors hired Morris Waldman, the former director of the influential United Hebrew Charities in New York City, to create a modern, decentralized program. Representatives of Boston's major Jewish child welfare agencies—the FJC, HJC, National Council of Jewish Women, and the newly organized Jewish Children's Aid Society—met in January 1918 to discuss the needs of dependent and delinquent children and adolescents.[154] They were frankly imitating the policies of the city's most progressive social work agencies—especially the BCAS and the reorganized NEHLW—emphasizing casework and child guidance. The primary concern of the FJC leadership was the backlog of applications and the placement of more than two hundred Jewish children in non-Jewish homes. "The immediate function is to find Jewish homes and pass upon cases referred." Waldman formed the General District Service Committee to oversee the five Jewish Community Centers, and he created the Children's Bureau Case Committee as "one of investigation and reference" for problem or chronic cases. His goal was to streamline and improve Boston Jewish child welfare as he had done in

Table 4.6

Selected Federated Jewish Charities Cases, Active, December 1926

Total Child Welfare Case Load	Average # Cases per Worker	
Boston	1,185	45.6
New York	2,101	28.4
Chicago	1,165	26.5
Philadelphia	1,063	32.3
Cleveland	617	28.0
Baltimore	514	24.5

SOURCE: Jewish Family and Children's Service, Archives, General District Service Committee Minutes, 17 March 1927.

New York. He found Boston social workers eager to offer the same "modern and professional social work" services that the prestigious Yankee agencies provided.[155]

The major way the FJC improved social services for children was to embrace the new techniques of psychiatric casework. When the first child guidance clinic, the Judge Baker Foundation, opened in Boston in 1917, the FJC created a scholarship in "applied psychology" for its staff, which was to be trained by Dr. William Healy and the Judge Baker Foundation co-director, Dr. Augusta Fox Bronner. The first student to receive this scholarship was May Bere (1917–19) followed by Dorothy Morgenthau (1919–21). These pioneer child psychologists were joined by Viola J. Rottenberg in 1920, an assistant psychologist working with Augusta Bronner.[156]

Children's Bureau reports in 1918 repeatedly mentioned Dr. Healy and the JBF as Freudian principles pervaded Jewish social work. An early example was the case of Irving Goldsmith, of whom "it is reported that this five-year-old child had bad sex tendencies and is being very closely observed."[157] Much of the FJC interest in child psychiatry was naive, but by 1922 Dr. Healy's diagnosis was usually prerequisite for admission of "mentally questionable" children to the HJC. In a typical case, the Children's Bureau case committee voted that only if Dr. Healy's examination of two boys "shows they are not mentally defective" may they be admitted. Deference to Healy's opinion about Louis Schwartz saved him from commitment to the Westborough Reform School in 1922; at the eleventh hour Dr. Healy recommended that he be placed in the HJC instead. Both the Boston Juvenile Court and the FJC agreed that this twelve-year-old boy, described as "delinquent, lying, stealing, playing truant from school, and in command of a gang of bad boys," was a "hard case," but Healy's interest in the case overcame all objections.[158]

Although Boston Jewish social workers won respect as early and eager advocates of psychology and psychiatry and admiration for their welfare organizations in the city, they sometimes encountered anti-Semitic attitudes. The Boston Juvenile Court referred some delinquent Jewish boys to the Hayden Goodwill Inn, a temporary home for juveniles in Dorchester. But when Dr. William H. Sheldon, America's leading somatotypist, studied a group of inmates there, he bordered on racism when he wrote about a sixteen-year-old "mesomorph" who had been in foster homes and reform schools since age seven:

> Outlook generally regarded as dubious, but it should not be forgotten that the boy is a Jew. . . . It is possible that Jews just now have a better sense of agglutination, or of group loyalty, than any other white group. This may be one reason why they have a better *espirit de corps* and tend to look out for one another better than some other groups do. At any rate they do this, and from it arises a kind of patriotism which may be among the important human virtues. Being Jewish, this youth is probably more likely to "wake up and come out of it" than he would be if he were Irish or a nondescript mongrel.[159]

The FJC was more fortunate when they encountered Dr. Douglas A. Thom, a child psychiatrist who founded the Boston Habit Clinic in 1921. FJC directors invited Dr. Thom to lecture to the staff and referred thumb-sucking, bed-wetting, head-banging, phobic, and sexually-precocious children to his clinic for diagnosis and treatment.[160] An even more influential child psychiatrist was Dr. Isidor Coriat (1875–1943), a Sephardic Jew who graduated from Tufts Medical School in 1900. He was a disciple of Sigmund Freud, founded the Boston Psychoanalytic Society, and was twice president of the American Psychoanalytic Association. As a training analyst, professor of psychiatry and department chairman at the Beth Israel Hospital, he was the strongest advocate for new psychiatric casework methods in Boston Jewish agencies.[161]

The Jewish agencies accepted these controversial methods much earlier than Protestant and Catholic agencies did, as the wider use of psychology, psychiatry, and psychoanalysis in FJC records indicates. But in every aspect of medicine, law, education, and social welfare, American Jews assumed a progressive stance. The old-fashioned "chevra doctors" (like Dr. Morris Kinstler, a Polish immigrant physician who practiced in the South End slums) were vanishing by the 1920s, just as the almsgiving rabbis and charity workers were replaced by the FJC professional social workers. When the Beth Israel Hospital moved into modern quarters in the Fenway area in 1928, it too included the most up-to-date psychiatric nursing and social services.[162] But when Maurice B. Hexter succeeded Morris Waldman as FJC director (1919–29), psychiatric casework was not yet the norm in Boston child welfare. Hexter trained in Cincinnati under Boris Bogen, the founder of Jewish social work in America. He earned a Ph.D. in social ethics under Dr. Richard C. Cabot at Harvard and taught at the Simmons College School of Social Work. His assistant, Maurice Taylor, was a native Bostonian who also earned a Ph.D. at Harvard and directed the FJC West End Community Center. Hexter and Taylor joined Saul Drucker, another Cabot protege, and the HJC superintendent, in promoting modern psychiatric casework for Jewish children and their families.[163]

These men and women trained the next generation of Jewish social workers and psychologists. By 1930, when the FJC was reorganized by Louis E. Kirstein as the Associated Jewish Philanthropies, Jewish child welfare services equaled all others in Boston and rivaled those of the trend-setting BCAS and the revamped NEHLW.[164] A relative newcomer compared to these old child-saving agencies, the FJC or new AJP matured rapidly and offered superior services to dependent, delinquent and emotionally disturbed children and adolescents. In 1932 the General District Service reformed as the Jewish Family Welfare Association, and embodied the AJP and the HJC child welfare responsibilities for all of metropolitan Boston. Since 1910, when Governor Eugene Foss appointed Lehman Pickert as a trustee of the Boston Psychopathic Hospital, Boston Jewish leaders had expanded charity and reform to embrace scientific social work, psychology, and medicine. In 1913 Maida Herman Solomon (1892–1988) became the first Jewish psychiatric social worker at this new mental hospital which facilitated cooperation between it and the FJC constituent agencies. The American mental hygiene movement struck a responsive chord with Boston Jewry, and by 1928 the FJC hired consulting psychiatrists Dr. Jacob A. Kasanin and Dr. Martha Gorovitz to train staff and to lecture to neighborhood groups on child guidance.[165]

All of which is to say that Boston Jews, for reasons still not fully understood, were early and strong proponents of psychology, psychiatry, and social work, seeing them as superior methods of understanding and preventing child welfare problems.[166] They traveled far from Temple Ohabei Sahlom's first *chevra,* and they proved to be as resourceful and progressive as the Boston Brahmin child-savers they emulated. Jewish charity demonstrated a dual purpose, to maintain ethnic integrity and to achieve social accommodation. Philanthropy for homeless and wayward children was a noncontroversial way of expressing their Judaic beliefs, and patrician practice in Boston commended it as socially useful while the ancient faith sanctified it as God's law.[167]

* * *

The third ethnic minority in Boston to develop its own child welfare and charity system was the Italians. Like the Jewish response to vulnerable

Table 4.7

Boston Residents Born in Italy, 1860–1920

	Italian-born Population	Percent of Population
1860	249	.14%
1870	263	.10
1880	1,277	.3
1890	4,718	1.1
1900	13,738	2.4
1910	31,380	4.6
1920	38,179	5.1

SOURCE: U.S. Census Bureau, Eighth to the Fourteenth Census, 1860–1920.

families, Italo-American child-saving should not be judged by modern social work standards. Its efforts were an internal response to family crisis not imposed externally by any Protestant or Irish Catholic leadership. Like Black Bostonians, the Italian immigrants did not create an institutional equivalent to established organizations, because their concept of family and children differed so much from those of the Irish and Yankee Americans.

Before the Civil War, Boston had fewer than three hundred Italians, but by 1890 they were the third largest immigrant group in the city. After 200,000 Irish and 20,000 Jews, came more than 15,000 Italians. In time this rapidly-growing and independent Italo-American community organized its own charity and child welfare system, but only after formidable obstacles were overcome.[168]

Although there were some Italians in antebellum Massachusetts, they were too few (see Table 4.7) to be regarded as a social problem. In fact, the scholars, musicians, dancing masters, sculptors, and artisans from Northern Italy were more colorful than controversial. When antebellum Boston reformers—romantic gentlemen like Samuel Gridley Howe, Theodore Parker, Theodore Lyman, and Henry I. Bowditch—thought of Italy, it was of the struggle for independence and national unification against the reactionary forces of the papacy, Austria, and France. Boston craftsmen, statue-makers, and organ-grinders from Italy were identified as fellow democrats or the innocent victims of foreign tyranny.[169]

The return of Pope Pius IX to Rome in 1850 under the protection of French and Austrian troops and the arrest of 58,000 Italian rebels prompted the Boston Transcript to express indignation at "these monstrous barbarities" and the "inherent vices of an ecclesiastical regime." These sentiments echoed the nativist tirades of the Know Nothing Party against Catholic immigrants, but had little effect on popular attitudes toward Italians in New England. It did, however, incite antagonism against the thousands of Irish Catholic immigrants in Massachusetts, and when the Know Nothing Party swept the state elections in 1852, anti-Catholicism reached a zenith with unrestrained condemnation of Irish Catholics as agents of papal despotism. Irishmen reacted with what was for most a new allegiance to their Church which set the stage for later antipathy between the sacerdotal Boston Irish and the anti-clerical Italian immigrants.[170]

Although not the only factor alienating Italians from the Archdiocese of Boston and its charity organizations, this difference of attitude toward the clergy and the Church created profound tensions. When Italians emigrated in large numbers to the United States in the 1890s, they encountered an Irish-American dominated Catholic church with French-Canadian, German, Polish, Lithuanian, and Portuguese Catholics on the fringes of organized Catholicism. Homeless Italian children entered St. Vincent's Asylum, the HAG, HDCC, HGS, and the Daly Industrial School from the first, but they occupied a minority status under the patronage of Irish Catholic clergy, nuns, and child-savers.[171]

Such charitable institutions were rare in Southern Italy where 90 percent of the Italian immigrants had lived, and they misconstrued them as another quaint American custom like school attendance laws, municipal hospitals, and public reform schools. As one child-saver maintained, "hot Italian blood" often led to wife desertion, and "the commitment of children to some charitable institution" often followed. "The Italian, indeed, has acquired a rather bad reputation on this score, being thought far too ready to throw off the burden of responsibility for his children." Like the Russian Jews, many Italian parents assumed that commitment of troublesome children to an orphanage or asylum was an American custom. Accustomed to a remote and indifferent, if not hostile, government, they were puzzled, but much was confusing in this new country. As another Progressive "expert" on the Italian immigrant claimed:

> With the doors of our asylums . . . flung hospitably open to every child for whom even a remote claim for support can be made, what wonder is it that the innocent immigrant, marvelling at the kindness of the great government, regards the 'collegio' as only another and superior variety of public school, needing no truant office to drive the children thither as it draws them with the attractions of free food and shelter?[172]

This unjust view was countenanced by the tradition of removing young children for whom there was still hope of moral regeneration from their "corrupt and immoral" parents. From the Children's Mission in the 1850s to the Massachusetts Tuberculosis Commission in the 1920s, private and public philanthropists assumed the working class needed the moral guidance of their "betters." Boston child-savers were far too eager to act as child-snatchers, and charity workers of all types were accustomed to removing children from "unsuitable" parents. Consequently, when Italian immigrants arrived in late-nineteenth-century Boston, they encountered new medical opinions that encouraged removal of sick children in much the same fashion:

> With the adults the doctor often has to compromise and demand only such measures as can be carried out along with the patient's regular occupation. In the case of children there should be *no compromise*. . . . The ailing child should be at once removed from school and "put out to grass," i.e., made to live out of doors in fresh air and sunshine. . . . The child should be sent to an open air school or some such institution."[173]

So, if the Italian or Jewish parents were too eager to surrender their morally or physically endangered children to American asylum-keepers, it was partly due to fear and ignorance, and partly because the do-gooders were so ready to take these children.

Immigrant parents were often frustrated by their too rapidly Americanized sons and daughters who were no longer as docile as they had been in the old country. Sometimes they blamed the public schools for corrupting their children with strange ideas and sent them to parochial schools or even to Catholic asylums like the HAG or HGS that they equated with the *collegio* or convent school of their homeland. In Italy only middle-class and upper-class children attended these strict boarding schools, and Italian peasants *(contadini)* thought themselves fortunate to have access to such schools in the United States. The *contadini* had no tradition of compulsory education or parochial schools, which they accepted only because of the problems of raising children in Boston slums.[174]

But because the Southern Italians had little experience with such schools (education was not compulsory in Italy until 1877 and not universal for a generation longer), and because of their ambivalence toward the Catholic church, they supported parochial schools and Catholic charities less enthusiastically than Irish, German, French-Canadian, or Polish Catholics in Massachusetts did.[175] If they occasionally turned to the parochial school to discipline a wayward child, more often they tried to send the child to a free public institution, such as the Lancaster, Westborough, and Shirley state reform schools, of which they had little dread. The Reverend Constantine Panunzio, an Italian immigrant who became a Methodist missionary in the North End in 1914, recalled an Italian fish vender who asked for help with his thirteen-year-old nephew. After two years in Boston, the boy was disrespectful, disobedient and profane. His uncle complained, "We don't know what to do with him. Do the schools in America teach boys to become bad? Will you help me to send him to jail?"[176]

A primary reason for the delinquency of the children of Italian immigrants had to do with the cultural stress they experienced, speaking Italian at home and English at school and at play. Parents, whose lives as peasants in a Southern Italian village equipped them poorly for urban industrial America, added to this alienation by recounting stories to their children of corrupt policemen, unethical lawyers, and larcenous jurists in the old country, where the government was distant and disruptive. From hearing stories of past injustice, they supposed that the Irish cop on the beat—who the school teachers said symbolized law, order, and democracy—was actually a villain underneath his blue tunic. On the basis of this outlook, some boys went so far as to ask their parents to conspire with them against tyrants like the school principal and the truant officer. Most parents, of course, refused, but child labor laws seemed unreasonable to peasants accustomed to family work in the fields, and many abetted children in evading school and work laws or winked at petty violations of the law. One Italian-American writer recalled immigrant parents who were

> not the least shocked or angered when the boys were caught stealing boxes of oranges and were only saved from arrest through the generosity of the store proprietor. Their attitude seemed to be that as long as the boys had escaped punishment, everything was fine, especially since they had dutifully been bringing home whatever oranges they did not sell. It was only when the boys began to steal from their own relatives that Mr. and Mrs. Panzienza became alarmed and requested the authorities to put their sons in a reform school for a while.[177]

This attitude, reflecting peasant customs and different child-rearing practices rather than any Italian criminality, shocked both the Irish street-level bureaucrats and Brahmin judges in Boston, who joined ranks to Americanize these "backward" immigrants from benighted Italy. But when Italians avoided commitment to the reform schools by recourse to the HAG or the HGS, they too were shocked by demands from the brothers or sisters for boarding fees. Strict rules concerning admission, conduct, visiting, and payments angered the somewhat anti-clerical Italians who regarded their institutional Church as rich and corrupt. Conflict occurred as soon as Italian children entered Boston Catholic asylums.[178] The first Italian boy in the HAG, who was kidnapped in Messina in 1859 by the cook of a frigate and jumped ship in Boston, was one of the waifs Father George F. Haskins picked up on the waterfront. The HAG registers listed no other Italian inmates until 1887, when two were admitted (0.8 percent of the 1887 admissions), another boy in 1897 (0.4 percent), five in 1907 (1 percent), five more in 1917 (1.5 percent), and two in 1927 (1, percent).[179] One immigrant placed in the HAG with his brother from 1918 to 1921 recalled the "terror" he felt at being among six hundred Irish-American boys under the "over-zealous discipline of gruff French-Canadian and Belgian Brothers of Charity." When his mother died in the influenza epidemic, his distraught father placed both of his young sons in the HAG until he settled his affairs and established a new home for them in the North End. Antonio was eleven years old when he entered the HAG, and "had been as free as a bird, just coming from Avellino to Boston, and then to be put behind those high walls, it frightened and angered me so much that I prayed to St. Anthony to burn the place down so I could go home to my father." Although he gradually became "as meek as a lamb," he eagerly awaited his father's visit on the first Sunday of each month and feared breaking a rule that might cost him even this privilege. His father, like 35 percent of the 246 parents in 1918, paid $12.00 per month for the care of each of his sons in the HAG, a very heavy burden on a poor laborer just arrived from Southern Italy.[180]

The Home for Destitute Catholic Children also welcomed Italian orphans, and two Italian boys were admitted to the HDCC in 1897, eight in 1907, four in 1917, and fourteen in 1927. Most of the inmates admitted from 1867 to 1927 were Irish or Irish-American (59 percent), but the next largest ethnic group (27 percent) in that period was Italian or Italian-American.[181] Similarly, the House of the Good Shepherd admitted one Italian girl in 1897 (2 percent of the inmate population), four others in 1907 (4 percent), and many more thereafter.[182] St. Vincent's Home and the Daly Industrial School also admitted Italian girls by 1900. There was no apparent discrimination against Italian children in these Catholic asylums, but the low numbers of Italian inmates suggest some Irish child-savers were cautious about the new immigrant groups. The existing Catholic institutions for children were adequate and available for Boston Italians. Why, then, did the Italian community establish the Home for Italian Children in 1921? This is especially puzzling because deinstitutionalization was sweeping child welfare by 1920, and many institutions closed or became temporary asylums for children awaiting foster family or adoption placements.[183]

The reason for this anomaly is found in the ethnic conflict of Boston's Irish, Italian, and Jewish working class neighborhoods and their sometimes violent assertion of group identity and autonomy. By 1900 the Irish were a well-entrenched "minority" (over 40 percent) in the city, who by 1920 dominated municipal government as an elaborate political fiefdom. The police, fire, school, water, and public works departments were predominantly Irish due to the extensive patronage system of the politically organized second generation Celts. This ethnic ascendancy almost excluded the Jews, Blacks, and Italians. Among the 110 elected City Councillors from 1924 to 1949 were 12 Jews, 9 Yankees, 4 Italians, 1 Black and

84 Irishmen. The first independent Italian ward boss was not elected to public office until 1939.[184]

The Jews and Blacks found refuge in the Republican Party, as did some Italians, but most Italians were politically passive and accepted their cool reception in the Irishmen's Democratic Party and local machines. Organized Catholic charity, which adopted methods and drew much support and leadership from ward politics, reflected this second-class status for Italians. They had little influence in the Catholic Charitable Bureau or in the congregate asylums which predated the CCB. Italian failure in Boston and state politics was echoed in charity work. They did not (or could not) organize or exert ethnic bloc strength in either politics or charity because regional and cultural divisions among Italian immigrants frustrated every effort.[185]

In Italy, the family and quasi-family bonds (*famigliari* and *conguinti*) were the only strong social ties. Friends counted for little and self-interest was paramount in most relationships. Strangers were suspect until made intimate as godparents (*compare* and *commare*) or as fictious uncles, aunts, and cousins. Even the spirit of *campanilismo,* or loyalty to fellow villagers born within the sound of the village church bells, was not sufficient to overcome centuries of peasant familism. Unfamiliar with disinterested benevolence by strangers, Boston Italians regarded precinct captains and social workers as policemen, spies, or fools. In southern Italy outsiders (*forestieri*) were ignored, except in case of almsgiving to ward off evil spirits disguised as beggars or lepers. Refusal to give alms did not mean one was miserly or inhospitable, because charity was a personal issue not demanded by the clergy or community. This attitude would frustrate Boston Italian community organization and self-help efforts for generations.[186]

Over 90 percent of the 4 million Italians who emigrated to the United States between 1820 and 1920 were *contadini* or landless day laborers (*giornalieri*) from the *Mezzogiorno* of Southern Italy. Both groups had been exploited at home by the literate merchant and professional class (*prominenti*) who formed the leadership of each Little Italy in American cities. But all these immigrants shared common attitudes expressed in the terms *campanilismo* and *paesano.* Each village, a collection of houses and shops clustered around the church, was a primary group with local customs, patron saints, festivals, and dialects. The *paesani* ventured outside the walls only as far as their fields around the village and identified with their village and region but seldom with Italy. The peasant brought this narrow spirit of *campanilismo* with him to Boston, and it severely limited his adaptation to American society. The formation of a single Italian-American culture was delayed by *campanilismo* as hundreds of regional subcultures fragmented Italians into rival factions.[187]

Accompanying this village-loyalty was the fatalism typical of most pre-industrial peasants. Limited opportunities, unremitting labor, and a harsh climate combined to make the *contadino* patient, persistent, subservient, and resigned to his fate. Obsequious to the *prominenti* and *padroni* (labor contractors), the peasant had no hope of rising in the world and little chance of fending off disaster. When trouble appeared, he was more accustomed to shrugging his shoulders than to clenching his fist or calling for help. This fatalism made him conservative, cautious, and self-sufficient. He distrusted the police, the schools, the clergy, the government, and the reformers by instinct, remembering that successive regimes in Italy had only despoiled his homeland. Despite the Sacco-Vanzetti legend and the Industrial Workers of the World leadership of the Lawrence, Massachusetts, textile strike, few southern Italians in New England joined radical organizations. Socialist and anarchist leaders like Arturo Giovannitti, Guiseppe Ettor, and Carlo Tresca were not representative of Italian-Americans.[188]

This suspicious outlook on the world retarded group cohesion and community organization in Boston. Unlike the Jewish *Landsmannschaften* and *chevra,* the one hundred Italian mutual aid societies in Boston were only ephemeral sickness and death benefit organizations for Italian men apart from their families in Italy. Often they were operated by *prominenti* in high-handed fashion for personal profit and prestige. In Italy such clubs or lodges existed mostly among urban craftsmen and unionized workers, and the *contadini* had little experience in self-help organizations. The extended family *(famiglia),* which included blood relatives and kinsmen to the fourth degree as well as godparents, was preferred to fraternal or benevolent societies. To members of the family, obligations were absolute, to outsiders, they were non-existent. The *famiglia* defined one's status in the community and pervaded every aspect of life. The individual counted for less than the fortune and reputation of the *famiglia.*[189]

The church was the only institution which rivaled the family, but it was far less important to Italians than it was to Catholics from northwestern Europe. Italian peasants paid scant attention to the clergy and their religion was superstitious to an extreme. Only women, children, and the elderly attended Mass regularly, and the habit of Italian men in talking and smoking outside church during Sunday Mass shocked Irish Catholics in Boston. Some men joined the religious confraternities organized by the clergy to provide charity to the poor, but often for their own purposes—to display power, to win prestige, or for love of ceremony and social life. The celebration of their patron saint's feast day was an opportunity for a holiday, and the *festa* came to the North End streets with the Italian immigrants. But these confraternities and festivals, emphasizing *cam-*

panilismo and regional differences, served to divide rather than unite Boston Italian charity.[190]

The two major charitable organizations for Boston Italians were formed by non-Italians. The Society of St. Raphael began in 1902 to send agents to the Immigration Station in East Boston to offer Italians advice, directions and translators. The Boston Society for the Protection of Italian Immigrants appeared in 1904 for the same purposes, but both were small, under-capitalized American organizations with little influence in Italian neighborhoods. The impersonal, bewildering East Boston Immigration Station was a small-scale Ellis Island. The process—with pickpockets, touts, pimps, and labor contractors hovering outside to prey upon unwary *paesani*—and the danger of deportation for unknown reasons by skeptical officials, confirmed the Italian's suspicion of strangers and his loyalty only to his family and his fellow villagers. The spirit of *campanilismo* became an entrenced attitude restricting the immigrants and their children to the tenements, shops, cafes, and streets of tiny neighborhoods in the North End and East Boston inhabited by relatives and friends from their home town.[191]

This group loyalty led the overwhelming majority of Boston Italians to become manual laborers or factory operatives, not only because of lack of funds, knowledge, and skills, but because they preferred urban poverty with *paesani* to the loneliness of rural New England or Midwestern agriculture as farm hands. The *prominenti* among them did little to encourage migration inland or to farms because their influence and income would vanish if their captive following scattered. Psychologically and financially depleted by emigration costs, and often planning to return to Italy as "birds of passage," most Boston Italians settled into regional enclaves in the city's North End near friends and jobs. Consequently, the North End had nine major Italian groups by 1920—from Abruzzi, Avellino, Calabria, Genoa, Naples, Salernitarni, Sicily, the Piedmont, and Tuscany. These groups even split into smaller enclaves occupying a single tenement or group of buildings on one street, recreating the village society left behind.[192]

But Boston was not Italy, and peasants unfamiliar with urban life ignored health and safety laws and deferred to greedy landlords and avaricious labor contractors *(padroni)*. The Jews, like the Irish and the Yankees before them, deserted the crowded North End on the arrival of this new wave of immigrants, many of whom were "birds of passage," or men who came to work hard and save assiduously to buy land in Italy. With no interest in becoming permanent residents of the United States, they had even weaker community ties than other Italians and were impossible to organize in charity or civic groups. Impoverished but desperate to succeed, they were more likely to put their wives and children to work at home or in small sweatshops than to send them to school or to settlement house Americanization classes.[193]

In some cases, Italian families were disrupted when the father or sons emigrated years in advance of the women and children. Worrisome social workers reported that some men lost contact with or simply deserted their families in Italy and married bigamously in Massachusetts. But little charity or court data has been discovered to indicate that emigration uprooted or disorganized Italian families. Death rather than divorce or desertion was the major hazard Boston Italians faced. However, even if the entire family emigrated, factory labor threatened the family unity so basic to Italian life. Family solidarity was undermined as each member went separately to a job or to school, and at night the home was crowded with boarders and kinsmen, often bachelor "birds of passage" living with a family to save rent costs. This too strained family life and produced child welfare problems. Immigrants adapted to urban industrial America in a variety of ways, but not as quickly or as successfully as some scholars have suggested.[194]

In Italy the wives and daughters of the *contadini* lived in a type of female seclusion after age twelve only slightly less rigid than the purdah in India or the Middle East. Naturally, this was impossible in Boston, and the wayward daughter became a familiar complaint in the Boston Juvenile Court.[195] The Italian family was father-dominated but mother-centered with the father's authority in the home final. Unlike most working-class parents who let their teenage children work before or after school to earn pocket money and to enjoy much freedom in recreation, most Italian parents expected adolescents to contribute earnings to the family budget and regarded play as a waste of time. The sweatshop system of home manufacture suited Italians because their wives and children could earn money by sewing, stitching, and as assembling small items at home. Despite social workers' fears about crowded living quarters and poverty, Italian families, unlike those of other immigrants in Boston, generally had high morale, infrequent resort to public welfare, few broken homes, and low desertion and illegitimacy rates. This was due to their maintenance of traditional values and avoidance of domestic service and outside work for the females.[196]

The Italian sexual code condoned the demure daughter who became a chaste, respectable wife and mother when her parents arranged her marriage. It condemned the unchaste female as *carogna* (whore), no matter how slight her indiscretion. This code denied the girl her natural propensity (in the progressive American view) to be independent, aggressive, dominant, or mischievous, with the result that daughters were often considered more troublesome than sons. Life in the crowded North End streets, with compulsory school attendance until the age of fourteen, weakened parents' customary control of girls, who were a source of anxiety to the entire family for what most American families regarded only as normal adolescent girlishness. If a girl was too plain or shy, the family worried about her failure to attract a good husband, but if she was too attractive or flirtatious, the possibility that she might be seduced was a terrifying threat to the whole family's honor. It was not sufficient that she remain chaste, or, if married, a faithful wife; she must appear respectable by rural Italian standards. If her behavior was too lively, no matter how innocent by American standards, immigrant parents worried constantly.[197]

Although bachelor "birds of passage" who roomed together in North End tenements were "as a rule very lax morally," and sometimes hired a Yankee or Irish housekeeper/mistress for a group of men, they did not relinquish their traditional values. When they married, it was usually with an Italian woman; but without the complex marriage arrangements of their native villages, problems arose. Parents suspected unknown Italian suitors, even decent men from neighboring villages in Italy, and were reluctant to give their consent. The *contadini* tradition of elopement, however, provided a remedy, and some rape cases in Boston courts were actually romantic "abductions" of willing brides whose parents had refused permission to marry.[198]

Some of these cases came to the Boston Juvenile Court, where Italian children accounted for 22 percent of the non-delinquent cases from 1907 to 1927. Most Italian or Italo-American cases (61 percent) were girls charged with sexual offenses. By 1907 one girl was committed to the Lancaster Reform School and another to the House of the Good Shepherd, while in a third case, Maria Petrillo's father warned Judge Baker that Pasquale De-Simone "was going to seduce Maria as he had eleven other women." He begged the judge to save Maria's honor by sending her to reform school, "Please do what you can to get my daughter put away."[199]

A decade later, not all Italian fathers were as cautious as Maria's. In the case of Josephine Gallo, Dr. William Healy noted, "home conditions . . . atrociously bad. Sleeps with father" who "leaves girl on streets at night" or "alone in the house with boarders, where immorality takes place." Josephine was born in Italy in 1903 with congenital syphilis and had "insufficient nourishment" as a child. She had to sleep in the same bed with her father who was a very "emotional and erratic man, nor normal mentally." He was a manual laborer in Boston earning $2.50 per day since his wife died of tuberculosis after three miscarriages, four still births, and five infant deaths. Josephine, the probation officer noted, suffered "ragged tonsils" and "some adenopathy" (which medical authorities considered a cause of emotional instability until the 1930s) and "bites her nails." Disgusted with this "disorganized home," the juvenile court committed her to the custody of the State Board of Charities for "foster home placement." This case, although not typical, demonstrates the many social, medical, emotional, and legal problems found in the most unfortunate immigrant families.[200]

Less disturbing to the court, though still troubling, was the case of Adelina Gagliardo, who was born in Italy in 1902 and came to Boston with her family in 1904. They lived in a "prosperous but crowded" apartment above her father's bakery on Hanover Street. When she eloped with Giacomo Cataldo in 1917, her parents appealed to the Boston Juvenile Court for a solution. The court asked the MSPCC to investigate and its physician, Dr. Martha E. Lovell, who specialized in wayward girl cases, examined Adelina. Then Dr. Healy was consulted but he found Adelina refused to cooperate as willingly as most children. Healy reported she "takes too much in the way of coffee and wine" and he complained that "it seems a pity that such a physically immature girl should have to stand an early chance of maternity."

How emotionally immature she was, we must wonder, because Adelina rejected a court-appointed attorney from the Boston Legal Aid Society and appeared in court with her own attorney upon whose advice she refused to testify or be examined by the Judge Baker Foundation psychiatrists. She eloped because she was dissatisfied when her father withdrew her from school after the sixth grade and forced her to work in his bakery without pay. Dr. Healy had Dr. Bronner see this precocious fourteen-year-old girl. Criminal charges against Giacomo and two other men attracted much newspaper attention and the MSPCC agents were clearly confounded by the sympathy these young lovers had won. Always cautious about public conflict, the MSPCC withdrew from the case, noting that "Dr. Bronner of the Judge Baker Foundation, was especially interested in Adelina, and thought the girl capable of being married and taking care of herself." Healy was also impressed by her and remarked in his court report, "If this marriage does not take place, or if it does, this girl has unusual ability for commercial occupation and could readily support herself well. She seems to have plenty of ambition." He concluded that her theft of $570.00 from her father's shop and the two week elopement was merely an "adolescent self-willed type reaction" to her father's injustice.

Adelina was placed on probation by Judge Cabot and married Giacomo with the Probate Court's permission. When last visited by her probation officer in 1927, she was happily married and living in Medford, but still rebelling against her father. The Gagliardo family moved to California, but Adelina refused to accompany them and insisted that she and her husband remain in Massachusetts.[201] Such a case illustrates the "Italian elopement problem" common in the juvenile and probate courts, as well as the uncertain authority of both juvenile courts and court psychiatrists and the long term follow-up in Massachusetts probation caseloads.

Like many immigrant parents, Boston social workers found Americanized Italian women perplexing whatever their age. Filomena Romano was arrested in 1917 as a fourteen-year-old stubborn child, to wit, "occupying a public street" to sell vegetables despite repeated warnings by the police. Her mother was "very scornful" of this charge, as she was "when the Overseers of the Poor threatened to withdraw $8.00 a week which they were giving if she did not improve home conditions." Josephina Romano was born in Italy and emigrated to Boston in 1901 with her husband and four children. When he died in 1916, she took in three Italian boarders, one of whom fathered her youngest child out of wedlock. The probation officer admitted "this is a trying case on account of the poverty of the family and the plucky struggle Mother made to keep them together." But the children were chronic truants, neglected, and badly clothed, and matters did not improve in 1916 when the Boston Overseers "refused to give further help because they learned that Mrs. Romano had spent over $300.00 on the funeral," and found that the "youngest boy is illegitimate" and that she continued to have two male boarders in the home.[202]

When the child neglect case came before Judge Baker, he had no alternative, as he told a Massachusetts General Hospital social worker who was interested in the case, but to commit the four children to the State Board of Charity's care for placement in the Home for Destitute Catholic Children. But their mother had learned well Amercian ways; she appealed this decision and furnished bail, claiming "she had $600.00 in cash in a bank." Her appeal to Superior Court was successful, and she regained custody of the children and married an Italian barber much younger than herself. The children later appeared in the juvenile court on various charges—peddling without a license, larceny of flour and a box of soap, and stubbornness—but their indomitable mother managed to keep them out of reform school. She continued to pick dandelions and catnip in the countryside to sell in the North End streets, and somehow kept her brood intact if unkempt. When her youngest son was ashamed to peddle vegetables in the market, a BCAS social worker placed him as a farm hand in New Hampshire in 1929, but Alfredo quickly returned to his family when the Yankee farmers "ridiculed his Italian customs."[203]

Like most Progressive Era child welfare experts, Dr. William Healy and his JBF staff were not sanguine about sexually precocious Italian girls. In the case of Julia Bertocci, who eloped with a movie theater usher in 1917, he advised "marriage if the man is decent, probably then she would settle down much," although her mentality was "defective in control—extreme Italian type." Julia was born in Italy in 1901 during her parents' "bird of passage" return to their home village. They brought Julia to Boston in 1902 where they established a modestly successful tailor shop. Like many Italo-American children, she found their old country manners and morals outmoded in the flapper era.[204] Julia was becoming an emancipated young woman and too Americanized for her own good, like her friend, Annunziata. This North End neighbor, Annunziata Bozza, admitted to her teacher that she engaged in sex play with another girl and two Italian boys at a local playground. A social worker at the North Bennett Street Nursery reported this crime to her parents and to the Boston Juvenile Court. The family and the court were both shocked by the sordid details, but Dr. Healy took a calmer view. He doubted that Annunziata was a "defective type, but very defective in control" and was certainly "suffering from a psycho-neurosis." He dismissed this childish incident, saying it was a "question whether sudden yielding to an impulse of a sex nature can be considered much of a delinquency." Judge Frank Leveroni filed this case after reading Healy's report, but the Bozza family was so embarrassed that they suddenly moved to Waltham. When visited by her probation officer a year later, Annunziata referred to the North End as a "pig pen" and her probation officer agreed that her new "surroundings are much different from her former place, much more air and healthier." She neglected to add that suburban Waltham was also much more American than the North End.[205]

Italians made substantial progress in Massachusetts by World War I and many immigrant families like the Bozzas moved from the initial settlement zone to more affluent suburbs around Boston. Old country values persisted, however, and when Elvira Calabrese ran away with her twenty-three-year-old boyfriend in 1917, her assimilated father appealed to the juvenile court for justice as frantically as less Americanized parents had done since 1906 when this court was established. Judge Cabot ordered Elvira to be examined by a physician and requested the Probate Court to waive the customary five day waiting period so the impetuous couple could marry immediately. Dr. Healy's psychiatric opinion was also requested, and, by now thoroughly familiar with such cases, he found Elvira to be the "slight and refined type, very mature for her years" but "quite normal." Healy was impressed with her family, who were an "unusually nice and intelligent type of Italians."[206]

However refined, nice, or genteel Boston Italians became in the 1920s, old country values endured despite social workers, settlement houses, schools, summer camps, Americanization classes, and the determined efforts of the court and the clinic. When Silvia Falcone was arrested for shoplifting at Filene's department store in downtown Boston, her family reacted with a stormy and emotional scene in the juvenile court. This fifteen-year-old girl was the daughter of a North End merchant of the *prominenti* class, who consulted his *paesani* when Judge Cabot sent Silvia to the court clinic for psychiatric evaluation. His friends advised him that Dr. Healy was a doctor for "crazy" people and might send the girl to a mental asylum. On the contrary, Healy diagnosed this as a "special temptation in the face of opportunity—an orgy of stealing" which required only probation and a new pair of eyeglasses for the girl. Her probation officer, however, learned that shoplifting was only a symptom of more serious family pathology. Silvia had stolen $3.25 worth of clothing with her older sister, Alicia, who had been raped in the cellar of their home by one her father's *paesani* while Mr. Falcone was in Italy settling an inheritance. Alicia had a child out of wedlock, to the shame of her entire family, who became extremely strict with both girls. Despite warnings from the probation officer, the parents beat the girls for minor infractions and denied them normal recreation. Silvia rebelled so much that her parents made a stubborn child complaint in court, hoping incarceration would prevent further disgrace. Again Dr. Healy was summoned, and he concluded that this was a "perfectly plain situation."

> Family is much disturbed on account of the experience with her sister. They are all excited about the matter. Much contradiction between father and girl. There has been much scandal and we know the family earlier were very sensitive about the shoplifting affair.

His suggestions were a new job for Silvia, supervised recreation at a North End settlement house, and continued efforts "to educate the family into a more sensible attitude.[207]
Like much of the new child guidance experts' advice, this was facile and futile because the juvenile court probation staff had only limited time and resources to "educate" the parents of mildly delinquent wayward girls. Silvia's probation officer, Miss May Burke, did visit the Falcone home, and she talked with her alone from time to time. Silvia complained that "her father caused scandal by following her on the street at night and this led to talk that she was a 'bad girl.'" Miss Burke agreed that the father was "over-strict," but there was little that she could do to change deeply-embedded cultural values. Matters came to a head when Alicia accused her father of incest; he was acquitted in court, but this shame was insurmountable. Italian daughters were changing rapidly in Boston from the obedient children of Italy to demi-vierges in America. Silvia was not reluctant to appeal to the juvenile court for help in 1926 when her father insisted on taking $12.00 of her $13.00 weekly wages at a biscuit factory and when he insisted that she marry one of his *paesani* or any boy she met more than once. He, in turn, accused Silvia of immoral conduct, and to allay his suspicions, the court ordered her examined by the Massachusetts

Society for the Prevention of Cruelty to Children physician. Dr. Elizabeth MacNaughton reported to the court that "the hymen is not ruptured" but "there is hypertropy of the labia minora" and "findings are consistent with masturbation." At this point, the juvenile court filed the case, and no more was heard from the Falcone family.[208]

By 1919 the Boston Italo-American community gradually began to substitute a spirit of *connazionali* (fellow countrymen) for *campanilismo* as the second generation matured. Italians were more sophisticated about charity and social service after decades of Americanization by Yankee and Irish-American do-gooders and they began to assert their group identity.[209] Like the Irish, Germans, French Canadians, and Poles, Italian Bostonians created their own child welfare institution.[210] Naturally, the oldest and largest group among them assumed leadership in this effort. These were the *prominenti* (or the most successful immigrants) from Avellino, a provincial market town in Italy's Campania region thirty miles east of Naples. The first immigrants from this hilly province arrived in Boston in 1875, beginning a steady chain migration until 1925. Many of these early North Enders achieved considerable success by World War I and held leadership positions in the community.[211]

Most prominent among the Avellino men were: Vincent Brogna (judge), Andrew DiPietro (banker), Felix Forte (judge), Carmine Antonio Martignetti (grocer), Ernest Martini (alderman), Thomas Nutile (fruit dealer), Antonio Polcari (restauranteur), Joseph Santosuosso (attorney), Principio Santosuosso (publisher), and James Sarni (drycleaner). Their families played major roles in the founding of the Home for Italian Children and were major contributors from 1919 to the present.[212] This orphanage, precipitated by the influenza epidemic of 1918, began with a fund-raising campaign in 1919 at St. Leonard's parish in the North End. The pastor, Father Antonio Sousa, a Portuguese Franciscan friar who shepherded the largest Italian parish in the archdiocese, received permission from Cardinal O'Connell to solicit funds for this new orphanage. The assimilated and successful men of Avellino responded as a group to his appeal for funds and support.[213]

Cardinal William Henry O'Connell (1859–1944) did not always enjoy cordial relations with his Italian flock, but he consented to this project partly to appease the most vocal and largest Catholic "national" minority, and partly because the campaign coincided with is own reorganization of Catholic charities.[214] O'Connell was increasingly critical of the older asylums for children that "had been allowed for years to go along in a haphazard way without any sort of supervision or inspection." He intended to change this, but not by professional social workers whom he found "materialistic" and too much like "the pedagogue with his myopic vision, rigid face and his hand on the ruler." O'Connell admired the

Brahmin philanthropies' business-like methods, and he envisioned a board of directors for each Catholic institution composed of pious, practical, and experienced businessmen and attorneys. The Avellino men were just such a group, and from the first the Home for Italian Children received the Cardinal's cautious support.[215]

This fund-raising campaign was very successful by 1921, not only because of O'Connell and the Avellino businessmen, but because Father Sousa and the archdiocesan chancellor, Monsignor Richard J. Haberlin, appealed to other wealthy Italians. A new source of philanthropy in Boston were men like Domenick Albiani, the proprietor of a chain of cafeterias; John Cifrino, a supermarket tycoon; Antonio Tomasello, a building contractor; and the oldest and most distinguished Italian in the city, Giovanni De Ferrari, founder of an import firm in 1856. De Ferrari's talented daughters, Emilia and Louisa, served on the board of directors and attracted other Italian ladies to the HIC. The Avellino *prominenti* founded and controlled the HIC, but Sousa and Haberlin continued to attract a wide range of Italians to this new asylum by appealing to awakening *connazionali* sentiments.[216]

When internal politics threatened the progress of the HIC, Cardinal O'Connell and Monsignor Haberlin, who was president of the corporation from 1919 to 1959, acted firmly to save the organization from the rivalries which had destroyed all previous Italian charities. Judge Frank Leveroni of the Boston Juvenile Court was proposed as a member of the board of directors, but he was identified with Dominic D'Alessandro, a controversial labor union leader and petty banker in the Italian community, and some HIC supporters objected to Leveroni's nomination. Haberlin diplomatically avoided conflict by naming Leveroni the HIC attorney and arranging private meetings for him with the cardinal.[217]

In the same way, when Judge Felix Forte objected to a role in the HIC for Father Mariano Milanese, Haberlin acted with tact and firmness. Forte complained that Milanese sided with the mill owners in the bitter 1912 Lawrence textile workers' strike and was therefore offensive to many New England Italians. There was a rumor that Father Milanese had been rewarded with $250,000 from the Yankee mill owners with which he renovated his Holy Rosary Church in Lawrence and built its school and orphanage. By some accounts he supported the strikers' demands and tolerated the radical leadership of the Industrial Workers of the World, but at the eleventh hour counseled his Italian parishioners to concede. Because this "subterfuge" was remarkably similar to the cardinal's own position on the strike, Haberlin dismissed Judge Forte's demurral.[218]

Forte wrote to the chancellor:

I gather that Father Milanese is not popular with the Italians in his own parish not to mention those who are not connected with this church. I seems that his unpopularity was furnished by the fact that in the last upheavals in Lawrence he has catered to the Mill Owners and not to his parishioners. As a result he has been able to receive enough funds from the Mill Owners and from American friends to build an Orphan Asylum and a School worth about $250,000.[219]

Haberlin replied for His Eminence, who as a boy spent a few weeks working in a Lowell mill but had become one of the most conservative Catholic bishops in the United States. He told Forte "that Father Milanese cannot be passed over or slurred" and must play an appropriate role in the campaign to raise $100,000 for the HIC. O'Connell was eager to secure businessmen and attorneys for his charitable boards, but he did not hesitate to let his flock know who was the shepherd and who were the sheep. Milanese stayed and Forte had to swallow his pride.[220]

O'Connell acted firmly when the contributions for the HIC lagged, donating $5,000 on his own in 1919. He also permitted Sister Mary Valentina, a Franciscan Sister of the Immaculate Conception who had taught at St. Anthony's School in the North End for many years, to operate the HIC with six members of her order. This convinced Italian immigrants who were suspicious of the new institution and unaccustomed to contributing to Catholic charities, that it was indeed their own institution. As another tactful step to build confidence in the HIC, Franciscan friars from St. Leonard's Church in the North End were appointed as the HIC chaplains.[221]

Slowly the larger Italian community was won over, and when Principio Santosuosso became editor and publisher of the Boston *Italian News* in 1921, the major English weekly newspaper for Massachusetts Italians, he too ballyhooed the HIC, as did his brother Joseph, who was a lawyer, physician and politician.[222]

The Home for Italian Children opened on 10 February 1921 with Sister Mary Valentina as superintendent and thirty girls aged four to fourteen in residence. The HIC consisted of a large farmhouse and barn on Centre Street in Jamaica Plain, and was actually a ten acre farm.[223] From 1921 to 1929 only girls were admitted, but due to pressure from Italian families and with the permission of the directors, Sister Valentina accepted boys from age four to twelve by 1929. From 1921 to 1941, there were 216 girls and 115 boys in the Home; the average age for inmates was ten, and the average stay was one year, although the ages ranged from two to seventeen and the children remained from six months to ten years.[224] No children were placed as domestic servants, not only because this practice was declining in Boston child welfare but, more importantly, because it was not customary for Italians to enter domestic service. No children were transferred to other institutions either, as was common at the HAG, HDCC, and HGS. Nor were foster or adoptive family placements made at the HIC prior to 1945. Most children simply remained there until they could return to their

Boston Italians opened their "own orphanage" for girls in 1921 at a Jamaica Plain farm. *(Italian Home for Children.)*

Cardinal O'Connell did not always agree with the *prominenti* on the Italian Home for Children board of directors, 1927. *(Italian Home for Children.)*

parents or relatives or until an older sibling was able to support them.[225] This made the HIC even more anachronistic than the other congregate Catholic institutions in Boston, but, as a recent HIC sister superior argued, "It is inappropriate to apply professional social work standards to Catholic institutions prior to the 1950s because they were doing apostolic work not social work."[226]

The HIC existed because Italian Catholics were dissatisfied with placing their homeless and wayward children in the "Irish institutions," the HDCC, HAG, Daly Industrial School, and St. Vincent's Asylum. Also they recognized that community spirit, something not deeply embedded in the *paesano* but which developed gradually in civic-minded Boston, demanded it. Left largely to their own devices, "because once the Home was established Cardinal O'Connell lost interest in it and Cardinal Cushing ignored it," according to one of the directors, Italian child-savers relied on traditional child-rearing practices like those of any working-class Italian-American family.[227] Young children were indulged, seldom suffered corporal punishment, and given a pasta-rich diet by the Franciscan Sisters. Unlike the Home for Jewish Children, the HIC had no social workers or psychologists on the staff or as consultants until 1960, and had no formal ties to the Boston Juvenile Court or the Judge Baker Foundation.[228] Even the Catholic Charitable Bureau formed only loose bonds with the HIC, although it functioned as a semi-autonomous archdiocesan directorate by 1925. No formal case records were maintained and only the barest data recorded. Like most Catholic asylums of the mid-twentieth century, great secrecy surrounded the HIC because some of the children were born out of wedlock or had parents in prison or mental hospitals. At the very time when most Boston institutions for children were embracing professional social work standards and employing modern psychiatric casework and clinical psychology to help homeless and wayward children, it was ironic that the children of the *contadini* trod this well-worn path to orphanage and Catholic child-saving.[229]

Did Boston Blacks, Jews, and Italians create child welfare services different from those established by the Brahmins and the Irish? It appears so, and these separate but unequal child-saving efforts represented different attitudes and practices in caring for homeless and wayward children. Quantification is neither possible nor useful in this aspect of child welfare, but visitors to asylums and orphanages noted it. Surviving photographs suggest it. Oral history interviews with former inmates and staff members return to this point again and again. "Our Home was as much like an Italian family as we could make it," one HIC orphan recalled. "The Home for Jewish Children was not one of those cold, austere orphanages. We made it very homey for the children and they were really part of the Dorchester and Mattapan Jewish community too," remembered an HJC graduate. Boston's oldest Black member of the St. Vincent de Paul Society insisted, "the Boston colored people before the Depression had too much pride to let a neighborhood child go into an orphanage." No such fond recollections of Pine Farm, the HAG, HGS, HDCC, or Lyman and Lancaster Schools have emerged.[230]

This is hardly the conclusive evidence historians seek, and further research may modify this testimony, but it does point to the pride and independence of the people Mayor James Michael Curley grandly called the "Newer Races." Not content with the increasingly brutal public institutions for wayward children in the 1890s and uncomfortable or unwelcomed in the secular, Protestant, and Irish Catholic private asylums, charitable Blacks, Jews, and Italians established their own child-saving methods for vulnerable working-class families in crisis. When numbers and resources permitted, these "other Bostonians" formed their own ethnic or racial shelters for their own wayward sons and daughters. But in the twentieth century, all child-savers encountered formidable new agencies that would transform child welfare in the generation before the Great Depression.[231]

5

The Boston Juvenile Court and Clinic

The work of the juvenile court is really a work of character building.

—Theodore Roosevelt, 1904

When the Massachusetts legislature established the Boston Juvenile Court on 1 September 1906, a century of charity, child welfare, and specialized juvenile justice coalesced in what was hailed as a humane judicial innovation. The Boston Juvenile Court actually was less an innovation than a combination of well-established concepts and methods with diverse roots in a variety of instruments and agencies of social control and benevolence. The Boston elite had forged a new humanitarian link in the chain which benignly bound the poor to community and control. In the Progressives' juvenile court movement, Bostonians were uncharacteristically tardy, waiting for American courts to recognize the new juvenile courts in other cities before proceeding to establish their own. When they did embrace the juvenile court movement in 1906, however, Boston social reformers quickly assumed a prominent position in this judicial crusade and made the Boston Juvenile Court and its psychiatric court clinic the foremost in the United States.

The juvenile court movement, according to the traditional explanation, was a product of the Progressive Era, launched in 1899 by Jane Addams and her coterie of Chicago settlement house workers, social scientists, reformers, and philanthropists.[1] Dependent and delinquent children were viewed as the innocent victims of poverty, ignorance, and slum conditions, who could be cured by scientific treatment prescribed by physician-like judges assisted by probation officers, social workers, and psychologists.[2] This explanation of the American juvenile court bears only a superficial relationship to the facts, and Chicago's claim to the invention of the juvenile court is questionable.[3] The Boston Police and Municipal Courts used probation in 1830, a practice sanctioned by the Massachusetts legislature in 1836, and had a probation officer in 1843. The Suffolk County district courts held separate juvenile sessions by 1869, and the Board of State Charities appointed agents to attend all trials of juveniles in 1870.[4]

Gardiner Tufts, the first such agent, interviewed the child, parents, police, complainant, and witnesses prior to the court hearing and acted as defense counsel—cross-examining witnesses, introducing evidence and recommending disposition of the case to the court. Tufts was an attorney in the state employ; although "the friend of the child, he also appear[ed] for the state." His aim was to serve the best interests of both the child and the community.[5]

Thus the major components of the juevenile court were devised and implemented in Massachusetts by 1870 and integrated smoothly with an extensive network of private and public child welfare agencies and institutions. Specialized juvenile justice was an early offshoot of the New England child welfare system and foreshadowed national trends by more than twenty years. The juvenile court was not invented in 1899 but had diverse roots—foster care, probation, institutional segregation, equity law, Probate Courts, separate judicial hearings, conferences in judges' chambers, rehabilitation instead of punishment, juvenile delinquency distinguished from crime, and treatment by educational correction. All of these elements contributed to the juvenile court, and Solomon's wise threat to cut the baby in two may have been the first manifestation of the unorthodox juvenile court judge.

Boston courts had been accustomed to dealing leniently with young children because juries and judges were reluctant to imprison those of "tender years" with adults. Even after the juvenile reformatories were established, most young lawbreakers managed to avoid incarceration. By the 1870s, however, the increasing number of juvenile delinquents, as wayward children were then styled, made specialized juvenile justice necessary. First offender's cases were usually placed on file by the court, or the child received a warning and a suspended sentence, especially if his family was known in the neighborhood and the home appeared respectable. Sometimes a local clergyman or politician vouched for the family, and this would satisfy the busy court. If the family was of doubtful character or recent arrival, the child was placed on probation and ordered to report weekly to the Board of State Charities visiting agent. Repeat offenders or juveniles from unsatisfactory families—those with intemperate, immoral, or destitute parents—were liable to be placed by the state agent in a foster home under indenture or sent by the court to private charities (like the Children's Mission, Boston Children's Aid Society, or Home for Destitute Catholic Children) for training and foster family placement. Serious or chronic offenders, despite the leniency of juries and judges toward young children, were incarcerated. The House of Reformation, the Lancaster Reform School and the Lyman Reform School (as the Westborough institution for boys was renamed), or the State primary School in Monson all served this purpose. In the 1870s the House of the

Angel Guardian and the House of the Good Shepherd became Catholic alternatives employed by the Boston courts as private reformatories as the Farm School on Thompson Island and the BCAS Newton and Foxborough farms had been earlier.[6]

Obviously, two or three state agents could not treat the thousands of juveniles appearing annually in Massachusetts courts, so the ubiquitous agents of the private charities quickly filled this need.[7] They made regular and even daily visits to the Boston courts and lock-ups in search of suitable children for their respective asylums, and gradually formed professional alliances among themselves, referring children to each other. Rufus Cook sent Catholic boys to Father Haskins' HAG and to the HDCC in the 1860s, and they in turn referred Protestant boys to the BCAS.[8]

The pioneer work in probation began in 1841 with John Augustus, the "saintly shoemaker." He volunteered to act as bail bondsman in the Boston Police Court for drunkards who seemed willing to reform. By 1843 Augustus paid bail for children accused of petty crimes and supervised their probation, school attendance, work, and home life.[9] After Augustus died in 1859, Joseph Barry of the Children's Mission, Rufus Cook of the BCAS, and Father Haskins of the HAG filled this unoffical role, and later the HDCC and NEHLW agents joined in haunting the courthouse in search of worthy children to save. Genteel asylums for girls, like St. Vincent's Home and the Boston Female Asylum, did not employ agents to recruit girls from the courts as these others did, because few worthy girls were expected to be found in the criminal courts of Victorian Boston. They did admit some "innocent" girls referred by the courts, however, and by 1888 the Society of St. Vincent de Paul employed a full-time agent to visit the jails and courts in search of Catholic boys and girls. These Vincentians formed professional relationships with their Protestant peers and a surprising degree of cooperation resulted, due to the organization's president, Thomas F. Ring, a wealthy member of the Boston Overseers of the Poor and a leading Catholic layman.[10]

All of these child-savers were volunteer probation officers who preferred dependent (i.e., homeless) children accused of no crime, but they also rescued delinquent (i.e., criminal) children charged with petty offenses. The treatment sought basically the same for both groups of children and adolescents—cleanliness, obedience, self-discipline, piety, and orderly work habits. To a lesser extent local clergymen, Sunday school teachers, and (after 1890) settlement house workers also served as unofficial probation juvenile officers with the consent of harried judges. A variety of forms of adult supervision and moral oversight were used to prevent working-class children from falling into the "dangerous classes" or whom commitment to reforms school was necessary. When Charles W. Birtwell succeeded Rufus Cook as the BCAS visiting agent (and later as

General Secretary), he introduced home libraries and savings banks to prevent delinquency by teaching moral values to lower class children.[11]

In this expanding network of child welfare, the courts willingly cooperated, grateful for the volunteer probation services the prestigious private charities provided. Truant officers, who assumed a policeman's role from their first appearance in Boston in 1852, also cooperated with private agencies (partly in the hope that professional prestige might rub off on them) and referred children to the BCAS, HDCC, and other asylums. Individual policemen frequently cooperated too, but more as a result of personal contacts with child-savers than as a result of Police Department policy. Even worried parents in the 1890s began turning to private child welfare agencies for advice about troublesome sons and daughters.[12]

Juvenile probation was clearly a common practice in antebellum Boston and continued throughout the nineteenth century, although the Boston courts did not employ salaried probation officers until 1878, and no juvenile probation officers until 1908. Private agency volunteers sufficed in this role until 1908, and with the cooperation and coercive power of the courts behind them, they exercised considerable influence over the wayward youth and troubled parents of the lower class in Victorian Boston.[13] When Chicago child-savers first considered the idea of a juvenile court in 1895, they dispatched Lucy L. Flower (1837–1921), a prominent Illinois philanthropist (who was born in Boston and adopted by a wealthy New Hampshire abolitionist), to investigate the Boston juvenile sessions and volunteer probation methods. She returned to Hull House with a favorable report of Boston's treatment of juvenile malefactors. Due to her report, Hull House lobbied the bar associations and Illinois legislature, which passed a law in 1899 creating the "first" juvenile court in the United States.[14] Judge Benjamin Lindsey in Denver was also aware of the Boston methods in 1899 when he persuaded the district attorney to prosecute all juvenile delinquents in the city under the state truancy law. From Judge Lindsey's efforts came America's "second" juvenile court in 1901.[15]

* * *

After Boston private charities observed the success of the Chicago and Denver experiments, they organized with the elite Massachusetts Civic League in 1905 to persuade the legislature to create the Boston Juvenile Court which began in September 1906.[16] But even this did not radically alter the juvenile justice and child welfare system that had been operating smoothly since the 1870s. The six Suffolk County (Boston area) district courts continued to hold separate juvenile sessions one day a week in the outlying communities—Brighton, Charlestown, Dorchester, East Boston, South Boston, Roxbury, and West Roxbury. The Boston Juvenile Court had jurisdiction only over the downtown business district and the area bounded by the harbor, the Charles River, and Massachusetts Avenue. More than half of its defendants lived in crowded tenements in the North End, South End, and West End, and only a few were suburban youths apprehended downtown. Even the first probation officers remained the same men as before, Samuel C. Lawrence of the BCAS and John A. Elliott of the Vincentians. Both men continued to act as unpaid probation officers until salaried positions were created in 1908. In most respects, the BJC was merely a codification of the previous juvenile justice and child welfare practices of the city.

Unlike Chicago and most other cities, Boston did not establish a juvenile detention center as part of the court because of the existing network of private institutions in which infants, children, and adolescents could be sheltered or confined until the court heard the cases. The House of the Angel Guardian, Home for Destitute Catholic Children, House of the Good Shepherd, the MSPCC, and other child welfare agencies willingly accepted children at the request of the Boston Juvenile Court probation department. Some children were placed in the MSPCC or BCAS temporary foster homes conveniently located near the courthouse while awaiting hearings. In certain cases, the Suffolk County Jail on Charles Street in the West End detained juveniles apart from adult inmates. Most children, however, were released in the custody of their parents or relatives.[17]

First offenders charged with what the court admitted were "trifling offences" were placed on probation and ordered to see the probation officer weekly at the courthouse, at a neighborhood settlement house or boys' club. The BCAS, Vincentians, and the National Council of Jewish Women routinely served as volunteer probation officers for many children and formed close working relationships with the presiding justice, Harvey H. Baker, and the part-time special justices, Frank Leveroni and Philip Rubenstein.[18]

Judge Baker was aware of the importance of continuing the traditional alliance between the courts and the city's well-established private charities, and he attempted to cooperate with them to avoid commitments to reform schools whenever possible. The private charities were his constituents and colleagues, and like them he believed "that the deterrent effect of commitment is greatly overestimated."[19] When permanent probation officers were appointed to the juvenile court, their work at first differed little from that of their volunteer predecessors. Until the 1930s, the example and influence of the private child welfare agencies remained dominant in the juvenile courts in Boston, Providence, New York, Chicago, and other cities. Moral training for the children of immigrants and lessons in middle-class American values—especially frugality, industriousness, honesty, and self-discipline—were more important in the eyes of judges and probation officers than legal adjudication of guilt or innocence. As one former probation officer remarked:

> Every kid was "guilty" of something! The point was to make sure he didn't return to court again and again and lose his fear of the law and tumble into the juvenile delinquent class.[20]

However much Judge Baker valued the traditional role of volunteers from private agencies, the juvenile court gradually lost its initial informality and systematized its interagency relations. This was partly due to the inevitable institutionalization of the court and bureaucratization of its politically appointed staff, and partly due to the emergence of social work as a career.[21] By 1920 juvenile courts existed in all but two states and judges relied upon written reports by professional probation officers, social workers, psychologists, psychiatrists, and pediatricians for detailed case histories of the individual child and his or her family.[22] The Confidential Exchange established in Boston in 1876 (and in most large cities by 1920) provided a complete list of each family's contact with charitable, social welfare, medical, and educational agencies. The Boston Juvenile Court used this information, which was quickly available by telephone or mail in standardized summary form, to assess the family background of each child. The Confidential Exchange listed the agencies who had assisted or advised the family before, and most of those agencies voluntarily provided the court with information in their records about the child, parents, and siblings. This access to personal information acquired by "friendly visitors" and social workers facilitated the court's investigation and enabled the judge to decide the case in the "best interest of the child."[23] That the Boston Juvenile Court might be prejudiced by unverified information collected in the past by untrained do-gooders was an issue that seemed less important than the court's desire for data upon which to make a scientific diagnosis.[24]

Was Judge Baker justified in this "spying" on the children and families who appeared in his court? This is a difficult question, and one not considered by the judiciary until 1966. To answer it we must consider the legal roots of the juvenile court. The court created in 1906 by the Massachusetts legislature harked back to the medieval English chancery courts of equity, which were designed to apply the dictates of conscience and principles of natural justice rather than the inflexible common law. Under the ancient doctrine of *parens patriae* the court assumed the state's right to act *in loco parentis* for any unsupervised minor.[25]

American courts drew their attitudes toward children from English law codified by William Blackstone (1723–80) in his *Commentaries*. Children were legally infants until the age of fourteen, and until the age of seven were incapable of crime. From age seven to fourteen the child was presumed incapable of committing a felony, although courts could ignore this at their discretion and sentence a young felon to prison or death. By the age of fourteen a child was liable to the full weight of the criminal law, but in American practice, minority often continued to age twenty-one. Victorian childhood imperceptibly merged into majority and adulthood, and adolescence was a term not used before 1900.[26]

Trial of children in adult courts had its roots in the English common law, modified only slightly by *parens patriae*. The state had the power to assume guardianship of any criminal child or one neglected, abandoned, or orphaned by his parents. Family law in America consisted almost entirely of state statutes and state court decisions (with federal courts providing only appellate review of constitutional issues) until the twentieth century. Residual powers gave the states jurisdiction in family matters, resulting in a patchwork of social legislation across the nation. In the 1820s the egalitarian integration of all social classes in public schools was the first major family issue settled. In the 1830s responsibility for dependent and delinquent children emerged as a controversial legal issue.[27] The romantic reformers of the 1840s and 1850s were reluctant to interfere with the apotheosized American family, but church-state separation became an issue when Roman Catholics were denied public funds for the traditional ecclesiastical prerogative of educating children and sheltering orphans and social deviants. The American Catholic Church asserted its protection of the family against encroaching state parenthood throughout the nineteenth century.[28] Yet *parens patriae* was seldom questioned as an inherent duty of American courts, and in the name of paternalism, courts exercised broad authority over minors. The father's legal rights to his children, which were superior to that of the mother, were slowly challenged by the state. Blackstone expressed little interest in children, and under eighteenth-century Anglo-American common law, the expression "children's rights" was a contradiction in terms. Children were the chattels of their father or the ward of the state (in the absence of a parent or guardian), but had no recognized political character, power, or status and few legal rights. The law emphasized the child's duty to his parents, but not the parent's obligations to his child.[29]

This harsh view slowly moderated under the influence of post-Revolutionary humanitarianism, the Enlightenment, positivism, and the rise of urban industrial society. By 1830 it was axiomatic in legal doctrine and educational thinking that children were more than miniature adults of "unripe years" as Americans once believed. They were seen as unique members of society who required special care for the common welfare. Blackstone's dictum that a child of seven years was criminally culpable no longer convinced Americans.

But increasing numbers of children were foundlings, orphans, and delinquents, especially in heterogeneous urban centers, and as states passed new laws and created specialized asylums for homeless and wayward children, the courts were asked to determine constitutional issues. The seminal decision incorporating *parens patriae* into American law was *Ex parte Crouse*. In 1838 a Philadelphia father petitioned the court for a writ of habeas corpus to release his daughter from the House of Refuge. The court ruled against the father on the grounds that juvenile reformatories were residential schools *in loco parentis* to which children could be committed by the state in the best interest of the child under the doctrine of *parens patriae*. This legal view prevailed until 1870 when the Illinois court ruled that reformatories were not schools but prisons for children and that the higher law of parenthood and natural rights preceded *parens patriae*. But this precedent, *People v. Turner,* was overturned in 1882 by the Chicago decision in the *Petition of Alexander Ferrier*. The constitutional basis for juvenile reformatories and child welfare policies was thus established with little controversy.[30] Having a sound foundation in law, the specialized juvenile law courts were an instrument reformers quickly grasped. Discretionary justice, intended to help the courts to help unfortunate children, gave wide latitude to the child-savers.

Proponents of the juvenile court consciously expanded *parens patriae* from dependent children (originally aristocrats' orphans inheriting estates) to the wayward children of the working class who filled congregate reform schools since the Jacksonian Era. Loss of confidence in the rehabilitative power of the reform school led to this expansion of the law and to the emergence of the juvenile court. Reform schools had long been the subject of repeated controversies because of chronic failure to accomplish the purposes for which they had been established. They were widely considered by the 1870s to be schools for crime and warehouses for social deviants. The less expensive, more humane and (it was hoped) more effective child welfare agency and child guidance clinic rose to replace the reform school. The newly professionalized child welfare specialists needed the coercive power of the court to compel parents and juveniles to consent to treatment in the clinics. This need explains the support Boston child welfare agencies gave to the Boston Juvenile Court.

Mugwump or Progressive political and economic ideas were reflected in the child welfare watchwords—efficiency, education, specialization, and individualization. Still, working-class immigrant parents were unfamiliar with middle-class American standards, especially those of Yankee Progressives, so specialized professionals intervened to adjust the "newer races" to American ways. Cultural, moral, physical and psychological defects in urban children were attributed to "unenlightened old country parents," but beneficent, knowledgeable professionals were hopeful that they could overcome these challenges. Progressives like Robert A. Woods of Boston's South End Settlement House led this confident assault on the working-class family in the name of Americanization. Their political ideals shaped a government characterized by pragmatism, utility, and efficiency. Basic research in the physical sciences was consigned to the universities, but for the new social sciences the ethnic community became a laboratory and the juvenile court "the out-patient department of the hospital."[31]

* * *

Harvey Humphrey Baker (1869–1915), who presided over the Boston Juvenile Court from 1906 to his sudden death, was just such a Progressive who influenced the juvenile court movement in the United States by reasons of his prestige and his association with national child welfare pacesetters like Charles W. Birtwell, Dr. Richard C. Cabot and the Boston School of Social Work (later Simmons College). Judge Baker's role has been overlooked in recent studies of juvenile justice and deserves scrutiny. He was a Republican and a Unitarian deacon with deep roots in the Boston Brahmin class. He graduated from Harvard College and Harvard Law School at a time when social work and social sciences were gaining prestige. Harvard Law School began to approach the law "scientifically" under Dean Christopher Columbus Langdell and President Charles W. Eliot (who was a chemist). As a student, Baker served as a friendly visitor to Birtwell's BCAS. Later he was Secretary of the Boston Conference of Child-Helping Agencies and wrote *A Manual for Use in Cases of Juvenile Offenders*. As a Progressive/Republican, he was appointed clerk and then special justice of the Brookline Police Court and was nominated by Governor Curtis Guild as Presiding Justice of the new Boston Juvenile Court. By all standards, Baker was a man eminently qualified for this new judicial position, and his enthusiasm and dedication are apparent from his correspondence in court files and his national reputation.[32]

But Judge Baker was a Victorian bachelor born in 1869 to an upper-class family, and unlike the dynamic Judge Ben B. Lindsey in Denver, he did not relate well or easily to the lower-class children who populated his court. Lindsey confidently discussed work, fighting, sex, venereal disease, and marriage with few inhibitions, while Baker never deviated from the distant, father-like role he created for himself in his court. He realized that "boys will be boys" and that a certain amount of rough-housing was to be expected in slum life, but he showed little understanding of girls who strayed from the cult of true womanhood. Female volunteers did most of the probation work and interviewing with female defendants, and all girls suspected of sexual misconduct were required to submit to gynecological

Judge Harvey H. Baker (1869–1915), first presiding justice of the Boston Juvenile Court in 1906. *(Boston Juvenile Court.)*

Judge Frederick Pickering Cabot succeeded Baker in 1916 and served until 1932.

examination by a MSPCC female physician, usually Dr. Mary F. Hobart, Dr. Elizabeth MacNaughton, or Dr. Martha E. Lovell. They sent reports to the court attesting to the health and virginity of the girl or the "sexual misbehavior" detected. Even "suspected masturbation" was cause for alarm to this extremely prudish judge. All was grist for the Baker mill in scientific diagnosis of wayward and stubborn girls.[33]

Baker was quite interested in making his court as scientific as possible, and to this end he visited the Juvenile Psychopathic Institute connected to the Chicago Juvenile Court. By 1912 he publically advocated establishing a similar court clinic in Boston for "baffling cases." After his death, such a clinic was created and named in his honor. But most of the children in the Boston Juvenile Court were more poor than psychopathic (see Table 5.1). Most of them were the victims of poverty and crowded slum conditions with inept or too strict parents trying to earn a living in an economically unrewarding community with little patience for slowly assimilating immigrant parents and their "maladaptive" children.[34]

Judge Baker assumed a key role in promoting scientific disposition of juvenile cases, but he discovered that this new brand of justice often had to be forced upon unwilling parents and resisting children of the Irish, Italian, and Jewish immigrant neighborhoods in his inner city jurisdiction.

Baker was unaware that it was nothing less than cultural imperialism to impose middle-class Protestant American standards on the children of the poor. When the BJC opened in September 1906 it was both a criminal and a civil court with an adversarial procedure, despite its avowed paternalism. The child appearing before this court risked being fined, committed to reform school or prison, placed in an asylum, sent to a foster family or placed on probation. He did not plead guilty or innocent but was usually cajoled into admitted wrong-doing. Lawyers could represent children in the BJC, but without a jury, an opposing prosecuting attorney, or many of the customary courtroom formalities, and in the face of the court's manifest goals of protecting the child's interests, lawyers' customary tactics had little value. Parents or lawyers who challenged the court risked loss of the child/client, as one witty Boston judge noted:

> Young children, when you prove unfit,
> Are whisked away by sovereign writ.[35]

The Boston Juvenile Court disregarded traditional courtroom procedure to help the child, but Judge Baker admitted he still sat on a raised platform to impress parents and children a little and to have a clear view of the child from his head to the "condition of his shoes." Only a probation officer was present in the courtroom, and if the child was reluctant to talk, Judge Baker spoke with the child alone. He sat near the child to give a friendly pat on the shoulder or a confidential word of encouragement when necessary. If the child denied committing the offense charged against him, "the judge sometimes talks with him at considerable length, reasoning with him, but never threatening him or offering inducements to him directly or indirectly, or asking him to inform on other children unless they are much older than he." Judge Baker believed it was necessary to get the child to admit his offense "because it greatly enhances the efficacy of the subse-

Table 5.1

Boston Juvenile Court, Occupation of Fathers, 1907–1927

	N = 216
High White Collar	3%
White Collar	16
Skilled	26
Semi-skilled	25
Unskilled	25
Unemployed	5

This sample from the Boston Juvenile Court consisted of all 514 children who appeared in the court in 1907, 1917, and 1927 as wayward, stubborn, or neglected children. Occupations of 216 could be determined. All charts in this chapter refer to this sample.

quent treatment of the case." It made the child more willing to follow the court's treatment plan, and it made his parents more willing "to accept the intervention of the judge and probation officers and to cooperate with them" if an admission of guilt was obtained. Otherwise, "they regard the judge as a tyrant and the probation officer as an intruder."[36]

Judge Baker presided over a court with a broad mandate, and he boasted that "the court does not confine its attention to just the particular offense which brought the child to its notice," which might only be a superficial symptom of more serious problems. "For example, a boy who comes to court for some such trifle as failing to wear his badge when selling papers may be held on probation for months because of difficulties at school; and a boy who comes in for playing ball in the street may (after the court has caused more serious charges to be preferred against him) be committed to a reform school because he is found to have habits of loafing, stealing, or gambling which cannot be corrected outside."[37] This court exercised wide discretion and disregarded constitutional rights of the defendants to provide even greater protection to children. Its good intentions notwithstanding, this practice degenerated into the tyranny of reform, as juvenile courts (presided over by men and women less lofty in spirit than Judge Baker) infringed on the equal protection clause of the Constitution and were under-inclusive by subjecting the child to legal sanctions while leaving the parent, who shares responsibility for his child's conduct, untouched by the law. Juvenile courts' willingness to impose state care and custody on children and to violate family privacy was tolerated because most defendants were young, poor, urban immigrants who needed "adjustment" or "Americanization." Not until 1966 did the United States Supreme Court restrain the juvenile court, noting, "The child receives the worst of both worlds; that he gets neither the protection accorded to adults nor the solicitous care and regenerate treatment postulated for children."[38]

The Supreme Court in 1966 condemned the "procedural arbitrariness" of the juvenile court which Judge Baker had obscured by attention to legal niceties, by notifying parents and children of court appearances, and by his courtesy to attorneys. The warning of Justice Louis Brandeis that "experience should teach us to be most on guard to protect liberty when the government's purposes are beneficent," did not seem to apply to the Boston Juvenile Court under the benevolent Judge Baker.[39] When he sent his probation officer, Clarence E. Fitzpatrick (1907–11), to a police station in the South End, Baker intended only to collect additional data upon which to make an objective, enlightened decision in the case of William Falls. This sixteen-year-old stubborn Black boy was well known to officers Murphy and McNally: "Both were of the opinion that the boy was lazy and would not work. At present not vicious or bad, but constant loafing as at present would soon make him bad." When Fitzpatrick questioned the headmaster of the Parental School (a special city truant school), he recalled William was "a good boy while here; not over-bright in his studies, but just about passable." With this testimony in hand, Fitzpatrick concluded in his probation report: "It is hard to do anything for him because he cannot adapt himself to any position. He can never do anything that will require brain work. Possibly the only thing that he will ever be able to do is washing windows, doing chores about a house or store, or similar work." Judge Baker read this report and concluded that this Black "boy was lazy and shiftless" and placed William on probation, ordering him to report weekly to Mr. Fitzpatrick, who had just collected all of this prejudicial evidence against him. This hardly seemed fair, but more remarkable is the fact that no other evidence or testimony existed against William Falls. He was adjudicated a juvenile delinquent and placed on probation indefinitely on the hearsay evidence of two neighborhood policemen and a truant school principal who had not seen him in two years. Ironically, he continued to live with his mother in a South End apartment and found himself a job as an elevator operator while on probation. Did William require court supervision? Why was he placed on probation? Perhaps another case will illustrate the Boston Juvenile Court "policy" on stubborn boys.[40]

John Cavello's father complained to the juvenile court clerk, Charles Williams, in 1907 that his sixteen-year-old son "could not hold a job" and was "out drunk every night." John and his father were summoned to Judge Baker's court a week later and Clarence Fitzpatrick was instructed to make an investigation. A month later, the busy Fitzpatrick reported that John was born in Boston but raised in Italy for ten years, and could speak no English. Still, he "seems to be a very nice boy anxious to work and ambitious. He was educated in Italy and is much smarter than the general run of Italian boys his age." With no other evidence but his own intuition, Fitzpatrick (who spoke no Italian) recommended probation, which Judge Baker imposed, and Fitzpatrick told John "to drop around once in a while to the court and let us know how things were progressing."[41]

Why such different attitudes toward two Boston boys charged with the same offense? Was it because William was Black and John was white, or one a Protestant and the other an Italian Catholic? William's mother made the complaint on the advice of the police while John's father was advised by North End *paesani* to teach the boy a lesson by bringing him to court. Did the origin of the complaints influence the court treatment of these two boys? These questions cannot be answered, because no data exists by which Boston Juvenile Court probation reports and case dispositions can be measured. They were idiosyncratic, arbitrary, and subjective decisions. The court made such decisions informally without prescriptive laws or rules, deciding each case individually "in the best interest of the child." But parents and the court often agreed, as demonstrated in the case of Harold Walsh.

This thirteen-year-old stubborn boy was sent to the Westborough State Reform School in 1907 by Judge Baker on equally intangible evidence. His mother had divorced Harold's father because he was "very intemperate" and she "fully realizes the danger the boy is in and fears—in view of the fact that the boy's father was such a dissipated character—that unless stringent measures are taken the boy may develop into a criminal." When the House of the Angel Guardian and the Working Boys' Home both failed to reform Harold to the satisfaction of his mother and the juvenile court, Judge Baker sent him to the Westborough school and persuaded his mother to pay $1.00 per week for his board. This was a case of preventive detention intended to preclude juvenile delinquency by the strict discipline of the reform school. Harold's crime under Massachusetts law was a status offense. He was a stubborn child who failed repeatedly to heed the commands of his mother, and when she applied to the juvenile court for help in controlling her son, the court complied with the protective custody of the state reform school.[42]

This case demonstrates the seriousness with which Judge Baker took his responsibility to be an "over-parent" to the children of the poor. In a case of a middle-class child who was in danger of becoming delinquent due to inadequate parental care, Judge Baker personally contacted the father of Edward Porter and suggested a private boarding school placement before court commitment was necessary. For lower-class children, he did not hesitate to use public institutions as a kind of boarding school to correct problems the child's parents would not or could not correct.[43] This was true with Sam Rosen, who appeared in the court for loitering at a railway station. Judge Baker regarded this as a "trifling matter in itself, but the condition of the boy's eyes, and the blindness of his mother, led us to hold him under oversight in order to make him wear his spectacles and use the medicines which the Eye and Ear Infirmary had prescribed." But Sam was "careless about keeping his engagements with the court and never seemed to be at all aroused to the seriousness of the trouble with his eyes." He continued to loiter with his gang on West End streetcorners and was suspected of petty theft and jack-rolling (robbing drunks). Finally, Judge Baker sent Sam to the Westborough reform school as a stubborn child, "first: to preserve his own eyesight, and second: to preserve the community from his wrong doing." It is important to note that Sam had been charged and proven guilty of nothing but too light a regard for Judge Baker's advice. He was accused of no crime, and the stubborn child complaint was made at Judge Baker's insistence.[44]

Boston "newsies" worked and played in city streets, often appearing in the Juvenile Court for trivial offences, 1917. *(Lewis W. Hine Collection, Library of Congress.)*

Clearly the Boston Juvenile Court exercised its power over the powerless with the best intentions in mind, but arbitrary authority is tyranny whether inflicted on the young or the old. Abe Perlmutter's only crime was that he "had a bad temper," and the court physician reported: "I do not find him insane or feeble-minded. . . . I believe that . . . he can learn to control himself to a safe degree." But Judge Baker kept a stubborn child charge pending to retain oversight of this case. He told Abe that the "new case was kept to steady him if he gets off his head."[45] This extraordinary judicial concern extended to Bart Greeley's bold request from the Westborough reform school for his girl friend's address, which the Clerk of Court refused to send because she was placed in a BCAS foster home.[46] Later John Murphy, who "had become addicted to the cigarette habit," was a worry to the court because, "This boy has done no work for two years, even though he has a widowed mother who has to work hard to support this big fellow. This fellow is one of the laziest, if not *the* laziest, that we have ever had in this court." Further investigation by the probation officer revealed John was a victim of the "self-abuse" habit, which was obvious (to the court!) from his appearance and demeanor. When he desisted, however, his appearance improved and "it will continue to improve if the boy can overcome this habit." A detailed list of the stores where John confessed to have purchased the cigarettes illegally was forwarded to the police for further action.[47]

As petty, trivial, inconsequential, and absurd as these cases may seem to the modern reader, they were quite serious indications to the Boston Juvenile Court of how children went astray. Serious, mature public officials investigated these puerile matters as part of a well-planned campaign to prevent juvenile delinquency in Boston. Occasionally, however, even the resourceful Judge Baker encountered an adolescent social deviant for whom nothing in the court's repertoire seemed appropriate.

Charles Harris was a very perplexing problem for his mother, his stepfather, the police, and all who met him. Charles was a sixteen-year-old hermaphrodite, with both male and female genitalia and severe enuresis. This made him a loathsome pariah, and his step-father abandoned the family when his mother refused to leave Charles. He was brought to the juvenile court by a policeman for being "wild, irresponsible, and rebellious" in the streets and for "bunking out in the subway and leading other boys astray." His mother was persuaded to sign a stubborn child complaint and the court ordered a thorough medical examination of the boy. When Charles ran away from the hospital, his probation officer, Samuel C. Lawrence reported that Charles continued

> to run wild about the streets, sleeping in doorways and sheds, associating with thieves, and causing anxiety to the police and citizens. His condition, owing to his infirmity, is so repulsive that the police have on one occasion turned him loose rather than hold him in the police station. He seems to be in mortal dread of hospitals.

The court found no solution or placement for this boy until the Boston Municipal Court committed him to the Concord Reformatory. The juvenile court closed this case in 1909, heaving an official sigh of relief that this troublesome boy was at last in custody.[48]

Still, few children were as disquieting as Charles Harris, and the juvenile court did not exercise arbitrary power in all cases. Judge Baker was aware of the low status of his court in the view of the Massachusetts judiciary, and he avoided reversal of his decisions by the Suffolk County Superior Court by prudent use of his authority. Parents dissatisfied with Baker's rulings could appeal the case to the Superior Court, which has appellate jurisdiction. The appeal consisted of a trial *de novo* with a judge (or judge and jury) unfamiliar with juvenile justice and more formal in its procedure. The rate of reversal, which Judge Baker estimated as six out of seven cases in 1910, was discouragingly high. In 1909 and 1910, for example, twenty-six of the thirty juvenile court decisions appealed resulted in reduced

Table 5.2

Boston Juvenile Court Defendants' Ethnicity, 1907–27

	1907 N = 226	1917 N = 170	1927 N = 118	Total N = 514
Irish	27%	21%	8%	21%
Jewish	11	9	6	9
American	8	2	9	7
Italian	6	22	17	14
Black	4	7	1	4
English	4	1	0	2
Canadian	1	6	2	3
Polish	1	3	5	3
Portuguese	1	1	1	1
German	0	1	1	.6
Syrian	0	1	0	.5
Other	0	5	35	10
Unknown	35	20	15	25

SOURCE: See Table 5.1.

Ethnicity was determined by birthplace of parents, by ethnic labels used in court records (i.e., Hebrew, Afro-American), and, in a few doubtful cases, by surnames.

sentences (probation instead of reform school), and the following year only two out of twenty-three appeal decisions upheld Judge Baker.[49]

This restraint on the Boston Juvenile Court was regretted by Judge Baker because it prevented him from committing as many children as he would have liked. He imposed milder sentences in many cases to avoid appeals that would result in less oversight of unsupervised wayward children. As he commented, the result was that children "will go without any oversight or control" when his court, "realizing how great the chance is that children will go free on appeal, refrains in many instances where parents will not acquiesce from insisting on much needed commitments." He rationalized his court's low rate of reform school commitment by arguing that the shame which middle-class families felt about reform schools did not inhibit lower-class immigrant families (see table 5.2).

But Judge Baker was too pessimistic when he said that the shame factor was "slight in the congested districts from which most of the court cases come." To argue that poor families valued respectability less than middle-class families was merely to repeat the age-old fallacy that the poor must love their children less because they provide less for them. It was a specious argument used traditionally to disparage poor relief, orphanages, reform schools, and other social welfare programs. The poor were misunderstood as cold, callous, heartless parents eager to abandon their children to the state's care to avoid the expense and trouble of raising them. This class warfare underlay the BJC view of shameless parents and saucy children for whom reform school was not a deterrent and the law was lightly regarded.[50]

Not only was this argument specious, but it is contradicted by later sociologists' labeling theory which contended that court appearances reinforced the predelinquent child's misbehavior and attached to him a stigma which translated into social handicaps. These were increased police surveillance of the child, rejection by teachers, classmates, neighbors, friends, relatives, and employers, and less tolerance by school authorities and his own family. This labeling process was ignored by juvenile courts, but not by adults responsible for children. An appearance in court for a trifling matter like violation of a city ordinance or for victimless crimes like status offenses could evoke bias in adults and cause in a child antisocial behavior and differential associational patterns (like shunning a "bad boy" as a troublemaker) that became a self-fulfilling prophecy. Recidivism had a basis in how the neighborhood treated a boy who had been to court, and this contributed to the evolution of a dependent child into a juvenile delinquent quite independent of the efficient paternal services the Boston Juvenile Court offered children.[51]

Max Cohen appeared in the juvenile court four times in two years, but he was hardly a chronic delinquent. Max was accused of selling fruit without a license and obstructing the sidewalk in his West End neighborhood. The "police complain he persists in peddling fruit in the street in front of George's Fruit Store and in North Station despite repeated warnings." He was the fourteen-year-old son of Jewish immigrants from Russia and had no license because he was ineligible for one while on probation.

Max was on probation for peddling without a license. This catch-22 predicament failed to impress Judge Leveroni, who gave the boy a suspended sentence to the Westborough reform school as a stubborn child. Was Max stubborn or persistent? His probation officer, Hans Weiss, who was himself a Swiss immigrant and sympathetic to many boys in the street trades, reported Max was a "rather bashful, self-conscious typical adolescent" whose "great ambition is to make money" as "a successful peddler." His Horatio Algeresque drive, however, was out of fashion in the Boston Juvenile Court by 1927, and his failure to keep appointments with Weiss and Judge Cabot proved very annoying to the court. The policemen in the West End tenement neighborhood continued to warn and to arrest Max, who earned quite a reputation as a nuisance. Further investigation by Weiss discovered that Max's father died as a psychotic patient at the Boston State Hospital and there was "considerable friction between the boy and his older brother" and "very lax discipline and much street life" was considered an aggravating factor.. On the other hand, Max had done well in school and his street life consisted of peddling fruit and hanging out with his peers outside a Jewish delicatessen in his old neighborhood several evenings from 6:00 to 9:00 p.m.[52]

Was Max a suitable candidate for juvenile court oversight and possible commitment to reform school? It is, of course, impossible to second-guess the court, but the comments of David F. Tilley, a contemporary Boston social worker, offer an insight. Tilley told the National Conference of Charities and Corrections session on prison and police administration that some of his problems in counseling boys on parole and probation arose from the overzealousness of the Boston Police. The cops on the neighborhood beat know the boy who has a record:

> When anything goes wrong in the neighborhood where that boy lives, the police officer is inclined to believe him responsible and it is almost impossible for him to get a fair start. I know from experience how hard it is to get an officer to feel an interest in that boy. He thinks he is no longer susceptible of anything good.[53]

The subjective opinion of the policeman accounted for the fact that few working-class boys reached maturity without a brush with the law. The Irish cops winked at gambling and drinking in the West End, but were more strict about violations of city ordinances and morals offenses. Also the genial Irish cop of legend was often anti-Semitic and not over-fond of the "newer races" from central and southeastern Europe. In Max's case, he was a young Jew selling fruit in competition with a licensed fruit store, and the Boston Police took a dim view of such unrestrained competition, especially when the store owner paid rent, taxes, and, perhaps, petty graft to the city authorities. It was easy for a persistent boy like Max to develop an unsavory reputation in the eyes of the local police and to compile a record in court which almost sent him to reform school. The cop on the beat, "a proud man drest in a little brief authority," was a street-level bureaucrat who Americanized the immigrants, much more practically than the settlement house or social worker.

It is ironic to recall that the "newer races" were assimilated by daily contact with Irish and Irish-American Bostonians, not with Yankee natives. The Italian, Jew, and Lithuanian heard the English language spoken with a Celtic lilt more often than with the accents of Beacon Hill or a Yankee twang.[54] In the ethnic ballet in every American city, the newly arrived immigrants succeeded those who had come in earlier waves from Europe. In Boston, the Irish moved from the North End and West End slums to more respectable residential districts in the South End, South Boston, and Dorchester, leaving their former tenement homes to the more recently arrived Jews and Italians. The Irish dominated the police and fire departments by 1880, as well as the streetcar jobs and lower echelon

Newspaper boy "stealing rides" on a Boston streetcar, 1909. *(Lewis W. Hine Collection, Library of Congress.)*

positions in public schools, courts, and government offices. It was these petty officeholders, not Yankees or Brahmins, who made the daily decisions affecting the lives of the "Hebes" and the "Guineas." As the journalist Theodore White recalled, it was an Irish motorman who decided if young Teddy could sell newspapers on a streetcar, not the School Department which issued his newsboy's badge or the Boston Elevated Train Company which permitted hawking in the cars. By such petty decisions was a boy's life made happy or horrible.[55]

Boston Juvenile Court reluctance to risk reversal by the Superior Court did not prevent the judges from committing a larger number of girls than boys to private and public institutions. More girls were institutionalized than boys, as Table 5.3 shows, because the Victorian double standard was still operative and most girls' offenses were sexual. The judges were more cautious about female cases and much less likely to dismiss or file a girl's case than they were a boy's. All girls on probation had female probation officers, but there were fewer female officers. Consequently fewer girls were placed on probation. Once a girl entered the benevolent BJC network, for whatever reason, she was retained under closer and longer court control than her brothers.

Sometimes the Americanized daughter of overly strict immigrant parents preferred Lancaster Reform School or the House of the Good Shepherd to her own home. This was true of Olympia Cappella, a sixteen-year-old girl whose father signed a stubborn child complaint in 1907: "That girl would not work except in a shop or office and was not fit for that. She flatly refused to work in a candy factory." She left home and lived for two weeks in a North End boarding house on her savings "to give her parents a scare and make them allow her more liberty and stop nagging her." Olympia's objection to work in a candy factory, which was a common job for Boston adolescents before WW II, was "based on the fact that Mother would call for her after work each day there." A volunteer probation officer from the Society of St. Raphael for the Protection of Italian Immigrants, Miss Eleanor Colleton, said "she was pretty sure the girl had not committed any immorality, but that even the girl herself realized she was in great danger and was agreeable to being sent to Lancaster." Olympia's older sister was a Lancaster alumna and Judge Baker accepted this solution because a foster family placement "was not acceptable to the parents." Like many working-class immmigrants, the Cappellas feared the loss of their daughter to middle-class values in a social worker's foster home, but they also feared the precocious sexuality of their Americanized daughter. To them the somewhat notorious Lancaster state reform school seemed an acceptable compromise. There she would be safe from designing males and would return home chastened and ready for a decent married life.[56]

The juvenile court found a more compelling reason to commit Pauline Axelrod to Lancaster when she was arrested at 2:00 A.M. in the Scollay Square redlight district. Pauline was the fourteen-year-old daughter of Russian Jewish Immigrants who lived in the West End, and "she has frequently been in company with a girl," Agnes Town, known as "a bad girl and an actress." Dr. Mary F. Hobart examined Pauline for the court and discovered that her hymen had been ruptured recently and that she had gonorrhea. With this report in hand, Judge Baker did not hesitate to send

Table 5.3

Boston Juvenile Court, 1907–1927, Disposition of Cases by Gender

	Dismissed	Filed	Probation	Public Instit.	Private Instit.	Public Agency	Private Agency
Male N = 245	11%	5%	15%	10%	20%	17%	22%
Female N = 220	1%	2%	6%	17%	34%	8%	32%
Total N = 474	7%	4%	11%	13%	26%	13%	26%

SOURCE: See Table 5.1.

Pauline to Lancaster. She was unsuitable for palliative methods by reason of "her unfeminine misconduct" and her parents did not appeal the judgment.[57]

Most girls were not arrested in such compromising circumstances, however. More commonly, distraught parents asked a child welfare agency or settlement house for advice on controlling their wayward daughters. Many of these cases were referred to the Boston Juvenile Court by the city's child welfare agencies. When Naomi Morris, a sixteen-year-old "American" girl born in Boston, came to the BCAS with her mother, the social worker recommended a stubborn child complaint. Naomi's mother, a spiritual adviser and the proprietor of a disreputable boarding house, consented. She told the court that Naomi "stayed out until eleven or twelve at night with any man who would ask her" and had been pregnant twice and "took drugs." The probation officer's investigation revealed that Naomi's sister "was constantly in the society of men" and Naomi "probably was in immoral relations with men" also. This sexual licentiousness and drug abuse was simply too deviant even for the progressive BCAS to treat. Without delay, the BCAS social workers supported the BJC probation officers' recommendation that Naomi be sent to Lancaster.[58]

The juvenile court admitted that reform school was an inappropriate remedy for most dependent children, especially girls who often adjusted to foster home placement more quickly than boys did. But sexual deviance constituted strong grounds for reform school commitment, and Judge Baker did not fear reversal on appeal in such cases. The story of Ellen Morelli illustrates the court's distinction between dependent and delinquent girls. When her immigrant father first asked the Clerk of Court to issue a stubborn child complaint, he was refused because of lack of sufficient evidence. Ellen had committed no illegal act and was only dissatisfied with home life and wanted to join her best friend, Olympia Cappella, at the Lancaster School. Three months later, Mr. Morelli again applied for a complaint and this time Ellen was summoned by Judge Baker. She was defiant in court and refused to return home, so Baker sent her to Mrs. Harvey's House, a temporary foster home operated by the MSPCC to detain children for the court. Two weeks later Ellen almost got her wish, she was sent by the court to the House of the Good Shepherd for one year. This disposition was made on the advice of Miss Colleton of the Society of St. Raphael, who was an Italian-speaking teacher at the Paul Revere School in the North End and familiar with both Olympia and Ellen.

After Ellen's discharge from the HGS, which some Italians in Boston regarded as a sort of convent school like those in the old country, Judge Baker retained oversight by simply not closing the Morelli case. In 1908 he was surprised to learn that Ellen had married without his consent and was living with her husband in East Boston. His final notes in the probation record demonstrates the deepening concern middle-class child-savers had for wayward working-class children. He grumbled that "as the marriage appears to be genuine I suspect there will be nothing for me to do but dismiss it."[59] Shortly thereafter, his probation officers were instructed to make periodic follow-up inquiries on all active cases, even when the child returned home from court ordered placements.

These are not the actions a harried judge or an indifferent bureaucrat overwhelmed with paper work. Judge Baker took his cases very seriously and was reluctant to end his oversight of a child until all the loose ends were tied. He was strict and aloof and unwilling to pose as a friend to a child like some avuncular juvenile court judges. To reform a stubborn girl known to be sexually active, Judge Baker even took the unusual step of detaining Minerva Talbot overnight in the Suffolk County Jail. He had personally investigated her case and "tried to arouse her by letting her spend a night in jail." This extraordinary step he dared to take because "I feel such a mixture of Indian and Negro blood as I understand exists in her case makes a very difficult character to deal with." He may have been racist, but he was hardly indifferent. When he committed Minerva to Lancaster, Baker wrote about her to Superintendent Fanny F. Morse asking to be informed of her progress. From time to time, Baker visited Lancaster, about thirty miles west of Boston, to see for himself how the girls from his court were being "adjusted."[60]

Judge Baker found girls' sexual misconduct especially troubling, and unlike his charismatic colleague in Denver, Judge Ben Lindsey, he "never talks with girls alone as he sometimes does with boys." His successor, Judge Frederick Pickering Cabot, another Boston Brahmin bachelor, also found delinquent girls embarrassing and depended on female probation officers or volunteers to interview them. Judge Baker found Italian girls particularly troubling and said, "I never entertain these complaints without having some woman familiar with the Italian language investigate."[61] The language barrier was not as formidable as the cultural barrier for the juvenile court and lingering prudery added to the embarrassment judges felt in dealing with sexual offenses by the more "volatile" Italian and Jewish girls.

Irish girls were also a problem, but of a more familiar type. Lillian Ryan was arrested for associating with a South End boys' gang, the Forty Thieves. The police reported she was constantly loitering with them in a public park and even judged a urinating contest late one night. She was not accused of sexual misconduct, however, and when she was committed as a wayward child to Lancaster or to the HGS, her family used political influence with the district attorney to thwart the commitment.[62] This was a less shocking issue for the genteel juvenile court, which bowed to the district attorney's clout.

Sexual deviance was a troubling and primarily female problem, but the juvenile court received little cooperation from social workers in prosecuting adults who seduced young girls. When Louise Harrigan "finally admitted to a great deal of wrong-doing with several persons," she was sent to Lancaster, but Judge Baker wanted to prosecute the man who paid her rent and reportedly seduced her. In this case, the BCAS was unwilling to become involved and Charles W. Birtwell asked Baker to discuss it with one of his female social workers acquainted with Louise:

> Tell me whether you think the girl is too reticent to make prosecution practicable, and as to whether, even if she would tell all she knew, it would be best, all things considered—the girl's welfare as well as that of the public—to prosecute.[63]

* * *

Most social workers were more interested in psychiatry by 1915 than in acting as an arm of the court or prosecuting lawbreakers. There was, however, one agency still eager to serve as the eyes and ears of the juvenile court. The Massachusetts Society for the Prevention of Cruelty to Children (MSPCC) had been founded in 1878 for such a purpose. The general secretary, Frank B. Fay, was a founder of the Lancaster School and a leading member of the Massachusetts Prisoners' Aid Association until he retired in 1903 at the age of eighty-two. MSPCC agents continued to work closely with Boston courts under Fay's successors, C.C. Carstens and Theodore A. Lothorp. Lothorp was a wealthy Boston attorney and author of a manual on child welfare laws. Judge Baker delegated all child abuse and neglect cases to the MSPCC, whose agents were in the court daily. The court and the MSPCC shared an activist approach more akin to the nineteenth-century child-savers than to the modern social workers, who were content to wait for clients to apply at their office for professional counseling.[64]

The case of Althea Ferguson illustrates the tenacity with which the juvenile court and the MSPCC attacked child abuse. She was a four-year-old child living in Boston with her mother, an Irish Catholic domestic servant. When her mother was reported to be living with a Chinese man and his white wife in a China Town tenement, the juvenile court asked the MSPCC in 1917 to investigate. Miss Claire Marstens, an MSPCC agent, visited the apartment with two Boston policemen, and in her report she described this raid:

> At the time of the investigation, the mother, Lee Jing and Sue Chin were in the kitchen. In the adjoining room a Chinaman was sleeping. Lee Jing was drunk, and was placed under arrest by the officers. An unlicensed dog was taken out of the house by the police.[65]

MSPCC agents investigated this West End immigrant family in a BJC neglect case in 1908. *(Massachusetts Society for the Prevention of Cruelty to Children.)*

Althea's mother was found to be "feeble-minded, mentality ten years, and is a moral imbecile." She worked as a maid for the Chin family for only $2.00 per week (and board for herself and her child) and was suspected of "engaging in immoral relations with men." The court ordered the child to be sent to her maternal grandparents in Lowell, but eight months later the MSPCC was still on the trail and found Althea boarded out with an interracial Chinese couple in Cambridge. Again a neglect charge was made in the juvenile court, and Althea was sent to the HDCC and later placed with her grandparents. But neither the court nor the MSPCC dropped the matter, and in 1922 the mother was investigated again and found to be "working for some Chinese caring for children brought there daily." She had three illegitimate children and had been aided by ten Boston charities. Only in 1923 did Judge Cabot file this case, but he announced that he was still willing to reopen it if Althea "was not doing well at the grandparents in Lowell."[66] The fact that this girl lived in a "broken home" was not remarkable, but an interracial and immoral home was so scandalous that the court and the MSPCC maintained an active interest in it for seven years.

This unrelenting vigilance was a hallmark of both the court and the MSPCC in cases involving "moral turpitude." Undoubtedly, sexual relations between white women and Chinese men inflamed the Ferguson case, but the feeble-mindedness of Mrs. Ferguson added to the debauchery. In the juvenile court's view, debauchery took many forms. Francois Martin was a neglected child in 1917 because of truancy. A truant officer reported his family to the MSPCC, who investigated for the court and found Francois' school record "serious," but his parents' "drunkenness" was the "immediate occasion for our asking for a complaint." Alfred F. Whitman, the MSPCC agent, found earlier complaints from the police about the Martin family, who were also the subject of repeated anonymous letters objecting to their chronic drinking. Visitors to the dirty basement apartment in the West End "found the boy well" but the parents engaged in a drunken "stormy scene." Francois was sent to the HDCC by Judge Cabot and placed in a respectable Cape Cod foster family. Later the boy was living with his uncle in Connecticut, and the Humane Society investigated a complaint that his uncle forced him "to do very hard work" in the uncle's restaurant. The juvenile court remained officially involved in this case for six years, demonstrating perseverance of the court and its resolute ally, the MSPCC, in neglected child cases. This French-Canadian alcoholic family was worthy of prolonged investigation, although no physical or psychological abuse was ever charged. It was purely a case of the "immoral influence" on an eleven-year-old boy by his chronically drunken immigrant parents. Such attention is evidence of the seriousness with which the Boston Juvenile Court considered child welfare issues in 1917.[67]

The low status of the juvenile court—demonstrated by the high rate of reversal by the appellate court and the rejection of moral police functions by scientific social workers—was to result in a new and self-conscious role for the Boston Juvenile Court. This court abandoned its judicial identity to a surprising degree in an attempt to redefine itself as something other than a short-pants criminal court. The court under Judge Baker was a new type of court less concerned with adjudicating than curing socially maladjusted youngsters, and placing "each child who comes before it in a normal relation to society as promptly and as permanently as possible."[68]

Judge Baker used a medical model to describe the function and purpose of his court. The judge was like a physician, the courtroom was equivalent to a doctor's examining room, and the probation officer an intern or "social physician" or nurse assisting the Doctor/Judge. Baker proudly claimed "there is no more formality of arrangement or attendance" in his court "than there is in a physician's examination room." In its daily process the juvenile court followed "the procedure of the physician."

Judge and probation officer consider together, like a physician and his junior, whether the outbreak which resulted in the arrest of the child was largely accidental, or whether it is habitual or likely to be so; whether it is due chiefly to some inherent physical or moral defect of the child, or whether some feature of his environment is an important factor; and then they address themselves to the question of how permanently to prevent the recurrence.[69]

In the case of a boy appearing for trivial offenses, such as violation of minor ordinances, and without aggravating circumstances in the family background report, "the judge sees him only once more, to examine him or his work," such as writing out the text of the city ordinance he violated "when it is finished, just as a physician might do in the case of a burn or a bruise." For more serious cases of dependency (i.e., a status offense like a stubborn or wayward child) or delinquency (i.e., larceny or assault), however, the judge saw the child more frequently, "just as with the patient and the physician in case of tuberculosis or typhoid."[70] This analogy continued, with reform school, court sentence, and lawbreaking compared to a hospital, medical treatment, and symptom of disease or injury. Still, it is doubtful that Boston Juvenile Court defendants imagined that they were in the Massachusetts General Hospital instead of the Suffolk County Courthouse, and the only equivalent in the minds of most youngsters may have been to the strong medicine "Dr. Baker" prescribed.

But why did Baker substitute a medical model for the more prestigious judicial model? It may have been because of his discontent with the low status of the Boston Juvenile Court in the ancient Massachusetts judiciary and a desire to compensate for this newborn court's unorthodoxy by affiliating with the increasingly respected science of medicine. The science of the law unabashedly borrowed from medicine and physical sciences; and in pretending to be like a physician, Judge Baker was only emulating his teachers at Harvard Law School. New leaders of the American bar and bench like Roscoe Pound and John H. Wigmore attempted to impose scientific exactitude on the empirical legal system.[71]

Because medicine had greater prestige than law in the minds of Progressives like Baker, the Boston Juvenile Court adopted this bogus medical model. It was a false analogy and unsound law because the defendants/patients were involuntarily submitting to treatment and were powerless to resist examination, diagnosis, or treatment. The court had the authority of the state to enforce its summons and decisions. This coercive power permitted the juvenile court to "recommend" extralegal dispositions, such as "voluntary" commitment to private reformatories like the House of the Angel Guardian and the House of the Good Shepherd."[72]

Judge Baker admitted that he had no statutory authority to send a child to a private institution, but in practice he made hundreds of such extralegal commitments by making it a condition of probation or an alternative to reform school. Parents agreed to place their children in these asylums for a set period and not to remove them without prior consent of the juvenile court. The court cooperated closely with these private asylums, and they kept the court, through the probation office, informed about the inmates' progress and destination at the time of discharge. The court was an important source of referrals for private asylums and they cooperated with the court as part of a collegial understanding. Occasionally, the Suffolk County District Attorney, who had little interest in juvenile court policies, disrupted this comfortable relationship by threatening to seek writs of habeas corpus to free HGS inmates being held against their will.[73] In the case of Lillian Ryan, as we have seen, the district attorney forced Judge Baker to reverse her commitment to the HGS when her family invoked political patronage. The influence of the Archdiocese of Boston, however, protected the Catholic asylums from much interference, but such threats proved the weakness of the juvenile court practices.[74]

For the most part, however, although this was patently illegal, the Boston Juvenile Court managed to avoid external challenges to its informal methods because few cases were important or controversial enough to attract attention. A child accused of a violent crime, as in the homicide case of an Episcopal choirboy in 1915, which the Boston newspapers made sensational news for a few weeks, was bound over for trial in the criminal court.[75] The juvenile court occupied a quiet and unobtrusive position in the Massachusetts judiciary and by its pretensions to the status of a physician or a social worker, it accrued to itself the prestige and perquisites of both while maintaining the judicial ermine as well.[76]

In time Judge Baker found the role of social physician impossible to maintain, and by 1912 he publically advocated a psychiatric court clinic like the Juvenile Psychopathic Institute established in Chicago in 1909 as an annex of the Cook County Juvenile Court. This court had despaired of serving as a judicial clinic for legally infected children, and the reasons must be understood prior to an analysis of the coming of psychology and child psychiatry to the Boston Juvenile Court.[77]

Boston Juvenile Court personnel reflected the heterogeneity of Boston in 1906. The child welfare administrators who shaped this court did so with cultural pluralism in mind. The presiding justice, Harvey Humphrey Baker, was, of course, a Boston Brahmin, a Republican, and a Unitarian like most of his seniors on the Massachusetts bench. The Brahmins clung tenaciously to the judiciary as a last vestige of their influence in government, but they were realistic as well.[78] The two special (or part-time) justices who sat in Judge Baker's absence, or when the docket was crowded, were representatives of the two largest groups of new immigrants. Frank Leveroni was an Italian-American and Philip J. Rubenstein was a Russian Jew, both attorneys interested in child welfare and ethnic charities.[79] The first probation officers appointed by Judge Baker, apart from the unpaid volunteers, were Irish Catholics. The Irish were politically powerful in Boston by 1860 and dominant after electing the first Irish Catholic mayors, Hugh O'Brien (1884–88) and Patrick Collins (1902–05). They dominated the Boston Police and Fire Departments by 1880 and most of the lower echelon civil service and political patronage positions by 1890. It was only to be expected that Irish politicians demanded their share of the court probation officer jobs, including those in the new juvenile court.[80] To balance the juvenile court staff further, Governor Curtis Guild appointed as Clerk of Court Charles Mack West Williams, a Black Republican attorney and former Alderman from the South End. With this carefully selected group, the Boston Juvenile Court was an ethnically well-balanced agency and certain to appear fair and equitable to potential critics. Whatever wheeling and dealing in State House corridors and City Hall antechambers accomplished this balance, it served to disarm critics.[81]

Chief among possible critics or foes was, of course, Archbishop William Henry O'Connell, who succeeded the conservative and timid Archbishop John J. Williams in 1907. O'Connell, however, made no overt criticism of the juvenile court and was content to exercise his considerable influence in social welfare behind the scenes or through the centralized welfare agency he created in 1907, the Boston Catholic Charitable Bureau.[82] By the time O'Connell became a cardinal, Baker had been succeeded by another Boston Brahmin, Frederick Pickering Cabot (1916–32), and later by John Forbes Perkins (1932–45).[83] Not until 1945, when a former Boston Juvenile Court probation officer and Irish Catholic attorney, John J. Connolly, was appointed to the court, did an Irish Catholic Democrat ascend to that not-so-elevated bench. The Black community had better fortune and the clerk of this court was always a Black man from 1906 to 1979, a singular accomplishment in view of the fact that no other Boston court had a Black clerk until 1980.[84]

This delicate ethnic and racial balancing might have been unnecessary in another city, but it was quite relevant and important to the sharply divided and ethnically conscious citizens of Boston before World War II. Religious prejudice had subsided, and Catholic priests were admitted to state institutions on an equal basis with Protestant clergymen by 1903, but fears and resentment lingered. To know that the juvenile court had a certain neutrality born of diversity in membership did much to dispel fears of favoritism or bias and contributed to the acceptance of the court by the heterogeneous community it served.[85]

In no area was this more important than in probation. The probation officer was a familiar if unloved figure in the working-class neighborhoods of Boston. Probation was common in Boston courts by 1840, and the legislature authorized the first salaried probation officer in Boston in 1878.

The highly-regarded chief of police, Edward H. Savage (1878–92), served as the first probation officer, and in 1880 and 1891 the legislature expanded probation to other courts.[86]

Still, juvenile probation officers served a somewhat different function when the Boston Juvenile Court opened in 1906, and they had to explain their role to new immigrants whose first impulse was to regard them as petty judges, policemen or government spies seeking evidence to justify sending their children to reform school. The probation officer faced a similar problem when he dealt with school personnel, who sometimes confused him with truant officers with whom they often dealt. Truant officers, humorously called "talent scouts for the reform school," were often superannuated teachers or policemen and did not enjoy professional status until 1930. The juvenile court probation officers had to instruct teachers, parents and the public about their role as investigators for the court as well as professional caseworkers for children under the guardianship of the court.[87]

The probation officers had a more serious problem in maintaining a neutral, judicial image because they employed a conflicting melange of police, casework, psychological, educational, and investigative techniques. They wore several hats and could not always deal consistently with a probationer. If, in friendly talks with a child, he discovered incriminating information, he was bound to investigate and, perhaps, to prosecute the child, his parents, siblings, playmates, or neighbors in court. He was an officer of the court first and a child-saver and social worker second. More than most courts, the Boston Juvenile Court was an activist court whose probation officers traveled daily in the neighborhoods as the eyes of the court. They often drifted across social welfare boundaries into law enforcement.[88]

The probation officer was increasingly unable to identify his role with professional social workers after 1920, when new graduate schools of social work in Massachusetts, New York, Pennsylvania, and Illinois produced a sufficient number of trained caseworkers and community organizers to give social work a distinct public image. These dedicated men and women often possessed a missionary zeal acquired from religious-minded professors and the influential settlement house workers with whom they had studied and lived. This evangelicalism set them apart from the law enforcement and court personnel they encountered in probation work. As social workers combined religion and science in the 1920s to help needy children and families, they discarded the old-fashioned charity worker's moral policing functions. Consequently, they distanced themselves from the probation officers who occupied an uncertain status between the policemen and the friendly visitor.[89]

Probation officers were appointed by the presiding justice of each court in Massachusetts (and many other states), and were, by 1920, usually politically active Republicans or Democrats, not Progressives or Independents. Although Judge Baker and Judge Cabot preferred to appoint experienced social workers, and relied upon settlement house head workers or the deans of social work schools to recommend candidates, few professionally educated social workers retained politicized probation jobs. Also, most judges preferred male social workers as probation officers because juvenile court caseloads were predominantly male. But men with the M.S.W. degree were in short supply and eagerly sought by private agencies, hospitals, clinics, institutions, and government bureaus as social service administrators.[90]

Social workers eschewed political activities, except for suffrage or child labor law campaigns, to protect their objectivity and professional status at the very time when, as the Progressive founders of the juvenile court had feared, the ward bosses and machine politicians used probation offices as a source of patronage. Despite the low pay, long hours, high caseloads, and poor working conditions, the probation officer had a secure white collar "government job" quite attractive to upwardly mobile men and women. Social workers recognized the difficulty of performing professional work in such a setting under the supervision of judges with little or no training in social work or psychology. The social worker in a probation officer's position worked under the daily direction of a lawyer who had been appointed as a juvenile court judge because of his political alliance with the governor. The judge might have little interest, experience, or knowledge of juvenile justice. In some states judges rotated from criminal or civil courts to juvenile courts. Almost certainly the judges had less expertise than a probation officer with an M.S.W. degree, and without professional autonomy and a career advancement path, the probation officer was merely an assistant to the judge. College-educated party workers increasingly sought these sinecures, which prompted apolitical social workers, intent upon prevention and scientific study of social problems, to opt for the private sector.[91]

Gradually social workers abandoned this field as the probation officer came to occupy a more bureaucratic role in the court system, and the Boston Juvenile Court sought another means of preventing crime and delinquency. Judge Baker's visit to the Chicago Juvenile Court in 1913 convinced him the psychiatric clinic attached to the court was the answer. It was the scientific laboratory he considered essential for his own court. When the director of this Juvenile Psychopathic Institute, Dr. William Healy, became dissatisfied with Cook County political interference and the insistence of Judge Merritt W. Pinckney that he sit beside him on the bench during hearings, he considered moving to Boston. Healy was a Harvard alumnus and had been a Harvard Medical School student before he transferred to Rush Medical School at the University of Chicago. He was attracted to the idea of returning to Boston, where he had been a protege of the philosophers William James and Josiah Royce.

In 1917 representatives of several major Boston social welfare organizations—J. Prentice Murphy of the BCAS; Frances Stern of the Boston Dispensary; Edith Burleigh of the Massachusetts General Hospital; Jessie Hodder of the Massachusetts Reformatory for Women; and Drs. Richard C. Cabot, Walter E. Fernald, and James Jackson Putnam—asked Healy to advise them on opening a juvenile court clinic in honor of the late Judge Baker. Healy's assistant, Dr. Augusta Fox Bronner, seized this opportunity to persuade her close friend and employer to abandon Chicago politics for Beacon Hill. When Herbert Parsons, the Massachusetts Commissioner of Probation, assured them they would have no political interference, they accepted the co-directorship of the clinic. On 1 April 1917 Healy and Bronner rented offices for the Judge Baker Foundation at 40 Court Street just two blocks south of the Boston Juvenile Court.[92]

This new out-patient psychiatric clinic was intended to diagnose, treat and study the "baffling cases" Judge Baker complained about in 1912. With Judge Cabot as president of the Judge Baker Foundation, and Boston's leading child welfare administrators in support, this clinic promised to fill the gap between probation and social work. The specialized juvenile court was one idea borrowed from Chicago which augmented Boston's traditional commitment to saving homeless and wayward children, and the city's child-saving agencies hoped that the court clinic would be the final link in their strong child welfare chain.

William Healy, the founder and director of the Judge Baker Foundation (1917–1949), was the first American criminologist to abandon the biological school of thought and to devote his career to research and theory independent of European criminology. Healy was the son of a middle-class English farmer (and bankrupt brick maker) who immigrated to Buffalo in 1878 and settled his family in Chicago a few months later. After grammar school, Healy was forced by his family's near poverty to work as a Chicago bank messenger and cashier. On this job he was tutored for college by a friendly banker. In 1897 at the age of twenty-eight, Healy entered Harvard College, where he studied under Josiah Royce, "the American Hegel," and William James, "the founder of pragmatism." From James, who became his mentor, Healy derived his psychological orientation, empiricism, and pragmatism.[93]

Healy graduated from Harvard in 1899 and immediately entered Harvard Medical School, but he transferred to Rush Medical School in Chicago, where he received his M.D. in 1900. The reasons for his return to Chicago are revealing. Financial exigencies were one factor, but more importantly, as Healy later admitted, he despaired of competing in medicine with his Brahmin classmates, men from "old Boston families," who would have a headstart on him in Boston but not in Chicago. This fear of and fascination with upper-class Bostonians, or his "snobbery and social climbing" as one of his colleagues said, was to be a major reason for his triumphant return to Boston. After his patrons in Chicago, Jane Addams, Julia Lathrop, and Ethel Dummer, moved on to other crusades and the county assumed control of his juvenile Psychopathic Institute in 1916, Healy became discontented. When Boston child-savers offered him a more prestigious position free of politics, he seized the opportunity, especially, as he said, when the BCAS, Children's Mission, and other children's agencies "a hundred years old" lent their support.[94]

At the Cook County Juvenile Court, Healy directed the nation's first child study clinic created by private philanthropy. One of its founders, Mrs. Ethel Dummer financed Healy's postgraduate study in Vienna, Berlin, and London in 1906 and 1907, a time when he was profoundly influenced by Sigmund Freud's work in psychoanalysis. When the Hull House trustees proposed the court clinic, Mrs. Dummer paid Healy to survey existing psychiatric centers throughout the United States. With William James' recommendation, Healy became the Juvenile Psychopathic Institute director (1909–17), operating the United States' first diagnostic treatment center for a court and an institute for research on the cause of juvenile delinquency. The court referred recidivist children with mental problems for scientific evaluation in exchange for medical examinations, social histories, and treatment recommendations.[95] Thus, when Healy taught at the Harvard Summer School in 1912 and 1913, he was a leading expert on child psychiatry and criminology. He was greatly pleased to discover senior physicians and leading social workers enrolled in his course. His major work, *The Individual Delinquent*—published in 1915 by the Boston firm, Little, Brown and Company, at the suggestion of John H. Wigmore, the dean of the Northwestern University Law School—established Healy's international reputation and strengthened his ties to Boston. When Dr. Bronner brought news of the proposed Judge Baker Foundation to Healy, he was prepared to capitalize on this opportunity.[96]

In the history of the Judge Baker Foundation, Augusta Fox Bronner (1881–67) played a central role concealed to a great extent by her exaggerated femininity and public deference to "the Chief," as Healy was called by the staff. Born in a wealthy Bavarian Jewish family in Louisville, Kentucky, "Gussie" joined Healy's Chicago staff in 1913 while completing her Ph.D. on female delinquency under Edward Lee Thorndike at Columbia University. She was one of the first female psychologists in the United States and quickly became Healy's alter ego. When Chicago political

Dr. William Healy (1869–1963) and Dr. Augusta Fox Bronner (1881–1966) directed the JBF from 1917 to 1949, making it a model for child guidance clinics. *(Print Department, Boston Public Library.)*

patronage jeopardized her job in 1914, Healy threatened to resign if she was displaced. This contretemps was resolved in her favor, but it prompted the pair to seek a more secure position elsewhere.[97]

Healy's first wife, Mary Tenney Healy, whom he met at Hull House while she was studying psychology at the University of Chicago, became a life-long invalid. This tragedy and Healy's close association with the vivacious and dynamic Bronner led to much gossip about the professional couple. Talk raged in proper Boston welfare circles, particularly when they spent long afternoons alone in his hideaway office at the Judge Baker Foundation. Whatever the true nature of their relationship, Healy depended on Bronner's administrative skill to operate the clinic smoothly. When Mary died in 1932, the Chief and Gussie married with the blessing of their families and a sigh of relief from their straitlaced colleagues.[98]

Although Bronner called Healy "the Chief," she handled the clinic finances, hired, and fired staff, arranged the case conferences and wrote most of the conference reports. It was Healy, however, who invented the case conference, a group meeting of all the social service professionals involved with a child or family. This simple concept was a basic contribution to social work because it brought together social workers, psychologists, psychiatrists, probation officers, and sometimes juvenile court judges. Seated around a large oval conference table in the Judge Baker Foundation on Beacon Hill, they each contributed their expertise and information about the child to arrive at a joint diagnosis and consensual treatment recommendation. Each conference was an interdisciplinary teaching and research session lasting one or two hours. It resulted in a concise, standardized two-page typewritten report. These "blue sheets" were sent to the court and to each of the participating agencies. They were a fundamental and much overlooked contribution by the JBF to individualized child welfare.[99]

Prior to the case conference, Dr. Healy skillfully and efficiently extracted the nucleus of the child's "own story" from him (Dr. Bronner saw all the girls) by asking simple questions and permitting the child to tell his side of the situation in a private session. With the child's "own story" in hand, Dr. Healy and Dr. Bronner convened the case conference at the clinic, usually with six or seven social workers and staff members present. Besides reviewing and interpreting the facts contained in available records and the child's "own story" to decide on a diagnosis and treatment plan, this was a didatic session in which junior staff learned the new psychoanalytically oriented casework. If Healy invented the child's "own story" and the case conference method, it was Bronner who often "invented the consensus."[100]

Interviews with former students of Healy and Bronner, social workers who attended case conferences while training with them, revealed that Dr. Healy was mild-mannered and given to understatement; but his wife, Dr. Bronner, was an aggressive, ambitious, and single-minded administrator intent upon efficiently "wrapping up the case with a minimum of discussion and no disagreement." She sat at one end of the long conference table and Healy sat at the other. "The social workers present from the JBF were generally students from Smith, Simmons or Boston University and not likely to have much to say. They were there to learn the process." The others were from an agency involved, like the BCAS or Federated Jewish Charities or the Family Welfare Society, "and if they talked too much or too long, Dr. Bronner would cut them off" and say, "Shall we summarize this now?" That was "the signal" that the conference was ending. "Often she would be dictating the report to a stenographer before we all were out of the room."[101]

The case conference report was typed that same day and copies sent to the judge, the referring agency and the child's therapist. With a page or two of "blue sheets" (from the color of the paper), the JBF concisely summarized the child in five areas: physical, mental, delinquencies, causative factors, and outlook. With this report in hand, the judge could feel confident that the child had been "scientifically analyzed" and given the "best work-up available" before the court made its disposition of the case.[102]

Healy and Bronner also contributed to the field of child guidance by teaching from time to time at Harvard, Yale, Simmons College, and Boston University. They often invited distinguished foreign visitors to attend case conferences to learn these new methods and procedures first hand. This was the culmination of the inter-agency cooperation and professionalism that Charles W. Birtwell introduced to the BCAS in 1885, and built upon the interdependency of the Boston Juvenile Court and the well-established agencies throughout Boston.[103] It was the hallmark of Boston child welfare in the early twentieth century, replacing the petty rivalries and fragmentation seen earlier.

Healy had not met Sigmund Freud in Vienna in 1907, but he quietly promoted the use of the child's "own story" and other psychoanalytic techniques in Chicago and Boston. Unlike Dr. James Jackson Putnam, who acted as a bellwether for Boston Freudians, Healy did not publicize his Freudianism. Still, their work made Boston something of a Freudian mecca in the United States by 1909 when Freud lectured at Clark University in nearby Worcester. Putnam, who was a Boston Brahmin professor of neurology at Harvard, could afford to risk his reputation by championing the controversial and blatantly sexual theories of Freud. Healy, an English immigrant from Chicago in charge of a new children's court clinic, realized that he must avoid unnecessary controversies to protect his work at the fledgling JBF. But he was psychoanalyzed by Franz Alexander, and Bronner undertook an analysis with Helene Deutsch. They encouraged the JBF staff to investigate psychoanalysis in the 1920s as did many of the social work schools in Massachusetts and New York.[104]

Perhaps because of his deliberately low profile and avoidance of public controversy, Healy had a long and productive career, writing scores of articles and seventeen books. Although best known as a criminologist for his first book, *The Individual Delinquent,* he was primarily a research psychiatrist and a psychotherapist for children suffering "conduct disorders." He was a founder and first president of the American Orthopsychiatric Association and president of the American Psychopathological Association. But perhaps his chief contribution was as founder and director of the first child guidance centers in the United States. Both the Juvenile Psychopathic Institute and the Judge Baker Foundation were models for hundreds of child psychiatry clinics that arose in American cities in the 1920s and 1930s. Most were publically funded in connection with juvenile courts but almost all followed Healy's JBF model.[105]

Not all of Healy's work in Boston, however, was an ideal model upon which to construct a juvenile court clinic, and by 1935 the JBF withdrew from its original intimacy with the Boston Juvenile Court. Crime and delinquency were the most distressing social problems of American society in the period following World War I, and American democracy itself seemed threatened by unrestricted immigration, cultural pluralism, urban overcrowding, and the maldistribution of wealth. As Healy wrote in 1930 in a popular magazine in an attempt to win public acceptance of his work:

> As I see it, our experiment in democracy is bound to suffer as much as it does, or even more from delinquency and crime unless there are more organized efforts and more legal and extra-legal cooperations in understanding and dealing with delinquents and criminals.[106]

He proposed to unite science and law to combat social disorder at the roots of crime—in children who violated the law or any social or moral convention. To Healy, lawbreaking, truancy, masturbation, sexual precocity, stealing, lying, cigarette smoking, drunkenness, or even unlicensed newspaper hawking were all offenses for which any boy or girl could be brought to court and remitted for examination by the JBF. The majority of children in the juvenile court and clinic were the offspring of impoverished immigrants. Boston, a center of the Immigration Restriction League efforts to close the Ellis Island floodgates, was gripped by fear that the uprooted and unassimilated children of the "New Immigrants" from Central and Southern Europe would subvert the American way of life. Social control of the young working class, a nativist goal since the Jacksonian Era, found scientific respectability in Healy's research. His scientific research was intended "for all concerned in understanding offenders" and he dedicated one book to parents and teachers:

> It is to be hoped that the work will serve as a book of direct reference when a case of stealing is encountered by home or school guardians of children.[107]

He offered himself as a self-appointed counsellor to courts, schools, institutions, social workers, and parents. He was the epitome of the Progressive Era expert, an efficient, economical, and humane source of authority.

In this ambitious role, however, Healy was to be disappointed. Although Hugo Munsterburg, a Harvard professor of psychology, had popularized psychology, and despite Healy's own articles in popular magazines on child guidance and the prevention of juvenile delinquency, the courts were not willing to concede the superiority of child psychiatry to traditional restraints on all children who broke the law. Judge Cabot, the brother-in-law of Dr. Putnam, was a conservative, shy bachelor; and as presiding justice of the juvenile court and president of the JBF, he was in a position to shape the clinic's role in juvenile justice. He opposed Healy's plan to provide short-term psychotherapy to all children referred by the court. Cabot insisted that the JBF only provide an evaluation, diagnosis and treatment recommendation. All "treatment" was to be provided by probation officers and private agencies—the BCAS, NEHLW, Children's Mission, and others—as usual.[108]

This was a decision that Healy accepted reluctantly, and he later regretted that he did not "stoutly insist" on treating more court cases as well as the private non-court cases who were drawn to the growing reputation of the clinic. By 1928, Healy and Bronner expanded their schedule of lectures to PTA and church groups in an effort to attract more private referrals from teachers, physicians, and parents worried about their own "problem children." Private cases who could afford the high fees of the Judge Baker Foundation made Healy less dependent on the court and gradually less interested in working-class cases.[109]

The juvenile court handled seven hundred to thirteen hundred children each year from 1907 to 1937, with only five probation officers. It was impossible for this small, untrained staff to treat all these children in a manner consistent with modern social work standards. Private agencies like the BCAS or NEHLW assigned only twenty or thirty cases at a time to each social worker, and the available support services (supervision, record-keeping, psychological testing, and vocational guidance, for example) were far superior to those at the court. In response to the overwhelming task it faced, the juvenile court created more formal bureaucratic procedures for referral of children to the private agencies from which the court had originally sprung as well as to the JBF it had spawned.[110]

Healy moved the JBF from rented offices on Court Street in 1932 to a large building on Beacon Hill at the corner of Walnut and Beacon Streets. This prestigious address reflected the clinic's growing stature in the community as well as a large endowment from Boston admirers, including $1.5 million from the Johns-Manville family and $2.5 million from an eccentric bachelor, Congressman George Holden Tinkham (1870–1956). Tinkham was a Massachusetts Republican and a Mayflower descendant who had never even met Healy, but had dropped by the clinic twice and chatted with the secretaries. These funds made the clinic independent of the juvenile court and were later used to build a larger facility uptown in the Fenway area adjacent to Boston Children's Hospital and Harvard Medical School.[111] The opening of the renamed Judge Baker Guidance Center in 1957 symbolized how far the clinic had traveled from its origin as a small juvenile court clinic. Although the clinic maintained a small office in the basement of the Suffolk County Courthouse to serve the needs of some of the juvenile court cases, the reality-based character disorders of most court children seldom benefitted from psychotherapy or psychoanalytically oriented casework. Most children in the juvenile court from 1930 to 1950 were considered not treatable by the sophisticated services of the JBF staff. These therapists were more comfortable and effective with articulate, middle-class voluntary patients who had social backgrounds more in common with social workers, psychologists, and psychiatrists than did lower-class juvenile delinquents.[112]

Even as mild a case as young Theodore White in 1929 found the JBF services more confusing than coherent. His mother brought this fourteen-year-old working-class Jewish boy to the clinic for vocational guidance. The "cold, severe technical" staff tested Teddy and recommended that he study engineering because of his aptitude for mathematics and manual dexterity. He recalled in a letter:

> I was kept there for three hours on each of two visits doing tests with pegs and peg boards, manual dexterity functions, quizzed with true and false questions and general information questions—in other words, the standard intelligence and aptitude tests of those days. At the end of this, my mother was told that I had an aptitude for electrical engineering.[113]

Perhaps other working-class families took JBF advice more to heart, but Theodore White went to Harvard, not MIT, with a Burroughs Newsboys' Foundation scholarship and had a brilliant career as an international journalist. His experience at the JBF probably was typical of the lower-class Boston children who found themselves before the stern Dr. Healy and his efficient co-director, Dr. Bronner. Without the authority of the court, child guidance clinics still had to earn the confidence of parents and children.[114]

Another obstacle to the Boston Juvenile Court's effective use of its clinic centered on the child welfare preoccupation with individual therapy instead of family therapy. Since the publication of G. Stanley Hall's influential 1904 book, *Adolescence,* social workers, psychologists, and the other child study advocates in the United States had focused on the individual child and his unique personality development. Although they blamed the "bad influence" of parents and family members for "inefficient" child development, treatment tended to be limited to the "nervous" or "wayward" child rather than the family constellation in which he lived. This reflected the earlier child-savers' eagerness to remove children from destitute or depraved homes and place them in congregate asylums or on rural family farms. Little thought was given to uplifting the child's family because of moral and hereditarian doubts about the ability of adult paupers to reform. The plasticity of the young individual child inspired an optimism which obscured the reformers' view of the nuclear family.[115]

This explains the emphasis by Healy and Bronner in their "blue sheets"

Dr. Bronner taught a new generation of Simmons College psychiatric social workers the JBF casework methods from 1930 to 1949. *(Simmons College Archives.)*

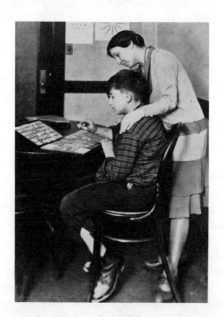

Dr. Bronner administers an IQ test to a young client in 1930. *(Harvard University, Countway Library.)*

on a child's individual personality traits and experiences. It was not merely a quirk in the JBF process, but a generalized strategy of twentieth-century child welfare specialists to limit efforts and energies to the individual. The earlier focus on family poverty or social problems was too ambitious, unsuccessful, and time-consuming for "efficient" and "scientific" social workers from 1900 to 1930. Not until the 1930s did social workers seriously consider family therapy an effective treatment for dependent and delinquent children. Prior to 1930, the Judge Baker Foundation and most child welfare agencies, like the field generally, focused on individual treatment of a child or a few siblings but seldom on the whole family unit.

* * *

The prevailing pattern in child welfare cases at the BCAS or NEHLW from 1900 to 1927 was for a parent, teacher, clergyman, or probation officer to refer a child for "adjustment" of a specific personality problem, such as lying, truancy, theft, running away, or some minor offense. The social worker collected family data and a life history of the child, interviewed him a few times and made a diagnosis and recommendation to the parent or court. Within this modality, the individual child was treated with little regard for broader issues, and when these issues impinged on the treatment, the child usually was placed in an institution or foster home for a temporary adjustment period. With this emphasis on the individual child, the Boston Juvenile Court could not expect to resolve the problems of dependent or delinquent children by the casework services of its clinic or agencies like the MSPCC or BCAS. The court had to solve its own problems with little support from social workers, and by 1934 Presiding Judge John Forbes Perkins was openly skeptical of child psychiatry.[116]

Instead of relying on child study experts and psychiatrists in the Depression era, the court emphasized community resources—the churches, clubs, settlement houses, schools, employers and the extended family—or children's organizations like the Boy Scouts, YMCA, and Morgan Memorial. These organizations could function as parental substitutes or supplements for absent, inept, or unassimilated immigrant parents of mildly wayward boys and girls appearing in court for a first or a minor offense. The juvenile court was extremely conscious of the changing nature of the urban community, but organized community resources offered hope that the "child in need of supervision" could avoid new-fangled psychiatry and the expensive, ineffective, and overcrowded reform schools. By connecting them to organized recreation centers and newly expanded youth clubs, the juvenile court might prevent these wayward teenagers from acquiring criminal records. For children who did not learn moral codes at home and were unaffiliated with these alternative forms of moral oversight, the probation officer was a compromise between the total asylum and total freedom from restraint. The private reformatories, the House of the Angel Guardian, the House of the Good Shepherd, and the George Junior Republic; or private orphanages, the Home for Jewish Children, the Home for Destitute Catholic Children, and the Home for Italian Children, were also employed by the juvenile court for some mild offenders.

The most reliable resource, however, remained the foster home, which was little changed since the colonial era Overseers of the Poor bound out pauper children to Massachusetts farmers. The White House Conference on the Care of Dependent Children in 1909 had criticized institutional life for innocent children and showered praise on family life. If a child's own family was no longer suitable, then the two hundred child-saving experts President Theodore Roosevelt gathered at the White House agreed that a foster home was usually the best solution. The Boston Juvenile Court apparently agreed also, because a large percentage of its children were placed in foster homes.[117]

Foster home placement, however effective, economical, and acceptable to the community as a solution for the homeless, wayward or emotionally disturbed child, no longer interested most social workers. Foster homes were considered an old-fashioned remedy in the modernist 1920–40 period. The expanding profession of American social work found psychiatric or clinical treatment more attractive. Recruiting, training, and supervising foster families for individual children smacked of friendly visiting and charity work. Massachusetts state law mandated quarterly home visits by the social worker to each foster child, and few children remained in one foster family for very long. This work was something the politically appointed visiting agents in the town or city departments of public welfare and the State Division of Minor Wards did but it now "seemed beneath the dignity of professional social workers." Graduates of the prestigious Simmons College, Smith College, and Boston University Schools of Social Work preferred to work in the elite and progressive private agencies and clinics rather than in public welfare or traditional child-placing agencies.[118]

Psychiatric social workers first appeared in 1907 at the Massachusetts General Hospital when Dr. James Jackson Putnam hired Edith N. Burleigh, a settlement worker, to assist him in treating the social problems of his mentally ill patients. This idea spread to the Boston Psychopathic Hospital opened by the state in 1912, and by 1917 Dr. Elmer E. Southard coined the term "psychiatric social worker." Their role was to use graduate training in social sciences, psychology, and social work to investigate and diagnose behavioral and personality problems. This scientific and educative approach included new psychometric methods and clinical interviews based on the "talking cure" developed by Freud.[119]

Yet the psychiatric social worker, for a combination of reasons having to do with her origins in nursing, professional rivalry by physicians, sexism, and the rising status of medicine, became the handmaiden of the psychiatrist. Social work was an overwhelmingly female career, and with less education and professional status than the psychiatrist, who was always a licensed physician and usually male, the social worker occupied a new and vague position in the hospital or clinic. By 1937 there were more than five hundred members in the American Association of Psychiatric Social Workers, but they exercised little power in medical institutions.[120] They collected and recorded data for the psychiatrists, made home visits, met with family members, and performed other ancillary functions. In children's institutions, like the Judge Baker Foundation or the NEHLW, social workers sometimes filled a more central role in treating patients. Dr. Healy profoundly influenced social work leaders like Mary Richmond, who admitted reading his writings with "more interest" than anything else in child guidance. Still, the close relationship that developed between psychiatry and social work lent the prestige of medicine to the new professionals in social work but also created a dependency inimical to professional autonomy. Analogies between doctors and nurses and psychiatrists and social workers did little to enhance the psychiatric social worker's image. In the public mind, she was more or less like the doctor's assistant, much as the probation officer remained the judge's henchman.[121]

As one social worker summarized the role of the court clinic social worker, it was to secure the social history, assist in evaluation of the case, locate community resources, and facilitate close working relationships between the clinic and other welfare agencies, as well as to observe the home, school, and recreation habits of the child. Burdened with these duties, there was little time for psychiatric treatment, which presumably was reserved for the more skillful "head-shrinker" doctor. Examples of the deference child welfare agencies gave to Dr. Healy illustrate the low self-esteem social workers possessed in this relationship. In 1924, for instance, when a thirteen-year-old boy stole four dollars from a neighbor, the court referred him to both the BCAS and the JBF. After a lengthy study of this case, the BCAS social worker recommended a foster home for Harvey Solomon; but, in a single interview with Dr. Healy, Harvey admitted he stole the money in a very clever manner. He substituted one dollar for the five-dollar bill in the wallet; and "because of this act, Dr. Healy, who had at first recommended placement, changed his recommendation to Reform School." Without objection, the BCAS staff supported this change in disposition and Harvey went to the Westborough School for nine months.[122]

Healy was critical of social workers who burdened families with frequent home visits, as in the case of Hubert Byers, a child who was mentally normal with "decidedly good ability" despite petty thefts and the poor "example of his older brothers," who were in reform school. Healy complained that Hubert's father had been "much approached by social workers and has had so much trouble" with them that further contact should be limited to consultations with the JBF staff and no further visiting by the importunate BCAS social workers.[123]

In 1927 the major Jewish child welfare agency in Boston, the Children's Bureau of the Federated Jewish Charities, decided to hire a staff psychiatrist because of "considerable dissatisfaction of its social workers with the Boston Psychopathic Hospital and the Nerve clinics of other hospitals." The agency proceeded cautiously in this innovative step and the man they chose was a highly recommended former student of Dr. Healy. Healy's prestige was sufficient to exclude all other candidates. The Children's Bureau enthusiastically decided this young child psychiatrist "would be good for clients and also help train the social work staff." Obviously, no matter how experienced a social worker might be, even a novice psychiatrist out-ranked her by virtue of his position as a physician.[124]

The role of the psychiatric social worker was further limited by Dr. Elmer E. Southard of the Boston Psychopathic Hospital, who frankly told an audience of social workers in 1916 that the social worker was merely "an intensive form of layman, as a sort of super-layman" who had the "task of cementing together the data of the physician, the psychologist, and other laymen endeavoring to influence the jurist's decision." The juvenile court clinic was a clearinghouse for delinquents and for potential delinquents who "require the best medical judgment, both for the bird's-eye view and for intensive work with delinquents." These wayward children were now considered a social-medical problem which "requires enlightened judicial review and presumably control." In this important work the social worker was clearly subservient to the psychiatrist and the judge, who had professional status obviously superior to the "super-layman" social worker.[125]

In a review of all the cases in the files of the Federated Jewish Charities from 1917 to 1927, 120 children were referred to the JBF by the juvenile court or the FJC Children's Bureau. Of these cases, one hundred recommendations by Dr. Healy or other members of his staff (for foster family placement or return to family care) were accepted by the FJC staff. It is important to understand that JBF recommendations had no binding power over this private agency and were rarely ordered by a court. This child welfare agency voluntarily complied with JBF suggestions even when it meant violating established agency policy.[126] The case of Bertha Levine illustrates the length to which the agency went to accommodate Dr. Healy's recommendations. Bertha was the seventeen-year-old daughter of a Russian Jewish peddler in the West End in 1924. Dr. Healy felt she "should have physical up-building, in order to be able to work and be self-supporting." The social worker noted, "Exception was made in this case since the girl is over the age limit of the Bureau, and placed her in a country foster home for physical upbuilding. Children's Bureau to pay."[127] Dr. Healy quite often recommended farm family placements for inner city children, and the Federated Jewish Charities was usually willing to comply, even if, in the case of Beth Schneider in 1918, "she may feel rather lonesome." Once again the social workers deferred to his wishes and merely acknowledged, "If this results, other homes will be found." No effort was too great if "Dr. Healy recommends" preceded the request in FJC child welfare cases.[128]

Healy's reputation was acknowledged by the national media in 1924 when Clarence Darrow called him to Chicago as an expert in the Leopold-Loeb kidnapping and murder trial. The "crime of the century" shocked the nation into the realization that even modern adolescents with every advantage could go bad. With Healy's expert testimony as an alienist, Darrow succeeded in preventing the death sentence for the two teenagers who confessed they killed a boy in an attempt to commit the perfect crime. Healy's role was to test their intelligence and sanity.[129] He recalled that Loeb had a mediocre IQ but that Leopold was "an extraordinary natural genius" and one of the two most brilliant men he ever met. He spent six weeks in Chicago at the urging of a committee of citizens of "high repute" and with ample funds from the boys' families. The two boys were members of a golden generation gone wrong, symbols of the post-war emancipation that was envied and feared by their Victorian elders. Yet even the testimony of the nation's leading child psychiatrist could not save them from a life sentence to prison.[130]

Interest in the mental hygiene movement added to the JBF luster, as psychotherapy, psychoanalysis, Freudianism, and World War I shell shock cases aroused American interest in the humane cure of mental diseases and the practical application of psychology to discover hidden motives. Hugo Munsterberg, the well-publicized Harvard psychologist, taught Americans that psychology was useful in evaluating court testimony, in advertising, schools, vocational guidance, self-improvement fads and increasing industrial productivity. Although anti-Semitism (against Freud) and wartime anti-Teutonicism, as well as prudery about sexual topics, hampered psychiatry and clinical psychology for a time, its usefulness quickly overcame these objections.[131]

Juvenile courts were the first to employ psychiatrists and psychologists, but adult courts were won over by 1930 because the mental health movement operated in the conducive milieu of religious reform, humanitarianism, positivism, individualism, conservative philanthropy, faith in education and bureaucratic organization. Psychiatry made no radical

242   BOSTON'S WAYWARD CHILDREN

changes in American society and no extreme demands on the capitalist system. It helped adjust deviant individuals who threatened the moral order by defining lawbreaking and dependency as anti-social behavior. The child welfare system endorsed psychiatry and attempted to absorb it for its own purposes. Psychoanalysis, the epitome of the Freudian system, however, was developed as a therapeutic tool for adult patients. It was seldom used for children or adolescents before 1950, although some of its techniques were obviously applied to children at progressive clinics like the Judge Baker Foundation. It was a humane method of investigating emotional problems, meant to help the patient resolve deep-seated emotional conflicts. To understand all, the therapist assumed, was to forgive all. Questions about the use to which a court clinic might put information revealed in therapy sessions seldom arose in the JBF. The child only saw the therapist for a few hours once or twice, and after he had interviewed the child and written his report, the obliging social workers assumed responsibility for carrying out the recommendations.[132]

Here the court and the clinic often parted company. Whatever Judge Baker might have envisioned, the court under Judge Cabot and his successor, Judge Perkins, frequently disagreed with or disregarded JBF treatment recommendations. In only 35 percent of the cases referred to the JBF by the juvenile court in 1917 and 1927 did the court follow the clinic's recommendation for disposition. The clinic recommended that 40 percent of the children be sent to private or public institutions or to foster homes, but the court acted on this plan in only 15 percent of the cases. When the clinic recommended that 42 percent of the children return home, the court sent over 61 percent of them home.[133] When the JBF recommended medical treatment for 707 children studied for one year, only 229 of them subsequently received the treatment (or 42 percent).[134]

Why did private agencies like the BCAS or Federated Jewish Charities accept JBF recommendations so often when the juvenile court ignored or rejected them? Unfortunately no data exist by which this intriguing question can be answered. Judicial decision-making is an arcane process and perhaps deliberately so. We cannot probe the minds of these judges. Judge Baker tended to avoid commitments to institutions when the parents were present and objected, but why his successors overrode the considered opinions of their court clinic is not known. It seems likely that the juvenile court was unwilling to disregard the wishes of parents who objected to foster homes or institutions for their children for the same reasons Judge Baker offered. He was not willing to risk reversal of his decision in the appellate court and to lose all oversight of children known to be "at risk" by reason of dependency or delinquency. If the child's parents were present in court and engaged an attorney to resist court action, perhaps the parents would be prodded into remedial action as effective as any remedy the juvenile court could offer. Even parents who used political patronage to free their wayward sons and daughters from the court offered some hope that they might be more vigilant over the child thereafter. One could not expect the ward boss to save a chronic delinquent every time he was hauled into the juvenile court.[135]

Still this does not answer the question of why the clinic and court disagreed so often on disposition of these cases. Again the answer is elusive, but the role of the scientific clinic and the lowly juvenile court suggests that the apolitical social workers and psychiatrists were free of mundane considerations under which the politically appointed Boston Juvenile Court judges and probation officers operated. The Judge Baker Foundation was a well-endowed, prestigious medical center, while the court had forgone its pretensions to the medical model. The clinic occupied a powerful position in its realm, one far superior to the more humble role the juvenile court had in the judicial realm. For the clinic, a misdiagnosis was unlikely to incur charges of malpractice, while misruling in the court had almost immediate consequences in reversal (an embarrassment to any judge) by the Superior Court.[136]

By 1930 the clinic's resources far exceeded that of its parent organization, the juvenile court; and the overworked, underpaid, untrained, ill-equipped probation officers were unequal to the task of providing the individualized treatment the JBF frequently recommended. It is true that the private agencies often took probation cases for the court, but they had developed their own sources of client referrals and were no longer at the service of the juvenile court as needed. They selected "interesting cases" and felt free to refuse others from the court.[137] Social workers had advanced far beyond the role probation officers occupied in the 1930s. Few graduates of social work schools were willing to accept the professional disadvantages of juvenile probation positions. Those who did become probation officers usually advanced rapidly to better jobs as social welfare administrators, having acquired practical experience at the juvenile court's expense early in their careers.[138]

By 1920 the juvenile court movement had failed in the opinion of many of its founders and footsoldiers. In 1921 Julia Lathrop admitted that the court was not a panacea, and although it had spread from Massachusetts and Illinois to 46 states, it staggered under heavy burdens. Miss Lathrop told a United States Children's Bureau audience that she was proud of her role in founding the Chicago juvenile court and clinic, but worried about the court's future effectiveness:

The juvenile court is 22 years old; we can never revert from its idea. Is it not possible to awaken fresh interest in a nation-wide realization of its ideal of justice?[139]

A decade earlier the perceptive Judge Ben Lindsey was equally disappointed that the court and juvenile probation proved to be only "palliatives" for wayward youngsters.[140] Other child welfare leaders, like Bernard Flexner, agreed that the juvenile court proved useful but that it was "not, alas, a cure-all."[141] This regretful litany continued throughout the 1920s, and the BCAS director, J. Prentice Murphy, complained in 1929 that the idea of juvenile courts as "separate and distinct from the spirit and practice of the criminal courts" had proved to be an experiment "at absolute variance with the facts."[142] Even the moderate and mild-mannered Dr. Healy told the National Probation Association in 1932 that the extent to which the "juvenile court system is effective is an open question."[143]

The Boston Juvenile Court's own Judge John Forbes Perkins had doubts about the whole juvenile justice system, but naturally he found fault not with the court so much as with the clinic. More than a decade of daily experience with Dr. Healy's clinical staff had dimmed his hopes:

> The value and power of psychiatry were exaggerated to the point of magic, and like the juvenile court, psychiatry was oversold to the public. The idea spread that delinquency was solely due to maladjustment or conflict and that all the court had to do was to send a boy to the clinic and have the maladjustment or conflict removed, like having a tooth pulled by a dentist.[144]

Judge Perkins dismissed the notion that wayward and homeless children should be treated like "sick people" or that the juvenile court should become a part of the child welfare system. The Depression years had convinced him that the more traditional view was wiser than scientific social work:

> It is the *function of the court to enforce the rules*. . . . Its role is enforcement, not prevention. It is an *authoritarian agency* not a *social agency*.[145]

To accomplish this authoritarian mission, in 1936 Judge Perkins established with private funds an adjunct to the Boston Juvenile Court called the Citizenship Training Group. This was a highly structured probation center with daily recreation programs, crafts, group therapy and individual counseling designed to keep unsupervised boys busy and involved with constructive activities.[146] It was widely acclaimed at the time, and still is recalled favorably by some Boston probation officers and social workers. Unfortunately, even this intensive effort was not a permanent solution: "Like most other innovations, it succumbed to bureaucratization and lack of funds. It was only a stopgap measure to shore up the sagging reputation the court had enjoyed in its heyday, 1917 to 1925."[147]

Boys were referred to this new center by the juvenile court, or by the established children's agencies, including the Morgan Memorial in the South End, the West End Settlement House, the Church Home Society, and the Hayden Goodwill Inn in Dorchester. The Citizenship Training Group earned an impressive reputation for a time, and its director, a juvenile court probation officer, John J. Connolly, succeeded Perkins as presiding justice in 1945. He managed to lower commitments to reform schools and other institutions from 15 percent to 3 percent by extensive use of this probation program.[148]

Nevertheless, the juvenile court was subject to criticism which was responsible for Judge Perkins's retreat to authoritarianism and Judge Connelly's reliance on the recreation and crafts approach to juvenile probation. The first direct criticism came from Healy and Bronner in 1926 when they published the results of their study of recidivism in Chicago and Boston juvenile courts. They found that 50 percent of the children in the Chicago court were recidivists who later appeared in the criminal court; but the figures for Boston were from 21 to 26 percent of the Boston Juvenile Court cases.[149] This rather encouraging report, however, was upset in 1934 when Sheldon and Eleanor Glueck reported that 88 percent of the Boston Juvenile Court children referred to the JBF were recidivists arrested within five years of their first juvenile court appearance.[150] Disturbed by these findings (and personally offended by the Gluecks' work according to Healy's colleagues), Healy and Bronner undertook another study. They were surprised and disappointed to find evidence confirming the Gluecks' pessimistic conclusions.

These reports disturbed many child welfare professionals, including the eminent Dr. Richard C. Cabot, the father of medical social work and a Judge Baker Foundation trustee. Cabot resigned from the JBF board and concluded that the Boston Juvenile Court and JBF efforts had been "an appallingly complete and costly failure, a stupendous waste of time, money, and effort in an attempt to check delinquency." He organized his own juvenile delinquency research project in Cambridge and Somerville without court or clinic affiliation.[151]

Meanwhile, Healy and Bronner concluded that, "If the roots of crime lie far back in the foundation of our social order, it may be that only a radical change can bring any large measure of cure." It was the unjust social and economic system in the United States which created wayward, homeless, and delinquent children, "and until a better social order exists, crime will probably flourish and society continue to pay the price." This disinterested view was hardly the scientific data or pragmatic program the juvenile court and the child welfare establishment expected to receive from the Judge Baker Foundation directors.

On this disquieting note, Dr. Healy and Dr. Bronner concluded their seventeen years of service at the Judge Baker Center, as the JBF was renamed in 1957 when it was relocated far away from the court which had fathered it. What, then, can be made of the court and the clinic in Boston's long child welfare history? The mingling of charity, law, medicine, and science proved a failure. The proof was no less distasteful when served up by Professor Glueck of the Harvard Law School which invented the scientific jurisprudence practiced in the Boston Juvenile Court. Perhaps Judge Cabot had found the answer to the riddle of child welfare and juvenile justice when he wrote a letter in 1918 about a pending case in his court. After elaborate and scientific investigation of the child and his family, the court and clinic were still at a loss to know how to help this pathetic little boy. Despite the best efforts of Boston's most prestigious social welfare agencies, no solution for this particular wayward child could be found. One remedy and then another were suggested, but the shy Brahmin judge, admitted ruefully:

His chief crime being the crime of poverty, the authorities do not know what to do with him.[152]

Epilogue

"I know histhry isn't thrue, Hinnissy, because it ain't like what I
see ivry day in Halsted Street. If any wan comes along with a
histhry iv Greece or Rome that'll show me th' people fightin',
gettin' dhrunk, makin' love, gettin' married, owin' th' grocery
man an' bein' without hard coal, I'll believe they was a Greece or
Rome, but not befure."

—Finley Peter Dunne, *Observations by Mr. Dooley* (New York, 1902)

Mr. Dooley voiced a common complaint about conventional history, but
now we are able to write a more credible history of Victorian America.
Historians have discovered that wayward and homeless working-class
children left behind extensive records from their institutional lives. Or
rather, middle-class child-savers wrote and preserved records which show
the common people "fightin', getting drunk, makin' love" and generally
living robust and rich lives. By studying these poor children in Boston
from the age of Jackson to the age of FDR, students can know their
history and themselves better. As the British historian R. H. Tawney
commented, "There is no touchstone, except the treatment of childhood,
which reveals the true character of a social philosophy more clearly than
the spirit in which it regards the misfortunes of those of its members who
fall by the way."[1]

If Tawney is correct, and I believe he is, then the history of wayward
children is essential to understanding American social philosophy. It
offers a twofold view of American society by focusing on both childhood
and children by the wayside. The Boston children's institutions and agencies studied here are, I think, representative of those formed simulta-
neously or later in other American cities. Further study in other
communities will offer useful insights into the lives of the poor and the
nearly poor, but never again can history be limited to the famous, wealthy,
and powerful.

Children have always been a problem; as early as 1641 Massachusetts
identified stubborn and disobedient juveniles as a special category under
the law. Constables and magistrates were directed to make special provi-
sion for any wayward minor who "habitually associates with vicious or
immoral persons or who is growing up in circumstances exposing him or

247

her to lead an immoral, vicious or criminal life." By 1830 the courts were authorized to give special care to these children and adolescents, care found most often in private charitable organizations. In the 1870s court jurisdiction over minors was refined further with probate and juvenile courts cooperating with the well-established children's societies. This cooperation blossomed in 1906 into the Boston Juvenile Court that was concerned with the "care, custody and discipline of the children brought before it and approximate as nearly as possible that which they should receive from their parents."[2]

Two modern bumper stickers sum up our continuing fascination with the wayward child. One says, "Huck Finn was a status offender," and the other says, "Children, you can't beat them." They mean, I suppose, that all children are ungovernable lawbreakers until socialized and that all children require kind discipline. Why, then, were Americans in the nineteenth century so concerned about lower-class children and adolescents who violated or ignored middle-class standards? I think the answer is that the triumph of the middle class in capitalist Europe and America enabled the bourgeoise to impose its values on all members of society. Because the family is the basis for all social organization, the lower-class family which deviated from middle-class standards aroused anxious reformers. In a chronic panic about the fate of the nation and the family, these do-gooders were determined to save society by saving children without "proper" homes.

By the 1830s heroic efforts were made to reform or rehabilitate social deviants—criminals, prostitutes, drunkards, lunatics, and paupers—but it is not easy to reform anyone. Wayward children, described with a catch-all term purposely not well-defined, were the most tempting target for rescue. The children of the urban poor seemed more plastic and promising to the reformers for whom "nip it in the bud" and "a stitch in time saves nine" sounded like a practical philosophy.

The urban working-class family was vulnerable to depressions, unemployment, strikes, fires, floods, illness, arrest, and death. Any tragedy could shatter home-life and turn school children into wayward children. Recent immigrants faced many obstacles as they adjusted to American life, and their children often bore the brunt of this turmoil. Middle-class members of the helping professions—clergymen, teachers, physicians, lawyers, and charity workers—were wary about these newcomers and were quick to disapprove of their family life. It was usually poverty that denied wayward children parental supervision satisfactory to middle-class critics, but the idea of eradicating poverty from society was too new and too radical for the Victorians. Calvinism taught the poor were sinners and Social Darwinism preached the strong survived. All this combined to place great stress on the poor family at the very time when the middle class increased supervision of their own children. As millions of peasants migrated to American cities, they were often overwhelmed by the urban industrial discipline. Working-class parents struggling for a foothold in a new world sometimes loosened or lost control of their children. Left to their own devices, the second-generation sons and daughters of European immmigrants were more at home in city than their parents ever would be. They played, worked, ate, drank, fought, loved, learned, and entertained themselves in the nineteenth and early twentieth-century city streets. In this urbanization process they created modern American culture, including the child welfare system for which they were as responsible and as active as the child-savers.[3]

While growing up American in the modern city, some of these hyphenated Americans ran afoul of the law. The focus here is not with juvenile delinquents, who are a fascinating and important topic; but rather with a larger and more amorphous group, those wayward children social workers later dubbed predelinquent children in need of services. Their parents were more destitute and confused than depraved, but the new breed of professional almsgiver or charity worker found their children an irresistible target for moral marksmanship. Lower-class migrants and immigrants produced wealth and disorder in the Victorian city, and into this chaos came the philanthropist or reformer and his employees—the charity worker; child-saver; settlement worker; and, finally, the social worker. In exchange for prestige, power, and professional status, these professional altruists tried to uplift and control the poor. Public aid to the poor was a moral impulse since Elizabethan days and it inspired rather than diminished private charity. The English secularized the idea of poverty, and for 350 years Americans followed their example until the welfare state emerged in the 1930s.

The French historian Philippe Aries argued persuasively that childhood as we know it was invented by the European bourgeoise. As this class dominated society in Europe and America, so did its ideals about child-rearing. These ideals were institutionalized in the church, law, schools, and government; and children who deviated from the new middle-class standards were defined as a problem. After the American Revolution, this problem received much attention. The discovery of poverty coincided with the discovery of the asylum, and the orphanage and child-placing society are as significant as the penitentiary or insane asylum. That is another lesson the Yankee child-savers demonstrated.[4]

The transformation of the antebellum philanthropist into the twentieth-century social worker can be seen in the contrasting careers of Joseph Tuckerman and Charles W. Birtwell. If it was narcissism that underlay the moralism of the child-savers, who beckoned backward to the idealized villages of agrarian America and prescribed rural domesticity for the social problems of wayward children, it was also Christian charity that inspired them. Economic analysis would illuminate the discussion of the origins and nature of American child welfare, but the available data are too fragmentary and subjective to permit meaningful quantification. We are left to ponder the asylum records and court cases used here. The subjectivity which hinders such social history is inevitable because it is inherent, and historians would be neither human nor historical to claim complete objectivity.

The so-called new social history accepts the elusive task of extracting from an unwilling record the role homeless children played in our collective past, and eventually the moral judgments, which are the inescapable task of the historian, may be rendered with more accuracy, grace, and compassion. But as Mr. Dooley complained:

> Histoyans is like doctors. They are always lookin' f'r symptoms. Those iv them that writes about their own times examines th' tongue an' feels th' pulse an' makes a wrong dygnosis. Th' other kind iv histhry is a post-mortem examination. It tells ye what a counrry died iv. But what I'd like to know what it lived iv.[5]

The post-mortem examination undertaken here is on a patient only recently deceased. The HDCC closed in 1985 and the HGS in 1986, but NEHLW still operates as a child welfare agency as do the (renamed) CM, BCAS, and BJC. The history of social welfare organizations does reveal much new and useful information about American society, but this work is still at a primitive stage. Moral judgment and accurate diagnosis await further evidence and investigation in more specialized local histories of welfare and penal organizations based on social work data. This study of selected child welfare agencies in one American city raises as many questions as it answers, it requires comparative data from other cities and states before conclusions may be reached.

In the meantime, I can venture some opinions based on the evidence presented here. Why did child-saving proliferate so early and so floridly in nineteenth-century Boston? The migration of peasants from Europe and the rural lower class from Canada and New England caused a social crisis which produced stricter social controls. Policing increased, and drunkenness, crime, vice, begging, loitering, street-walking, and poverty were suppressed by native Bostonians to reinforce the endangered social order. The children of the "disorderly" Irish Catholics and later immigrants presented attractive targets for romantic reformers and evangelical missionaries alike. Child welfare and juvenile justice machinery hummed with zealous benevolence by the 1830s.

In the 1830s and again in the 1850s, Boston suppressed prostitution, crime, and public disorder by vigorous police surveillance of the riotous

West End and North End slums where children played and loitered on the streets amid appalling sin and squalor. The solution offered by Boston child-saving societies was to shape children as self-sufficient, moral citizens trained and socialized by private philanthropy with middle-class values and working-class jobs.

Before the watershed of the Industrial Revolution, and certainly by the Civil War, Boston underwent a transformation in every respect. The wealthy could no longer maintain an intimate relationship with the poor, but private charity was stimulated, not squelched, by the challenge of urban poverty. Reformers saw poor children as a perfect target for their growing empire of benevolence. The immigration of the Irish, Jews, Italians, and "newer races" gave the lower class a size and complexity impossible for private philanthropy to accommodate. In the fragmented metropolis, the Boston elite lost political power but not social influence. The Catholic Church and organized Jewry accepted Brahmin direction in exchange for religious toleration until middle-class Irish power brokers shook off prejudice and patronage in the twentieth century.

The public welfare sector, which we have considered only in contrast to the private system, was largely social control rather than benevolent uplift. It acted as a coercive threat behind and beneath the private system, and was an inferior system chiefly for the hopeless, violent, chronic, or recalcitrant juveniles. Victorian child-savers divided the wayward children into the worthy and the unworthy much as the Elizabethans had done. The former constituted their clientele from 1830 to 1930, and the latter were relegated to the less fastidious public institutions.

The twentieth century brought the specialized juvenile court and its child guidance or psychiatric clinic, both of which imposed moral sanctions in medical jargon. The wayward child was no longer immoral, but rather he was sick, emotionally disturbed, maladjusted, or neurotic. Both court and clinic were merely the latest solutions for the problem children of the dangerous classes; and like their predecessors, they found only limited success and narrow acceptance. Straightening bent twigs was no less difficult for social workers in the 1930s than it had been for child-savers in the 1830s. The economic system underlying urban industrial poverty had changed little and the same kinds of child welfare problems confront Americans today much as they did in antebellum and Depression Boston.[6]

Recent solutions to child welfare problems offered by the Reagan and Bush administrations focus on the need for stronger family life and moarlity. These are hardly new concepts, and newspaper reports of urban violence by teenagers are quickly followed by demands for reopening state reform schools and transferring serious cases from the juvenile to the criminal courts. Are we coddling young hoodlums, editorialists wonder?

What can be done about the cycle of poverty that sees welfare mothers with pregnant teenagers? Have our public schools failed us? Should immigration be limited and electric fences built to stem the flood of unwashed masses across our borders?"

These queries would sound familiar to Victorian Boston newspaper readers. Poverty is endemic and expanding, and the children of the poor are again in the headlines. The welfare of the young is a problem because their parents do not meet our middle-class standards. We are again anxious about the next generation of ill-educated, untrained, and immoral poor. What is to be done?

History does not provide concrete answers, but it does prove that social problems are recurrent and manageable. It is useful to understand that hand-bag snatching and auto theft are not new vices, but only jackrolling and misappropriation of a horse and buggy renewed. Loitering on Boston Common and rowdiness in the subway cars by young Bostonians are perennial problems, not a unique threat to the yuppie commuter. The "chickenhawk" preying on homeless boys at the bus station today is only the Victorian pederast in 1980s clothing.[8]

Americans profess to love children and cherish the family, but still we abuse, neglect, and shun poor children and disdain families in poverty. Early in the last century, proper Bostonians endeavored to uplift the poor but found the task too difficult. These prototypical philanthropists did not surrender but prudently chose more manageable goals, the homeless and wayward children of the working-class immigrants. But working-class Bostonians resisted this class warfare, however well-intentioned or holy it pretended to be, and the city saw wayward children become a battleground and a testing ground. The upper and middle class Protestants were successful until challenged by Catholics and later by Jews who had their own self-image and self-help methods. St. Vincent's Asylum—like the HAG, HDCC, HGS, Daly Industrial School, and Working Boys' Home—was an Irish immigrant affirmation of ethnic, sectarian, and class identity. The Home for Italian Children was an Italian reaction to both Yankee and Irish Catholic cultural imperialism, as was the Black community's use of kinship fostering and the small but significant St. Augustine's Farm. Jewish immigrants resented Yankees, Catholics, and German Jews who disparaged and dominated their poor, and Boston Jewish social welfare was shaped to an important and unrecognized degree by working-class Eastern European Jews' determination to uplift themselves.

But how is this ethnic ballet (or battle) in Boston relevant to American history? In a sense, this question is irrelevant. Like any city, Boston's history is an important subject for its own sake, yet it is relevant to the history of social welfare throughout the nation. Boston child savers made an impact beyond their own era, and Bostonians played a major role in

American reform movements and charitable and welfare organizations of all kinds. In reforming the wayward child, Massachusetts men and women pioneered and prosleytized for more humane, effective, and permanent methods of alternative child care.

In a sense, the struggles of the child-savers to rescue poor children from their inadequate or missing parents failed. Individual children were sheltered, fed, clothed, healed, and educated, and some found new and loving homes. But child welfare in the United States never will be successful. It cannot escape the self-contradictions of its goals—compassion and control, uplift and discipline. Child welfare is one part of the problem of social welfare, largely an economic and political issue. When immigrants achieved sufficient political power in Boston, they created their own children's institutions and had fewer poor children to institutionalize in them. With political power came greater economic security that protected the working-class family from disruption.

The debate over charity and pauperization has continued for two centuries with no result. Americans, like all people, prefer independence to dependence and meaningful work to welfare. All parents want to love and provide and protect their children. It was and is the economic system that produced wayward and homeless children.

Voluntary efforts to relieve poverty have always been inadequate, however well-intentioned. Public institutions always sheltered more children than the quaintly-named asylums considered here. Both private and public child welfare efforts have always been a cooperative attempt to resolve the problem of poor children, and never more so than since 1930. As a public agency child welfare caseworker in Boston in the 1970s, I saw the same private agencies discussed here—HGS, HDCC, BCAS, NEHLW, CM, and JBF—(or their successors)—grapple with public child welfare cases on a fee-for-service basis. Since 1930 the public sector has financially outdistanced the more prestigious private sector and converted the private agencies into clients. The results, unfortunately, are disappointing.

In the 1980s the debate reverted to the ancient (and false) myth that character prevents poverty. Most of the wayward children of Victorian Boston were the victims of economic and social forces, sickness, disability, old age, mental illness, and unemployment. They were not poor because they or their parents were immoral. The distinction between the worthy and unworthy poor is a fiction comforting to the affluent but false and degrading to the poor. Recent statistics indicate that many neglected and abused children (the incidence of which rose from 101 cases per 10,000 children in 1978 to 272 per 10,000 in 1984) are found in single-female headed (40 percent) white (70 percent) families. The average age of these boys and girls is seven and their mothers are 32 years old and receiving (45 percent) public welfare assistance. Also 17 percent of all persons arrested in the United States in 1985 were under age 18 and 5.7 percent under age fifteen.[9]

It does not stretch the imagination or the facts to suggest a connection between poverty, child neglect or abuse, and juvenile arrests. Poor children populated Victorian Boston orphanages and the Progressives' Boston Juvenile Court as they fill child welfare agencies and juvenile courts today. Bostonians fear lower-class juvenile crime now as their grandparents did in the last century. Efforts to solve these social problems continue with the best intentions but with as little success (and perhaps less) as the efforts of child-savers in the nineteenth century and social workers in the 1920s.

What is the solution? Historians examine the past and are not expected to predict the future, but they can hazard a guess based on the facts presented here. Children will be malnourished, poorly-clothed, ill-educated, neglected, abused, and abandoned, and they will turn to crime as often in the 1990s as they did in the 1890s if poverty continues to debilitate lower-class families. It is time for a national examination of poverty, disease, and crime with a new agenda and new determination to eradicate the causes and consequences of poverty and ignorance. Private philanthropy cannot suffice; it has never been sufficient, however far-sighted and earnest. Public welfare must provide adequate incomes, medical care, and meaningful employment if the next generation is to avoid the social problems of all past generations. This will require that all Americans accept poverty and crime as relics of the benighted past, problems that can be solved and prevented.

The cautious and conservative policies of American leaders have failed to solve these problems, but perhaps far-sighted men and women of new administrations in state houses and in Washington will be more effective. But no permanent solutions can be devised and implemented without an understanding of the history of the wayward child and efforts to save him in the past.

Notes

Introduction

1. David G. Gil and John H. Nobel, "Public Knowledge, Attitudes and Opinions about Child Abuse in the U.S.," *Child Welfare* 48 (July 1969): 395–401; *Boston Globe*, 6 October 1986, 9.

2. *Statistical Abstract of the United States, 1987* (Washington, D.C., 1987), 161–71; Betty Reid Mandell, ed., *Welfare in America* (Englewood Cliffs, N.J., 1975), 57.

3. Alfred Kadushin, *Child Welfare Services* (New York, 1974), 6.

4. Barbara M. Brenzel, *Daughters of the State: A Social Portrait of the First Reform School for Girls in North America, 1856–1905* (Cambridge, 1983), 95.

5. Walter I. Trattner, *From Poor Law to Welfare State: A History of Social Welfare in America* (New York, 1975), 11.

6. Franklin B. Sanborn, *The Public Charities of Massachusetts* (Boston, 1876), 110–27; Bernard Bailyn, *Education in the Formation of American Society* (New York, 1960).

7. Edmund S. Morgan, *The Puritan Family: Religion and Domestic Relations in Seventeenth Century New England* (New York, 1966), 87, 110.

8. Robert F. Seybolt, *The Town Officials of Colonial Boston, 1634–1775* (Cambridge, 1939).

9. Josiah H. Benton, *Warning Out in New England, 1656–1817* (Boston, 1911), 5–30.

10. Samuel Freeman, *The Town Officer: Or the Power and Duty of Selectmen* (Boston, 1808), pp. 212–14.

11. Joseph F. Kett, *Rites of Passage: Adolescence in America, 1790 to the Present* (New York, 1977), 18; Nathaniel B. Shutleff, *A Topographical and Historical Description of Boston* (Boston, 1872), 310.

12. Robert W. Kelso, *The History of Public Poor Relief in Massachusetts, 1620–1920* (Boston, 1922), 115; Gary B. Nash, *The Urban Crucible: Social Change, Political Consciousness, and the Origins of the American Revolution* (Cambridge, 1979), 108–17.

13. John P. Demos, *A Little Commonwealth: Family Life in Plymouth Colony* (New York, 1970), 135; Abbot Emerson Smith, *Colonists in Bondage: White Servitude and Convict Labor in America, 1607–1776* (New York, 1971), 166; Nathaniel B. Shurtleff, ed., *Records of New Plymouth Colony, Court Orders* (Boston, 1855), 3:72.

14. Philippe Aries, *Centuries of Childhood: A Social History of Family Life* (New York, 1962), 128; Bernard Wishy, *The Child and the Republic: The Dawn of Modern American Child Nuture* (Philadelphia, 1972).

15. Michael B. Katz, *Class, Bureaucracy and Schools: The Illusion of Educational Change in America* (New York, 1971); Stanley K. Schultz, *The Culture Factory: Boston Public Schools, 1789–1860* (New York, 1973); J. Leslie Dunstan,

A Light to the City: 150 Years of the City Missionary Society of Boston, 1816–1966 (Boston, 1966), 32.

16. Michael B. Katz, ed., *School Reform: Past and Present* (Boston, 1971), 12, 141, 170.

17. Peter Dobkin Hall, "The Model of Boston Charity: A Theory of Charitable Benevolence and Class Development," *Science and Society* 38 (Winter 1975–76): 464–77; Ronald D. Story, *The Forging of an Aristocracy: Harvard and the Boston Upper Class, 1800–1879* (Middletown, 1980).

18. Peter Dobkin Hall, "Family Structure and Economic Organization: Massachusetts Merchants, 1700–1850," in *Family and Kin in Urban Communities, 1700–1930*, ed. Tamara K. Hareven (New York, 1977), 47.

19. Justin Winsor, *The Memorial History of Boston*, (Boston, 1882), 4:659.

20. Catharine Maria Sedgwick, *Home* (Boston, 1835); Walt Whitman, *Franklin Evans, Or, The Inebriate: A Tale of the Times* (New York, 1929); Christopher Lasch, *Haven in a Heartless World: The Family Besieged* (New York, 1977).

21. Massachusetts, *Report of a General Plan for the Promotion of Public and Personal Health, Devised, Prepared and Recommended by the Commissioners Appointed Under Resolve of the Legislature of Massachusetts, Relating to a Sanitary Survey of the State* (Boston, 1850), 153–55; Michael B. Katz, *The Irony of Early School Reform: Educational Innovation in Mid-Nineteenth Century Massachusetts* (Boston, 1968), 174.

Chapter 1. Boston Protestant Charity for Children

1. Homer Folks, *The Care of Destitute, Neglected, and Delinquent Children* (Albany, 1907), 30–36; see also Peter Dobkin Hall, *The Organization of American Culture, 1700–1900: Private Institutions, Elites, and the Origins of American Nationality* (New York, 1984), 109–10.

2. Gustave de Beaumont and Alexis de Tocqueville, *On the Penitentiary System in the United States*, ed. Thorsten Sellin (Carbondale, 1964), 136–50.

3. George W. Pierson, *Tocqueville and Beaumont in America* (New York, 1938), 69.

4. Robert A. McCaughey, "From Town to City: Boston in the 1820's," *Political Science Quarterly* 88 (June 1973): 191–213; Robert H. Bremner, *From the Depths: The Discovery of Poverty in the United States* (New York, 1956), 85–88.

5. Robert S. Pickett, *House of Refuge: Origins of Juvenile Reform in New York State, 1815–1857* (Syracuse, 1969); Justin Winsor, *The Memorial History of Boston* (Boston, 1882), 4:646.

6. Michael Ignatieff, *A Just Measure of Pain: The Penitentiary in the Industrial Revolution, 1750–1850* (New York, 1978); Stanley K. Schultz, *The Culture Factory: Boston Schools, 1789–1860* (New York, 1973), 248–93.

7. Enoch C. Wines and Theodore W. Dwight, *Report on the Prisons and Reformatories in the United States and Canada* (Albany, 1867), 354–55; Arthur Wellington Brayley, *Schools and Schoolboys of Old Boston* (Boston, 1894), 108–11; and John F. Richmond, "The House of Reformation," *New England Magazine* 3 (November 1832): 382–90.

8. Beaumont and Tocqueville, *Penitentiary System*, pp. 163–64.

9. W. David Lewis, *From Newgate to Dannemora: The Rise of the Penitentiary in New York* (New York, 1965); and on the tension between custody and curing due to public apathy and political interference in Massachusetts; see Gerald N. Grob, *The State and the Mentally Ill* (Chapel Hill, 1966), and Mary Ann Jiminez,

Changing Faces of Madness: Early American Attitudes and Treatment of the Insane (Hanover, 1987).

10. Prison Discipline Society, *Fourth Annual Report* (Boston, 1829), 297–98; Harold Garfinkel, "Conditions of Successful Degradation Ceremonies," *American Journal of Sociology* 61 (March 1956): 420–24.

11. Edward Everett Hale, *James Russell Lowell and His Friends* (Boston, 1899), 55; David J. Rothman, *The Discovery of the Asylum: Social Order and Disorder in the New Republic* (Boston, 1971), and his sequel, *Conscience and Convenience: The Asylum and its Alternatives in Progressive America* (Boston, 1980).

12. Christopher Lasch, *The World of Nations: Reflections on American History, Politics and Culture* (New York, 1972), 3–17; John J. Toomey and Edward P. F. Rankin, *History of South Boston* (Boston, 1901), 152–54.

13. Grob, *The State and the Mentally Ill*, 227–29; Massachusetts, State Board of Education, *Sixty-first Annual Report* (1898), 14; "A Parental School," *Lend A Hand* 8 (February 1892): 90–96.

14. Boston, in *Report of the Committee of the Overseers of the Poor on Street-Begging* (Boston, 1865), 5, reported 477 boys panhandling or selling newspapers in 1865, often truants or petty thieves; and this problem continued; see *Report on the Treatment of the Poor* (Boston, 1878), on flexible "justice" for children in the Boston Police Court; see Massachusetts, State Board of Education, *Twenty seventh Annual Report* (Boston, 1864), 83–88.

15. Lydia M. Child, *The Mother's Book* (New York, 1844); Jacob Abbott, *The Rollo Code of Morals* (Boston, 1841); Catharine E. Beecher, *A Treatise on Domestic Economy for the Use of Young Ladies at Home and at School* (Boston, 1842); Carroll Smith Rosenberg, *Religion and the Rise of the American City: The New York City Mission Movement, 1812–1870* (Ithaca, 1971), 216.

16. Ruth H. Bloch, "American Feminine Ideals in Transition: The Rise of the Moral Mother, 1785–1815," *Feminist Studies* 4 (June 1978): 103–13; Boston opened a municipal orphanage in 1878 which was soon criticized for overcrowding; see *Report of the Commission on the Treatment of the Poor*, 23 and Boston City Documents, No. 122, *Special Committee to Inspect the Public Institutions, Final Report* (1892), 46–48.

17. Daniel T. McColgan, *Joseph Tuckerman: Pioneer in American Social Work* (Washington, D.C., 1940); Joseph Tuckerman, *On the Elevation of the Poor: A Selection from His Reports as Minister-at-Large in Boston* (Boston, 1874, reprint ed., New York, 1971), 70–72.

18. Nathan I. Huggins, *Protestants Against Poverty, Boston's Charities, 1870–1900* (Westport, Conn. 1971), 15–27.

19. Steven L. Schlossman, "The 'Culture of Poverty' in Ante-Bellum Social Thought," *Science and Society* 38 (Summer 1974): 150–66.

20. Theodore M. Hammett, "Two Mobs of Jacksonian Boston: Ideology and Interest," *Journal of American History* 62 (March 1976): 845–68; Roger Lane, *Policing the City—Boston, 1822–1885* (New York, 1971), 62–69.

21. Schultz, *The Culture Factory*, 275–80; Boston Police, *Annual Reports* (1850–66); John William Perrin, "The Truancy Problems in Massachusetts, 1845–1890," *Journal of Pedagogy* 17 (March 1905): 214–24.

22. Jane Riblett Wilkie, "Social Status, Acculturation and School Attendance in 1850 Boston," *Journal of Social History* 11 (Winter 1977): 179–90; Michael B. Katz, *The Irony of Early School Reform: Education Innovation in Mid-Nineteenth Century Massachusetts* (Cambridge, 1968), 162.

23. David Tyack and Michael Berkowitz, "The Man Nobody Liked: Toward a Social History of the Truant Officer, 1840–1940," *American Quarterly* 29 (Spring 1977): 31–51; Michael B. Katz, "Who Went to School?" *History of Educational Quarterly* 7 (Fall 1972): 432–54.

24. Joseph F. Kett, *Rites of Passage: Adolescence in America, 1790 to the Present* (New York, 1977), 46–50; David B. Tyack, *The One Best System: A History of American Urban Education* (Cambridge, 1974), 35–47; and Brayley, *Schools and Schoolboys,* 44–66, 90–92.

25. John Koren, *Boston, 1822–1922* (Boston, 1923, 136–48; Picket, *House of Refuge,* 87; for a visitor's account of the House of Reformation, see Marian Lawrence Peabody, *To Be Young Was Very Heaven* (Boston, 1967), 62–63.

26. McColgan, *Joseph Tuckerman,* p. 149; details on Wells and the decline of the House of Reformation are scattered in Boston City Documents, *Annual Reports of the Board of Directors for Public Institutions* (Boston, 1834–66).

27. Laura E. Richards, ed., *Letters and Journals of Samuel Gridley Howe,* 2 vols. (Boston, 1906–09) 2:511.

28. Forest C. Ensign, *Compulsory School Attendance and Child Labor* (Iowa City, 1921), 60–65; Charles Loring Brace, *The Dangerous Classes of New York and Twenty Years Work Among Them* (New York, 1872).

29. Thomas Bender, *Toward an Urban Vision: Ideas and Institutions in Nineteenth-Century America* (Lexington, Mass., 1975), 145–50; John L. Thomas, "Romantic Reform in America, 1815–1865," *American Quarterly* 17 (Winter 1965): 656–82.

30. Barbara J. Berg, *The Remembered Gate: Origins of American Feminism, the Woman and the City, 1800–1860* (New York, 1978), 159; Nancy F. Cott, *The Bonds of Womanhood: Woman's Sphere in New England, 1780–1835* (New Haven, 1977), 151–54.

31. Lois W. Banner, "Religious Benevolence as Social Control: A Critique of an Interpretation," *Journal of American History* 60 (June 1973): 23–41; Carl Scaburg and Stanley Paterson, *Merchant Prince of Boston: Colonel T. H. Perkins, 1764–1854* (Cambridge, 1971), 425; Barbara Welter, "The Feminization of American Religion: 1800–1860," in *Clio's Consciousness Raised* ed., Mary Hartman and Lois W. Banner (New York, 1973), 137–57.

32. Winsor, *Memorial History,* 4:662; Boston Female Asylum, *An Account of the Rise, Progress and Present State of the Boston Female Asylum* (Boston, 1803); Abby L. Wade, *Reminiscences of the Boston Female Asylum* (Boston, 1844).

33. BFA, Record Book, 1857–1887, 2 July 1887; see also two recent studies, Carol S. Lasser, "Mistress, Maid and Market: The Transformation of Domestic Service in New England, 1790–1870" (Ph.D. diss., Harvard University, 1981), Susan L. Porter, "The Benevolent Asylum: Image and Reality, the Care and Training of Female Orphans in Boston, 1800–1840" (Ph.D. diss., Boston University, 1984).

34. Boston Society for the Care of Girls (BSCG), *One Hundred Years of Work With Girls in Boston* (Boston, 1919), 5.

35. BFA, Record Book, 1892–1893, 13; Huggins, *Protestants Against,* 89.

36. BSCG, Letter File, 1926, passim.

37. Huggins, *Protestants Against,* 88.

38. Ibid., 85.

39. Robert H. Bremner, et al., eds., *Children and Youth in America: A Documentary History* (Cambridge, 1970), 1:667.

40. Boston Children's Service Association, BFA Photograph Collection, Box III, contains newspaper files and photographs of socially prominent trustees active

in 1927–33 fund-raising campaigns, including an ancestor of Mrs. Hannah Still-man; Henry W. Thurston, *The Dependent Child* (New York, 1930), 54–58.

41. Wade, *Reminiscences, 57–62; and Berg, The Remembered Gate,* 158; under the common law, married women had no legal status and could not sue in court or manage property in many states until the 1870s.

42. McColgan, *Joseph Tuckerman,* 135; Bremner, *Children and Youth,* 1:729; Brayley, *Schools,* 155; Nathaniel Hawthorne, *The American Notebooks* (New Haven, 1932), 24; Boston Asylum and Farm School, *Report for 1842* (Boston, 1842), 507; Charles Dickens, *American Notes for General Circulation,* (London, 1842), 1:64–117.

43. Nathaniel B. Shurtleff, *A Topographical and Historical Description of Boston* (Boston, 1872), 505.

44. Robert Rich, "'A Wilderness of Whigs': The Wealthy Men of Boston," *Journal of Social History* 4 (Winter 1971): 263–71; Frederic Cople Jaher, "Nineteenth-Century Elites in Boston and New York," *Journal of Social History* 6 (Fall 1972): 32–77.

45. Robert W. Kelso, *The History of Public Poor Relief in Massachusetts, 1620–1920* (Boston, 1922), 165; Michael B. Katz and Mark J. Stern, "Fertility, Class, and Industrial Capitalism: Erie County, New York, 1855–1915," *American Quarterly* 33 (Spring 1981): 63–92.

46. Robert M. Mennel, *Thorns & Thistles: Juvenile Delinquents in the United States, 1824–1940* (Hanover, N.H., 1973), 41; Joseph M. Hawes, *Children in Urban Society: Juvenile Delinquency in Nineteenth Century America* (New York, 1971), 81; Parents' and Children's Service Association of Boston, Archives, Children's Mission, Scrapbook, Volume II (1849–79).

47. Edith Rivers, *Working and Trusting: or, Sketches Drawn from the Records of the Children's Mission* (Boston, 1859); Children's Mission, *Light Dawning: or, Fruits of the Children's Mission* (Boston, 1856); Children's Mission, *First Annual Report* (Boston, 1850), 5; the New England Home for Little Wanderers was also supported by "energetic boys and girls all over New England" in Sunday schools according to the NEHLW, *Seventh Annual Report* (Boston, 1872), 5.

48. Children's Mission, *Third Annual Report* (1852); CM, *Scrapbooks: Early Days*; CM, *The Children's Mission: What It Is and What It Does* (Boston, 1884); CM, *Fourteenth Annual Report* (1863); a more recent analysis is in Paul Boyer, *Urban Masses and Moral Order in America, 1820–1920* (Cambridge, 1978), 17–18.

49. Brace, *The Dangerous Classes,* 86; Miriam Z. Langsam, *Children West: A History of the Placing-out System in the New York Children's Aid Society, 1853–1890* (Madison, Wisc., 1964); CM, *Ninth Annual Report* (1858); Donald Dale Jackson, "It Took Trains to Put Street Kids on the Right Track Out of the Slums," *Smithsonian* 17 (August 1986): 94–102.

50. Raymond Williams, *The Country and the City* (New York, 1973); Horatio Alger, Jr., *Julius the Street Boy* (New York, 1874); but Vida Scudder, *A Listener in Babel* (Boston, 1903), 71, noted that Boston Irish girls dreaded the country.

51. CM, *Tenth Annual Report* (1859), 3; *Eleventh Annual Report* (1860), 5; Mrs. Glendower Evans, "What Do You Know of the Children After They Leave Your Home or Institutions: Do You Supervise Them?" National Conference of Charities and Corrections, *Proceedings* (1907), 274–78.

52. Langsam, *Children West,* 25–27; Annette Riley Fry, "The Children's Migration," *American Heritage* 26 (December 1974): 4–10, 79–81.

53. Frances E. Lane, *American Charities and the Child of the Immigrant* (Washington, D.C., 1932), 47; Massachusetts, State Board of Education, *Twenty-third Annual Report* (1860), 61.

54. Critics of the unprofessional, haphazard orphan train method include, Thurston, *The Dependent Child,* 136; Bremner, *From the Depths,* 40; Amos Warner, *American Charities* (New York, 1919), 272; and Lyman P. Alden, "The Shady Side of the 'Placing-Out System' " NCCC, *Proceedings* (1892), an interview with Robert I. Beers, former executive director of the NEHLW (1 June 1987), revealed that he met elderly Boston orphan train passengers in Illinois in 1962 who were traumatized by their childhood experiences.

55. CM, *First Annual Report* (1850), 6.

56. Thomas M. Johnson and Barry Supple, *Boston Capitalists and Western Railroads* (Cambridge, 1967); John F. Stover, *History of the Illinois Central Railroad* (New York, 1975), 115–16; Boston Brahmin railroad directors cooperated with child-savers; see BCAS, Temporary Home Records, 26 September 1874.

57. William D. Kelly, *The Life of Father Haskins* (Boston, 1899), 70–73; George F. Haskins, *Report, 1851–1864* (Boston, 1865), 5; Haskins, *Six Weeks Abroad in Ireland, England and Belgium* (Boston, 1872).

58. George F. Haskins, *House of the Angel Guardian Report* (Boston, 1868), 23–25.

59. CM, *Eleventh Annual Report* (1860), 12, noted the demand for children exceeded the supply but that efforts would be expanded to fill this need.

60. Philip Greven, *The Protestant Temperment: Patterns of Child-Rearing, Religious Experience, and the Self in Early America* (New York, 1977); Lawrence Stone, *The Family, Sex and Marriage in England, 1500–1800* (New York, 1977), 475.

61. George C. Needham, *Street Arabs and Gutter Snipes* (Philadelphia, 1888); and Steven L. Schlossman, *Love and the American Delinquent: The Theory and Practice of "Progressive" Juvenile Justice, 1825–1920* (Chicago, 1977).

62. Boston Children's Aid Society, *First Annual Report* (1865), 3.

63. Cook was not unique because many New England clergymen were attracted from rural parsonages to urban bureaucracies; see Donald M. Scott, *From Office to Profession: The New England Ministry, 1750–1850* (Philadelphia, 1978); Donna Merwick, *Boston Priests, 1848–1910: A Study of Social and Intellectual Change* (Cambridge, 1973), 80–83.

64. Jonathan Katz, *Gay American History* (New York, 1976), 27–28, reports homosexual abuse of boys in Massachusetts jails; concerning probation, see National Probation Association, *John Augustus, First Probation Officer* (New York, 1939); BCAS, *First Report of the Executive Committee* (1865), 5–15.

65. Massachusetts, Board of State Charities, *Fourth Annual Report* (1868), 58; Mennel, *Thorns & Thistles,* 43–45; BCAS, Pine Farm Visitor's Book, Volume IV, July 1882.

66. Horace Mann, Theodore Parker, Samuel Gridley Howe, and Julia Ward Howe investigated asylums in Europe in 1843. Charles Dickens, who supervised a London refuge for homeless women, guided the Howes to London asylums as they had done for him in Boston; see Deborah Pickman Clifford, *Mine Eyes Have Seen the Glory: A Biography of Julia Ward Howe* (Boston, 1979), 70–77.

67. Brace, *The Dangerous Classes,* 115; BCAS, *Second Annual Report* (1866), 10.

68. Board of State Charities, *Fourth Annual Report* (1868), 56; *Fifth Annual Report* (1869), lxviii; and BCAS, *Third Annual Report* (1867), 6.

69. Haskins, *Report* (1868), 25; BCAS, *Third Annual Report,* 7; *Ninth Annual Report* (1869), 4.

70. Roy Lubove, *The Professional Altruist: The Emergence of Social Work as a*

Career, 1880–1930 (Cambridge, 1965), 28; BCAS, *Ninth Annual Report,* 3–4; *Thirteenth Annual Report* (1877), 3.

71. BCAS, Boston North End Mission Records, Committee Minutes, (14 November 1898), eulogized one trustee for his lifelong volunteer charity work. On BCAS leader, Robert Treat Paine; see *Dictionary of American Biography,* 14 : 158–59; and on BCAS social worker, Emily Green Balch; see Sam Bass Warner, Jr., *Province of Reason* (Cambridge, 1984), 90–115; social control by self-control is treated in Robert H. Bremner, *The Public Good: Philanthropy and Welfare in the Civil War Era* (New York, 1980).

72. BCAS, *Twenty-Second Annual Report* (1885), 8–11; Katz, *The Irony of Early School Reform,* p. 199; and *Boston Transcript,* 30 March, 6 April, 13 April, and 7 December 1877.

73. Thurston, *The Dependent Child,* 181; William H. Pear, "The Full Measure of Responsibility," NCCC, *Proceedings* (1906); BCAS, Pine Farm Visitor's Book, Volume 1, January 1869, 20; on Douglass, see Irving H. Bartlett, *Wendell Phillips: Brahmin Radical* (Boston, 1961), 82–86.

74. Peter J. Schmitt, *Back to Nature: The Arcadian Myth in Urban America* (New York, 1969), 77–79; G. Kitson Clark, *The Making of Victorian England* (Cambridge, 1962), 95; Gordon Milne, *George William Curtis and the Genteel Tradition* (Bloomington, 1956), 130; and Massachusetts, Board of State Charities, *Second Annual Report* (1866), xcix.

75. Thomas L. Harris, *Juvenile Depravity and Crime in Our City* (New York, 1850), 10–13; Edward Everett Hale, "The State's Care of its Children: Considered as a Check on Juvenile Delinquency," in *Prize Essays on Juvenile Delinquency* (Philadelphia, 1855), 25–27.

76. Mennel, *Thorns & Thistles,* 43–44; BCAS, Pine Farm Visitor's Book, Volume IV, July 1882, 34.

77. BCAS, *Eighth Annual Report* (1872), 6.

78. BCAS, *Thirteenth Annual Report* (1877), 3–4; Clyde S. Griffen, "Rich Laymen and Early Social Christianity," *Church History* 36 (March 1967): 3–23.

79. BCAS, Directors' Minutes Book I, October 1866, 23; Barbara M. Cross, *Horace Bushnell, Minister to a Changing America* (Chicago, 1958), 55; Daniel T. Rodgers, "Socializing Middle-Class Children: Institutions, Fables, and Work Values in Nineteenth-Century America," *Journal of Social History* 13 (Spring 1980): 354–67.

80. Abraham Lincoln, *Second Inaugural Address,* 4 March 1865; NEHLW, *Advocate* (May 1870), 60; and HDCC, Superintendent's Journal, 27 November 1865.

81. James H. Moorhead, *American Apocalypse: Yankee Protestants and the Civil War, 1860–1869* (New Haven, 1978), 65; Massachusetts, Board of State Charities, *Secretary's Supplementary Report* (1865), 77.

82. BCAS, *Twentieth Annual Report* (1884), 6–7; Thurston, *The Dependent Child,* 181–87.

83. BCAS, *Twenty-third Annual Report* (1887), 11–13.

84. BCAS, *Twenty-sixth Annual Report* (1890), 5; *Proceedings of the Conference on the Care of Dependent Children* (Washington, D.C., 1909), 133–34.

85. Charles W. Birtwell, "Home Libraries," *BCAS Report* (1893), formed 68 libraries with 52 volunteer home visitors in 1887–1893 for 646 children ages 7 to 16; later he added savings banks and home gardens, as well as written reports by staff on lawbreaking and immorality in working-class homes they visited as "librarians."

86. BCAS, Ledger for Savings Accounts, October 1915, records 126 children with savings accounts ranging from $9.00 to $990.00; the BCAS, *Forty-seventh Annual Report* (1911), was Birtwell's last report summarizing his multifaceted approach to child welfare; on vocational training, see Isabel C. Barrows, ed., *A Conference on Manual Training* (Boston, 1891), and Myron E. Adams, "Children in American Street Trades," *Annals of the American Academy* 25 (May 1905): 437–58.

87. Frank J. Bruno, *Trends in Social Work, 1874–1946* (New York, 1948), 133–35; BCAS, Correspondence Book II (June 1890), 20; New England Watch and Ward Society, *Annual Report* (1888), 26.

88. BCAS, *Twenty-seventh Annual Report* (1891), 9; Massachusetts Bureau of Labor Statistics, *Thirteenth Annual Report* (1882), and Robert Treat Paine, "Address to the Board," BCAS, Records, 24 March 1890.

89. R. Jackson Wilson, *In Quest of Community: Social Philosophy in the United States, 1860–1920* (New York, 1968), 173; BCAS, *Thirty-third Annual Report* (1896), 21; Robert A. Woods, et al., *The Poor in Great Cities* (New York, 1895), 191; and James C. Whorton, *Crusaders for Fitness: The History of American Health Reformers* (Princeton, 1982), 290.

90. Hastings H. Hart, "The Care of the Dependent Child in the Family," *The Pedagogical Seminary* 16 (June 1909).

91. Lubove, *The Professional Altruist,* 42–43.

92. Bremner, *From the Depths,* 201–03; Charles W. Birtwell, "Discussion on Destitute Children," NCCC, *Proceedings* (1902), 396–417; BCAS, *Twenty-third Annual Report,* 12.

93. Joseph Lee, *Constructive and Preventive Philanthropy* (New York, 1910), 16; Huggins, *Protestants Against,* 106; Boston Children's Aid Association, *Annual Report* (1930), 2.

94. Gregory H. Singleton, "Protestant Voluntary Organizations and the Shaping of Victorian America," *American Quarterly* 27 (December 1975): 549–60; Barbara Miller Solomon, *Ancestors and Immigrants: A Changing New England Tradition* (New York, 1965), 40–42.

95. Ronald Story, *The Forging of an Aristocracy: Harvard and the Boston Upper Class, 1800–1879* (Middletown, Conn., 1980); Lance Edwin Davis and Peter Lester Payne, "From Benevolence to Business: The Story of Two Savings Banks," *Business History Review* 32 (Winter 1958): 386–406.

Chapter 2. Boston Catholic Charity for Children

1. City Missionary Society, *Annual Report* (Boston, 1854), 28; Herbert G. Gutman, *Work, Culture, and Society in Industrializing America: Essays in Working-Class and Social History* (New York, 1976).

2. William V. Shannon, *The American Irish* (New York, 1963), 182–200; Charles Loring Brace, *The Dangerous Classes of New York and Twenty Years Work Among Them* (New York, 1872).

3. A. J. P. Taylor, *Essays in English History* (London, 1976), 75; Robert E. Kennedy, Jr., *The Irish: Emigration, Marriage, and Family* (Berkeley, Cal., 1973), 19–20.

4. Cecil Woodham-Smith, *The Great Hunger: Ireland, 1845–1849* (New York, 1962); Lewis Perry Curtis, Jr., *Apes and Angels* (Washington, D.C., 1971).

5. Herman Melville, *Redburn, His First Voyage* (New York, 1963), chap. 57; Lynn Hollen Lees, *Exiles of Erin: Irish Migration in Victorian London* (Ithaca, N.Y., 1979), 42–44.

6. Oscar Handlin, *Boston's Immigrants, 1790–1880: A Study in Acculturation* (New York, 1971), 114–23, rescues the Irish from the Paddy stereotype but ignores positive aspects of Celtic culture.

7. Samuel Eliot Morison, *Harrison Gray Otis, 1765–1848, The Urbane Federalist* (Boston, 1969), 107–09, 478–80; Doris Kearns Goodwin, *The Fitzgeralds and the Kennedys* (New York, 1987).

8. Paul S. Boyer, *Urban Masses and Moral Order in America, 1820–1920* (Cambridge, 1978), 37; and Stanley K. Schultz, *The Culture Factory: Boston Public Schools, 1789–1860* (New York, 1973).

9. Brace, *The Dangerous Classes*, 15–22.

10. Thomas Bender, *Toward an Urban Vision: Ideas and Institutions in Nineteenth-Century America* (Lexington, Mass., 1975), 132–57.

11. Maria Monk, *Awful Disclosures of the Hotel Dieu Nunnery* (New York, 1836); Ray Allen Billington, *The Protestant Crusade, 1800–1860* (New York, 1964), 32–45.

12. Donna Merwick, *Boston Priests, 1848–1910: A Study of Social and Intellectual Change* (Cambridge, 1973), 1–2; Emmet Larkin, "The Devotional Resolution in Ireland, 1850–75," *American Historical Review* 77 (June 1967).

13. James W. Sanders, "19th Century Boston Catholics and the School Question," *University of Notre Dame Working Papers* (Fall 1977), 17.

14. As late as 1892, the president of the Society of St. Vincent de Paul lectured Boston seminarians on NEHLW and BCAS hostility to Catholicism; see Thomas F. Ring Papers, Volume I, 7–10, Boston College Archives.

15. Timothy Walch, "Catholic Social Institutions and the Urban Development: The View from Nineteenth-Century Chicago and Milwaukee," *Catholic Historical Review* 64 (January 1978): 16–32.

16. Andrew W. Greeley, *That Most Distressful Nation: The Taming of the American Irish* (Chicago, 1972), 32–48, notes the profound Irish suspicion of do-gooders and formal authority; see also Kenneth H. Connell, *Irish Peasant Society* (Oxford, 1968), 20–30.

17. Robert H. Lord, John E. Sexton, and Edward T. Harrington, *History of the Archdiocese of Boston* (Boston, 1944), 3:368–70, 645; see also Lawrence J. McCaffrey, *The Irish Diaspora in America* (Bloomington, Ind., 1976), 53.

18. Daniel T. McColgan, *Joseph Tuckerman: Pioneer in American Social Work* (Washington, D.C., 1940), 127–28.

19. Annabelle M. Melville, *Jean Lebvre de Cheverus, 1768–1836* (Milwaukee, 1958); *Boston Pilot*, 13 March 1875; *Daughters of Charity, 1809–1959* (Emitsburg, Md., 1959).

20. Annabelle M. Melville, *Elizabeth Bayley Seton, 1774–1821* (New York, 1951); Charles E. Rosenberg, *The Cholera Years: The United States in 1832, 1849, and 1866* (Chicago, 1962), 64, 95, 139; John Gilmary Shea, *History of the Catholic Church in the United States* (New York, 1886), 1:195.

21. William Byrne, *History of the Catholic Church in the New England States* (Boston, 1899), 1:182–95; St. Vincent Asylum, *Annual Report* (Boston, 1843), 5; *Boston Pilot*, 26 October 1850, 27 October 1855.

22. For unwed mothers, the Daughters of Charity opened the St. Mary Infant Asylum and Lying-in Hospital in 1874; see Douglass Shand Tucci, *The Second Settlement, 1875–1925* (Boston, 1974), 13; see also Archdiocese of Boston Archives, St. Vincent Asylum Records, File I and Bishop's Journal, Volume IV, 19 July 1859, 239.

23. Sister Mary Elizabeth McHugh (a former St. Vincent's Asylum student) and Sister Thecla Robinson (a former St. Vincent's Asylum teacher), interview

with author, Boston, 20 March 1979.

24. Reverend Francis Sullivan (HDCC chaplin), interview with author, Boston, 6 May 1979.

25. *Boston Post,* 11 February 1912; *Boston Pilot,* 19 October 1912.

26. *Boston Pilot,* 22 March 1922; *Boston Post,* 10 November 1929.

27. Lord, *History,* 2:330; Handlin, *Boston's Immigrants,* 258; St. Vincent Asylum, *Annual Reports* (Boston, 1843–1913) show inmate populations from 200 to 600 girls, but an average of 300 in 1860–1913.

28. Byrne, *History,* 1:182–83, 195–97; Lord, *History,* 2:329–31, 630–31; *Boston Pilot,* 27 March 1875.

29. St. Vincent Asylum, Records, Box 10.

30. HDCC, Superintendent's Journal, 11 September 1865; Shea, *History,* 2:414, 3:468, 511.

31. Lord, *History,* 2:631; St. Vincent Asylum, Scrapbook.

32. "Jacob Sleeper," *Dictionary of American Biography,* 17:208; Shea, *History,* 4:511.

33. John A. Garraty, *Henry Cabot Lodge: A Biography* (New York, 1968), 4–13; Henry Cabot Lodge, *Early Memories* (New York, 1913), 56.

34. Merwick, *Boston Priests,* 6; Vincent Y. Bowditch, *Life and Correspondence of Henry Ingersoll Bowditch* (Boston, 1902), 1:80; and Lord, *History,* 2:631, 3:358.

35. Handlin, *Boston's Immigrants,* 221–29; Merwick, *Boston Priests,* 6–8; Lynn H. Lees and John Modell, "The Irish Countryman Urbanized: A Comparative Perspective on the Famine Migration," *Journal of Urban History* 3 (August 1977): 391–408.

36. Jay Dolan, *The Immigrant Church: New York's Irish and German Catholics, 1815–1865* (Baltimore, 1975), 4; Merwick, *Boston's Priests,* 88–90.

37. Theodore M. Hammett, "Two Mobs of Jacksonian Boston: Ideology and Interest," *Journal of American History* 62 (March 1976): 845–68; and Dorah Mahony, *Six Months in a House of Correction, or the Narrative of Dorah Mahony, Who Was Under the Influence of the Protestants about a Year* (Boston, 1835).

38. Richard J. Grozier, "The Life and Times of John Bernard Fitzpatrick, Third Roman Catholic Bishop of Boston," (Ph.D. diss., Boston College, 1966), p. 15.

39. John Higham, *Strangers in the Land: Patterns of American Nativism, 1860–1925* (New Brunswick, N.J., 1955), 28–30, 58–60, 178–82; Donald L. Kinzer, *An Episode of Anti-Catholicism: The American Protective Association* (Seattle, Wash., 1964).

40. John Gaffey, "The Changing of the Guard: The Rise of Cardinal O'Connell of Boston," *Catholic Historical Review* 59 (July 1973); 225–44.

41. Robert Aidan O'Leary, "William Henry Cardinal O'Connell: A Social and Intellectual Biography" (Ph.D. diss., Tufts University, 1980), pp. 220–30; William Henry Cardinal O'Connell, *Sermons and Addresses,* (Boston, 1915–38), 10:192.

42. St. Vincent Asylum Register, 1908, 63; NEHLW, Admission Record, 1883–86, 37.

43. Bishop William Lawrence, *Memories of a Happy Life* (Boston, 1926), 70; and "The Summer Work," *The Church Militant* 7 (October 1904): 28–29.

44. *Boston Pilot,* 4 November 1916 and 4 March 1922.

45. Rudolph Reeder, *How Two Hundred Children Live and Learn* (New York, 1910), 194, provides a rare view of asylum life; Sanford M. Portnoy, Henry S. Miller, and Anthony Davids, "The Influence of the Child Care Worker in Residential Treatment," *American Journal of Orthopsychiatry* 42 (July 1972): 719–22.

46. Sister Marie de Loudres Walsh, *The Sisters of Charity of New York, 1809–1959,* (New York, 1960) 3:64–84; and *Boston Pilot,* 24 July 1858 and 7 July 1877.

47. Sister Mary Elizabeth McHugh (St. Vincent Home alumna), and Sister Thecla Robinson (HDCC staff), and Reverend Francis Sullivan (HDCC chaplain) interviews with author, Boston, 1979; Reverend Francis Stannell (HDCC chaplain); also see Massachusetts, Board of State Charities, *Eighth Annual Report* (1872), 41–53; Reverend James Moynihan, S.J., the first Catholic psychologist in Boston, revealed no psychology services were used in Catholic asylums until 1945, "and then only very gradually," interview with author, Boston, 23 April 1979.

48. Florence Clothier, "Problems in Placement of Illegitimate Children," *Child Welfare* 40 (March 1941); 1–8; Sister Rose Quinlivan, letter to author, 8 June 1979.

49. Sister Marie Cassidy, (teacher, St. Vincent Asylum, 1920), letter to author, 30 April 1979.

50. Morris J. Vogel, *The Invention of the Modern Hospital, Boston 1870–1930* (Chicago, 1980), 40–46; Sister Rose Quinlivan, letter.

51. Barbara Gutman Rosenkrantz, *Public Health and the State: Changing Views in Massachusetts, 1842–1920* (Cambridge, 1972), 70–76.

52. Sister Rose Quinlivan, letter; Sister Zoe Hyland, (teacher, St. Vincent Asylum, 1929), letter to author, 23 May 1979.

53. Monsignor James H. Doyle (director, Boston Catholic Charitable Bureau) interview with author, Boston, 4 March 1979; Monsignor Charles A. Finn (1877–1982), recalled the sister superior in 1920 was "autonomous," interview with author, Boston, 8 March 1979.

54. Sister Rose Quinlivan, letter.

55. Ibid.; Mary Ewens, *The Role of the Nun in Nineteenth-Century America: Variations on the International Theme* (New York, 1978), 250–65.

56. *Boston Pilot,* 15 November 1876; two middle-class accounts are revealing; see Mary McCarthy, *Memoirs of a Catholic Girlhood* (New York, 1957), and Eileen Simpson, *Orphans, Real and Imaginary* (New York, 1987).

57. Elizabeth Oakes Smith, *The Newsboy* (New York, 1854), chap. 3.

58. David R. Johnson, *Policing the Urban Underworld* (Philadelphia, 1978); Herbert J. Gans, *The Urban Villagers: Group and Class in the Life of Italian-Americans* (Glencoe, Ill., 1962), 23–30; and Harry E. Burroughs, *Boys in Men's Shoes: A World of Working Children* (New York, 1944).

59. Children's Mission, *Light Dawning: or, Fruits of the Children's Mission* (Boston, 1856); *Boston Morning Post, Selections from the Court Reports, 1834 to 1837* (New York, 1974).

60. William D. Kelly, *The Life of Father Haskins* (Boston, 1899), 5–15; Barbara Miller Solomon, *Ancestors and Immigrants: A Changing New England Tradition* (Cambridge, 1956), p. 46.

61. George F. Haskins, "Asylum and Reformatory of San Michele," *American Journal of Education* 3 (March 1858): 580–82; Archdiocese of Boston Archives, Bishop's Journal, Volume IV, 23 November 1851, 62; Merwick, *Boston Priests,* 71–83.

62. Lord, *History,* 2:632–35; HDCC, Superintendent's Journal, 16 February 1865; *The Irish Pictorial,* 28 January 1860, 15.

63. Byrne, *History,* 1:192–93; *Boston Pilot,* 19 May, 26 May, and 2 June 1849.

64. George F. Haskins, *Report, Historical, Statistical and Financial of the House of the Angel Guardian from the Beginning in 1851 to October 1864 . . . with other Later Reports Appended* (Boston, 1864), 10–12.

65. George F. Haskins, *House of the Angel Guardian Report* (Boston, 1868), 25–27.

266   BOSTON'S WAYWARD CHILDREN

66. David B. Tyack, *George Ticknor and the Boston Brahmins* (Cambridge, 1967), 222; Thomas H. O'Connor, *Fitzpatrick's Boston, 1846–1866: John Bernard Fitzpatrick, Third Bishop of Boston* (Boston, 1984), 116.

67. Handlin, *Boston's Immigrants,* 162; Lord, *History,* 2:632.

68. BCAS, Pine Farm Visitor's Book, Volume IV, February 1883; Haskins, *Report* (1868), 26.

69. Lord, *History,* 3:359; Massachusetts, Board of State Charities, *Fourth Annual Report* (1868), 58; and *Boston Pilot,* 28 January 1861, 26 November 1864.

70. Joseph A. Allen, *Westboro State Reform School Reminiscences* (Boston, 1877), 23, was "convinced by experience that boys placed with farmers in the country are almost certain to do well . . . while those placed in large towns and cities are about equally sure to return to their former evil habits;" but Haskins and most Catholic child-savers, like Father Levi Silliman Ives in New York City, disagreed; see Aaron I. Abell, *American Catholicism and Social Action: A Search for Social Justice, 1865–1950* (New York, 1960), 50–55; and Haskins, *Six Weeks Abroad,* 82.

71. *Boston Pilot,* 26 May 1855, reprints Haskins's eulogy of Father William Wiley (1803–55), a runaway orphaned apprentice converted in Boston by Bishop Fenwick, Wiley converted Haskins and interested him in Catholic orphans; see *Boston Pilot,* 2 August 1851 and 26 June 1852 on the lack of municipal cooperation with Haskins.

72. Haskins, *Report, Historical,* 10, 21.

73. Ibid., 29–39, Haskins considered the notion that a juvenile asylum could be self-supporting "moonshine" by impractical "theorists."

74. Ibid., 26–29.

75. Kelly, *Life of Haskins,* 75–79; and other Catholic asylums sent Haskins unmanageable boys at their expense; see HDCC, Superintendent's Journal, 2 January 1867.

76. Haskins, *Six Weeks Abroad,* 124; *Boston Pilot,* 10 April 1915.

77. Ibid., 37–39, 48.

78. Kelly, *Life of Haskins,* 70.

79. Haskins, *Six Weeks Abroad,* 79–82.

80. Ibid.; Thomas T. McAvoy, *A History of the Catholic Church in the United States* (Notre Dame, 1969), 195.

81. Haskins, *Report, Historical,* 5.

82. Ibid., 32–34.

83. Merwick, *Boston Priests,* pp. 81–82; Haskins, *Six Weeks Abroad,* p. 128.

84. House of the Angel Guardian, Register I, 8 September 1860, Archdiocese Archives; Roland Aube, interview with author, Boston, 17 May 1978; Jerry Palmer, interview with author, Boston, 9 January 1979; Joseph E. Saul, interview with author, Boston, 3 February 1979; all are HAG alumni.

85. Lord, *History,* 3:632–35; Boyer, *Urban Masses,* 118; and HAG, Register IV, 5 November 1885; for example, interviewees recalled HDCC boys transferred to the HAG were known as "Harrys" (from the HDCC address on Harrison Avenue) and formed a clique in the HAG population.

86. The Reverend Antonio Ubaldus DiPrizio (a former inmate), interview with author, Boston, 17 November 1980; Monsignor James J. Keating (HAG chaplain in 1939), interview with author, Boston, 29 April 1978 *Boston Pilot,* October 7, 1908.

87. David J. Rothman, *The Discovery of the Asylum: Social Order and Disorder in the New Republic* (Boston, 1971), 207; *Boston Pilot,* 10 October 1908; HAG, *Silver Jubilee of the Brothers of Charity of the House of the Angel Guardian, Boston* (Boston, 1899).

88. Kelly, *Life of Haskins,* 140–49; Lord, *History,* 3:360; HAG, Record Book IV, November 1885; HAG, Record Book V, March 1905; when the HAG asked the Gloucester Overseers to pay $3.00 per week for a boy, the city officials suggested transferring the boy to the NEHLW or to the state; see Record Book X, July 1919.

89. Joseph E. Saul, Jerry Palmer, Roland Aube and Reverend Antonio Ubaldus DiPrizio, interviews, (quotes are from Father DiPrizio, a Franciscan priest); see also HAG, Record Book X, 23 May 1919 for a dunning letter to an Ohio mother.

90. Quotes from Roland Aube, interviews; see Thomas A. Dwyer, *Glimpses of the Brotherhood of Charity* (Boston, 1893); Erving Goffman, *Asylums: Essays on the Social Structure of Mental Patients and Other Inmates* (New York, 1961).

91. Lord, *History,* 3:575; O'Leary, "Cardinal O'Connell," 124–30; William Henry Cardinal O'Connell, *Recollections of Seventy Years* (Boston, 1934), 277; Monsignor James J. Keating, interview.

92. Figures on 1,665 boys compiled from HAG, Register, 1877, 1887, 1897, 1907, 1917, and 1927. Foreign-born boys were French Canadian (5 percent), Irish (2 percent) and Italian (1 percent); among the 16 percent who remained more than two years were many who stayed as long as six years.

93. Haskins, *Report, Historical,* 27; John O'Grady, *Levi Silliman Ives, Pioneer Leader in Catholic Charities* (New York, 1933), 57–61.

94. Haskins, *HAG Report* (1868), 10–12.

95. Judge Baker Foundation, *Harvey Humphrey Baker: Upbuilder of the Juvenile Court* (Boston, no date), 53; Boston Juvenile Court, Probation Case 672 contains a friendly letter from Brother Jude to Judge Baker.

96. HAG, Register, 1877–1927; HDCC, Register III, 8 January 1887.

97. Ibid.; Associated Charities of Boston, *Directory of Charitable and Beneficent Organizations* (Boston, 1914), 101; and John M. Cooper, *Children's Institutions: A Study of Programs and Policies in Catholic Children's Institutions in the United States* (Philadelphia, 1931), 570–76.

98. The Reverend Vincent J. Kelly (a visiting chaplain at the HAG), interview with author, Boston, 9 May 1978; Massachusetts, Department of Public Welfare, *Annual Reports* (Boston, 1911–37).

99. Joseph E. Saul and Roland Aube, interviews; Saul and Aube still live within sight of the HAG.

100. Lord, *History,* 2:635–38, 3:361–62; Byrne, *History,* 1:183–84; Samuel Eliot Morison, *One Boy's Boston, 1897–1901* (Boston, 1962), 60–64, asserts his grandfather "could believe no ill of the Irish."

101. Sister Mary Alphonsine Frawley, *Patrick Donahoe* (Washington, D.C., 1946); Francis E. Lane, *American Charities and the Child of the Immigrant* (Washington, D.C., 1932), 124–26.

102. Lord, *History,* 3:404; Society of St. Vincent de Paul, *Nineteenth Annual Report* (Boston, 1907), 74–76; Katherine E. Conway and Mabel Ward Cameron, *Charles Francis Donnelly: A Memoir* (New York, 1909).

103. O'Connor, *Fitzpatrick's Boston,* 115–17; Schultz, *The Culture Factory,* 307–08; Lord, *History,* 2:584–601.

104. Richard J. Quinlan, "Growth and Development of Catholic Education in the Archdiocese of Boston," *Catholic Historical Review* 22 (April 1963): 30–37.

105. Sanders, "19th Century Boston Catholics," 8; Timothy L. Smith, "Protestant Schooling and American Nationality," *Journal of American History* 53 (March 1967): 679–95; James W. Sanders, *The Education of an Urban Minority,* 18–19.

106. Lord, *History,* 2:547–609, 3:404; Alfred S. Foley, *Bishop Healy: Beloved Outcaste* (New York, 1954), 97–98; Conway and Cameron, *Donnelly,* 25–30.

107. *Boston Pilot,* 8 October 1864; HDCC, *Third Annual Report* (1867), 9; the State Supreme Court ruled the HDCC had the right to "bind out" children of unfit parents in the O'Connell case, HDCC, Superintendent's Journal, 25 February 1865.

108. HDCC, Superintendent's Journal, 11 February, 18 February and 14 March 1865; Donahoe advocated midwestern migration in his newspaper, *Boston Pilot,* 8 September 1849, perhaps because he and Mayor Jerome V. C. Smith sold Iowa land in the New England Land Company; see Handlin, *Boston's Immigrants,* 67, and *Boston Pilot,* 6 March 1850.

109. HDCC, Superintendent's Journal, 12 September 1865.

110. Ibid., 14 March 1865.

111. Ibid., 21 January 1865, and the Superintendent did not object when the court committed second offenders to reform school in other cases.

112. Ibid., 18 February 1865.

113. Children's Mission, *Fourteenth Annual Report* (1863), 11; NEHLW, *Advocate,* April 1870, 58.

114. HDCC, Superintendent's Journal, 18 January, 23 January, 3 March, and 10 March 1865, Adams took immediate steps "to counteract the efforts of the new so-called Home about to be established" on Baldwin Place. He promised that "we shall look out for the children in that place," later named the NEHLW.

115. Ibid., 15 February, 18 September, 20 December 1865, Rufus Cook of the BCAS befriended Adams, gave him a copy of the BCAS annual report and referred 57 children to the HDCC in 1865; see BCAS, *First Annual Report* (1865), 16.

116. HDCC, Superintendent's Journal, 23 February, 2 March, 10 March 1865.

117. Ibid., 2 February 1865.

118. Ibid., 17 March 1865, 23 December 1864, 11 January 1865; children accompanied their mothers to the House of Correction as late as 1907; see Boston Juvenile Court, Case 601.

119. Ibid., 18 November 1865; common drunkard was the most frequent offense listed, for example: "Three persons up as C.D.'s having children. . . . The women were put under bonds for good behavior. Joe Dever has two children, he was sent to [House of Correction] 6 months"; Ibid., 31 August 1866.

120. Ibid., 24 February 1865; *Boston Pilot,* 5 December 1864.

121. Ibid., 14 March 1865; many New England widows and orphans migrated to Midwest states; see Lewis O. Stilwell, *Migration from Vermont* (Montpelier, VT., 1948), 208–14.

122. Ibid., 20 January, 25 February, 1 March 1865, 23 October 1866; anti-Catholicism was responsible for delays, Adams wrote that a new Clerk of Public Institutions was to be appointed and "I consider it to be a great assistance to have a liberal man in that position."

123. Ibid., 27 August 1866.

124. Ibid., 28 August 1866.

125. Ibid., 15 February 1867.

126. Ibid., 27 August 1866.

127. Ibid., 21 September 1865, 28 December 1871, in addition to child-saving, the busy superintendent "went to . . . have plastering done in the kitchen & also to have the drain cleaned by order of the Board of Health" and "collected subscriptions" and "received donations."

128. Ibid., 19 March 1872.

129. Ibid., 28 May 1872, many priests perferred city placements for children Merwick, *Boston Priests,* 95–96.

130. HDCC, Visiting Agent Journal, 6 May 1891, 33; and hostility between the

HDCC and NEHLW subsided enough to permit the rivals to refer children to one another, even three Irish children "Booked for the west by Mr. Tole"; see HDCC, Superintendent's Journal, 30 May 1877, 288.

131. James Bernard Cullen, ed., *The Story of the Irish in Boston* (Boston, 1899), 128, 156–58, 383; Leslie G. Ainley, *Boston Mahatma* (Boston, 1949), 26, 246, noted Duggan, the mentor of Wardboss Martin Lomasney, instructed him "a politician should be like a clergyman or doctor" to his constituents.

132. Byrne, *History,* 1 : 183–84; *Boston Pilot,* 4 November 1908; Cullen, *The Story,* 383; Duggan's job was easier when HDCC president John B. O'Brien was elected Sheriff, and by 1880 Irish success in politics provided access to public institutions.

133. Byrne, *History,* 1 : 184; and John Lancaster Spalding, *The Religious Mission of the Irish People and Catholic Colonization* (New York, 1880), on efforts to settle the Boston Irish in the Middle West; and *New York Times,* 31 May 1987, reports on survivors of Bishop Fenwick's effort to relocate the Boston Irish in rural Maine.

134. HDCC, Superintendent's Journal, 18 October 1877; James P. Shannon, *Catholic Colonization on the Western Frontier* (New Haven, 1957), 64–66.

135. HDCC, Superintendent's Journal, January, 1887, 112–14.

136. HDCC, *Annual Report* (1896), 5; Thomas F. Ring, "Catholic Child-Helping Agencies in the United States," NCCC, *Proceedings* (1896), 328–29; Merwick, *Boston Priests,* 110.

137. HDCC, Superintendent's Journal, 24 February 1901; about 24 percent of children placed out were replaced or returned to the HDCC in 1877–97.

138. HDCC, Visiting Agent's Journal, 18 April 1891, 28.

139. HDCC, Register III, 22 March 1887, 120.

140. HDCC, Superintendent's Journal, 28 August 1866.

141. HDCC, *Sixteenth Annual Report* (1880), 10–12, the sisters sometimes corresponded with children placed out.

142. Mary Snow, (HDCC inmate in 1917), interview with author, Boston, 3 June 1981; neglected child referred to HDCC by a court could be placed out and, if he or she ran away, then committed to reform school, as in Boston Juvenile Court, Case 544; in 1907, 26 percent of the 131 neglected children in this court entered the HDCC.

143. Pauline Dever (HGS inmate in 1937), interview with author, Boston, 18 January 1979.

144. Ewens, "The Role of the Nun," 227; Mary J. Oates, "Organized Voluntarism: The Catholic Sisters in Massachusetts, 1870–1940," *American Quarterly* 30 (Winter 1978): 652–80.

145. HDCC, Registers, 1867–97, show a trend toward a longer stay; in 1867, 70 percent of 229 children admitted were placed out; by 1887 this fell to 52 percent of 498 children, and to 40 percent of 1,097 admitted in 1897; see *Boston Pilot,* 14 October 1916.

146. *Boston Pilot,* 26 June 1918.

147. Ibid., 23 December, 4 November 1916; Merwick, *Boston Priests,* 190.

148. Boston Juvenile Court, Probation Records, 1907, 1917, 1927.

149. *Upbuilder,* 25, 102; and BJC, Case 987; Pyne (1912–17) was a Malden city councillor active in Catholic charities for thirty years; see *Boston Pilot,* 13 May 1917; his assistant, Patrick Hayden, was in the BJC daily and Pyne's successor, William J. Driscoll (1917–23) had a close relationship with this court.

150. HDCC, Superintendent's Journal, 1907, 242; figures compiled from registers for 1867, 1877, 1897, and 1907.

151. HDCC, Case Record Cover Sheets, 1887–1947, indicate health data was first collected in 1928 and expanded in 1947. By 1907 the court placed neglected children in the HDCC but gave the more professional MSPCC all casework responsibility; see BJC Case 1043, 115.

152. Monsignor James J. Keating, interview; John O'Grady, *Catholic Charities in the United States* (Washington, D.C., 1930), 90, 125; Lane, *American Charities,* 216.

153. HDCC, Superintendent's Journal, 8 January 1888, 210; HDCC, Executive Committee Records, 22 August 1923; Ewens, *The Role of the Nun,* 230–40.

154. Monsignor Augustine C. Dalton (HGS and Catholic Hospital Board trustee), interview with author, Boston, 15 March 1979; Herbert Dwight McConnell (Congregational minister who converted to Catholicism, HDCC agent in 1935–75), interview with author, Boston, 13 June 1979.

155. Monsignor Charles A. Finn (1877–1982) saw his first "slave auction" in 1904.

156. The Reverend James Moynihan, S.J. (a HDCC psychologist in 1952), interview with author, Boston, 2 May 1979; *Boston Post,* 12 January 1906.

157. The Reverend Francis Sullivan (a HDCC chaplain), interview with author, Boston, 6 May 1979.

158. Sister Marcella Rettew and Sister Thecla Robinson of the HDCC, interviews with author, Boston, 19–20 May 1979; quote from the Reverend Francis Scannell, S.J., interview with author, Boston, 24 May 1978.

159. Herbert Dwight McConnell, interview; Sister Ursulita Toomey's family took a boy from a parish slave auction in 1927, interview with author, Boston, 21 May 1981.

160. Reverend Vincent J. Kelly (HGS chaplain), interview with author, Boston, 9 May 1979.

161. Monsignor James H. Doyle, interview.

162. HDCC, Ladies Aid Society File, 1950; *Boston Pilot,* 11 April 1914.

Chapter 3. Wayward Girls in Boston

1. Helen Campbell, *Darkness and Daylight; or, Lights and Shadows of New York Life* (Hartford, 1895), 154; Carroll Smith-Rosenberg, "Puberty to Menopause: The Cycle of Femininity in Nineteenth-Century America," in *Clio's Consciousness Raised,* ed., Mary Hartman and Lois W. Banner (New York, 1974) 23–37.

2. Greer Litton Fox, " 'Nice Girl': Social Control of Women Through a Value Construct," *Signs* 2 (Summer 1977): 805–17; Horatio Alger, Jr., *Ragged Dick and Mark the Match Boy* (New York, 1962).

3. Boston Female Moral Reform Society, *Third Annual Report* (1838), 16, describes prostitutes as "abandoned girls"; BCAS, *Second Annual Report* (1866), 8–10; Charles Loring Brace, *The Dangerous Classes of New York and Twenty Years Work Among Them* (New York, 1872), 116; on middle-class intervention into lower-class female behavior, see Judith R. Walkowitz, *Prostitution and Victorian Society: Women, Class, and the State* (New York, 1980).

4. Boston Juvenile Court, Case 973, contains a letter from Dr. Laura Hughes on 10 November 1915 that states, "I find that the hymen has not been ruptured, and I believe that she is of virtuous character."

5. Campbell, *Darkness,* 157; John F. Richmond, *New York and Its Institutions, 1609–1871* (New York, 1871), 333; Massachusetts, *Annual Reports of the Trustees of the State Industrial School for Girls* (Boston, 1857–1937); Carroll Smith-Rosenberg, "Beauty, the Beast and the Militant Woman: A Case Study in

Sex Roles and Social Stress in Jacksonian America," *American Quarterly* 23 (October 1971): 562–84; the State Industrial School for Girls at Lancaster and the State Reform School for Boys at Westborough will be referred to as the Lancaster School and the Lyman School (having been renamed for Boston philanthropist Theodore Lyman in 1884).

6. Barbara Welter, "The Cult of True Womanhood: 1820–1860," *American Quarterly* 18 (Summer 1966): 151–74.

7. Peter Gabriel Filene, *Him/Her Self: Sex Roles in Modern America* (New York, 1974), 88–95.

8. Keith E. Melder, *Beginnings of Sisterhood: The American Woman's Rights Movement, 1800–1850* (New York, 1977, 10; Allan Nevins and Milton H. Thomas, eds., *The Diary of George Templeton Strong* (New York, 1952), 2:56.

9. Kathryn Kish Sklar, *Catharine Beecher: A Study in American Domesticity* (New Haven, 1973), 150–60; Carroll Smith-Rosenberg, *Religion and the Rise of the American City: The New York City Mission Movement, 1812–1870* (Ithaca, N.Y., 1971), 215–20, analyzes female moral reformers' motives.

10. Boston Female Asylum, Records, June 1857, 20; David M. Kennedy, *Birth Control in America: The Career of Margaret Sanger* (New Haven, 1970), 50–58; NEHLW, Boston Penitent Refuge Society, Register of Inmates, 1821–1856, Case 259; about 25 percent of inmates were placed out as servants.

11. Nancy F. Cott, *The Bonds of Womanhood: "Women's Sphere in New England, 1780–1835* (New Haven, 1977), 151–54; Martha Vicinus, ed., *Suffer and Be Still: Women in the Victorian Age* (Bloomington, Ind., 1972), 160–70; Children's Mission, *Sixth Annual Report* (1855), 7.

12. Nathan I. Huggins, *Protestants Against Poverty: Boston's Charities, 1870–1900* (Westport, Conn., 1971), 90; Massachusetts, State Board of Education, *Nineteenth Annual Report* (1856), 120.

13. Ruth Miller Elson, *Guardians of Tradition: American Schoolbooks of the Nineteenth Century* (Lincoln, Neb., 1964), 262–81; Richard N. Bernard and Maris A. Vinonskis, "The Female School Teacher in Ante-Bellum Massachusetts," *Journal of Social History* 10 (March 1977): 332–45; Massachusetts, State Board of Education, *Twentieth Annual Report* (1857), 11; the *Eighteenth Annual Report* (1855), 128, claimed teachers imparted "morals and manners."

14. Brace, *The Dangerous Classes,* 117; Jane Riblett Wilkie, "Social Status, Acculturation and School Attendance in 1850 Boston," *Journal of Social History* 11 (Winter 1977): 179–90; Massachusetts, State Board of Education, *First Annual Report* (1838), 5; Michael B. Katz, "Who Went to School?" *History of Education Quarterly* 12 (Fall 1972): 432–54.

15. Ann C. Butler, *Notes of Inmates in the Female Department of the House of Reformation at South Boston* (Boston, 1834); Robert M. Mennell, *Thorns & Thistles: Juvenile Delinquents in the United States 1824–40* (Hanover, N.H., 1973); Enoch C. Wines and Theodore W. Dwight, *Report on the Prisons and Reformatories of the United States and Canada* (Albany, 1867), 354–55.

16. Boston City Documents, No. 8, *Report on the House of Reformation* (1838), 7–9; Boston, *Report of the Commission on the Treatment of the Poor* (1878); Boston City Documents, *Annual Report of the Directors of Public Institutions* (1890); Boston Common Council, *City Document No. 14* (1841), 18–22; Boston Common Council, *Report of the Committee Appointed to Investigate Alleged Abuses at the House of Reformation and House of Correction* (1864), 22–24.

17. Barbara M. Brenzel, *Daughters of the State: A Social Portrait of the First Reform School for Girls in North America, 1856–1905* (Cambridge, Mass., 1983);

Phyllis M. Cosand (director of the Florence Crittendon Home in Boston), interview with author, Boston, 17 January 1981, confirms that female delinquents were seldom as sexually experienced as reformers feared.

18. NEHLW, *Advocate,* May 1870, 66; John S. Haller and Robin M. Haller, *The Physician and Sexuality in Victorian America* (Urbana, Ill., 1974), 100; John Griscom, *Memoir* (New York, 1859), 198, estimated 70 percent of the 1,687 girls admitted to the New York House of Refuge in 1825–1858 were reformed.

19. Barbara M. Brenzel, "Lancaster Industrial School for Girls: A Social Portrait of a Nineteenth-Century Reform School for Girls," *Feminist Studies* 3 (Fall 1975): 40–53; Joseph M. Hawes, *Children in Urban Society: Juvenile Delinquency in Nineteenth-Century America* (New York, 1971), pp. 84–86.

20. John Clark Wirkkala, "Juvenile Delinquency and Reform in Nineteenth Century Massachusetts: The Formative Era in State Care, 1846–79" (Ph.D. diss., Clark University, 1973); Theodore Parker, *Social Classes in a Republic* (Boston, 1907), 238; C. D. Randall, ed., *History of Child-Saving in the United States* (Boston, 1893), 62–68; and Bradford K. Peirce, *A Half-Century with Juvenile Delinquents, or; The New York House of Refuge and its Times* (New York, 1869), 239–46; and Massachusetts, State Board of Education, *Twenty-third Annual Report* (1860), 61; and *Twenty-fourth Annual Report* (1861), 167–69; Massachusetts, Trustees of the State Industrial School for Girls, *First Annual Report* (1857), 6–12.

21. Barbara M. Brenzel, "Domestication as Reform: A Study of the Socialization of Wayward Girls, 1856–1905," *Harvard Educational Review* 50 (May 1980): 196–213; Ray S. Hubbard, *Crusading for Children: The Massachusetts Society for the Prevention of Cruelty to Children* (Boston, 1943), 14; Steven L. Schlossman, *Love and the American Delinquent: The Theory and Practice of "Progressive" Juvenile Justice, 1825–1920* (Chicago, 1977), 39–42.

22. Massachusetts, *Acts and Resolves of 1870,* Chap. 359, Sec. 8; *Acts of 1871,* Chap. 365, admitted girls aged seventeen to Lancaster and transferred inmates to other state institutions; Laura F. Richards, *Letters and Journals of Samuel Gridley Howe,* (Boston, 1909), 2:188; Lancaster, *Annual Report* (1861), 8.; Peirce is quoted in State Board of Education, *Twenty-fourth Annual Report,* 169; on visiting agents, see Gardiner Tufts, Letter Books, 1869–1890, Tufts Papers, Massachusetts Historical Society.

23. Laura E. Richards, *Samuel Gridley Howe* (New York, 1835), 166; Samuel Gridley Howe, *A Letter to the Commissioners of Massachusetts for the State Reform School for Girls* (Boston, 1854), 26–28; Laura E. Richards, "Horace Mann to Samuel G. Howe," *New England Quarterly* 12 (December 1939): 730–44; efforts to abolish Lancaster in 1878 were unsuccessful and the institution survived for a century longer; see W. F. Spaulding, "Report from Massachusetts," NCCC, *Proceedings* (1879), 22–23.

24. Frank B. Sanborn, *Dr. S. G. Howe, the Philanthropist* (New York, 1891), 212 notes that reformers' debates "led to heated and protracted controversy, carried on, as such things always are in Boston, with much personal bitterness."

25. Estelle B. Freedman, *Their Sisters' Keepers: Women's Prison Reform in America, 1830–1930* (Ann Arbor, Mich., 1981), 83–86, makes a comparable case for the Massachusetts Reformatory for Women to which many Lancaster inmates were transferred; *Boston Globe,* 4 March 1979; Harold Schwartz, *Samuel Gridley Howe: Social Reformer, 1801–1876* (Cambridge, 1956), p. 275; Lancaster, *Annual Report* (1858), 7; Henry Barnard, "Samuel Gridley Howe," *American Journal of Education* 11 (1862): 389–99.

26. Associated Charities, *Directory of Charitable and Benevolent Organizations* (Boston, 1914), 99; Massachusetts, State Board of Charities, *Annual Reports*

of the State Primary School and Reform Schools (Boston, 1879–86); Tufts, Letter Books, 174.

27. Massachusetts, State Board of Education, *Twenty-fourth Annual Report,* 167–69, reports Lancaster was not called a reform school "to save its inmates from any stigma;" but its reputation declined as the average age rose; see Randall, *History of Child-Saving,* 247–58; Irene McAuliffe was Boston's first female police officer in 1921–34; see *Boston Globe Magazine,* 4 January 1987, 61; see also Roger Lane, *Policing the City—Boston, 1822–1885* (Cambridge, 1967), 62–69.

28. Edward H. Savage, *Police Records and Recollections: Or, Boston By Daylight and Gaslight for Two Hundred and Forty Years* (Boston, 1873), 173–82.

29. Elijah Adlow, *Threshold of Justice—A Judge's Life Story* (Boston, 1973), describes the rough justice in nineteenth-century Boston police stations, families, and courts; see also James F. Richardson, *The New York Police: Colonial Times to 1901* (New York, 1970), 19.

30. Michael Lipsky, "Toward a Theory of Street-Level Bureaucracy," in *State, School and Politics,* ed. Michael Kirst (Lexington, Mass., 1972); Sanford J. Fox, "Juvenile Justice Reform: An Historical Perspective," *Stanford Law Review* 22 (June 1970): 1187–1239.

31. *Boston Post, Selections from the Court Reports, 1834 to 1837* (New York, 1974), 70, describes an Irish mother who "fought like a tiger" to prevent Police Court officers from taking her sons (aged nine and twelve) to jail; only by the 1860s were child-savers in court to aid in such cases; see NEHLW, *Advocate,* March 1870, 35.

32. Horatio Woodman, ed., *Reports of Criminal Cases Tried in the Municipal Court of the City of Boston* (Boston, 1845), 165–67, reports Judge Peter Oxenbridge Thacher (1776–1843) dealt compassionately with children and ruled that a thirteen-year-old boy was "mentally deranged" by gin and cigars when he stole a watch; judges exercised wide discretionary power over children in Victorian courts; see Michael Lipsky, *Street-Level Bureaucracy: Dilemmas of the Individual in Public Service* (New York, 1980), and Susan E. Houston, "Victorian Origins of Juvenile Delinquency: A Canadian Experience," *History of Education Quarterly* 12 (Fall 1972): 254–80.

33. William T. Davis, *Bench and Bar of the Commonwealth of Massachusetts* (Boston, 1895), 2:80–90; HDCC, Superintendent's Journal, 23 February, 8 March 1865.

34. HDCC Superintendent's Journal, 24 February 1865.

35. Ibid., 20 April 1877, 284.

36. Ibid., 24 February 1865; on Judge Sebeus C. Main, see William T. Davis, *History of the Judiciary of Massachusetts* (Boston, 1900), 208–29.

37. HDCC, Superintendent's Journal, 7 August 1877; 5 September 1866.

38. Ibid., 13 December 1877; 11 July 1918, 389; NEHLW, *Advocate* (June 1892), 9.

39. HDCC, Superintendent's Journal, 28 April 1872.

40. Ibid., 2 February 1865.

41. Massachusetts, Board of State Charities, *Fourth Annual Report* (1868), 157–58, has state visiting agent Gordon M. Fisk's report of visits to Lancaster, Lyman, and Monson schools to place out inmates who, he claims, are "looking to him as a protector in times of need, and the pacificator of all their difficulties;" this claim is questionable, but reflects the child-savers' missionary zeal as does his hard work, 609 home visits and 442 letters to children or parents in one year.

42. Social workers distinguished between prostitutes and girls who experimented with sex by 1890; see Roy Lubove, "The Progressives and the Prostitute,"

Historian 25 (May 1962); 308–30; Linda Gordon, *Woman's Body, Woman's Right: A Social History of Birth Control in America* (New York, 1977), 200–205; and this liberal trend continued; see Paula S. Fass, *The Damned and the Beautiful: American Youth in the 1920's* (New York, 1977), 70, although lower-class sexual mores were more permissive than those of the middle class.

43. Edith N. Burleigh, "Some Principles for Parole for Girls," NCCC, *Proceedings* (1918), 147–48, denied her inmates were feeble-minded slatterns as earlier alleged, and the Lancaster, *Annual Report* (1912), 93–95, recognized private asylums attracted the better-behaved girls; Winifred Richmond, *The Adolescent Girl* (New York, 1925), 115–17, argued the modern girl was a "young animal" but seldom promiscuous; also see Katz, *The Irony,* 176–85; Eric C. Schneider, "A Fountain of Corruption: Female Delinquency in Boston, 1870–1920" (Paper presented at the Fourth Berkshire Conference on the History of Women, Mt. Holyoke College, August 1878); on Civil War widows and orphans; see William Schouler, *A History of Massachusetts in the Civil War* (Boston, 1871), 1 : 479–81, 2 : 530, 667; James L. Bowen, *Massachusetts in the War, 1861–65* (Springfield, 1889), 872–73; Thomas Wentworth Higginson, *Massachusetts in the Army and Navy During the War of 1861–65,* (Boston, 1896), 1 : 568; Edith Abbott, "Civil War and the Crime Wave of 1861–70," *Social Service Review* 1 (June 1927); 212–34.

44. NEHLW, *Advocates,* May 1870, 66, and March 1870, 36, admitted, "We have been called excessively rigid, but if we have been we intend to be more so in the future;" the directors succumbed to the myth of the promiscuous teenage girl by excluding all "babes not born in wedlock," in *Seventh Annual Report* (1872), 3.

45. Persistent parents could win release of their daughters because private child-savers feared legal challenges, as in BFA, Admission Records, 1896–97, 5, but not so public institutions; see Margaret Reeves, *Training Schools for Delinquent Girls* (New York, 1929), 382–83.

46. Paul Thompson, *The Edwardians: The Remaking of British Society* (Bloomington, Ind., 1975), 70–80; on both sides of the Atlantic, middle-class ladies organized private societies to elevate public morals by forming semi-maternal relationships with mill girls and maids; see Brian Harrison, "For Church, Queen and Family: The Girls' Friendly Society 1874–1920," *Past & Present* 61 (November 1973): 108–38; in 1877 this Anglican society opened a branch in the United States, but no reform school alumnae were recruited.

47. Thurston, *The Dependent Child,* 170; BCAS, *Fifth Annual Report* (1868), 7.

48. BCAS, *Sixth Annual Report* (1869), 9; BCAS, Directors' Minutes, Volume I, October 1866, 4; Huggins, *Protestants Against,* 93.

49. BCAS, Pine Farm Visitors Book, Volume II, December 1870, 15; Massachusetts, Board of State Charities, *Fourth Annual Report* (1868), 58; contains an inspection report on the Girls' Home; on "Auntie" Pomeroy, see Anna L. Boyden, *Echoes from Hospital and White House: A Record of Mrs. Rebecca R. Pomeroy's Experience in Wartimes* (Boston, 1884); Lucy Ellis Allen, "The Rebecca Pomeroy Newton Home for Orphan Girls," in *The Mirror of Newton Past and Present* (Newton, 1907), 89–90.

50. BCAS, *Sixth Annual Report,* 6; when the BCAS closed the Girls' Home, Mrs. Pomeroy reopened it the day after the great Boston fire of 1872 as a non-denominational orphanage placing girls as maids or foster children; see *Boston Globe,* 29 March 1981, and Massachusetts, Department of Public Welfare, *Annual Report* (1925), 96.

51. BCAS, Directors' Minutes, Volume I, June 1872, 9.; masturbation was a serious moral offense; see Haller, *The Physician and Sexuality,* 105, on the "solitary vice."

52. BCAS, Pine Farm Visitors Book, Volume II, April 1872, 25; Laura Crites, *The Female Offender* (Lexington, Mass., 1976), 27, analyzes the sexist, racist, and class bias wayward girls faced from social workers and courts.

53. Mild punishments at Pine Farm reflected the Pestalozzian evocative therapy BCAS preferred to the inculcative penal discipline; Robert Treat Paine noted that one boy "has now run away some half dozen times. He was punished by being kept in bed all the next day," in BCAS, Pine Farm Visitors Book, Volume IV, July 1882, 8; this indulgent attitude was in sharp contrast to the anxiety provoked by girls.

54. Carroll Smith-Rosenberg, "The Hysterical Woman: Sex Roles and Role Conflict in Nineteenth-Century America," in *Our Selves/Our Past: Psychological Approaches to American History,* ed. Robert J. Brugger (Baltimore, 1981), 205–27.

55. BCAS, *Sixteenth Annual Report* (1879), 9; and Peter L. Tyor, " 'Denied the Power to Choose the Good': Sexuality and Mental Defect in American Medical Practice, 1850–1920," *Journal of Social History* 10 (June 1977): 472–89.

56. Thurston, *The Dependent Child,* 108–10, 273–75, and Bremner, *Children and Youth,* 1 : 669, 2 : 259–63, both document the Civil War origins of the NEHLW.

57. NEHLW, Admission Register, 1883, 35.

58. Ibid.; on the expansion of Methodist missions among the urban poor in Boston and Maine; see Timothy L. Smith, *Revivalism and Social Reform in Mid-Nineteenth-Century America* (New York, 1957), 135–44, 165–76.

59. Huggins, *Protestants Against,* 96; NEHLW, Admission Records, 1889–1906, 131; The NEHLW monthly magazine, *Advocate,* January 1918, outlines the history of the home, as does Edward C. Winslow, *How it Came to Be, What it Is, and How They Did It* (Boston, 1929), and NEHLW, *Frederick Harrison Knight, 1859–1922* (Boston, 1922), on the superintendent who transformed it into a prestigious child study center; the NEHLW differed from the BFA, CM, BCAS and other elite Boston charities because of its *nouveau riche* Yankee Methodist origins and founders, self-made millionaire businessmen Jacob Sleeper, Isaac Rich, and William Claflin, who also founded Boston University in 1869.

60. NEHLW, Admission Records, 1889–1905, 235, and Marie Therese de Solms, *The Condition of Women in the United States* (Boston, 1895), 133, for a critical view of generous but coldhearted Boston charities.

61. NEHLW, Industrial School, Dorchester, Records, 26 January 1889.

62. Ibid.; George C. Needham, *Street Arabs and Gutter Snipes* (Philadelphia, 1888), 281; NEHLW, *Eighth Annual Report* (1873), 9, which reported 4,877 children had been admitted and 500 children sent on orphan trains to the Midwest.

63. Sentimental appeals were frequently found in NEHLW publications; see, for example, *Advocate,* February 1870, 21; on child-savers' rescue fantasies, see Kathleen Woodroofe, *From Charity to Social Work: In England and the United States* (Toronto, 1962), 83; Robert H. Bremner, *American Philanthropy* (Chicago, 1960), 114–16; much information on NEHLW child-saving was provided in an interview on 6 January 1986 with Robert I. Beers, former NEHLW director, and on 17 January 1986 with Phyllis M. Cosand, former assistant director.

64. NEHLW sent orphan trains to six Midwestern states by 1867, usually companies of forty children consisting of "boys and families of brothers and sisters" rather than the young girls child-savers were reluctant to place alone; funds were raised by the Orphans' Choir which toured New England and the Maritime Provinces; see *Advocates,* June 1870, 87; sexual abuse of foster children was a universal problem, then and now; see NEHLW, Records, 1900–1918, Case T6299; *Advocate,* April 1918, 26; Florence Rush, *The Best Kept Secret: Sexual Abuse of Children* (Englewood Cliffs, 1980); and David G. Gil, *Violence Against Children: Physical Abuse in the United States* (Cambridge, 1973). Massachusetts

had 23,000 such cases in 1878–1901, according to MSPCC, *Twenty-first Annual Report* (1901), 24.

65. Robert H. Lord, John E. Sexton, and Edward T. Harrington, *History of the Archdiocese of Boston* (Boston, 1945), 3:373–75; Katherine E. Conway, *The Good Shepherd in Boston, 1867–1892: Silver Jubilee Memorial* (Boston, 1892), accustomed to monasteries and convents in Europe, immigrant Catholics did not fear the HGS as much as Yankee Protestants did; see NEHLW, *Advocate,* June 1872 68, prostitution was uncommon among Irish women, which may account for the delay in opening the Boston HGS; see Hasia R. Diner, *Erin's Daughters in America: Irish Immigrant Women in the Nineteenth Century* (Baltimore, 1983), 116–18.

66. Gaetan Beronville, *Saint Mary Euphrasia Pelletier: Foundress of the Good Shepherd Sisters* (Westminster, MD., 1959), 167; and Louis Chevalier, *Labouring Classes and Dangerous Classes in Paris during the first half of the Nineteenth Century* (London, 1973), 277.

67. George Paul Jacoby, *Catholic Child Care in Nineteenth Century New York* (Washington, D.C., 1941), 198–201; James J. McGovern, *The Life and Writings of the Right Rev. John McMullen, D.D.* (Chicago, 1888), 130; Sister Mary of St. Marine Verger, *Practical Rules for the Use of the Religious of the Good Shepherd for the Direction of the Classes* (Angers, 1898).

68. Verger, *Practical Rules,* 134; Lord, *History,* 3:107; Katherine E. Conway, *The Golden Year of the Good Shepherd in Boston* (Boston, 1918), 7; and HGS, Annals of the Monastery of Our Lady of Charity of the Good Shepherd of Angers at Boston, 1867, 10.

69. Verger, *Practical Rules,* p. 67; and on the training of Catholic nuns, see Monica Baldwin, *I Leap Over the Wall* (New York, 1950), 98; inspiration, enthusiasm, and dedication substituted for formal training in the HGS.

70. Barbara Misner, "Highly Respectable and Accomplished Ladies: Early American Women Religious, 1790–1850," *University of Notre Dame Working Papers* (Fall 1980); Andrew M. Greeley, *That Most Distressful Nation: The Taming of the American Irish* (Chicago, 1972), 82–86.

71. HGS, St. Mary Register, 1907, 311, contains daily admission data, most of which refer to judges and probation officers by name and Overseers of the Poor who paid $2.50 per week to keep each girl there, the "sentence" was six, nine, or twelve months, renewable by the court; girls who ran away or were unmanageable were committed by the court to Lancaster, as in HGS, Case 4961.

72. BJC, Case 145 (1909), shows friendly correspondence between the HGS Superior and the judge informally transferring a girl from the Boston HGS to the Springfield HGS, in which the sister wrote, "We have nothing at heart but the child's future welfare, and we have confidence if she is properly placed when she leaves this Home, that she will turn out to be an excellent woman"; Chicago juvenile courts also relied on the HGS; see William I. Thomas and Florian Znaniecki, *The Polish Peasant in Europe and America* (New York, 1927), 2:1811–15.

73. In HGS, Register, 1907, Case 1214, Judge Baker of the BJC wrote the HGS Superior that he had "no power by law to keep her there, and she is not before this court on a sufficiently serious charge to enable me to send her anywhere else"; but HGS, St. Joseph, and St. Mary Registers, 1900–1927, contain typewritten lists of every Boston female probation officer and handwritten notes, "Catholic," "Non-Catholic" and "brings girls here herself"; by 1890 the "courts have acknowledged its worth by entering into semi-official relations with it," according to William Byrne, *History of the Catholic Church in the United States* (Boston, 1899), 1:194.

74. Richmond, *New York and Its Institutions,* 340; and BCAS, Children's Aid Association, Face Sheets, Case 40969, shows private agency cooperation with HGS; a fourteen-year-old Italio-American girl with gonorrhea was sent to the HGS because her parents "wished to give her one more chance" before asking the court to commit her to Lancaster.

75. Richmond, *New York and Its Institutions,* 341; and Eugenia C. Lekkerkerker, *Reformatories for Women in the United States* (The Hague, 1931), 90–98, notes Boston Quakers founded the Temporary Asylum for Discharged female Prisoners in Dedham in 1864 for similar aims.

76. Lord, *History,* 3:107–10; Margaret L. Shepherd, *My Life in the Convent* (Columbus, Ohio, 1892); for the best perspective, see John Higham, *Strangers in the Land: Patterns of American Nativism 1860–1925* (New Brunswick, N.J., 1955), 58–66, 77–86.

77. HGS, St. Mary Register, 1867, 5, records the first inmate who entered on 9 May 1867 was a twenty-year-old "American" born in Maine and sent "from the court"; Conway, *The Golden Year,* 7, notes the HGS admitted Protestants, Jews, and Blacks, although most inmates were Catholics.

78. Monsignor Charles A. Finn interview with author, Boston, 8 March 1979 provided information on Healy; Alfred S. Foley, *Bishop Healy: Beloved Outcaste* (New York, 1954), 97–111, notes Healy maintained close relations despite the racial prejudice that caused his sister to transfer from the HGS to a Montreal convent, Healy was overseer of all archdiocesan charities and wrote the HGS *Annual Report* for many years.

79. Rhoda Truax, *The Doctors Warren of Boston, First Family of Surgery* (Boston, 1868), 241, 294; St. Vincent Orphan Asylum, "In Memoriam to Dr. Thomas Dwight," *Annual Report* (1911), 6; and Lord, *History,* 2:640.

80. Conway, *The Golden Year,* 199; benefactors are listed in the HGS Annals, 1891; and Lord, *History,* 3:373, discusses state funds granted in 1870 "for once only."

81. Lord, *History,* 3:372; *Boston Pilot,* 17 October 1908, outlines the early days; by 1890 the HGS had thirty-four sisters and 324 inmates and had admitted over 4,000 inmates since 1867.

82. HGS, Annals, 1870, 35, listed twelve sisters, all with Irish surnames; Sister Bertha Collins, Sister Mary Canavan and Sister Mary Beatrice Carrigan, interviews with author, Boston, 21 March 1979, noted the working-class Irish-American origins of most HGS sisters; for a list of Boston Irish novices in the Good Shepherd Sisters, see John F. Byrne, *The Glories of Mary in Boston* (Boston, 1921), 483; HGS, Annals, 1867–1887, passim, notes many sisters died of "consumption" or tuberculosis.

83. Mary J. Oates, "Organized Voluntarism: The Catholic Sisters in Massachusetts, 1870–1940," *American Quarterly* 30 (Winter 1978): 652–80, notes 40 percent of the sisters in 1880 did charity work or nursing and few were college graduates; the important role of the calm HGS atmosphere to soothe easily distracted girls was noted in interviews by the author, on 17 May 1978 with Francis Toomey, an HGS employee from 1938 to 1960; on 24 May 1978 with the Reverend Francis Scannell, HGS chaplain; on 9 May 1978 with the Reverend Vincent J. Kelly, HGS chaplain; and on 8 March 1979 with Monsignor Charles A. Finn, who first visited HGS in 1900.

84. Monsignor Augustine C. Dalton, interview with author, Boston, 15 March 1979, a member of the HGS board in 1959–64, revealed the case history data was unavailable to the sisters "who were not trained as social workers" due to the rigid hierarchy and strict control by the sister superior; Dalton placed girls at the HGS

in the 1930s; some were placed as domestic servants in families he visited in the 1930s and "did quite well after the training the sisters had given them."

85. In 1887, 12 percent of the girls left for domestic service jobs, but only 7 percent by 1907, and most girls (57 to 85 percent in any given year) returned to parents; see HGS, St. Mary Register, 1867–1907; St. Joseph Register, 1885–1907; Most Reverend Richard J. Cushing, *The House of the Good Shepherd* (Boston, 1944); HGS, *Thirty-sixth Annual Report* (1903), 7.

86. Sister Bertha Collins' memories (interview with author on 21 March 1979) of the "wild and rowdy girls" are similar to the HGS, Annals, 1867, 10, which reported inmates "who were alas! for the most part violent and difficult characters." Few inmates were prostitutes, only adolescent victims of the criminal justice system; see C. C. Carstens, "The Rural Community and Prostitution," NCCC, *Proceedings* (1907): 267.

87. Kingsley Davis, "The Sociology of Prostitution," *American Sociological Review* 2 (March 1937): 744–755, found parental neglect and abuse commonly experienced by young prostitutes. Byrne, *History,* 1:194 described the Magdalens in 1890; and Conway, *The Good Shepherd,* 14, observed the besmirched past of Magdalens prevented them from ever becoming Sisters of the Good Shepherd, to protect the status and reputation of the sisters.

88. Sister Cecelia O'Brien (HGS social worker), interview with author, Boston, 4 April 1979, revealed few Magdalens were former prostitutes, but rather pious young women who felt a vocation to a life of prayer and penance for the sins of the world; also most St. Joseph girls were virgins and St. Mary inmates were usually anxious for the "Josies" to avoid the unhappy life they had led; HGS girls committed to Lancaster formed a clique there of "Josies" in 1920–60.

89. Raymond J. Adamek and Edward Z. Dager, "Social Structure, Identification and Change in a Treatment-Oriented Institution," *American Sociological Review* 33 (December 1968): 931–44; and Sister Cecelia O'Brien commented, "It is a mistake to impose a social work model on the House of the Good Shepherd and other Catholic institutions prior to 1950."

90. Katherine O'Brien, interview with author, Boston, 11 May 1979, a BJC probation officer, who attested to the willingness of many girls to enter the HGS instead of Lancaster; but even Thomas F. Ring, the president of the Boston Conference of the Society of St. Vincent de Paul and an Overseer of the Poor, misunderstood the mission of the HGS; see Thomas F. Ring, "Catholic Child-Helping Agencies in the United States," NCCC, *Proceedings* (1896), 337–38; see also Barbara Meil Hobson, *Uneasy Virtue: The Politics of Prostitution and the American Reform Tradition* (New York, 1987).

91. Recidivism was very common in the St. Mary Class, but no record shows a St. Joseph girl who later entered the St. Mary Class; on HGS management, see Mary J. Oates, " 'The Good Sisters': The Work and Position of Catholic Churchwomen in Boston, 1870–1940" in *Catholic Boston: Studies in Religion and Community, 1870–1970,* eds. Robert E. Sullivan and James M. O'Toole (Boston, 1985).

Chapter 4. Separate but Unequal: Black, Jewish, and Italian Childsaving

1. Homer Folks, *The Care of Destitute, Neglected, and Delinquent Children* (New York, 1907), 59–60; Leonard P. Curry, *The Free Black in Urban America 1800–1850: The Shadow of The Dream* (Chicago, 1981), 133–35.

2. Oscar Handlin, *Boston's Immigrants, 1790–1880: A Study in Acculturation* (New York, 1971), 52–53; Adelaide C. Hill, "The Negro Upper Class in Boston—

Its Development and Present Social structure" (Ph.D. diss., Radcliffe College, 1952), 54–60.

3. Quoted in C. Vann Woodward, *The Strange Career of Jim Crow* (New York, 1966), 19–20; Robert P. Smith, "William Cooper Nell: Crusading Black Abolitionist," *Journal of Negro History* 55 (July 1970): 182–99; Curry, *The Free Negro*, 70, declared Boston the most segregated (by residence and occupation) of the fifteen largest cities in antebellum America.

4. Odell Shepard, *Pedlar's Progress: The Life of Bronson Alcott* (New York, 1968), 210; Herbert Aptheker, ed., *A Documentary History of the Negro People in the United States* (New York, 1951), 1 : 147–48.

5. Leonard W. Levy and Douglas L. Jones, *Jim Crow in Boston: The Origin of the Separate but Equal Doctrine* (New York, 1974); Aptheker, *History*, 1 : 376–78; Leonard W. Levy, *The Law of the Commonwealth and Chief Justice Lemuel Shaw* (Cambridge, 1957), 109–116; Michael B. Katz, *School Reform: Past and Present* (Boston, 1971), 178–196, notes Massachusetts prohibited racial discrimination in public schools in 1855.

6. Arthur O. White, "Prince Saunders: An Instance of Social Mobility Among Antebellum New England Blacks," *Journal of Negro History* 55 (October 1975): 526–35, counted three hundred Black students and four teachers in the Smith School in 1837; James Oliver Horton and Lois E. Horton, *Black Bostonians: Family Life and Community Struggle in the Antebellum North* (New York, 1979), 2–5.

7. Quoted in John Daniels, *In Freedom's Birthplace: A Study of Boston Negroes* (New York, 1914), 27; and Donald M. Jacobs, "A History of the Boston Negro from the Revolution to the Civil War" (Ph.D. diss., Boston University, 1968).

8. Boston Prison Discipline Society, *First Annual Report* (1826), 35–38; Leon F. Litwack, *North of Slavery: The Negro in the Free States, 1790–1860* (Chicago, 1961), 68–72.

9. Arthur O. White, "Antebellum School Reform in Boston: Integrationists and Separatists," *Phylon* 34 (June 1973): 203–17.

10. Arthur O. White, "The Black Leadership Class and Education in Antebellum Boston," *Journal of Negro Education* 42 (Fall 1973): 504–15; John Hope Franklin, *From Slavery to Freedom: A History of Negro Americans* (New York, 1967), 237–40, points out colonization efforts were unpopular with Black Americans.

11. Philip S. Foner and Ronald L. Lewis, eds., *The Black Worker to 1869* (Philadelphia, 1978), 129–33; Donald M. Jacobs, "William Lloyd Garrison and Boston's Blacks, 1830–1865," *New England Quarterly* 44 (June 1971): 259–77.

12. Arthur O. White, "Salem's Antebellum Black Community: Seedbed of the School Integration Movement," *Essex Institute Historical Collections* 108 (April 1973): 99–118.

13. Curry, *The Free Negro*, pp. 113–25, found the Boston Almshouse in 1813 had 20 percent Black inmates but this declined to 1 percent by 1850 due to racial bias; blacks were over-represented (by four times) in the House of Correction by 1850, usually for sexual offenses (33 percent) of drunkenness (25 percent), suggesting little "criminality."

14. Robert S. Pickett, *House of Refuge: Origins of Juvenile Reform in New York State, 1815–1857* (Syracuse, N.Y., 1969), 6–8; Charles Dickens, *American Notes* (New York, 1957), 62; and see Society for the Reformation of Juvenile Delinquents in New York, *Eleventh Annual Report* (1838), 6, on Black boys committed to the city jail rather than to this new asylum.

280   BOSTON'S WAYWARD CHILDREN

15. Quoted in Robert M. Mennel, *Thorns & Thistles: Juvenile Delinquents in the United States, 1825–1840* (Hanover, N.H., 1973), 18; see George Wilson Pierson, *Tocqueville and Beaumont in America* (New York, 1938), 512.

16. Jacobs, "A History," 104–22; the account is in *The Liberator,* 12 March 1831, 43; see also Franklin, *From Slavery,* 236.

17. Andrew Billingsley and Jeanne M. Giovannoni, *Children of the Storm: Black Children and American Child Welfare* (New York, 1972), 8–12.

18. Barbara Brenzel, "Domestication as Reform: A Study of Wayward Girls, 1856–1905," *Harvard Educational Review* 50 (May 1980): 196–213, found Blacks were 6 percent of the Lancaster inmates while only 2 percent of the state population; Horton, *Black Bostonians,* 35, found reform schools and penal institutions had 5 to 15 percent black inmates in 1840–60; *See* Massachusetts, State Archives, Monson Primary School, Records (1876) and Board of State Charities, *Twelfth Annual Report* (1876), 12–17.

19. Henry Quarles, interview with author, Boston, 13 November 1981, a Black attorney born in the West End in 1907, who was BJC Clerk and a member of the Society of St. Vincent de Paul, noted the disproportionate commitment of Blacks to public asylums.

20. Grace Abbott, *The Child and the State* (Chicago, 1938), 1:191; W. E. B. DuBois, *The Black North in 1901: A Social Study* (New York, 1969), 30–38.

21. Herbert G. Gutman, *The Black Family in Slavery and Freedom, 1750–1925* (New York, 1976), 220–22; Paul D. Escott, *Slavery Remembered: A Record of Twentieth-Century Slave Narratives* (Chapel Hill, 1979), 46–48, reported 21 percent of slave families were disrupted by the slave trade.

22. August Meier and Elliott Rudnick, *From Plantation to Ghetto* (New York, 1966), 55–57.

23. Curry, *The Free Negro,* 132–35; John L. Thomas, *The Liberator, William Lloyd Garrison: A Biography* (Boston, 1963), 198–201; John F. Richmond, *New York and Its Institutions, 1609–1871* (New York, 1871), 302–5 is the most detailed account of the Colored Orphan Asylum.

24. Homer Folks, *Care,* 57.

25. NYCAS, *Third Annual Report* (1857), 30, notes "one clever little black boy" who was the flagbearer for an orphan train company, but this was rare; A. Blake Brophy, *Foundlings on the Frontier* (Tucson, 1972), discusses outrage in 1904 when white children were placed with Mexican-American families.

26. Elizabeth H. Pleck, "The Two-Parent Household: Black Family Structure in Late Nineteenth Century Boston," *Journal of Social History* 6 (Fall 1972): 3–31; Isabel Burke (Massachusetts Division of Minor Wards) interview with author, Boston, 12 April 1979, noted informal adoption of Black children "was very common in Boston in the 1930s."

27. Carol B. Stack, *All Our Kin: Strategies for Survival in a Black Community* (New York, 1974), 22.

28. Nehemiah Adams, *A South Side View of Slavery* (Boston, 1854), 85; this misconception continued in Howard W. Odum, *Social and Mental Traits of the Negro* (New York, 1910), 39.

29. Horton, *Black Bostonians,* 18; yet the press reported sensational cases of Black family breakdown; see *Boston Post,* 22 September 1906, on a Black South End mother who drank carbolic acid when a teacher threatened to send her daughter to reform school.

30. Elizabeth H. Pleck, *Black Migration and Poverty, Boston, 1865–1900* (New York, 1979), 164, refutes views of migrant Black urban families as weak, disorganized, and matriarchal, such as E. Franklin Frazier, *The Negro in the United States* (New York, 1939) or Daniel P. Moynihan, *The Negro Family: The Case for*

National Action (Washington, D.C., 1965); see William Monroe Trotter's warning in the *Boston Guardian,* 29 November 1902, about a fraudulent "Jim Crow" charity that did little "rescuing of wayward boys and girls from the temptations of the street."

31. Horton, *Black Bostonians,* 19; E. Franklin Frazier, *Black Bourgeoise* (Glencoe, Ill., 1957), 10–14; and Stack, *All Our Kin,* 23, on urban Black extended families and kinship fostering of homeless children.

32. Gutman, *The Black Family,* argues high illegitimacy rates are not *prima facie* evidence of family disorganization.

33. Lee Rainwater, "Crucible of Identity: The Negro Lower-Class Family," *Daedalus* 95 (Winter 1966): 172–216; Elsie Johnson McDougald, "The Double Task: The Struggle of Negro Women for Sex and Race Emancipation," *Survey Graphic* 6 (March 1925): 690–91, argues that "contrary to popular belief, illegitimacy among Negroes is cause for shame and grief. . . . Generally, the married aunt, or even the mother, claims that the illegitimate child is her own. The foundling asylum is seldom sought"; the best analysis is Herbert G. Gutman, "Persistent Myths About the Afro-American Family," *Journal of Interdisciplinary History* 6 (Fall 1975): 181–210.

34. Henry Quarles, interview with author, Quarles led the Vincentians' St. Peter Claver Conference in 1925–63 and noted "the Boston colored people before the Depression had too much pride to let a neighborhood child go into an orphanage" although he visited some Black children in the HDCC and Working Boys' Home.

35. Walter G. Sharrow, "John Hughes and a Catholic Response to Slavery in Antebellum America," *Journal of Negro History* 57 (July 1972): 254–69; Bishop Fitzpatrick in Boston, unlike Hughes in NYC, was a strong supporter of Blacks and the Union cause.

36. HGS, St. Mary Register, 1867–1916, Case 1537, in which a mulatto girl born in Virginia was admitted in 1880 and placed out four months later.

37. Robert H. Lord, John E. Sexton, and Edward T. Harrington, *History of the Archdiocese of Boston,* (Boston, 1944), 2:488; Donna Merwick, *Boston Priests, 1848–1910: A Study of Social and Intellectual Change* (Cambridge, 1973), 83–87; the best source on the Healy family is Alfred S. Foley, *Bishop Healy: Beloved Outcaste* (New York, 1954), but integration of Catholic asylums was debated at the Baltimore Plenary Council in 1866, according to Thomas W. Spalding, *Martin John Spalding: American Churchman* (Washington, D.C., 1973).

38. HDCC, Visiting Agent's Journal, 7 April 1891, 26, describes "a colored child who will be taken out about 1 May" to a Boston foster home; see also Annabelle M. Melville, *Elizabeth Bayley Seton, 1774–1821* (New York, 1951), for the foundress' anti-slavery background; Sister Marcella Rettew, interview with author, Boston, 9 March 1979, noted the HDCC admitted Black children "a few at a time" without "any fuss or controversy" and there "were even some Negro sisters" in the 1920s.

39. Lord, *History,* 3:364–67; George Paul Jacoby, *Catholic Child Care in Nineteenth Century New York* (Washington, D.C., 1941), 198.

40. Lord, *History,* 3:368; the Archives of the Sisters of St. Joseph, Boston, Daly Industrial School, show no Black students ever listed; Sister Ursulita Toomey (archivist of Daly Industrial School), interview with author, Boston, 27 May 1981, confirmed this policy, as do Archdiocese of Boston Archives, Daly Industrial School, Records, 1899–1960.

41. Foley, *Bishop Healy,* p. 121; Msgr. Charles A. Finn, interview with author, Boston, 9 May 1979.

42. Albert S. Foley, *God's Men of Color: The Colored Catholic Priests of the*

United States, 1854–1954 (New York, 1955); Lord, *History*, 1:647; Daniel T. McColgan, *A Century of Charity: The First One Hundred Years of the Society of St. Vincent de Paul in the United States* (Milwaukee, 1959), 1:337; and John T. Gillard, *The Catholic Church and the American Negro* (Baltimore, 1929), 208.

43. John R. Betts, "The Negro and the New England Conscience in the Days of John Boyle O'Reilly, *Journal of Negro History* 51 (October 1966): 246–61.

44. Francis R. Walsh, "The Boston *Pilot:* A Newspaper for the Irish Immigrant, 1829–1908" (Ph.D. diss., Boston University, 1968), 165–72.

45. Handlin, *Boston's Immigrants,* 205; HDCC, Superintendent's Journal, 28 February 1865, found: "In the Police Court 2 girls . . . of those dens where young girls are harboured for illicit purposes. The house is in Church St., is kept by a black woman, and girls of the age of 12 and upwards, are there taught all kinds of crime."

46. Handlin, *Boston's Immigrants,* 204.

47. Tension increased as the groups grew in size (52,000 Irish versus 2,100 Blacks in 1850) and the *Liberator* and the *Pilot* constantly sniped at each other; see Jacobs, "History," 331–33.

48. Edward H. Savage, *A Chronological History of the Boston Watch and Police, from 1631 to 1865* (Boston, 1865), 66–67.

49. W. E. B. DuBois, *The Philadelphia Negro: A Social Study* (Philadelphia, 1899), 357–58.

50. John J. Toomey and Edward P. B. Rankin, *History of South Boston* (Boston, 1901), 420–21; C. Bancroft Gillespie, *Illustrated History of South Boston* (Boston, 1900), 257; Episcopal Diocese of Massachusetts, Archives, Church Home Society Records, Box I; "The Church Home for Orphans and Destitute Children," *The Church Militant* 7 (October 1904): 133–34; Sibley Higginbotham (former CHS director) interview with author, Boston, 6 April 1981.

51. Robert Cheney Smith, *The Cowley Fathers in America: The Early Years* (Boston, n.d.); Robert Cheney Smith, *The Shrine on Bowdoin Street, 1883–1958: The Story of the Mission Church of St. John the Evangelist* (Boston, 1959).

52. Reverend Frederick C. Gross (Society of St. John the Evangelist), interview with author, Cambridge, 3 June 1978, a colleague of Fr. Field; Henry Quarles, BJC Clerk, interview with author; BJC, Case 937 and 10118 note Black girls who ran away from the CHS and BCAS. Both were sent to Lancaster when Fr. Field declined to accept responsibility for them.

53. Barbara M. Brenzel, *Daughters of the State: A Social Portrait of the First Reform School for Girls in North America, 1856–1905* (Cambridge, 1983), 116.

54. Rose Giallombardo, *The Social World of Imprisoned Girls* (New York, 1974), 33–53, analyzes one New England reform school with 62 percent Black female inmates and chronic homosexual black-white relationships; this confirms reports of similar "discipline problems" by Sister Cecelia O'Brien at the HGS in New York City and Boston.

55. Sister Mary Beatrice Carrigan, interview with author, Boston, 21 March 1979, revealed that naive nuns were shocked by interracial homosexuality among HGS inmates. See Albert Deutsch, *Our Rejected Children* (Boston, 1950), 69, on "black and tan lesbian relations in reform schools"; HGS and Lancaster tolerated some of this because "it reduced discipline problems among the girls," according to Henry Quarles, BJC Clerk and juvenile justice attorney.

56. Stella Goostrag, *Memoirs: Half a Century in Nursing* (Boston, 1969); Sister Catherine Louise, *House of My Pilgrimage: History of the American House of the Society of St. Margaret* (Boston, n.d.), 260; and Paul Boyer, *Purity in Print: the Vice-Society Movement and Book Censorship in America* (New York, 1968), 14, reports on Boston Episcopal organizations.

57. NEHLW, *Advocate,* January 1918, 2; and Norris Magnuson, *Salvation in the Slums: Evangelical Social Work, 1865–1920* (Metuchen, 1977), notes the absence of racial bias in Methodist charities.

58. Robert H. Bremner, et al., eds., *Children and Youth in America: A Documentary History* (Cambridge, 1971), 1:699, cites "a smart, intelligent contraband comes to us from the sunny South. Once a slave but now free" as evidence of NEHLW enthusiasm for Black orphans.

60. NEHLW, Admissions Register, February 1884.

61. Ibid., January 1884, 40–45.

62. NEHLW, *Frederic Harrison Knight, October 22, 1859–October 15, 1922* (Boston, 1923), 37.

63. BCAS, Pine Farm Visitors' Book, Volume I, January 1869; and Huggins, *Protestants Against,* p. 96, report one director objected to "a racially mixed boy" and questioned whether the BCAS should "take charge of children of such an unnatural union."

64. BCAS, *Fifteenth Annual Report* (1879), 3–5; and *Twenty-first Annual Report* (1885), 7.

65. Thurston, *The Dependent Child,* 181–83.

66. Massachusetts Infant Asylum, *Fifth Annual Report* (1872), 18; and *Thirteenth Annual Report* (1897), 16–29.

67. John L. Morse, "The History of Pediatrics," *New England Journal of Medicine* 204 (March 1931): 170–179, reviews the history of the MIA from 1867 to 1912 when it merged with the BCAS; also BCAS, *Fifty-first Annual Report* (1915) discussed the merger and BCAS Case 666, MIA Case 876, 5 January 1879 reveals admission criteria.

68. BCAS, BFA Records, 1907, 35.

69. Boston Children's Aid Association, *Annual Report* (1927), 5.

70. Francis Aldrich, Interview with author, Boston, 27 March 1981, a BCAS and Boston Family Welfare Society social worker, who lived at the South End Settlement House in the 1920's with extensive contact in the Black community; see also Clarke A. Chambers, *Seedtime of Reform: American Social Service and Social Action, 1918–1933* (Minneapolis, 1963), 18–22.

71. Charles W. Birtwell, "Introduction to Discussion," NCCC, *Proceedings* (1902), 400–401.

72. BCAA, Case Record Face Sheets, Case 40779.

73. Thurston, *The Dependent Child,* 181, noted it was the BCAS "avowed policy" to experiment and "to undertake a piece of work as a needed demonstration and as soon as it was adopted by public agencies to drop it and go on to another"; this was Birtwell's major contribution to social work; in BJC, Case 1073 (1907), for instance, he encouraged his staff to cooperate with Black social workers at the Sojourner Truth Club in the South End House.

74. Sexual misconduct included prostitution, fornication, bastardy, and homosexuality by children or parents; Black children represented 4 percent of my BJC sample; see chap. 5.

75. BJC, Case 147 (1906), in which Judge Baker unwittingly relied upon kinship fostering in lieu of institutionalization; he wrote the volunteer probation officer of a Black boy, "You will be interested to know that Arthur Roland by arrangement with this court, has left his father and mother and gone to live with his aunt. . . . Now that he is under a better home influence, you will find him a more fruitful subject to cultivate."

76. Robert A. Woods, ed., *Americans in Process: A Settlement Study* (Boston, 1903), 248–62; and BJC, Charles West Mack Williams File, Court Personnel Records, describes this Black Republican Common Councillor, who Governor

Curtis Guild appointed the first BJC Clerk in 1906; Williams (1870–1931) was a Sunday school superintendent who used his court position discreetly to aid the Black community; see also *Boston Guardian,* 14 March 1931, 3.

77. BJC, Case 342.

78. BJC, Case 10161; bunking out refers to runaway children who slept in doorways, alleys, sheds, or parks.

79. BJC, Case 1089.

80. BJC, Case 1192; and racial prejudice as a cause of the disproportionate incarceration of Blacks is well established; see Pleck, *Black Migration,* 92; Wiley Britton Sanders, *Negro Child Welfare in North Carolina* (Chapel Hill, No. Ca., 1933), 191; Yona Cohn, "Criteria for the Probation Officer's Recommendation to the Juvenile Court Judge," *Crime and Delinquency* 9 (July 1963): 262–75.

81. BJC, Case 10800; and Belle Boone Bard, *Juvenile Probation* (New York, 1934), 18–26 reports on five hundred BJC children treated at the JBF in 1929–32, of whom six percent were black; Healy endorsed this book, and apparently Beard's conclusion confirming "the popular conception of the Negro as impetuous, sensual, wandering and philandering but not vicious."

82. BJC, Case 10800; Benedict S. Alper, interview with author, Boston, 14 September 1981, a former BJC probation officer and Healy's colleague and co-author at the JBF in 1930–42; Henry Quarles (BJC Clerk and juvenile court attorney), interview with author, noted that Judge Cabot and Judge Perkins were fair but "influenced by the attitudes of those times against the colored people."

83. Msgr. James J. Keating (HAG chaplain, 1937–46), interview with author, Boston, 29 April 1978; Jerry Palmer, Joseph E. Saul, and Roland Aube, interviews with author.

84. Quote in Louis R. Harlan, *Booker T. Washington: The Making of a Black Leader, 1856–1901* (New York, 1972), 236; on Black children in Catholic schools, see Sandra N. Smith, "Parochial Schools in the Black Cities," *Journal of Negro Education* 42 (Summer 1973): 379–91.

85. Robert V. Guthrie, *Even the Rat Was White: A Historical View of Psychology* (New York, 1976), analyzes the impact of racism on American psychology and social work.

86. United States Bureau of the Census, *Historical Statistics of the United States* (Washington, D.C., 1960), 95–122.

87. Lee M. Friedman, "Boston in American Jewish History," *American Jewish Historical Quarterly* 42 (June 1953): 333–40.

88. Lee M. Friedman, *Jewish Pioneers and Patriots* (Philadelphia, 1943), 250.

89. Albert Ehrenfried, *A Chronicle of Boston Jewry: From the Colonial Settlement to 1900* (Boston, 1963), 260, 330; Nathaniel I. Bowditch, *A History of the Massachusetts General Hospital* (Boston, 1851), 64, 778.

90. George B. Emerson, ed., *Memoirs of Samuel Joseph May* (Boston, 1873), 15; Jacob R. Marcus, *The Colonial American Jew, 1492–1776* (Detroit, 1970), 1:297.

91. Friedman, *Jewish Pioneers,* 125; Handlin, *Boston's Immigrants,* 164, 183, 219.

92. Thomas C. Gratton, *Civilized America* (London, 1859), 1:95; Anita Libman Lebeson, *Pilgrim People* (New York, 1950), 333, found 337 members, 60 pupils and 44 births at Temple Ohabei Shalom in 1860.

93. Jonathan D. Sarna, *Jacksonian Jew: The Two Worlds of Mordecai Noah* (New York, 1981); and Paul Kurt Ackermann, *Germans in Boston* (Boston, 1981), 77–83.

94. Joseph L. Blau and Salo W. Baron, *The Jews of the United States, 1790–*

1840: A Documentary History (New York, 1963), 2:597–601; and Jacob R. Marcus, *Early American Jewry* (Philadelphia, 1955), 2:43–60, 282, found one temple spent 23 percent of its budget on charity.

95. Boris D. Bogen, *Jewish Philanthropy* (New York, 1917), 18–26, notes raising an orphan is extolled in the Midrash as the highest form of charity.

96. Louis Finkelstein, ed., *The Jews: Their History, Culture, and Religion* (New York, 1949), 1:724; Marcus, *Early American Jewry,* 2:485, claims American synagogues transferred charity work to the semi-autonomous *chevra* in imitation of American Christians.

97. Mark Zborowski and Elizabeth Herzog, *Life Is With People: The Culture of the Shtetl* (New York, 1952), 191–213.

98. *Encyclopedia of the Jewish Religion,* 1966 ed., 84–85.

99. Ephraim Frisch, *An Historical Survey of Jewish Philanthropy* (New York, 1924), 78.

100. Blau and Baron, *Jews of the United States,* 1:44–55.

101. Priscilla Fishman, ed., *The Jews of the United States* (New York, 1973), 10–24.

102. Lloyd P. Gartner, "Immigration and the Formation of American Jewry," in *The Jew in American Society,* ed. Marshall Sklare (New York, 1974), 33–55.

103. Moses Rischin, *The Promised Land: New York's Jews, 1870–1914* (Cambridge, 1962), 95–99.

104. Barbara Miller Solomon, *Pioneers in Service: The History of the Associated Jewish Philanthropies of Boston* (Boston, 1956), 2–8.

105. Ibid.; some Jews learned Yankee values from an unimpeachable source, Horatio Alger, Jr., who was a private tutor from 1869 to 1881 to the sons of Joseph Seligman, America's leading Jewish banker; see Gary Scharnhost, *Horatio Alger, Jr.* (Boston, 1980), 36.

106. Abraham J. Karp, *Golden Door to America: The Jewish Immigrant Experience* (New York, 1976), 54–58.

107. Rischin, *Promised City,* 105; and National Council of Jewish Women, *The First Fifty Years: A History of the National Council of Jewish Women, 1893–1943* (New York, 1943), 35, reports on thieves, pimps, and "cadets" preying on Jewish girls at the Boston seaport.

108. Solomon, *Pioneers in Service,* 12–15; Rabbi Schindler's casework is documented in UHBA Archives, Box I (1894), American Jewish Historical Society, Waltham, Massachusetts.

109. Harold M. Silver, "The Russian Jew Looks at Charity—A Study of the Attitudes of Russian Jewish Immigrants Toward Organized Jewish Charitable Agencies in the United States in 1890–1900," *Jewish Social Service Quarterly* 4 (December 1927): 129–44; and Ehrenfried, *Chronicle,* 560–62.

110. Solomon, *Pioneers in Service,* 10–16; Ehrenfried, *Chronicle,* 554–57, 643; and Julia Ward Howe, ed., *Representative Women of New England* (Boston, 1904), 334.

111. Arthur Mann, *Yankee Reformers in the Urban Age: Social Reform in Boston, 1880–1900* (Cambridge, 1954), 52–72; Arthur Mann, ed., *Growth and Achievement: Temple Israel, 1854–1954* (Cambridge, 1954), pp. 45–62.

112. Solomon, *Pioneers in Service,* 13–15; Massachusetts, Department of Education, *Annual Report* (1922), 37, describes the changing nature of immigration in the Commonwealth.

113. Ehrenfried, *Chronicle,* 624–627; Huggins, *Protestants Against,* 181–82.

114. Boston Provident Association, *Thirty-second Annual Report* (1883), 9; Nora Levin, *While Messiah Tarried: Jewish Socialist Movements, 1871–1917* (New

York, 1977), 70, describes the disgust with which German-American Jews received the "wild Russian Jews"; see Hebrew Immigrant Aid Society Archives, American Jewish Historical Society, Waltham, for registration of all Jews arriving at the Port of Boston in 1895–1924.

115. Massachusetts reorganized its Bureau of Immigration in 1919 as the Department of Education's Division of Immigration and Naturalization to cope with the flood of "New Immigrants"; fear of the Jewish and Italian immigrants was expressed by Immigration Restriction Leaguers, like Henry Pratt Fairchild, *Immigration* (New York, 1913) or educators, Leonard P. Ayres, *Laggards in Our Schools* (New York, 1909).

116. Jewish Family and Children's Service, Archives, General District Service Committee, Minutes, June 15, 1923, show the close cooperation of Jewish social workers with city, state, and legislative leaders; the GDSC aided five hundred families annually in the 1920s but voted not to give funds to families who violated Prohibition laws, to avoid controversy and demonstrate good citizenship; see also Ehrenfried, *Chronicle,* 656–58; and Samuel Joseph, *History of the Baron De Hirsch Fund: The Americanization of the Jewish Immigrant* (Philadelphia, 1935), 248, 272, on the Boston branch founded in 1894.

117. Ehrenfried, *Chronicle,* 541–49; Rosnosky (1846–1907) was the first Jew elected to the City Council, 1877, and to the state legislature, 1880; Morse (1831–92) was a Cleveland Democrat and the first New England Jew elected to Congress, in 1876.

118. Solomon, *Pioneers in Service,* 45–50; Isaac Goldberg, "A Boston Boyhood," *American Mercury* 17 (July 1929): 354–61.

119. Jabob Neusner, "The Impact of Immigration and Philanthropy Upon the Boston Jewish Community, 1880–1914," *American Jewish Historical Quarterly* 46 (September 1956): 71–85; Saul Drucker, *Reasons for Separate Orthodox Institutions* (Buffalo, 1909), 14, explains how tensions between Reformed and Orthodox Jews affected charities.

120. Anna Fleischer (HJC fund-raiser, 1925–1931) interview with author, Boston, 10 December 1979; Ehrenfried, *Chronicle,* 552, 624–31.

121. UHBA, *Annual Report* (1894), 6; Ehrenfried, *Chronicle,* 649; although the FJC had 489 subscribers and a $12,000 budget in 1895, many assimilated Boston Jewish leaders remained aloof; see Saul Engelbourg, "Edward A. Filene: Merchant, Civic Leader, and Jew," *American Jewish Historical Quarterly* 66 (September 1976): 106–22.

122. Rose Pave Roazen (president of the HJC), interview with author, Boston, 22 May 1979; on Jews in the HDCC, see HDCC, Records 1871, 23 November 1871," The Father is a German Jew. The Mother is Irish, he beats all of them because they don't go to his meeting"; the HAG, Register 1890–1916, 187–203, lists three Russian Jews admitted; Sister Mary Bertha Collins, interview with author, Boston, 21 March 1979, recalled "many Jewish girls" in the HGS from the courts in the 1920s.

123. On BCAS Jewish cases, see JFCS, Case 20293 (1928) and BJC, Case 143 (1906); JFCS, Children's Bureau Case Committee, Minutes, 1 March 1918 "decided if Jewish home cannot be obtained, that worker will cooperate with the Children's Aid Society"; this committee placed children at the NEHLW on 24 May 1918 and 23 December 1923; Brenzel, *Daughters of the State,* 116, found 16 to 38 percent of the Lancaster inmates in 1885–1905 were Jews, Italians, and others.

124. Frances E. Cohen, "From Institution to Foster Home: A Study of the Adjustment of Forty-five Children Who Went from the Home for Jewish Children to Foster Homes" (M.S. thesis, Simmons College, 1945); Cyrus L. Jacobs (a HJC

alumnus) interview with author, Boston, 26 May 1979; Solomon, *Pioneers in Service,* 47–50, 74–76.

125. Ehrenfried, *Chronicle,* 552–533; Saul Drucker and Maurice Beck Hexter, *Children Astray* (Cambridge, 1923), an account of the HJC by its superintendent and the FJC director.

126. Sam Bass Warner, Jr., *Streetcar Suburbs: The Process of Growth in Boston, 1870–1900* (Cambridge, 1962), 113–15; Francis Russell, *The Great Interlude* (New York, 1964), 85–110; HJC children's magazines and correspondence are revealing; see HJC, Archives, American Jewish Historical Society.

127. Frederick A. Bushee, *Ethnic Factors in the Population of Boston* (New York, 1903), 111; Solomon, *Pioneers in Service,* 43–45; Cohen, "From Institution," 30, found 16 of 45 children were admitted due to desertion, divorce, or separation of parents.

128. Bushee, *Ethnic Factors,* 110; Woods, *Americans in Process,* 112–13; family disruption was a serious problem among Jewish immigrants; see Charles Zunser, "The National Desertion Bureau," National Conference of Jewish Social Service, *Proceedings* (1923), 386–404.

129. Morris D. Waldman, *Nor by Power* (New York, 1953), 307–17, is the autobiography of the NDB founder who was the Boston FJC director in 1917–19.

130. Peter Romanofsky, ed., *Social Service Organizations* (Westport, Conn., 1978), 1:297–301; Ronald Sanders, *The Downtown Jews: Portraits of an Immigrant Generation* (New York, 1969), 357–65.

131. Irving Howe, *The World of Our Fathers* (New York, 1976), 177–90; Charles Reznikoff, "Boston's Jewish Community: Earlier Days," *Commentary* 15 (January 1953): 490–99.

132. Romanofsky, *Social Service Organizations,* 1:300; Waldman, *Nor by Power,* 312.

133. JFCS, CBCC, Minutes, Case 632, 21 July 1922.

134. Ibid., 10 May 1918.

135. Ibid., Case 143.

136. Solomon, *Pioneers in Service,* 15, 45–48.

137. Ibid.; Eugene T. Lies, "Country Outings for City Children," *Charities* 12 (2 July 1904): 694–95, contended "mere contact with a form of existence that is peaceful, unrushing, undisturbed by the money-mad chase of city life, is a tonic worth more than gold."

138. BJC, Case 41, concerned an immigrant Jewish boy who stole a horse and wagon; he was sent "into the country to get him away from his companions and surroundings in the North End" and out of his "slack, shiftless home" in a "cheap tenement house district."

139. Federation of Jewish Charities, *First Annual Report* (1896), 5; Ehrenfried, *Chronicle,* 649.

140. Solomon, *Pioneers in Service,* 47; South End Settlement House workers encouraged city children to move to rural New England; see Alvan F. Sanborn, "The Future of Rural New England," *Atlantic Monthly* 80 (May 1897): 74–79.

141. Max Mitchell, "The Boston Federation," National Conference of Jewish Charities, *Proceedings* (1902); Anthony Platt, *The Child Savers: The Invention of Delinquency* (Chicago, 1969), 40; although Boston Jewish child-savers agreed with the deinstitutionalization policy of the first White House Conference on Children, they supported the HJC until 1930; see Frank J. Cohen, "The Institution: Its Place and Function Today," *Jewish Social Service Quarterly* 10 (September 1938): 82–87.

142. JFCS, CBCC, Minutes, 1918–19, 1; Anzia Yezierska, *Bread Givers* (New

York, 1925), chap. 3, is a vivid portrait of how some immigrant parents saw their children as a source of income.

143. Frank L. Kozol, "Lee M. Friedman: A Biographical Profile," *American Jewish Historical Quarterly* 56 (March 1967): 261–70, discusses his role in the creation of the BJC, Judge Rubenstein (1871–1957) was his law partner and ally; see also Solomon, *Pioneers in Service,* 52–63; and JFCS, CBCC, Minutes, 22 August 1924.

144. Judge Baker Foundation, *Harvey Humphrey Baker: Upbuilder of the Juvenile Court* (Boston, n.d.), 17, 66, notes NCJW agents in the court, Rosa Z. Krokyn (1906–09) and Katherine Weisman (1909–18), as does JFCS, CBCC, Minutes, 12 July 1918.

145. JFCS, CBCC, Minutes, 14 November 1922.

146. BJC, Case 582, concerned Max Fogelson whose "parents have requested several times that he be sent back to the Parental School" but the court found Max "a worthy fellow" and dismissed the stubborn child complaint.

147. Golde Bamber, "Russian Jews in Boston," *Lend a Hand* 8 (March 1892): 168–71, reports some immigrants concealed assets and feigned poverty to avoid official attention; BJC, Case 957, concerned a pregnant sixteen-year-old whose family felt "it was imperative that institutional treatment should be given her"; this was interpreted as greedy or cruel by the suspicious court.

148. Peter Romanofsky, " 'To Save . . . Their Souls': The Care of Dependent Jewish Children in New York City, 1900–1905," *Jewish Social Studies* 36 (July–August 1974): 253–61.

149. Otto Pollak, "Social Determinants of Family Behavior," *Social Work* 8 (July 1963), analyzes differences between WASP and Jewish clients and social workers; Egal Feldman, "The Social Gospel and the Jews," *American Jewish Historical Quarterly* 58 (March 1969): 308–22.

150. BJC, Case 10145.

151. Herman D. Stein, "Jewish Social Work in the United States, 1920–1955," in *The Jews: Social Patterns of an American Group,* ed. Marshall Sklare (New York, 1955), 173–204.

152. JFCS, General District Service Committee, Minutes, 17 March 1927.

153. Ibid.

154. Ibid.; Waldman, *Nor by Power,* 409–11; the FJC limited social work caseloads to thirty clients, but recognized excess cases must be ignored and "this is a tremendous psychological burden" and "a very unhealthy situation."

155. JFCS, CBCC, Minutes, 11 January 1918.

156. Ibid., 1 September 1917.

157. Ibid., 31 May 1918; at this time the HJC sheltered 150 children and 25 percent of these had been examined by the JBF.

158. Ibid., 5 May 1922; 12 December 1922.

159. William H. Sheldon, *Varieties of Delinquent Youth* (New York, 1949), 604; Emil M. Hartll (Sheldon's assistant), interview with author, Boston, 12 May 1981.

160. JFCS, CBCC, Minutes, 18 May 1923; Douglas A. Thom, "Habit Clinics for Children of the Pre-School Age," *American Journal of Psychiatry* 79 (1922–23): 31–38.

161. Eveoleen N. Rexford (JBF child psychiatrist and director of the Thom Clinic), interview with author, Cambridge, 9 November 1981; Ehrenfried, *Chronicle,* 744–52; Dennis B. Klein, *Jewish Origins of the Psychoanalytic Movement* (New York, 1981).

162. Solomon, *Pioneers in Service,* 118–23; Rudolph Allers, "Holding Up the Mirror to Psychoanalysis," *Catholic Charities Review* 20 (March 1939): 70–72;

Robert Morris and Michael Freund, eds., *Trends and Issues in Jewish Social Welfare in the United States, 1899–1958* (Philadelphia, 1966).

163. Drucker and Hexter, *Children Astray,* 275–76; Henry B. Elkind and Maurice Taylor, "'One Thousand Juvenile Delinquents', A Critique," *Mental Hygiene* 28 (October 1934): 531–52, is a strong defense of the JBF by Associated Jewish Philanthropies directors.

164. Leon Harris, *Merchant Princes* (New York, 1979); Charles H. Trout, *Boston, the Great Depression and the New Deal* (New York, 1977), 267–68.

165. JFCS, CBCC, Minutes, 17 March 1927; Solomon, *Pioneers in Service,* p. 113–30.

166. JFCS, CBCC, Minutes, 1 July 1922; the HJC closed in 1931 in recognition of the deinstitutionalization and psychiatric casework policies sweeping child welfare.

167. Arthur A. Goren, *New York Jews and the Quest for Community: The Kehillah Experiment, 1908–22* (New York, 1970).

168. Grace Abbott, *The Problem of Immigration in Massachusetts: Report of the Commission on Immigration* (Boston, 1914).

169. Eric Amfitheatrof, *The Children of Columbus* (Boston, 1973), 100–104; and Vincent Y. Bowditch, *Life and Correspondence of Henry Ingersoll Bowditch* (Boston, 1902), 2:111–17, relates how thrilled Bowditch was in 1867 to see Garibaldi in Paris.

170. Handlin, *Boston's Immigrants,* 68.

171. The Reverend Antonio Ubaldus DiPrizio (St. Leonard Church) interview with author, Boston, 17 November 1980; Richard M. Linkh, *American Catholicism and European Immigrants* (New York, 1975).

172. Kate Holladay Claghorn, "The Italian Under Economic Stress," in *The Italian in America, the Progressive View, 1891–1914,* ed. Lydio F. Tomasi (New York, 1972), 131–34.

173. John B. Hawes, *Consumption* (Boston, 1915), 62.

174. Claghorn, "The Italian," 132; Frank P. Fasano, "The Italian-American Home as Influenced by Factors of Family Disorganization Peculiar to the American Environment" (M.A. thesis, Boston University, 1931).

175. Peter H. Rossi and Alice S. Rossi, "Background and Consequences of Parochial School Education," *Harvard Educational Review* 37 (Summer 1957): 168–99; and James W. Sanders, *The Education of an Urban Minority: Catholics in Chicago, 1833–1965* (New York, 1977), 67–71.

176. Constantine M. Panunzio, *The Soul of an Immigrant* (New York, 1928), 255.

177. Gerre Mangione, *Mount Allegro* (Boston, 1943), 211–12.

178. Kate Holladay Claghorn, *The Immigrant's Day in Court* (New York, 1923), 278; Herbert Dwight McConnell interview with author, Boston, 13 June 1979, recalled "many problems" with Italian immigrants at the HDCC.

179. HAG, Register I, 1851–1859; Registers, 1860–1927.

180. The Reverend Antonio Ubaldus DiPrizio interview; Rudolph J. Vecoli, "Prelates and Peasants: Italian Immigrants and the Catholic Church," *Journal of Social History* 2 (Spring 1969): 217–66.

181. Figures compiled from the HDCC, Superintendent's Journal and Registers for 1867–1927.

182. HGS, St. Joseph Register, 1887–1927; based on birthplace, parentage and names, I estimate 20 percent of the St. Joseph Class inmates were Italian in 1907–27.

183. Sister Mary Elizabeth McHugh (St. Vincent's Home), interview with au-

thor, Boston, 20 March 1979; with Sister Ursulita Toomey (Daly Industrial School), interview with author, Boston, 27 May 1981, whose family took an Italian boy from an HDCC parish "slave auction" in 1937.

184. John F. Stack, Jr., *International Conflict in an American City: Boston's Irish, Italians and Jews, 1935–1946* (Westport, Conn., 1979), 33–35.

185. Msgr. James H. Doyle (Boston Catholic Charitable Bureau), interview with author, Boston, 4 March 1979; Eliot Lord, J. D. Trenor, and Samuel J. Barrows, *The Italian in America* (New York, 1905), 190–96; Howard Ralph Weisz, *Irish-American and Italian-American Educational Views and Activities, 1870–1900: A Comparison* (New York, 1976), 363–65.

186. A. L. Maraspini, *The Study of an Italian Village* (Paris, 1968), 200–210; Edward C. Banfield, *The Moral Basis of a Backward Society* (Glencoe, Ill., 1958).

187. Leonard Covello, *The Social Background of the Italo-American Child* (Leiden, Netherlands, 1967), 173–75; Ann Cornelisen, *Women of the Shadows: A Study of the Wives and Mothers of Southern Italy* (Boston, 1976).

188. Associated Charities of Boston, *Twenty-third Annual Report* (1902), 3; Edwin Fenton, *Immigrants and Unions, A Case Study: Italians and American Labor, 1870–1920* (New York, 1975), 122–24.

189. Mutual benefit societies were important according to John W. Briggs, *An Italian Passage: Immigrants to Three American Cities, 1890–1930* (New Haven, 1978); Jan Brogger, *Montevarese: A Study of Peasant Society and Culture in Southern Italy* (Oslo, Norway, 1971), 100–25.

190. Fenton, *Immigrants,* 50–55; Reverend Antonio Ubaldus DiPrizio, interview.

191. Society of St. Raphael for the Protection of Italian Immigrants, *First Annual Report* (1903), 5; "The Protection of Italian Immigrants," *Charities* 8 (10 May 1904): 435; Baron Gustavo Tosti, the Italian consul in Boston, subsidized the Benevolent Aid Society to aid immigrants also.

192. William M. DeMarco, *Ethnics and Enclaves: Boston's Italian North End* (Ann Arbor, Mich., 1981); Fenton, *Immigrants,* 123–30.

193. Louis C. Odencrantz, *Italian Women in Industry* (New York, 1919), 13, 165; Vida Scudder, "Experiments in Fellowship Work with Italians in Boston," *Survey* 22 (3 April 1909): 47–51.

194. No cases of divorce or desertion were found in the Italo-American charity and court records I studied; see Virginia Yans-McLaughlin, *Family and Community: Italians Immigrants in Buffalo, 1880–1930* (Urbana, Ill., 1982), 88–95, for comparable data; this may have been a problem in some Italian families; see Robert E. Forester, *Italian Emigration in Our Times* (Cambridge, 1919); Phyllis H. Williams, *South Italian Folkways in Europe and America* (New Haven, 1948).

195. Brogger, *Montevarese,* 179; Humbert S. Nelli, *Italians in Chicago, 1880–1930: A Study in Ethnic Mobility* (New York, 1970), 66–72.

196. Virginia Yans McLaughlin, *Family and Community: Italian Immigrants in Buffalo, 1880–1930* (Ithaca, N.Y., 1977).

197. Brogger, *Montevarese,* 180; Silvano M. Tomasi and Madeline H. Engel, eds., *The Italian Experience in the United States* (New York, 1970) 125–45.

198. Woods, *Americans in Process,* 252; Claghorn, *The Immigrant's Day,* 100; Sophonisba P. Breckinridge, *The Family and the State: Select Documents* (Chicago, 1934), 67–74, reported 6,575 "child marriages" in Massachusetts in 1929; *Boston Post,* 3 January 1906, reported an attempted suicide by Emma De Fossi, a thirteen-year-old bride.

199. Figures from BJC, Probation Records, 1906–27, which contain 44 cases of Italian girls appearing as stubborn, wayward, or neglected children; in 27 of these

cases, sexual misconduct (masturbation, loitering in Scollay Square or Boston Common, and nightwalking, for example) were alleged, as in BJC Case 445, 580, 1274.

200. BJC, Case 10458.

201. MSPCC, Case 48289 and BJC, Case 10514.

202. BJC, Case 10667, 10990; and MSPCC, Case 48232 demonstrates the "star boarder problem" in which immigrant women had sexual relations with male boarders and children were removed from such homes.

203. BJC, Case 10704.

204. BJC, Case 10253.

205. BJC Case, 10760, 10761; MSPCC, Case 48266, in which an Italian son "ruled the household" and beat his Americanized sister for unchaperoned dating.

206. BJC, Case 10776.

207. BJC, Case 25831.

208. BJC, Case 19460; and May Burke, a young Irish Catholic probation officer (1916–29), urged that "something should immediately be done to Americanize this girl."

209. Michael J. Parenti, *Ethnic and Political Attitudes: A Depth Study of Italian Americans* (New York, 1976), 32–37; and Deanna P. Gumina, *The Italians of San Francisco, 1850–1930* (New York, 1978), 163–71.

210. Lord, *History,* 3:368–69, 645.

211. The Reverend Antonio Ubaldus DiPrizio, interview; Joseph W. Carlevale, *Leading Americans of Italian Descent in Massachusetts* (Plymouth, Mass., 1946).

212. HIC, Photograph Collection, 1919–88, demonstrates continuous support by the founders' families who serve on the board and annually donate funds, goods, and services; Michael LaScelia, interview with author, Boston, 29 June 1987, a staff member who entered the home as an orphan in 1933; Anthony S. J. Tomasello (HIC director), interview with author, Boston, 3 November 1980; see Carlevale, *Leading Americans,* passim.

213. Orfanotrofio Italiano, *Home for Italian Children Report* (1922), 3; Giovanni Schiavo, *Italian American History,* (New York, 1949), 2:631.

214. Robert Aidan O'Leary, "William Henry Cardinal O'Connell: A Social and Intellectual Biography" (Ph.D. diss., Tufts University, 1980), 130, 220; James Gaffey, "The Changing of the Guard: The Rise of Cardinal O'Connell of Boston," *Catholic Historical Review* 59 (July 1973).

215. William Henry Cardinal O'Connell, *Recollections of Seventy Years* (Boston, 1934), 270; *Boston Pilot,* 23 December 1919.

216. Carlevale, *Leading Americans,* 11, 174, 229, 778; HIC, Correspondence File, Archdiocese of Boston Archives, 12 June 1919.

217. HIC, Correspondence File, 11 March 1920; *Boston Globe,* 29 February, 30 May 1904.

218. Fenton, *Immigrants,* 344–45; Lord, *History,* 3:310–12, 569–70.

219. HIC, Correspondence File, 11 March 1920.

220. Ibid., 18 March 1920.

221. Ibid., 12 November 1920, 20 December 1922; Anthony Martignetti (HIC board member), interview with author, 19 November 1980.

222. Carlevale, *Leading Americans,* 705–06; *Boston Italian News,* 8 July 1938.

223. *Boston Post,* 10 February 1921; United States Department of Commerce, Bureau of the Census, *Children Under Institutional Care, 1923* (Washington, D.C., 1927), 80–81.

224. HIC, Register, 1921–64; and HIC, Correspondence File, Archdiocese Archives, Folder 1921, "Rules for the Home for Italian Children."

225. Sister Solanus Cerio, Sister Biagia Carbone, and Sister Catherine Donnelly (HIC Staff), interviews with author, Boston, 3–17 November 1980.

226. Ibid.

227. Quote from Anthony S.J. Tomasello, interview; *Boston Globe,* 25 October 1954.

228. Msgr. James H. Doyle, interview; Claghorn, *The Immigrant's Day,* 99, discusses how Italian child-rearing customs appalled Yankee child-savers.

229. HIC, *Fiftieth Anniversary, 1919–1969 Bulletin;* Sister Margaret Yennock (HIC), interview with author, Boston, 29 June 1987.

230. Quotes from Michael LaScelia, Cyrus L. Jacobs, and Henry Quarles, interviews.

231. James Michael Curley, *I'd Do It Again* (Englewood Cliffs, N.J., 1957), 67.

Chapter 5. The Boston Juvenile Court and Clinic

1. Allen F. Davis, *American Heroine: The Life and Legend of Jane Addams* (New York, 1973), 76–80, 150; Murray Levine and Adeline Levine, *A Social History of the Helping Services: Clinic, Court, School and Community* (New York, 1970), 4.

2. Ellen Ryerson, *The Best-Laid Plans: America's Juvenile Court Experiment* (New York, 1978).

3. Anthony M. Platt, *The Child Savers: The Invention of Delinquency* (Chicago, 1969).

4. *Boston Morning Post, Selections from the Court Reports, 1834 to 1837* (New York, 1974), 70, gives vivid accounts of Irish children in the Boston Police Court; Frank W. Grinnell, "The Common Law History of Probation: An Illustration of the 'Equitable' Growth of Criminal Law," *Journal of Criminal Law and Criminology* 32 (May–June 1941): 15–34.

5. Gardiner Tufts, Letter Books, 1869–1872, Tufts Papers, Massachusetts Historical Society, Boston, 130–34, estimated the courts tried 1,800 juveniles in 1870, not including an equal number of children charged with violation of town or city ordinances or the small number charged with serious crimes; Tufts claimed only 20 percent of the 1,800 his agency oversaw were committed to reform schools.

6. Judge Peter Oxenbridge Thacher (1776–1843) anticipated John Augustus by releasing juveniles on personal recognizance in 1830, a practice approved by the legislature in 1836; see *Comparative Survey of Juvenile Delinquency, Part I: North America* (New York, 1958), 12.

7. Massachusetts, Board of State Charities, *Fifth Annual Report* (1868), lxviii, contended the courts should "provide for every minor, a defender, to whom it should be as much a matter of duty and of pride to acquit the accused, as it is of the State's attorney to convict him"; Tufts was not such a "defender"; see Gardiner Tufts, "The Massachusetts Statutes Relating to Juvenile Offenders and the Methods of Dealing with Them," NCCC, *Proceedings* (1880), 200–09.

8. HDCC, Superintendent's Journal, 15 February 1872; BCAS, Pine Farm Visitors' Book, Volume IV, February 1883; Frances E. Lane, *American Charities and the Child of the Immigrant* (New York, 1932), 84.

9. National Probation Association, *John Augustus, First Probation Officer* (New York, 1939); Nicholas S. Timasheff, *One Hundred Years of Probation, 1841–1941* (New York, 1941), 1:8–9; and Frank W. Grinnell, "Probation as an Orthodox Common Law Practice in Massachusetts Prior to the Statutory System," *Massachusetts Law Quarterly* 2 (August 1917): 591–639.

10. Donna Merwick, *Boston Priests, 1848–1910: A Study of Social and Intel-

lectual Change (Cambridge, 1973), 65, 97; Daniel T. McColgan, *A Century of Charity: The First One Hundred Years of the Society of St. Vincent de Paul in the United States* (Milwaukee, 1951), 1:334–44; Society of St. Vincent de Paul, *Annual Report* (Boston, 1888), 5.

11. BCAS, *Twenty-fifth Annual Report* (1889), 14; Robert A. Woods and Albert J. Kennedy, *The Settlement Horizon* (New York, 1922), 268.

12. David Tyack and Michael Berkowitz, "The Man Nobody Liked: Toward a Social History of the Truant Officer, 1840–1940," *American Quarterly* 19 (Spring 1977): 31–54; HDCC, Superintendent's Journal, 23 January 1865.

13. Lenient treatment of juveniles by judges and juries was recognized as a problem by 1840, and state reform schools were built to eliminate this evil; see "Theodore Lyman," *American Journal of Education* 24 (March 1861): 5–14; Robert M. Mennel, *Thorns & Thistles: Juvenile Delinquents in the United States, 1825–1940* (Hanover, N.H., 1973); Joseph M. Hawes, *Children in Urban Society: Juvenile Delinquency in Nineteenth-Century America* (New York, 1971).

14. Most sources exaggerate the originality of the Chicago and Denver juvenile courts and overlook the earlier Boston juvenile sessions due to the national reputation of Hull House reformers; see *Notable American Women,* "Lucy L. Flower," 1:635–37; Harriet S. Farwell, *Lucy Louise Flower, 1837–1920: Her Contribution to Education and Child Welfare in Chicago* (Chicago, 1924); Hawes, *Children,* 165.

15. Charles Larsen, *The Good Fight: The Life and Times of Ben B. Lindsey* (Chicago, 1972), focuses more his life than his times; see also Peter G. Slater, "Ben Lindsey and the Juvenile Court of Denver: A Progressive Looks at Human Nature," *American Quarterly* 20 (Summer 1968): 211–23; and Ben B. Lindsey and Wainwright Evans, *The Revolt of Modern Youth* (Garden City, N.J., 1925), 39–41, 115.

16. Massachusetts Civic League, *State House Newsletter* 2 (January 1951): 1–2, analyzes the origin of the BJC, which was neither a civil nor a criminal court, and certainly not the "clinic" its founders intended; David J. Rothman, *Conscience and Convenience: The Asylum and its Alternatives in Progressive America* (Boston, 1980), 236, errs in designating the BJC a criminal court; Massachusetts *Acts and Resolves* (1906), chap. 413, 489, were written by Joseph Lee to blend chancery and criminal court procedures in creating the BJC; see *Boston Post,* 6 January 1906; *Boston Post,* 9 September 1906; Joseph Lee, "Report from Massachusetts," NCCC, *Proceedings* (1905), 55–60.

17. Florence M. Warner, *Juvenile Detention in the United States* (Chicago, 1933), 207–10; Robert M. Mennel, "Origins of the Juvenile Court: Changing Perspectives in Legal Rights of Juvenile Delinquents," *Crime and Delinquency* 18 (January 1972): 68–78; Robert H. Bremner, et al., eds., *Children and Youth in America: A Documentary History* (Cambridge, 1970), 2:494.

18. Harvey H. Baker, "Procedure of the Boston Juvenile Court," *Survey* 23 (February 1910): 649–50; Philip Davis, ed., *The Field of Social Service* (Boston, 1915), 201; Boston Juvenile Court, *In Memoriam to the Presiding Justices of the Boston Juvenile Court* (Boston, 1940); Bremner, *Children and Youth,* 2:536–38.

19. Judge Baker Foundation, *Harvey Humphrey Baker: Upbuilder of the Juvenile Court* (Boston, n.d.), 47; BCAS, *Forty-first Annual Report* (1905), 15; St. Vincent de Paul Society, *Annual Report* (1907), 6.; BJC, Probation Files, 1906–09, contain many letters by Baker to the first probation officers, Samuel C. Lawrence and John A. Elliott.

20. Quote in Robert I. Beers, interview with author, Boston, 23 June 1986, a probation officer and NEHLW director; much information on the BJC was pro-

vided by the author's interviews with these 1930s probation officers and social work administrators: Phyllis M. Cosand, (NEHLW), 7 January 1981; Sibley Higginbotham (Boston Church Home Society), 6 April 1981; Robert Mulford (MSPCC), 11 April 1981; and Roland D. Elderkin (MSPCC), 12 April 1981.

21. Roy Lubove, *The Professional Altruist: The Emergence of Social Work as a Career, 1880–1930* (Cambridge, 1965); Jack M. Holl, *Juvenile Reform in the Progressive Era: William R. George and the Junior Republic Movement* (Ithaca, N.Y., 1971), 161; Social workers seldom made probation a career because it required political appointment, not professional training.

22. Herbert H. Lou, *Juvenile Courts in the United States* (Chapel Hill, N.C., 1927), 116–20; Edwin L. Cooley, *Probation and Delinquency* (New York, 1927).

23. Arthur C. Holden, *The Settlement Idea: A Vision of Social Justice* (New York, 1922), 58; Margaret F. Byington, *The Confidential Exchange: A Form of Social Cooperation* (New York, 1912), 5; Laura Woodbury, the director from 1902 to 1947, was highly regarded according to Frances Aldrich, interview with author, Boston, 27 March 1981, of the South End House and Boston Family Welfare Society; the rights of welfare clients were subordinate to the social worker's "need to be thorough, and not a single client ever objected" to this invasion of privacy, as Miss Aldrich recalled.

24. David Wigdor, *Roscoe Pound, Philosopher of Law* (Westport, Conn., 1974), 35, 242–47, analyzes America's foremost legal scholar and Dean of Harvard Law School, who was trained as a biologist and applied science to courts; especially in juvenile courts, according to Hawes, *Children,* 261.

25. Rothman, *Conscience,* 212; Roscoe Pound, *Interpretations of Legal History* (New York, 1923), 134–35; *Boston Post,* 11 September 1906, 7; and Roscoe Pound, *Criminal Justice in America* (New York, 1930), 33, 62.

26. Hillary Rodham, "Children Under the Law," *Harvard Educational Review* 43 (November 1973): 487–514; and Florence Kelley, "On Some Changes in the Legal Status of the Child Since Blackstone," *International Review* (August 1882): 83–98, argues that American courts in 1870 protected the individual rights of the child rather than parents' rights, calling the trend a "blow struck at the legal family."

27. Bernard Greenblatt, *Responsibility for Child Care* (San Francisco, 1977), 7–9, summarizes these laws.

28. Arthur Mann, *Yankee Reformers in the Urban Age: Social Reform in Boston, 1880–1900* (Cambridge, 1954), 24–27.

29. Steven L. Schlossman, *Love and the American Delinquent: The Theory and Practice of "Progressive" Juvenile Justice, 1825–1920* (Chicago, 1977), 8–14, outlines the court cases.

30. Ibid.; Robert H. Mnookin, "Foster Care—In Whose Best Interest," *Harvard Educational Review* 43 (November 1973): 599–638.

31. Ryerson, *The Best-Laid Plans,* 8–11; and Albert Warren Stearns, "A Program for the Control of Crime in the State of Massachusetts," *New England Journal of Medicine* 204 (March 1931): 529–34.

32. John Gould Curtis, *History of the Town of Brookline* (Boston, 1933), 331, notes Baker was a BCAS member, wrote *A Manual for Use in Cases of Juvenile Offenders* (Boston, 1895) as the Secretary of the Boston Conference of Child-Helping Agencies and was Clerk and Special Justice of the Brookline Police Court in 1895–1906; see also Charles E. Silberman, *Criminal Violence, Criminal Justice* (New York, 1978), p. 315; and Arthur E. Sutherland, *The Law at Harvard: A History of Ideas and Men, 1817–1967* (Cambridge, 1967), 174–80.

33. Peggy Lamson, *Roger Baldwin: Founder of the American Civil Liberties Union* (Boston, 1976), 34, describes Baldwin's work as chief probation officer of the St. Louis Juvenile Court, establishment of the National Probation Association and preference for his fellow Bostonian, Baker, to the more daring Ben Lindsey.

34. McColgan, *A Century of Charity,* 1:344; BJC, Case 1280, 1313.

35. Robert Grant, *Fourscore: An Autobiography* (Boston, 1934), 244.

36. Baker, "Procedure of the Juvenile Court," 650.

37. Ibid.

38. *Kent v. United States,* 383 U.S. 541, 545 (1966); for earlier criticism of juvenile court judges, see Hannah Kent Schoff, *The Wayward Child* (Indianapolis, Ind., 1915), 220; Edwin H. Sutherland, *Criminology* (Philadelphia, 1924), 278.

39. Brandeis is quoted in Silberman, *Criminal Violence,* 309.

40. BJC, Case 342.

41. BJC, Case 440.

42. BJC, Case 660, 672.

43. BJC, Case 842, in which Baker wrote to the boy's father, "We do not like as a rule to place a boy of his mental caliber in an institution"; see also James McLachlan, *American Boarding Schools: A Historical Study* (New York, 1970).

44. BJC, Case 824.

45. BJC, Case 844; Julian W. Mack, "Juvenile Courts as Part of the School System of the Country," NCCC, *Proceedings* (1908): 375–76, admitted that as the Chicago Juvenile Court judge his probation officers and the public saw him "as all-powerful, as one who can exercise his arbitrary and tyrannical good-will just as it may please him."

46. BJC, Case 896; and Julian W. Mack, "The Juvenile Court," *Harvard Law Review* 23 (1910): 119–20.

47. BJC, Case 945; many reformers were alarmed by young "cigarette fiends"; see Gordon L. Dillow, "Thank You For Not Smoking," *American Heritage* 32 (February–March 1981): 94–107.

48. BJC, Case 975.

49. BJC, Case 1107, shows Baker acquiesced to one Irish family's political influence with the District Attorney to substitute probation for commitment to reform school; but in BJC, Case 1053, Baker wrote, "even politicians agree not much hope for this family"; on the role of the Boston ward boss as the "neighborhood adviser, father confessor, foster parent, social service worker, and court of personal appeal"; see John Henry Cutler, *Honey Fitz, Three Steps to the White House: The Life and Times of John F. Fitzgerald* (New York, 1962), 46–48.

50. *Baker, Upbuilder,* 59–60; BJC, Case, 10892; and James F. Richardson, *Urban Police in the United States* (Port Washington, N.Y., 1974), 172, points out that slum children were perceived as lawless by police and courts due to radical, ethnic, class, and religious bias, which accounts for higher arrest rates for the poor.

51. Francis A. Allen, *The Borderland of Criminal Justice* (Chicago, 1964), 45; Gustav L. Schramm, "Philosophy of the Juvenile Court," in *The Problem of Delinquency,* ed. Sheldon Glueck (Boston, 1959), 271–72; Arthur Lewis Wood, *Deviant Behavior and Control Strategies* (Lexington, Mass., 1974), 140.

52. BJC, Case 25753.

53. David F. Tilley, "Discussion on the Committee Report and Prison Problems," NCCC, *Proceedings* (1907): 98–108; see also *Boston Post,* 10 September 1906, on a police crack down on young fruit peddlers littering streets.

54. Theodore H. White, *In Search of History: A Personal Adventure* (New

York, 1978), 28–40; Roger Lane, *Policing the City—Boston, 1822–1885* (Cambridge, 1967), 126–27.

55. White, *In Search,* 39; Russell Sage Foundation, *Boyhood and Lawlessness* (New York, 1914), 14; and Cornelius F. Cahalane, *The Policeman* (New York, 1923), 258–260.

56. BJC, Case 445; and Kate Holladay Claghorn, *The Immigrant's Day in Court* (New York, 1923), 193–206, contains information supplied by Judge Cabot and BJC staff; Americanized girls who preferred shop or office work to factory jobs faced many obstacles; see Katharine Anthony, *Mothers Who Must Earn* (New York, 1914), 51, and Frances R. Donovan, *The Saleslady* (Chicago, 1929); but schools sent most working-class girls to dead-end jobs in Boston's candy and box factories rather than to the secretarial pool, due to the demand for cheap labor and slow growth of vocational education; see Marvin Lazerson and W. Norton Grubb, eds., *American Education and Vocationalism* (New York, 1974).

57. BJC, Case 466; and in BJC, Case 10145, the brother of two Jewish flappers begged the judge to send them to Lancaster "because if you don't you will be getting them into court for bad girls"; the dance craze of 1912–17 produced many flappers and sheiks in the court, as in BJC, Case 26399 and 26403.

58. BJC, Case 552; rape and sexual abuse of children was a growing concern to social workers and juvenile courts in the 1920s; see C. C. Carstens, "The Next Step in the Work of Child Protection," National Conference of Social Work, *Proceedings* (1924): 135–39; the Boston police and juvenile court bureaucratic process sometimes had the effect of labeling girls as immoral or mentally defective according to Ruth Rosen, *The Lost Sisterhood: Prostitution in America, 1900–1918* (Baltimore, 1982), 22–23.

59. BJC, Case 580; Jane Addams, *The Spirit of Youth and the City Streets* (New York, 1909), 6, believed overly strict old country parents made their daughters wayward; Thomas Travis, *The Young Malefactor* (New York, 1908), 125, agreed and noted these "recently arrived immigrants who display small adaptability in American standards are by no means slow in learning about this and other institutions where they may safely leave their children to be fed, clothed, and cared for at public expense."

60. BJC, Case 957; and for a discussion of Boston Brahmins' prudish, class-bound view of sex, see George E. Vaillant, *Adaptation to Life* (Boston, 1977), 138; see also Steven L. Schlossman and Stephanie Wallach, "The Crime of Precocious Sexuality: Female Juvenile Delinquency in the Progressive Era," *Harvard Educational Review* 48 (February 1978): 65–94.

61. Baker, "Procedure of the Boston Juvenile Court," 651; Bremner, *Children,* 2 :520; and *Boston Post,* 4 January 1906, reported that the national dance craze responsible for many "bad girls" who are "starting their downward career" is not evident in Boston.

62. BJC, Case 1107; but changes in sexual mores alarmed many; see Kenneth A. Yellis, "Prosperity's Child: Some Thoughts on the Flapper," *American Quarterly* 21 (Spring 1969): 44–64.

63. BJC, Case 1238; and James R. McGovern, "The American Woman's Pre-World War I Freedom in Manners and Morals," *Journal of American History* 55 (September 1968): 315–33.

64. MSPCC, *Twenty-sixth Annual Report* (1906) 5; Roy S. Hubbard, *Crusading for Children* (Boston, 1943); and in BJC, Case 126, Baker wrote to Christian Carl Carstens, the MSPCC director and founder of the Child Welfare League of America, that all BJC neglect cases will be "handled by your agents" and then asked for advice.

65. BJC, Case 10866; but the MSPCC slowly shifted from police functions to casework as reported in MSPCC, *Twenty-seventh Annual Report* (1907), 16; Robert Mulford (MSPCC director), interview with author, Boston, 11 May 1981, noted that the close working relationship between the BJC and MSPCC still existed in the 1930s "but on a more professional basis."

66. BJC, Case 10866.

67. BJC, Case 10088.

68. Baker, "Procedure of the Juvenile Court," 651.

69. Ibid; and Timothy D. Hurley, "Juvenile Probation," NCCC, *Proceedings* (1907): 225–32, said the probation officer "must also in many cases become the doctor, nurse, peacemaker, even missionary."

70. Ibid.; Stearns, "Program for the Control of Crime," 532, continued the analogy of court to hospital; Dr. Stearns was the Dean of Tufts University Medical School and Massachusetts Commissioner of Corrections when he praised "scientific judges" who looked to social work and medicine for guidance.

71. Sutherland, *The Law at Harvard,* 176; and Boston City Hospital, *Fifteenth Annual Report* (1879), 19.

72. Massachusetts, Department of Health, *First Annual Report* (1916), 20, showed this new scientific attitude toward syphilis and the courts agreed; but moral condemnation of illicit sex persisted; see Leon Harris, *Only to God: The Extraordinary Life of Godfrey Lowell Cabot* (New York, 1967), on the Boston Watch and Ward Society.

73. Katherine E. Conway, *The Golden Year of the Good Shepherd in Boston: Compiled from the Annals of the Convent* (Boston, 1918), 193, reports Archbishop O'Connell visited the HGS in 1906 to assure the sisters that the District Attorney would not disturb their relationship with the court.

74. BJC, Case 1107; and Robert A. Woods, *The Neighborhood in Nation-Building* (Boston, 1923), 69, admitted settlement houses were powerless "to win away the following of local politicians."

75. BJC, Case 8842; *Boston Globe,* 13 January 1915, *Boston Traveller,* 14 January 1915, note the BJC waived jurisdiction in this lurid case.

76. On the increasing role of medical experts in legal matters, see Barbara G. Rosenkrantz, *Public Health and the State: Changing Views in Massachusetts, 1842–1936* (Cambridge, Mass., 1972), 129, 171–75.

77. *Upbuilder,* 79–80.

78. William V. Shannon, *The American Irish: A Political and Social Portrait* (New York, 1963), 217, analyzes tensions between the Irish and Yankees which excluded Irish-Americans from the Massachusetts bench despite their political success.

79. BJC, Personnel File; HIC, Correspondence File, 1919–1940, Archdiocese of Boston Archives, discusses Leveroni, who was the HIC attorney, a Boston Overseer of the Poor and a leader of the Italo-American community; Rubenstein is discussed in Barbara Miller Solomon, *Pioneers in Service: The History of the Associated Jewish Philanthropies of Boston* (Boston, 1956), 52, 63.

80. Shannon, *The American Irish,* 187; and Joseph Dinneen, *Ward Eight* (New York, 1936), in which a North End ward boss summed up Irish contempt for the Brahmin reformer when he said, "He's as bad down here as an informer, and as cordially hated"; Robert Grant, *The Law-Breakers and Other Stories* (New York, 1906).

81. Orlando Patterson, *Ethnic Chauvinism: The Reactionary Impulse* (New York, 1977), 150, 177, points out the melting pot thesis was challenged by romantic, relativist, anti-modern ethnic leaders most successfully in politics; on Wil-

298 BOSTON'S WAYWARD CHILDREN

liams, see BJC, Personnel File and Adlow, *Threshold of Justice,* 154.

82. Robert H. Lord, John E. Sexton, and Edward T. Harrington, *History of the Archdiocese of Boston* (Boston, 1944), 3:533.

83. Mark A. Howe, *The Children's Judge: Frederick Pickering Cabot* (Boston, 1932); Helen Howe, *The Gentle Americans: Biography of a Breed* (New York, 1965), 277; Harry E. Burroughs, *Boys in Men's Shoes: A World of Working Children* (New York, 1944), 27; Bremner, *Children and Youth,* 3:1053–57; and BJC, Personnel File.

84. BJC, Judge Connelly File; *Boston Globe,* 9 January 1980, places the BJC tradition of black Clerks of Court in perspective; as did Henry Quarles, interview with author, Boston, 13 November 1981, the BJC Clerk in 1933–42.

85. Trout, *Boston, the Great Depression and the New Deal,* 15–17; and John F. Stack, *International Conflict in an American City: Boston's Irish, Italians and Jews, 1935–1944* (Westport, Conn., 1979).

86. Charlton J. Lewis, "The Probation System," NCCC, *Proceedings* (1897): 38–46.

87. Donald Brieland and John Lemmon, *Social Work and the Law* (St. Paul, 1977), 163; Robert M. Emerson, *Judging Delinquents* (Chicago, 1969), 23; and George W. Stubbs, "The Mission of the Juvenile Court," NCCC, *Proceedings* (1904): 356.

88. Orin C. Baker, *Travelers Aid Society in America: Principles and Methods* (New York, 1917), p. 118; and Paula Clare, "Discussion," National Probation Association, *Yearbook* (1929), p. 204 complained about role conflict that made children parents distrust the probation officer.

89. Walter I. Trattner, *Homer Folks: Pioneer in Social Welfare* (New York, 1968), 87–92; Emil M. Hartl (Hayden Goodwill Inn), interview with author, Boston, 12 May 1981, revealed that limited opportunities for casework, "the politics of the job" and "the poor working conditions and low pay" made juvenile probation unattractive to professional social workers by 1940.

90. Author's interviews with BJC probation officers, Joseph O'Reilly, Boston, 5 March 1978; Katherine O'Brien, Boston, 4 April 1978; Louis G. Maglio, Boston 5 May 1978; Peter G. Garabedian and Don C. Gibbons, eds., *Becoming Delinquent: Young Offenders and the Correction System* (Chicago, 1970).

91. Mennel, *Thorns & Thistles,* 140–42; and Shirley D. McCune and Daniel L. Skoler, "Juvenile Court Judges in the United States, Part I, A National Profile," *Crime and Delinquency* 11 (May 1965): 121–31.

92. John C. Burnham, "Oral History Interviews of William Healy and Augusta F. Bronner, January 1960, June 1961," Houghton Library, Harvard University, Cambridge, 86–97, 170.

93. Ibid., 10–20; Jon Snodgrass, "The American Criminological Tradition: Portraits of the Men and Ideology in a Discipline," (Ph.D. diss., University of Pennsylvania, 1972), 58–60.

94. Burnham, "Oral History," 30–40; Benedict S. Alper (Boston College), interview with author, Boston, 14 September 1981, Healy's co-author of *Criminal Youth and the Borstal System* (New York, 1941).

95. George E. Garner, "In Memoriam: William Healy, M.D.—1869–1963," *American Journal of Orthopsychiatry* 34 (October 1964): 960–63; George S. Stevenson and Geddes Smith, *Child Guidance Clinics: A Quarter Century of Development* (New York, 1934), 15–17; Ethel S. Dummer Papers, Correspondence File, Schlesinger Library, Radcliffe College, Cambridge, Mass.

96. William Healy, *The Individual Delinquent* (Boston, 1915).

97. Emil M. Hartl and Roland D. Elderkin, interviews with the author, Boston, 12 May 1981, JBF students of Healy and Bronner, case conference participants; also Robert I. Watson, "A Brief History of Clinical Psychology," *Psychological Bulletin* 50 (September 1953): 321–42.

98. Snodgrass, "American Criminological," 63–64. Healy's long love affair with Bronner was rather daring in proper Bostonian circles of the 1920s and surprising considering his criticism of his patients' "irregular sex practices."

99. BJC, Probation Files, 1917–37, contain hundreds of "blue sheets" dictated by Healy or Bronner, others are found in JFCS, CBCC Files, and Judge Baker Children's Center, Archives, 1917–37, Countway Library, Harvard University, Boston.

100. Benedict S. Alper interview; on Bronner, see American Historical Society, *The Story of Massachusetts: Personal and Family History* (New York, 1938), 4:93–95.

101. Quotes from Emil M. Hartl, interview, which were confirmed by interviews with Roland D. Elderkin, Morgan Memorial, Boston; and Sibley Higginbotham, Church Home Society, Boston; Bronner was recalled by all interviewees as "formidable" and "commanding."

102. Two hundred randomly selected JBF case reports in 1917, 1927 and 1937 were examined in BJC, JFCS, BCAS, and Countway Library archives, Frances Aldrich, Boston Family Welfare Society, interpreted sample "blue sheets" for me.

103. Eveoleen N. Rexford, interview with author, Cambridge, 9 November 1981, a JBF child psychiatrist trained by Healy; also Nathan G. Hale, Jr., *Freud and the Americans: The Beginnings of Psychoanalysis in the United States, 1876–1917* (New York, 1971), 75–77; Healy's interviews in which the child was encouraged to tell "his own story" foreshadowed Freud's "talking cure" and psychoanalytic interviews.

104. Burnham, "Oral History," 220–28; E. Bruce Tucker, "James Jackson Putnam: An American Perspective on the Uses of Psychoanalysis, 1885–1918," *New England Quarterly* 51 (December 1978): 527–46; John C. Burnham, "Psychiatry, Psychology, and the Progressive Movement," *American Quarterly* 12 (Winter 1960): 457–65.

105. Snodgrass, "American Criminological," 65–66; Burnham, "Oral History," 183, notes six hundred American child guidance clinics appeared by 1942 but were not foreseen by Healy or Bronner; on Healy's connection with emigre Freudians, see Paul Roazen, *Helene Deutsch, A Psychoanalyst's Life* (New York, 1985), 275–81.

106. William Healy, "The Devil's Workshop," *The Century* 120 (January 1930): 122–32.

107. Healy, *The Individual Delinquent*, 6; and Healy, *Honesty* (Indianapolis, Ind., 1915), 9.

108. Matthew Hale, Jr., *Human Science and Social Order: Hugo Munsterberg and the Origins of Applied Psychology* (Philadelphia, 1980), 9; and Burnham, "Oral History," 90–95, 235–38.

109. Burnham, "Oral History," 97, 200–204.

110. Henry D. Thurston, "Some Phases of the Probation Work of the Juvenile Court," NCCC, Proceedings (1905): 177–85; Hans Weiss, "The Child on Probation," National Probation Association, *Yearbook* (1929), 94–108, claimed the BJC probation officers had the chief responsibility, "He takes up the threads laid bare by judge and clinic."

111. Burnham, "Oral History," 250–65.

112. August B. Hollingshead and Frederick C. Redlich, *Social Class and Mental Illness: A Community Study* (New York, 1958), 345; Eric H. Erikson, *Childhood and Society* (New York, 1950), 224.

113. White, *In Search of History,* 61–62.

114. Emil M. Hartl, interview, said, "Healy was more stern and Bronner much more an efficient administrator, but they worked very well together as a pair. She was his alter ego."

115. G. Stanley Hall, *Adolescence* (New York, 1904); Dorothy Ross, *G. Stanley Hall* (Chicago, 1972), places "the father of child study" in perspective; Arthur W. Calhoun, *A Social History of the American Family* (Cleveland, 1919), made the decline of the family a by-word; and Travis, *The Young Malefactor,* 183, claimed juvenile delinquents "spring most directly of all from defective home conditions."

116. Jane Addams, *The Spirit of Youth,* 454, was the most authoritative source for social workers' decisions to concentrate their efforts on the individual child rather than on the "disorganized" family; see also Addams, *Democracy and Social Ethics* (New York, 1907); Judge Perkins expressed his doubts about child psychiatry and social work in *Common Sense and Bad Boys and Other Essays* (Boston, 1946), 18–20.

117. Social workers and settlement houses created institutions to which lower-class children were attracted for socialization and supervision in the guise of recreation; see Roy Rosenzweig, *Eight Hours for What We Will: Workers and Leisure in an Industrial City, 1870–1920* (Cambridge, England, 1983), 150; Woods and Kennedy, *Settlement Horizon* 60; and David Nasaw, *Children of the City: At Work and At Play* (New York, 1985), 152–57.

118. Quote is from Robert Mulford, interview; Elvena Bage Tillman, "The Rights of Childhood: The National Child Welfare Movement, 1880–1919" (Ph.D. diss., University of Wisconsin, 1968), 140–42.

119. Burnham, "Oral History," 208, notes Healy preferred foster homes or "New England academies" for non-delinquent boys; Benedict S. Alper, interview, recalled this was done occasionally with private funds.

120. Lubove, *The Professional Altruist,* 61–66; William Healy, "Memorial to Elmer Ernest Southard," *Journal of Juvenile Research* 12 (July 1920): 176–77.

121. Lubove, *The Professional Altruist,* 55–66; Paul L. Schroeder, et al., *Child Guidance Procedures* (New York, 1937), 35–37; and Mary E. Richmond, *Social Diagnosis* (New York, 1917).

122. Frances Aldrich, interview; BCAS, Case 41121.

123. BCAS, Case 40773.

124. JFCS, General District Service Committee, Directors' Minutes, 17 March 1927.

125. Elmer E. Southard, "Psychopathic Delinquents," NCCC, *Proceedings* (1916): 529–38.

126. BJC and JFCS archives contain 135 cases aided by the Federated Jewish Charities in 1917–1927, which comprised this sample.

127. JFCS, Children's Bureau Central Committee, Minutes, 18 January 1924.

128. Burnham, "Oral History," 175–80.

129. Kevin Tierney, *Darrow, a Biography* (New York, 1979), 328–30.

130. Burnham, "Oral History," 180–83.

131. John C. Burnham, *Psychoanalysis and American Medicine, 1894–1918: Medicine, Science and Culture* (New York, 1967).

132. Burnham, "Psychiatry, Psychology, and the Progressive Movement," 457–65; Nathan G. Hale, *Freud and the Americans,* 75–77; and Matthew Hale, Jr., *Human Science and Social Order,* 8.

133. Figures from my BJC sample of 1917 and 1927 cases.

134. Beard, *Juvenile Probation,* 61–62; Henry B. Elkind and Maurice Taylor, " 'One Thousand Juvenile Delinquents,' A Critique," *Mental Hygiene* 18 (October 1934): 531–52, pointed out that only 40 percent of the BJC cases were referred to the JBF; about 80 percent of these children visited the clinic only once and saw a psychiatrist for a single interview; only 20 percent of the JBF recommendations were carried out by the court or another agency.

135. *Baker, Upbuilder,* 59–62; and this explanation of the discrepancy between JBF and BJC disposition of cases is consistent with author's interviews with Benedict S. Alper, Robert Mulford, Roland D. Elderkin, Frances Aldrich, Emil M. Hartl, and Sibley Higginbotham.

136. Francis H. Hiller, "The Juvenile Court as a Case-Working Agency: Its Limitations and Its Possibilities," NCCC, *Proceedings* (1926): 144, complained that "political hangers-on" and "untrained, uneducated weaklings" appointed as probation officers often impeded the functions of the juvenile court; anecdotal evidence in personal interviews cited above suggest this was sometimes a problem in the BJC after 1930.

137. Henry Quarles and Benedict S. Alper, interviews; Perkins, *Common Sense and Bad Boys,* 130–32, forcefully rejected advice from the JBF, in turn Healy called Perkins a "legalist."

138. Judge Harry L. Eastham, "Letter," *Survey* 70 (June 1934): 20, criticizes the BJC, whose decisions "have frequently been temporized by the fear of appeal" and which lacked the "necessary support and cooperation from other social agencies without which no juvenile court can function effectively."

139. Julia Lathrop, "Introduction," *Proceedings of the Conference on Juvenile Court Standards,* U.S. Children's Bureau Publication No. 97 (Washington, D.C., 1922), 8.

140. Ben B. Lindsey, "My Lesson from the Juvenile Court," *Survey* 5 (February 1910), 652.

141. Bernard Flexner, "A Decade of the Juvenile Court," NCCC, *Proceedings* (1910): 116.

142. J. Prentice Murphy, "The Juvenile Court at the Bar: A National Challenge," *Annals* 145 (September–November 1929): 90–92.

143. William Healy, "Knowing Your Individual," *Yearbook of the National Probation Association* (New York, 1932), 230.

144. Perkins, *Common Sense and Bad Boys,* 19–20.

145. Ibid., 39–41.

146. 131–33; Louis G. Maglio, *A Court Reaches Out to the Child in Trouble with the Law: The Story of the Citizenship Training Group, Inc. Affiliated with the Boston Juvenile Court* (Boston, n.d.).

147. Quote from Roland D. Elderkin and author's interviews on Judge Perkins with Frances Aldrich, Emil M. Hartl, and Katherine O'Brien.

148. BJC, *In Memorandum to the Presiding Justices,* 9.

149. William Healy and Augusta F. Bronner, *Delinquents and Criminals: Their Making and Unmaking* (New York, 1926), 62–66; but this report was challenged by Harvard Law School criminologists, Sheldon and Eleanor Glueck, who were "personal rivals of Healy and Bronner," according to Edwin Powers, interview with author, Boston, 24 February 1979, and Benedict S. Alper, interview.

150. Sheldon Glueck and Eleanor T. Glueck, *One Thousand Juvenile Delinquents* (Cambridge, 1934), 165–67, 180–84; JBF trustee Dr. Richard C. Cabot, the father of medical social work in Boston, was shocked by the Glueck study and concluded that the BJC-JBF efforts were a complete failure. See *Cabot,* "One

Thousand Delinquent Boys: First Findings of the Harvard Law School's Survey of Crime," *Survey* 70 (February 1934): 38–40; Cabot resigned from the JBF and began his Cambridge-Somerville Study; see Powers and Witmer, *An Experiment*.

151. William Healy, Augusta F. Bronner, and Myra E. Shimberg, "The Close of Another Chapter in Criminology," *Mental Hygiene* 19 (April 1935): 208–22.

152. BJC, Case 10889.

Epilogue

1. Gertrude Himmelfarb, *The Idea of Poverty: England in the Early Industrial Age* (New York, 1984); R. H. Tawney, *Religion and the Rise of Capitalism* (New York, 1947), 222.

2. Catherine S. Menand, *A Research Guide to the Massachusetts Courts and Their Records* (Boston, 1987), 97.

3. David Nasaw, *Children of the City: At Work and At Play* (New York, 1985).

4. Philippe Aries, *Centuries of Childhood: A Social History of Family Life* (New York, 1962).

5. Finley Peter Dunne, *Observations by Mr. Dooley* (New York, 1902), 15.

6. John H. Ehrenreich, *The Altruistic Imagination: A History of Social Work and Social Policy in the United States* (Ithaca, N.Y., 1985), 75.

7. Boston *Globe*, 5 April 1987; 19 August 1987; 18 October 1987; New York *Times*, 31 May 1987.

8. Judith Ennew, *The Sexual Exploitation of Children* (New York, 1986), 85.

9. U.S. House of Representatives, *Children, Youth and Families: 1983, A Year-End Report on the Activities of the Select Committee on Children, Youth and Families* (Washington, D.C., 1984), 113–27.

Select Bibliography

A. Manuscripts

1. Private Organizations

Boston Children's Aid Society. Archives, in the possession of the University of Massachusetts-Boston Library, Boston.

Boston Female Asylum. Archives, in the possession of the University of Massachusetts-Boston Library, Boston.

Boston Provident Society. Archives, in the possession of the Family Service of Greater Boston, Boston.

Children's Mission to the Children of the Destitute. Archives, in the possession of Parents' and Children's Service Association, Boston.

St. Vincent Orphan Asylum Records. Chancery of the Archdiocese of Boston, Archives, Boston.

Home for Destitute Catholic Children Records. Chancery of the Archdiocese of Boston, Archives, Boston.

House of the Angel Guardian Records. Chancery of the Archdiocese of Boston, Archives, Boston.

Church Home Society Records. Chancery of the Episcopal Diocese of Massachusetts, Archives, Boston.

Daly Industrial School for Girls Records. Motherhouse of the Sisters of St. Joseph, Archives, Boston.

Jewish Family and Children's Service. Archives, Boston.

Gardiner Tufts Papers. Massachusetts Historical Society, Boston.

School of Social Work Records. Simmons College. Archives, Boston.

Massachusetts Society for the Prevention of Cruelty to Children. Archives, in the possession of the University of Massachusetts-Boston Library, Boston.

New England Home for Little Wanderers, Archives, Boston.

Healy, William, and Augusta Bronner. Oral History. Houghton Library. Harvard University, Cambridge, Mass.

Mary Kenney Papers. Schlesinger Library. Harvard University, Cambridge, Mass.

School of Social Work Records. Boston College. University Archives, Chestnut Hill, Mass.

Society of St. Vincent de Paul Records. Boston College. University Archives, Chestnut Hill, Mass.

House of the Good Shepherd Records. Madonna Hall Center, Archives, Marlboro, Mass.

Boston Home for Jewish Children, Hecht House and United Hebrew Benevolent

Association Records. American Jewish Historical Society, Archives, Waltham, Mass.

National Association of Social Workers Records. Temple University. Urban History Archives, Philadelphia.

2. Public Organizations

Boston Juvenile Court. Probation Records, 1906–40, Boston.

Commonwealth of Massachusetts. Department of Youth Services. Records for inmates of the Lyman School for Boys in Westborough, the Industrial School for Boys in Shirley, and the State Industrial School for Girls in Lancaster are on microfilm for period after 1900. Records for the earlier period are available in manuscript volumes at the Schlesinger Library, Harvard University, Cambridge, Mass.

Commonwealth of Massachusetts. Secretary of the Commonwealth. State Archives, State Primary School at Monson Records, Boston.

Commonwealth of Massachusetts. State Library. Reports of Legislative Committees, Boston.

3. Interviews

Aldrich, Frances. Family Welfare Society. Interview with author. 27 March 1981.

Aube, Roland. House of the Angel Guardian. Interview with author. Boston, Mass. 17 May 1978.

Beers, Robert I. New England Home for Little Wanderers. Interview with author. Boston, 23 June 1986.

Bradshaw, Francis A. Essex County Training School. Interview with author. Lawrence, Mass., 25 October 1978.

Burke, Isabel. Division of Child Guardianship. Interview with author. Boston, Mass. 12 April 1979.

Canavan, Sister Mary of the Good Shepherd. House of the Good Shepherd. Interview with author. Marlboro, Mass., 21 March 1979.

Carbone, Sister Biagia. Home for Italian Children. Interview with author. Boston, 3 November 1980.

Carrigan, Sister Mary Beatrice. House of the Good Shepherd. Interview with author. Marlboro, Mass. 21 March 1979.

Cerio, Sister Solanus. Home for Italian Children. Interview with author. Boston, 3 November 1980.

Chamberlain, Tony. Boston Farm Trade School. Interview with author. Boston, 14 July 1987.

Collins, Sister Mary Bertha. House of the Good Shepherd. Interview with author. Marlboro, Mass., 21 March 1979.

Cosand, Phyllis M. New England Home for Little Wanderers. Interview with author. Boston, 7 January 1986.

Dalton, Msgr. Augustine C. Boston Catholic Charitable Bureau. Interview with author. 15 March 1979.

Dever, Pauline. House of the Good Shepherd. Interview with author. Boston, 18 January 1979.

DiPrizio, Rev. Antonio Ubaldus. House of the Angel Guardian. Interview with author. Boston, 17 November 1980.

Donnelly, Sister Catherine. Home for Italian Children. Interview with author. Boston, 17 November 1980.

Doyle, Msgr. James H. Boston Catholic Charitable Bureau. Interview with author. Boston, 4 March 1979.

Elderkin, Roland D. Hayden Goodwill Inn. Interview with author. 12 May 1981.

Finn, Msgr. Charles A. Boston Catholic Charitable Bureau. Interview with author. Boston, 8 March 1979.

Fleischer, Anna. Home for Jewish Children. Interview with author. Boston, 10 December 1979.

Hartl, Emil M. Hayden Goodwill Inn. Interview with author. Boston, 12 May 1981.

Higginbotham, Sibley. Church Home Society. Interview with author. Boston, 6 April 1981.

Jacobs, Cyrus L. Home for Jewish Children. Interview with author. Boston, 26 May 1979.

Kahalas, Max. West End House. Interview with author. Boston, 12 January 1977.

Keating, Msgr. James J. House of the Angel Guardian. Interview with author. Boston, 29 April 1978.

Kelly, Rev. Vincent J. House of the Good Shepherd. Interview with author. Boston, 9 May 1978.

LaScelia, Michael. Home for Italian Children. Interview with author. Boston, 29 June 1987.

McConnell, Herbert Dwight. Home for Destitute Catholic Children. Interview with author. Boston, 13 June 1979.

McHugh, Sister Mary Elizabeth. St. Vincent's Asylum. Interview with author. Boston, 20 March 1979.

Maglio, Louis G. Boston Juvenile Court. Interview with author. Boston, 10 May 1978.

Martignetti, Anthony. Home for Italian Children. Interview with author. Boston, 19 November 1980.

Moreland, Donald W. Family Service Association of Greater Boston. Interview with author. Cambridge, 9 July 1987.

Moynihan, Rev. James. Home for Destitute Catholic Children. Interview with author. Boston, 2 May 1979.

Mulford, Robert. Massachusetts Society for the Prevention of Cruelty to Children. Interview with author. Boston, 11 May 1981.

O'Brien, Katherine. Boston Juvenile Court. Interview with author. Boston, 11 May 1978.

O'Reilly, Joseph M. Boston Juvenile Court. Interview with author. Boston, 11 May 1978.

Palmer, Jerry. House of the Angel Guardian. Interview with author. Boston, 9 January 1978.

Powers, Edwin. Boston Juvenile Court. Interview with author. 24 February 1979.

Rettew, Sister Marcella. Home for Destitute Catholic Children. Interview with author. Boston, 19 March 1979.

Roazen, Rose Pave. Home for Jewish Children. Interview with author. Boston, 22 May 1979.

Robinson, Sister Thecla. Home for Destitute Catholic Children. Interview with author. Boston, 20 March 1979.

Saul, Joseph E. House of the Angel Guardian. Interview with author. Boston, 3 February 1979.

Scannell, Rev. Francis. House of the Good Shepherd. Interview with author. Boston, 24 May 1978.

Snow, Mary M. Home for Destitute Catholic Children. Interview with author. Boston, 3 June 1981.

Sullivan, Rev. Francis. Home for Destitute Catholic Children. Interview with author. Boston, 6 May 1979.

Tomasello, Anthony. Home for Italian Children. Interview with author. Boston, 3 November 1980.

Toomey, Francis. House of the Good Shepherd. Interview with author. Boston, 17 May 1978.

Toomey, Sister Ursulita. Daly Industrial School. Interview with author. Boston, 27 May 1981.

Yennock, Sister Margaret. Home for Italian Children. Interview with author. Boston, 29 June 1987.

B. Published Records of Private Organizations

Boston Children's Aid Society. *Annual Reports*, 1865–1921. Boston.

Boston Farm Trade School. *Annual Reports*, 1834–1930. Boston.

Boston Society for the Prevention of Pauperism (Industrial Aid Society). *Annual Reports*, 1852–1925. Boston.

Children's Aid Society of New York. *Annual Reports*, 1854–95. New York.

Children's Friend Society. *Annual Reports*, 1834–1920. Boston.

Children's Mission to the Children of the Destitute. *Annual Reports*, 1850–1930. Boston.

Society of St. Vincent de Paul. *Annual Reports*, 1868–1930. Boston.

Watch and Ward Society (New England Society for the Suppression of Vice). *Annual Reports*, 1879–1925. Boston.

C. Government Documents

1. Boston

Boston Police Commission. *Annual Reports, 1851–1940.*

Boston School Committee. Annual Reports, 1854–1940.

Documents of the City of Boston. 1826–1940.

2. Massachusetts

Board of State Charities. *Annual Reports*, 1864–1940. *See* reports under these titles:

Board of State Charities, 1864–78.

State Board of Health, Lunacy and Charity, 1878–85.

State Board of Lunacy and Charity, 1885–96.

State Board of Charity, 1897–1919.

Department of Public Welfare, 1919–40.

Industrial School for Boys (Shirley). *Annual Reports,* 1909–40.

State Industrial School for Girls (Lancaster). *Annual Reports,* 1856–40.

State Reform School for Boys (Westborough). *Annual Reports,* 1847–1940.

D. Books and Articles

Abbott, Edith. "Civil War and the Crime Wave of 1865–1870." *Social Service Review* 1 (June 1927): 212–34.

Abbott, Grace. *The Problem of Immigration in Massachusetts: Report of the Commission on Immigration.* Boston: Wright and Potter, 1914.

Abell, Aaron Ignatius. *American Catholicism and Social Action: A Search for Social Justice, 1865–1950.* Garden City, N.J., Hanover House, 1960.

Addams, Jane. *The Spirit of Youth and City Streets.* New York: Macmillan, 1909.

Allen, Lucy Ellis. "The Rebecca Pomroy Newton Home for Orphan Girls." In *The Mirror of Newton Past and Present.* Newton, Mass.: Newton Federation of Women's Clubs, 1907.

Amfitheatrof, Erik. *The Children of Columbus: An Informal History of the Italians in the New World.* Boston: Little, Brown, 1973.

Antler, Joyce, and Stephen Antler. "From Child Rescue to Family Protection: The Evolution of the Child Protective Movement in the United States." *Children and Youth Service Review* 1 (1979), 177–204.

Ashby, LeRoy. *Saving the Waifs: Reformers and Dependent Children, 1890–1917.* Philadelphia: Temple University Press, 1984.

Associated Charities of Boston. *Directory of the Charitable and Beneficent Organizations of Boston.* Boston, 1891.

Baker, Harvey H. "Procedure of the Boston Juvenile Court." *Survey* 23 (February 1910): 649–50.

Baltzell, E. Digby. *Puritan Boston and Quaker Philadelphia: Two Protestant Ethics and the Spirit of Class Authority and Leadership.* New York: Free Press, 1979.

Bamer, Golde. "Russians in Boston." *Lend a Hand* 8 (March 1892) 168–71.

Banner, Lois W. "Religious Benevolence as Social Control: A Critique of an Interpretation," *Journal of American History* 60 (June 1973): 23–41.

Beard, Belle Boone. *Juvenile Probation: An Analysis of the Case Records of Five Hundred Children Studied at the Judge Baker Guidance Clinic and Placed on Probation in the Juvenile Court of Boston.* New York: American Book Company, 1934.

Berg, Barbara J. *The Remembered Gate: Origins of American Feminism: The Woman and the City, 1800–1860.* New York: Oxford University Press, 1978.

Billingsley, Andrew and Jeanne M. Giovannoni. *Children of the Storm: Black Children and American Child Welfare.* New York: Harcourt Brace Jovanovich, 1972.

Bodnar, John. *The Transplanted: A History of Immigrants in Urban America.* Bloomington: Indiana University Press, 1985.

Boston Female Asylum. *An Account of the Rise, Progress, and Present State of the Boston Female Asylum.* Boston, 1803.

———. *Reminiscences of the Boston Female Orphan Asylum.* Boston, 1844.

Boston Juvenile Court. *In Memoriam of the Presiding Justices of the Boston Juvenile Court.* Boston: Boston Juvenile Court, 1940.

Boston Morning Post. *Selections from the Court Reports Originally Published in the Boston Morning Post, from 1834 to 1837.* New York: Arno Press, 1974.

Boston Society for the Care of Girls. *One Hundred Years of Work With Girls in Boston.* Boston: BSCG, 1919.

Boyer, Paul S. *Urban Masses and Moral Order in America, 1820–1920.* Cambridge: Harvard University Press, 1978.

Brace, Charles Loring. *The Dangerous Classes of New York and Twenty Years Work Among Them.* New York, 1872.

Brayley, Arthur Wellington. *Schools and School Boys of Old Boston.* Boston, 1894.

Breckinridge, Sophonisba and Edith Abbott. *The Delinquent Child and the Home.* New York: Survey Associates, 1912.

Bremner, Robert H. *From the Depths: The Discovery of Poverty in the United States.* New York: New York University Press, 1956.

———. *Children and Youth in America: A Documentary History.* 3 vols. Cambridge: Harvard University Press, 1970.

———. *The Public Good: Philanthropy and Welfare in the Civil War Era.* New York: Knopf, 1980.

Brenzel, Barbara M. *Daughters of the State: A Social Portrait of the First Reform School for Girls in North America, 1856–1905.* Cambridge: MIT Press, 1983.

Briggs, John W. *An Italian Passage: Immigrants to Three American Cities, 1890–1930.* New Haven: Yale University Press, 1978.

Bruno, Frank J. *Trends in Social Work as Reflected in the Proceedings of the National Conference of Social Work, 1874–1946.* New York: Columbia University Press, 1948.

Burnham, John C. *Psychoanalysis and American Medicine, 1874–1918: Medicine, Science and Culture.* New York: International Universities Press, 1967.

Burleigh, Edith N. and Frances R. Harris. *The Delinquent Girl.* New York: New York School of Social Work, 1923.

Burroughs, Harry E. *Boys in Men's Shoes: A World of Working Children.* New York: Macmillan, 1944.

Butler, Ann. *Notes of Inmates in the Female Department of the House of Reformation at South Boston.* Boston, 1834.

Byington, Margaret F. *The Confidential Exchange: A Form of Social Cooperation.* New York: Russell Sage Foundation, 1912.

Byrne, William. *History of the Catholic Church in the United States.* 2 vols. Boston, 1899.

Carlevale, Joseph William. *Leading Americans of Italian Descent in Massachusetts.* Plymouth: Memorial Press, 1946.

Chambers, Clarke A. *Seedtime of Reform: American Social Service and Social Action, 1918–33.* Minneapolis: University of Minnesota Press, 1963.

Child, Irvin L. *Italian or American? The Second Generation in Conflict.* New Haven: Yale University Press, 1943.

Children's Mission. *Light Dawning: or, Fruits of the Children's Mission.* Boston, 1856.

———. *The Children's Mission: What It Is and What It Does.* Boston, 1884.

Claghorn, Kate Holladay. *The Immigrant's Day in Court.* New York: Harper and Brothers, 1923.

Clement, Priscilla Ferguson. *Welfare and the Poor in the Nineteenth-Century City: Philadelphia, 1800–1854.* Rutherford, N.J.: Fairleigh Dickinson University Press, 1985.

Conway, Katherine E. *The Good Shepherd in Boston, 1867–1892: Silver Jubilee Memorial.* Boston, 1892.

Conway, Katherine E., and Mabel Ward Cameron. *Charles Francis Donnelly: A Memoir.* New York: J. T. White, 1909.

Conway, Katherine E. *The Golden Year of the Good Shepherd in Boston: Compiled from the Annals of the Convent.* Boston: Thomas J. Flynn, 1918.

Cooper, John M. *Children's Institutions: A Study of the Programs and Policies in Catholic Children's Institutions in the United States.* Philadelphia: Dolphin Press, 1931.

Cott, Nancy F. *The Bonds of Womanhood: "Women's Sphere:" in New England, 1780–1835.* New Haven: Yale University Press, 1977.

Covello, Leonard. *The Social Background of the Italo-American School Child.* Leiden, Netherlands: E. J. Brill, 1967.

Cullen, James Bernard. *The Story of the Irish in Boston.* Boston, 1889.

Cumbler, John T. *Working-Class Community in Industrial America: Work, Leisure, and Struggle in Two Industrial Cities, 1880–1930.* Westport, Conn. Greenwood Press, 1979.

Daniels, John. *In Freedom's Birthplace.* Boston: Houghton Mifflin, 1914.

Davis, Allen F. *Spearheads for Reform: The Social Settlements and the Progressive Movement, 1890–1914.* New York: Oxford University Press, 1967.

———. *American Heroine: The Life and Legend of Jane Addams.* New York: Oxford University Press, 1973.

Davis, Philip. *Street-Land: Its Little People and Big Problems.* Boston: Small, Maynard, 1915.

Davis, William T. *Bench and Bar of the Commonwealth of Massachusetts.* 2 vols. Boston, 1895.

Dawley, Alan. *Class and Community: The Industrial Revolution in Lynn.* Cambridge: Harvard University Press, 1976.

de Beaumont, Gustave and Alexis de Tocqueville. *On the Penitentiary System in the United States and its Application in France.* Carbondale: Southern Illinois University Press, 1979.

De Marco, William M. *Ethnics and Enclaves: Boston's Italian North End.* Ann Arbor, Mich.: UMI Research Press, 1981.

Devine, Edward T. *The Spirit of Social Work.* New York: Charities Publication, 1911.

Diner, Hasia R. *Erin's Daughters in America: Irish Immigrant Women in the Nineteenth Century.* Baltimore: Johns Hopkins University Press, 1983.

310   BOSTON'S WAYWARD CHILDREN

Donzelot, Jacques. *The Policing of Families.* New York: Random House, 1979.

Drucker, Saul, and Maurice Beck Hexter. *Children Astray.* Cambridge: Harvard University Press, 1923.

Dudden, Faye E. *Serving Women: Household Service in Nineteenth-Century America.* Middletown, Conn.: Wesleyan University Press, 1983.

Dunstan, J. Leslie. *A Light to the City: 150 Years of the City Missionary Society, 1816–1966.* Boston: Beacon Press, 1966.

Dyer, Thomas A. *Glimpses of the Brotherhood of Charity.* Boston, 1893.

Ehrenfried, Albert. *A Chronicle of Boston Jewry: From the Colonial Settlement to 1900.* Boston: n.p., 1966.

Ehrenreich, John H. *The Altruistic Imagination: A History of Social Work and Social Policy in the United States.* Ithaca: Cornell University Press, 1985.

Ewens, Mary. *The Role of the Nun in Nineteenth-Century America: Variations on the International Theme.* New York: Arno Press, 1978.

Farwell, Harriet S. *Lucy Louise Flower, 1837–1920: Her Contribution to Education and Child Welfare in Chicago.* Chicago: n.p., 1924.

Fass, Paula S. *The Damned and the Beautiful: American Youth in the 1920's.* New York: Oxford University Press, 1977.

Fenton, Edwin. *Immigrants and Unions, A Case Study: Italians and American Labor, 1870–1920.* New York: Arno Press, 1975.

Finkelhor, David. *Child Sexual Abuse: New Theory and Research.* New York: Free Press, 1984.

Flexner, Bernard, and Roger N. Baldwin. *Juvenile Courts and Probation.* New York: Century Company, 1916.

Foley, Alfred S. *Bishop Healy: Beloved Outcaste.* New York: Arno Press, 1969.

Folks, Homer. *The Care of Destitute, Neglected, and Delinquent Children.* New York: Macmillan, 1902.

Foote, Elizabeth L. "The Children's Home Library Movement." *The Outlook* 57 (September 1897): 172–73.

Fox, Sanford J. "Juvenile Justice Reform: An Historical Perspective." *Stanford Law Review* 22 (June 1970): 1187–1239.

Freedman. Estelle B. *Their Sisters' Keepers: Women's Prison Reform in America, 1830–1930.* Ann Arbor: University of Michigan Press, 1981.

Friedman, Lee M. "Boston in American Jewish History." *American Jewish Historical Quarterly* 42 (June 1953): 333–40.

Fry, Annette Riley. "The Children's Migration." *American Heritage* 26 (December 1974): 4–10, 79–81.

Gaffey, James. "The Changing of the Guard: The Rise of Cardinal O'Connell of Boston." *Catholic Historical Review* 59 (July 1973): 225–44.

Gavin, Donald P. *The National Conference of Catholic Charities, 1910–1960.* Milwaukee: Catholic Life Publications, 1962.

Gil, David G. *Violence Against Children: Physical Abuse in the United States.* Cambridge: Harvard University Press, 1970.

Glueck, Sheldon, and Eleanor T. Glueck. *Five Hundred Delinquent Women.* New York: Knopf, 1934.

———. *One Thousand Juvenile Delinquents.* Cambridge: Harvard University Press, 1934.

Goodwin, Doris Kearns. *The Fitzgeralds and the Kennedys*. New York: Simon and Schuster, 1987.

Gordon, Linda. *Woman's Body, Woman's Right: A Social History of Birth Control in America*. New York: Grossman, 1976.

——. "Single Mothers and Child Neglect, 1880–1920." *American Quarterly* 37 (Summer 1985): 173–192.

——. *Heroes of Their Own Lives: The Politics and History of Family Violence, Boston 1880–1960*. New York: Viking Books, 1988.

Griffin, Clifford S. *Their Brothers' Keepers: Moral Stewardship in the United States, 1800–1865*. New Brunswick, N.J.: Rutgers University Press, 1960.

Grinnell, Frank W. "Probation as an Orthodox Common Law Practice in Massachusetts Prior to the Statutory System." *Massachusetts Law Quarterly* 2 (August 1917): 591–639.

Grob, Gerald N. *Mental Institutions in America: Social Policy to 1875*. New York: Free Press, 1973.

Gutman, Herbert G. *The Black Family in Slavery and Freedom, 1750–1925*. Oxford: Basil Blackwell, 1976.

Hall, Peter Dobkin. *The Organization of American Culture, 1700–1900: Private Institutions, Elites, and the Origins of American Nationality*. New York: New York University Press, 1984.

Haller, John S., and Robin M. Haller. *The Physician and Sexuality in Victorian America*. Urbana: Ill.: University of Illinois Press, 1974.

Haller, Mark H. *Eugenics: Hereditarian Attitudes in American Thought*. New Brunswick, N.J.: Rutgers University Press, 1963.

Halsey, William M. *The Survival of American Innocence: Catholicism in an Era of Disillusionment, 1920–1940*. Notre Dame, Ind.: Unviersity of Notre Dame Press, 1980.

Hammet, Theodore M. "Two Mobs of Jacksonian Boston: Ideology and Interest." *Journal of American History* 62 (March 1976), 845–68.

Handlin, Oscar. *Boston's Immigrants, 1790–1880: A Study in Acculturation*. Cambridge: Harvard University Press, 1959.

Hareven, Tamara K., ed. *Family and Kin in Urban Communities, 1700–1930*. New York: New Viewpoints, 1977.

Harris, Leon. *Only to God: The Extraordinary Life of Godfrey Lowell Cabot*. New York: Atheneum, 1967.

Hart, Hastings H., ed. *Juvenile Court Laws in the United States*. New York: Charities Publication, 1910.

Haskins, George F. *House of the Angel Guardian Report*. Boston, 1868.

——. *Six Weeks Abroad in Ireland, England and Belgium*. Boston, 1872.

Hawes, Joseph M. *Children in Urban Society: Juvenile Delinquency in Nineteenth-Century America*. New York: Oxford University Press, 1971.

Healy, William. *The Individual Delinquent*. Boston: Little Brown, 1915.

Healy, William, and Augusta F. Bronner. *Delinquents and Criminals: Their Making and Unmaking*. New York: Macmillan, 1926.

Higham, John. *Strangers in the Land: Patterns of Nativism, 1860–1925*. New York: Atheneum, 1972.

Hiner, N. Ray, and Joseph M. Hawes, eds. *Growing Up in America: Children in Historical Perspective*. Urbana: University of Illinois Press, 1985.

Hobson, Barbara Meil. *Uneasy Virtue: The Politics of Prostitution and the American Reform Tradition*. New York: Basic Books, 1987.

Horton, James Oliver, and Lois E. Horton. *Black Bostonians: Family Life and Community Struggle in the Antebellum North*. New York: Holmes & Meier, 1979.

Howe, Helen. *The Gentle Americans, 1864–1960: Biography of a Breed*. New York: Harper & Row, 1965.

Howe, Mark A. De Wolfe. *The Children's Judge: Frederick Pickering Cabot*. Boston: Houghton Mifflin, 1932.

Howe, Samuel Gridley. *An Essay on Separate and Congregate System of Prison Discipline*. Boston, 1846.

———. *A Letter to the Commissioners of Massachusetts for the State Reform School for Girls*. Boston, 1854.

House of the Angel Guardian. *Silver Jubilee of the Brothers of Charity of the House of the Angel Guardian, Boston*. Boston, 1899.

House of the Good Shepherd. *Shall the State Give Money to Aid a Charity Managed on a Sectarian Basis?* Boston, 1888.

Houston, Susan E. "Victorian Origins of Juvenile Delinquency: A Canadian Experience." *History of Education Quarterly* 12 (Fall 1972): 254–80.

Hubbard, Ray S. *Crusading for Children: The Massachusetts Society for the Prevention of Cruelty to Children, 1878–1943*. Boston: MSPCC, 1943.

Jacobs, Donald M. "A History of the Boston Negro from the Revolution to the Civil War." Ph.D. diss., Boston University, 1968.

Jacoby, George Paul. *Catholic Child Care in Nineteenth-Century New York*. Washington, D.C.: Catholic University of America Press, 1941.

Jaher, Frederick Cople. *The Urban Establishment: Upper Strata in Boston, New York, Charleston, Chicago and Los Angeles*. Urbana: University of Illinois Press, 1982.

Judge Baker Foundation. *Case Studies, Series I*. Boston: Judge Baker Foundation, 1922.

———. *Harvey Humphrey Baker, Upbuilder of the Juvenile Court*. Boston: Judge Baker Foundaton, 1921.

Kadushin, Alfred. *Child Welfare Services*. New York: Macmillan, 1974.

Katz, Michael B. *The Irony of Early School Reform: Educational Innovation in Mid-Nineteenth Century Massachusetts*. Cambridge: Harvard Unversity Press, 1968.

———. *Class, Bureaucracy, and Schools: The Illusion of Education Change in America*. New York: Praeger Publishers, 1971.

———. *Poverty and Public Policy in American History*. New York: Academic Press, 1983.

———. *In the Shadow of the Poorhouse: A Social History of Welfare in America*. New York: Basic Books, 1986.

Kelley, Florence. *Some Ethical Gains Through Legislation*. New York: Macmillan, 1905.

Kelly, William D. *The Life of Father Haskins*. Boston, 1899.

Kelso, Robert W. *The History of Public Poor Relief in Massachusetts, 1620–1920.* Boston: Houghton Mifflin, 1922.

Kennedy, David M. *Birth Control in America: The Career of Margaret Sanger.* New Haven: Yale University Press, 1970.

Kennedy, Robert E., Jr. *The Irish: Emigration, Marriage, and Family.* Berkeley: University of California Press, 1973.

Kett, Joseph F. *Rites of Passage: Adolescence in America, 1790 to the Present.* New York: Basic Books, 1977.

Knights, Peter R. *The Plain People of Boston, 1830–1860: A Study of City Growth.* New York: Oxford University Press, 1971.

Lamson, Peggy. *Roger Baldwin, Founder of the American Civil Liberties Union: A Portrait.* Boston: Houghton Mifflin, 1976.

Lane, Frances E. *American Charities and the Child of the Immigrant.* New York: Arno Press, 1974.

Lane, Roger. *Policing the City: Boston, 1822–1885.* Cambridge: Harvard University Press, 1967.

Langsam, Miriam Z. *Children West: A History of the Placing-Out System of the New York Children's Aid Society.* Madison:State Historical Society of Wisconsin. 1964.

Larsen, Charles. *The Good Fight: The Life and Times of Ben B. Lindsey.* Chicago: Quadrangle Books, 1972.

Lasch, Christopher. *Haven in a Heartless World: The Family Besieged.* New York: Basic Books, 1977.

Lazerson, Marvin. *The Origins of the Urban School: Public Education in Massachusetts, 1870–1915.* Cambridge: Harvard University Press, 1971.

———. "Understanding American Catholic Educational History." *History of Education Quarterly* 17 (Fall 1977): 297–317.

Lees, Lynn H., and John Modell. "The Irish Countryman Urbanized: A Comparative Perspective on the Famine Migration." *Journal of Urban History* 3 (August 1977): 391–408.

Leiby, James. *A History of Social Welfare and Social Work in the United States.* New York: Columbia University Press, 1978.

Levy, Leonard W. *The Law of the Commonwealth and Chief Justice Shaw.* New York: Oxford University Press, 1987.

Levy, Leonard W., and Douglas L. Jones, eds. *Jim Crow in Boston: The Origin of the Separate but Equal Doctrine.* New York: Da Capo Press, 1974.

Lipsky, Michael. *Street-Level Bureaucracy: Dilemmas of the Individual in Public Service.* New York: Russell Sage Foundation, 1980.

Lord, Robert H., John E. Sexton, and Edward T. Harrington. *History of the Archdiocese of Boston.* 3 vols. Boston: Pilot Publishing Company, 1945.

Lou, Herbert H. *Juvenile Courts in the United States.* Chapel Hill: University of North Carolina Press, 1927.

Louise, Sister Catherine. *The House of My Pilgrimage: History of the American House of the Society of St. Margaret.* Boston, n.d.

Lubove, Roy. *The Professional Altruist: The Emergence of Social Work as a Career, 1880–1930.* Cambridge: Harvard University Press, 1965.

McAvoy, Thomas T. *A History of the Catholic Church in the United States.* Notre Dame, Ind.: University of Notre Dame Press, 1969.

McCaughey, Robert A. "From Town to City: Boston in the 1820's." *Political Science Quarterly* 88 (June 1973): 191–213.

McColgan, Daniel T. *Joseph Tuckerman: Pioneer in American Social Work.* Washington, D.C.: Catholic University of America Press, 1940.

———. *A Century of Charity: The First One Hundred Years of the Society of St. Vincent de Paul in the United States.* Milwaukee, Wisc.: Bruce Publishers, 1951.

McCune, Shirley D., and Daniel L. Skoler. "Juvenile Court Judges in the United States: Part I. A National Profile." *Crime and Delinquency.* 11 (May 1956): 121–131.

Mack, Julian W. "The Juvenile Court." *Harvard Law Review* 23 (1910): 119–20.

Marcus, Steven. *The Other Victorians: A Study of Sexuality and Pornography in Mid-Nineteenth Century England.* New York: Basic Books, 1966.

Melder, Keith E. *Beginnings of Sisterhood: The American Woman's Rights Movement, 1800–1850.* New York: Schocken Books, 1977.

Melville, Annabelle M. *Elizabeth Bayley Seton, 1774–1821.* New York: Charles Scribner's Sons, 1951.

Mennel, Robert M. *Thorns & Thistles: Juvenile Delinquency in the United States 1825–1940.* Hanover, N.H.: University Press of New England, 1973.

Merwick, Donna. *Boston Priests, 1848–1910: A Study of Social and Intellectual Change.* Cambridge: Harvard University Press, 1973.

Misner, Barbara. "Highly Respectable and Accomplished Ladies: Early American Women Religious, 1790–1850." *University of Notre Dame Working Papers Series* (Fall 1980): 40–46.

Mnookin, Robert H. "Foster Care—In Whose Best Interest." *Harvard Educational Review* 43 (November 1973): 599–638.

Muraskin, William A. "The Social Control Theory in American History: A Critique." *Journal of Social History* 9 (Summer 1976): 559–69.

Nasaw, David. *Children of the City: At Work and At Play.* Garden City, N.J.: Doubleday, 1985.

National Conference of Charities and Corrections. *Proceedings, 1874–1930.*

National Council of Jewish Women. *The First Fifty Years: A History of the National Council of Jewish Women, 1893–1943.* New York: NCJW, 1943.

National Probation Association. *John Augustus, First Probation Officer.* New York: National Probation Association, 1939.

Needham, George C. *Street Arabs and Guttersnipes.* Philadelphia, 1888.

Nelli, Humbert S. *Italians in Chicago, 1880–1930: A Study in Ethnic Mobility.* New York: Oxford University Press, 1970.

Neusner, Jacob. "The Impact of Immigration and Philanthropy Upon the Boston Jewish Community, 1880–1914." *American Jewish Historical Quarterly 47 (September 1956), 71–85.*

New England Home for Little Wanderers. Frederic Harrison Knight. Boston: New England Home for Little Wanderers, 1922.

Oates , Mary J. "Organized Voluntarism: The Catholic Sisters in Massachusetts, 1870–1940." *American Quarterly* 30 (Winter 1978): 652–80.

O'Connell, William Henry Cardinal. *Recollections of Seventy Years.* Boston: Houghton Mifflin, 1934.

O'Grady, John. *Catholic Charities in the United States.* Washington, D.C.: National Conference of Catholic Charities, 1930.

O'Leary, Robert Aidan. "William Henry Cardinal O'Connell: A Social and Intellectual Biography." Ph.D. diss., Tufts University, 1980.

Panunzio, Constantine M. *The Soul of an Immigrant.* New York: Macmillan, 1921.

Peirce, Bradford Kinney. *A Half-Century with Juvenile Delinquents or the House of Refuge and its Times.* New York, 1869.

Perkins, John Forbes. *Common Sense and Bad Boys and Other Essays.* Boston: Citizenship Training Department, 1946.

Pickett, Robert S. *House of Refuge: The Origins of Juvenile Reformation in New York State, 1815–1857.* Syracuse, N.Y.: Syracuse University Press, 1969.

Pivar, David J. *Purity Crusade: Sexual Morality and Social Control, 1868–1900.* Westport, Conn., Greenwood Press, 1973.

Platt, Anthony M. *The Child-Savers: The Invention of Delinquency.* Chicago: University of Chicago Press, 1969.

Pleck, Elizabeth Hafkin. *Black Migration and Poverty, Boston 1865–1900.* New York: Academic Press, 1979.

————. *Domestic Tyranny: The Making of Social Policy Against Family Violence from Colonial Times to the Present.* New York: Oxford University Press, 1987.

Powers, Edwin, and Helen Witmer. *An Experiment in the Prevention of Delinquency: The Cambridge-Somerville Youth Study.* New York: Columbia University Press, 1951.

Quinlan, Richard J. "Growth and Development of Catholic Education in the Archdiocese of Boston." *Catholic Historical Review* 22 (April 1936): 30–37.

Randall, C. D., ed. *History of Child Saving in the United States.* Boston, 1893.

Reeves, Margaret. *Training Schools for Delinquent Girls.* New York: Russell Sage Foundation, 1929.

Richmond, Mary E. *Friendly Visiting Among the Poor.* New York, 1899.

Richards, Laura E. *Samuel Gridley Howe.* New York: D. Appleton-Century Company, 1935.

Rischin, Moses. *The Promised City: New York's Jews, 1870–1914.* Cambridge: Harvard University Press, 1962.

Rivers, Edith. *Working and Trusting: or, Sketches Drawn from the Records of the Children's Mission.* Boston, 1859.

Rodham, Hillary. "Children Under the Law." *Harvard Educational Review* 43 (November 1973): 487–514.

Rolle, Andrew. *The Italian Americans: Troubled Roots.* New York: Free Press, 1980.

Rosen, Ruth. *The Lost Sisterhood: Prostitution in America, 1900–1918.* Baltimore: Johns Hopkins University Press, 1982.

Rosenberg, Carroll Smith. *Religion and the Rise of the American City: The New York City Mission Movement, 1812–1870.* Ithaca: Cornell University Press, 1971.

————. *Disorderly Conduct: Visions of Gender in Victorian America.* New York: Knopf, 1985.

Rosenberg, Charles E. *The Cholera Years: The United States in 1832, 1849, and 1866*. Chicago: University of Chicago Press, 1962.

———. *No Other Gods: On Science and American Social Thought*. Baltimore: Johns Hopkins University Press, 1976.

———. *The Care of Strangers: The Rise of America's Hospital System*. New York: Basic Books, 1987.

Ross, Dorothy. *G. Stanley Hall: The Psychologist as Prophet*. Chicago: University of Chicago Press, 1972.

Ross, Edyth L., ed. *Black Heritage in Social Welfare, 1860–1930*. Metuchen, N.J.: Scarecrow Press, 1978.

Rossi, Peter H., and Alice S. Rossi. "Background and Consequences of Parochial School Education." *Harvard Educational Review* 27 (Summer 1957): 168–99.

Rothman, David J. *The Discovery of the Asylum: Social Order and Disorder in the New Republic*. Boston: Little, Brown, 1971.

———. *Conscience and Convenience: The Asylum and Its Alternatives in Progressive America*. Boston: Little, Brown, 1980.

Rush, Florence. *The Best Kept Secret: Sexual Abuse of Children*. New York: McGraw-Hill, 1980.

Russell, Francis. *A City in Terror: The 1919 Boston Police Strike*. New York: Viking Press, 1975.

Ryerson, Ellen. *The Best-Laid Plans: America's Juvenile Court Experiment*. New York: Hill and Wang, 1978.

Salmon, Lucy Maynard. *Domestic Service*. New York, 1897.

Sanborn, Franklin B. *The Public Charities of Massachusetts During the Century Ending Jan. 1, 1876*. Boston, 1876.

———. *Dr. S. G. Howe, the Philanthropist*. New York, 1891.

———. *Recollections of Seventy Years*. 2 vols. Boston: R. G. Badger, 1909.

Sanders, James W. *The Education of an Urban Minority: Catholics in Chicago, 1833–1965*. New York: Oxford University Press, 1977.

———. "19th Century Boston Catholics and the School Question." *University of Notre Dame Working Papers Series* (Fall 1977): 3–30.

Savage, Edward H. *Police Recollections: or, Boston by Daylight and Gaslight for Two Hundred and Fifty Years*. Boston, 1873.

Schlossman. Steven L. *Love and the American Delinquent: The Theory and Practice of "Progressive" Juvenile Justice, 1825–1920*. Chicago: University of Chicago Press, 1977.

Schlossman, Steven L., and Stephanie Wallach. "The Crime of Precocious Sexuality: Female Juvenile Delinquency in the Progressive Era." *Harvard Educational Review* 48 (February 1978): 65–94.

Schob, David E. *Hired Hands and Plowboys: Farm Labor in the Midwest, 1815–60*. Urbana, Ill.: University of Illinois Press, 1975.

Schroeder, Paul L. et al. *Child Guidance Procedures*. New York: D. Appleton-Century Company, 1937.

Schultz, J. Lawrence. "The Cycle of the Juvenile Court History." *Crime and Delinquency* 19 (October 1973): 457–76.

Schultz, Stanley K. *The Culture Factory: Boston Public Schools, 1789–1860*. New York: Oxford University Press, 1973.

Schwartz, Harold. *Samuel Gridley Howe: Social Reformer 1801–1876*. Cambridge: Harvard University Press, 1956.

Shannon, William V. *American Irish*. New York: Macmillan, 1966.

Shea, John Gilmary. *History of the Catholic Church in the United States*. 4 vols. New York, 1886.

Sheldon, William H. *Varieties of Delinquent Youth: An Introduction to Constitutional Psychiatry*. New York: Harper & Row, 1949.

Shepherd, Margaret L. *My Life in the Convent*. Toledo: Book and Bible House, 1938.

Silver, Harold M. "The Russian Jew Looks at Charity—A Study of the Attitudes of Russian Jewish Immigrants Toward Organized Jewish Charitable Agencies in the United States in 1890–1900." *Jewish Social Service Quarterly* 4 (December 1927): 129–44.

Sisters of Charity. *Sisters of Charity, Emitsburg, 1809–1959*. Emitsburg, MD. Motherhouse of the Sisters of Charity, 1959.

Skillern, Harriet M. "A Socio-legal Analysis of the Massachusetts Stubborn Child Law." Ph.D. diss., Brandeis University, 1977.

Sklar, Kathryn Kish. *Catharine Beecher: A Study in Domesticity*. New Haven: Yale University Press, 1973.

Slater, Peter G. "Ben Lindsey and the Juvenile Court of Denver: A Progressive Looks at Human Nature." *American Quarterly* 20 (Summer 1968): 211–23.

Smith, Daniel Scott, and Michael S. Hindus. "Premarital Pregnancy in America, 1640–1971: An Overview and Interpretation." *Journal of Interdisciplinary History* 5 (Spring 1975): 537–70.

Smith, Elizabeth Oakes. *The Newsboy*. New York, 1854.

Smith, Robert Cheney. *The Cowley Fathers in America: The Early Years*. Boston: Society of St. John the Evangelist, 1958.

Smith, Robert P. "William Cooper Nell: Crusading Black Abolitionist." *Journal of Negro History* 55 (July 1970): 182–99.

Solomon, Barbara Miller. *Ancestors and Immigrants: A Changing New England Tradition*. Cambridge: Harvard University Press, 1956.

Spalding, John Lancaster. *The Religious Mission of the Irish People and Catholic Colonization*. New York, 1880.

Spellman, Francis Cardinal. *The Foundling*. New York: Charles Scribner's Sons, 1951.

Stack, Carol B. *All Our Kin: Strategies for Survival in a Black Community*. New York: Harper & Row, 1974.

Stack, John F., Jr. *International Conflict in an American City: Boston's Irish, Italians, and Jews, 1935–1944*. Westport, Conn., Greenwood Press, 1979.

Stansell, Christine. *City of Women: Sex and Class in New York, 1789–1860*. New York: Knopf, 1986.

Steinmetz, Suzanne, and Murray A. Straus, eds. *Violence in the Family*. New York: Dodd, Mead, 1974.

Story, Ronald D. *The Forging of an Aristocracy: Harvard and the Boston Upper Class, 1800–1879*. Middletown, Conn., Wesleyan University Press, 1980.

Sullivan, Robert E., and James M. O'Toole. *Catholic Boston: Studies in Religion and Community, 1870–1970*. Boston: Archbishop of Boston, 1985.

Thernstrom, Stephan. *The Other Bostonians: Poverty and Progress in the American Metropolis, 1880–1970*. Cambridge: Harvard University Press, 1973.

Thomas, John L. "Romantic Reform in America, 1815–1865." *American Quarterly* 17 (Winter 1965): 656–81.

Thomas, William I., and Florian Znaniecki. *The Polish Peasant in Europe and America*. 2 vols. New York: Knopf, 1927.

Thurston, Henry W. *The Dependent Child*. New York: Columbia University Press, 1930.

Tiffin, Susan. *In Whose Best Interest? Child Welfare Reform in the Progressive Era*. Westport, Conn., Greenwood Press, 1982.

Timasheff, Nicholas S. *One Hundred Years of Probation, 1841–1941*. 2 vols. New York: Fordham University Press, 1941.

Trattner, Walter I. *Crusade for Children: A History of the National Child Labor Committee and Child Labor Reform in America*. Chicago: Quadrangle, 1970.

———. *From Poor Law to Welfare State: A History of Social Welfare in America*. New York: Free Press, 1974.

Travis, Thomas. *The Young Malefactor*. New York: Thomas Y. Crowell, 1908.

Tyack, David B. *The One Best System: A History of American Education*. Cambridge: Harvard University Press, 1974.

Tyack, David B., and Michael Berkowitz. "The Man Nobody Liked: Toward a Social History of the Truant Officer, 1840–1940." *American Quarterly* 29 (Spring 1977): 31–54.

Tucci, Douglass Shand. *The Second Settlement, 1875–1925*. Boston: St. Margaret's Hospital, 1974.

Tuckerman, Joseph. *On the Elevation of the Poor: A Selection from His Reports as Minister-at-Large in Boston*. New York: Arno Press, 1971.

U.S. Congress, Senate, *Proceedings of the Conference on the Care of Dependent Children, held at Washington, D.C., January 25–29, 1909*. 60th Congress, 2nd Session, S. Doc. 721. Washington, D.C., 1909.

U.S. Department of Commerce, Bureau of the Census. *Benevolent Institutions*. Washington, D.C., 1910.

———. *Children Under Institutional Care 1923*. Washington, D.C., 1927.

———. *Children Under Institutional Care and in Foster Homes, 1933*. Washington, D.C., 1935.

Vogel, Morris J. *The Invention of the Modern Hospital: Boston, 1870–1930*. Chicago: University of Chicago Press, 1980.

Wade, Abby L. *Reminiscences of the Boston Female Asylum*. Boston, 1844.

Waldman, Morris D. *Nor by Power*. New York: International Universities Press, 1953.

Walkowitz, Judith R. *Prostitution and Victorian Society: Women, Class, and the State*. New York: Cambridge University Press, 1980.

Walsh, Francis R. "The Boston *Pilot:* A Newspaper for the Irish Immigrant, 1829–1908." Ph.D. diss., Boston University, 1968.

Wandersee, Winifred D. *Women's Work & Family Values, 1920–1940* Cambridge: Harvard University Press, 1981.

Warner, Florence M. *Juvenile Detention in the United States*. Chicago: University of Chicago Press, 1933.

Weisz, Howard Ralph. *Irish-American and Italian-American Educational Views and Activities, 1870–1900: A Comparison.* New York: Arno Press, 1976.

Welter, Barbara. "The Cult of True Womanhood: 1820–1860." *American Quarterly* 18 (Summer 1966): 151–74.

White, Arthur. "Antebellum School Reform in Boston: Integrationists and Separatists." *Phylon* 34 (June 1973): 203–17.

Whittaker, James K. "Colonial Child Care Institutions: Our Heritage of Care." *Child Welfare* 50 (July 1971): 396–400.

Wilentz, Sean. *Chants Democratic: New York City & the Rise of the American Working Class, 1788–1850.* New York: Oxford University Press, 1984.

Wilkie, Jane Riblett. "Social Status, Acculturation and School Attendance in 1850 Boston." *Journal of Social History* 11 11 (Winter 1977): 179–90.

Williams, Phyllis H. *South Italian Folkways in Europe and America: A Handbook for Social Workers, Visiting Nurses, School Teachers, and Physicians.* New Haven: Yale University Press, 1938.

Winslow, Edward C. *How It Came To Be What It Is, and How They Did It.* Boston: New England Home for Little Wanderers, 1929.

Woodham-Smith, Cecil. *The Great Hunger: Ireland, 1845–1849.* New York: Harper & Row, 1962.

Woods, Robert A. *Young Working Girls.* Boston: Houghton Mifflin, 1913.

———. *The Neighborhood in Nation-Building: The Running Comment of Thirty Years at the South End House.* Boston: Houghton Mifflin, 1923.

Wright, Carroll D. *The Working Girls of Boston.* New York: Arno Press, 1969.

Yans-McLaughlin, Virginia. *Family and Community: Italian Immigrants in Buffalo, 1880–1930.* Ithaca: Cornell University Press, 1977.

Zainaldin, Jamil S., and Peter L. Tyor. "Asylums and Society: An Approach to Industrial Change." *Journal of Social History* 13 (Fall 1979), 23–48.

Zelizer, Viviana A. *Pricing the Priceless Child: The Changing Social Value of Children.* New York: Basic Books, 1985.

Index

References to illustrations are printed in boldface type.

Pelletier, Rose Virginnie (Mother Euphrasia), 128
Pelletier, William, 93
Penology, 111
People v. Turner, 204
Perkins, John Forbes, 225, 237, 242, 244, 245
Petition of Alexander Ferrier, 204
Philadelphia House of Refuge, 141
Pickert, Lehman, 166, 176
Pilot, 75–76, 92, 94, 96, 147
Pinckney, Merritt W., 227
Pine Farm, 52, **54**, 56, 61, 119, 121; Black children at, 151–52; closing of, 57, 60; described, 53–55; establishment of, 51
Polcari, Antonio, 191
Pomeroy, Rebecca R., 120
Poorhouse, 24, 53
Poor laws, 16–17, 18
Portuguese immigrants, 178
Pound, Roscoe, 223
Prescott, William, 39
Probation: juvenile, 200; officers, 170, 225–27, 237–38, 239, 243, 276nn. 71 and 73, 297n.69; poineer work in, 199
Progressives, 55, 197, 204–5, 223, 233
Prominenti, 182, 183, 184, 189–90, 191, 192
Proselytizing, 46–47, 81, 164, 170
Prostitution, 58, 107, 114, 117–18, 218, 282; among Black women, 139, 153, 279; and reform, 108; at HGS, 116, 127–28, 131, 132, 134–36
Psychiatry, 176, 195, 220, 224, 228, 238, 241–42. *See also* Judge Baker Foundation
Psychoanalysis, 229, 232, 242
Puritans, 20, 27, 35, 60, 75, 157
Putnam, James Jackson, 228, 232, 233, 238
Pyne, Daniel J., 102, 103

Quakers, 138, 148
Quincy, Josiah, 24, 33
Quinlivan, Sister Rose, 76–77, 78–79

Racism: and Blacks, 137–56. *See also* Anti-Catholicism; Anti-Semitism
Reformatory for Women (Sherborn), 112
Reform schools, 23, 34, 39, 41; and the

State School Ships, 50; segregation of, 143
Rich, Isaac, 125
Richmond, Mary, 239
Ring, Thomas F., 99–100, **102**, 199
Roberts v. Boston (1849), 138
Rock Lawn Farm (Foxborough), 52, **54**, 57, 152
Roosevelt, Theodore, 197, 238
Rosnosky, Issac, 163
Rottenberg, Viola J., 174
Royce, Josiah, 228
Rubenstein, Philip J., 170, 171, 201, 224
Russian Jews, 161, 163, 164, 167, 170, 172

Sacco-Vanzetti legend, 183
St. Augustine's Farm (Foxborough), 148, 150, 252
St. Joseph Class (HGS), 132, 134, 135, 136
St. Mary Class (HGS), 132, 134, 136
St. Mary's Infant Asylum, 67, **106**
St. Monica's Home for Sick Colored Women and Children, 150
St. Peter Claver Conference of Colored Men (Vincentians), 147
St. Vincent de Paul Society (Vincentians), 77, 89, 90, 98, 99, 147, 196, 199
St. Vincent Female Orphan Asylum (St. Vincent Home), 16, **68**, **70**, 81, 84, 87, 91, 252; admission to, 67, 71; assessment of, 79–80; and BFA, 72, 74, 94; and Andrew Carney, 72–73; and courts, 199; daily life at, 69, 76–78; education at, 69–71; establishment of, 67; and Italian children, 178, 181, 195; jobs for girls, 67–69, 71, 79; legal surrender, 71–72; location of, 72; *Pilot* on, 75–76; Protestant supporters of, 73, 74; purpose of, 74; and HGS, 130
Sanborn, Franklin B., 113
Santosuosso, Joseph, 191, 193
Sarni, James, 191
Savage, Edward H., 226
Sawyer, William, 23
Schindler, Solomon, 162, 163, 164, 165, 169
Scollary Square, 217, 291
Sedgwick, Catharine Maria: *Home*, 22
Seton, Elizabeth B., 67, 146